Crossing Linguistic Boundaries

Also available from Bloomsbury

Contemporary Linguistic Parameters, edited by Antonio Fábregas,
Jaume Mateu and Michael Putnam
The Bloomsbury Companion to Historical Linguistics,
edited by Silvia Luraghi and Vit Bubenik
World Englishes: A Critical Analysis, by Mario Saraceni
World Englishes Volumes I–III Set, edited by Tometro Hopkins,
Kendall Decker and John McKenny

Crossing Linguistic Boundaries

Systemic, Synchronic and Diachronic Variation in English

Edited by
Paloma Núñez-Pertejo, María José López-Couso,
Belén Méndez-Naya and Javier Pérez-Guerra

BLOOMSBURY ACADEMIC
LONDON • NEW YORK • OXFORD • NEW DELHI • SYDNEY

BLOOMSBURY ACADEMIC
Bloomsbury Publishing Plc
50 Bedford Square, London, WC1B 3DP, UK
1385 Broadway, New York, NY 10018, USA
29 Earlsfort Terrace, Dublin 2, Ireland

BLOOMSBURY, BLOOMSBURY ACADEMIC and the Diana logo are trademarks of
Bloomsbury Publishing Plc

First published in Great Britain 2020
Paperback edition published 2021

ISBN: HB: 978-1-3500-5385-4
        PB: 978-1-3502-6745-9
      ePDF: 978-1-3500-5386-1
     eBook: 978-1-3500-5387-8

Typeset by RefineCatch Limited, Bungay, Suffolk

To find out more about our authors and books visit www.bloomsbury.com
and sign up for our newsletters.

Contents

Tables

Figures

Contributors

Andreas Baumann is Lecturer at the Department of English and American Studies, University of Vienna. He has an academic background in cognitive science, linguistics, and mathematics, and his research focuses on quantitative, cognitive and evolutionary linguistics, as well as on the mathematical modelling of language change.

Bert Cornillie is Associate Professor of Spanish Linguistics at the University of Leuven. He has published on modality, evidentiality, (inter)subjectivity, diachronic morphosyntactic variation and discourse traditions, modal particles and discourse markers.

Kristin Davidse is Professor of English Linguistics at the University of Leuven. Her main research interest is the description of English grammar from a functional perspective. She has published on clefting, transitivization, and especially on grammaticalization, deictification and intersubjectification processes, as they affect the English noun phrase in particular.

Ryan B. Doran is Assistant Professor in the Department of Philosophy and Classics at the University of Regina. He has research interests in the philosophy of language, focusing on areas such as reference and pragmatics.

Raymond Hickey is Professor of English Linguistics at the University of Duisburg and Essen. His research has included work on varieties of English, especially Irish English, the history and the standardisation of English, language contact and areal linguistics, as well as sociolinguistic variation and change.

Marianne Hundt is Professor of English Linguistics at the University of Zürich. She has published extensively on grammatical change in contemporary and Late Modern English, and on linguistic varieties in which English is either a first or a second language.

Manfred Krug is Professor of English and Historical Linguistics at the University of Bamberg. His research has dealt with modal verbal constructions, grammaticalization, phonological issues such as the Great Vowel Shift, World Englishes, and related aspects of linguistic globalization.

Christophe Lenoble is currently a doctoral student at Paris 3 – Sorbonne Nouvelle University, where he received his Master's degree in English Linguistics. His PhD involves a study of the imperfective aspect in Singapore English. He has been granted a USPC – NUS scholarship.

Diana M. Lewis is Associate Professor of English Linguistics at Aix Marseille University and a member of the 'Laboratoire Parole et Langage'. She has published in the areas of semantic and morphosyntactic change, discourse relations, and contrastive linguistics. Her current research focuses on adverbial grammaticalization in English.

María José López-Couso is Associate Professor of English at the University of Santiago de Compostela and a member of the research group VLCG. Her research interests are morphosyntactic and pragmatic change and grammaticalization in English.

Lucía Loureiro-Porto is Associate Professor of English Linguistics at the University of the Balearic Islands and a member of the team 'Variation in English Worldwide' (ViEW; University of Vigo). Her research interests include morphosyntactic variation in varieties of English, grammaticalization, and global processes such as colloquialization and democratization.

Belén Méndez-Naya is Associate Professor at the University of Santiago de Compostela and a member of the research group VLCG. She works on grammaticalization in the history of English, especially the development of intensifiers and pragmatic markers.

Paloma Núñez-Pertejo is Associate Professor of English at the University of Santiago de Compostela and a member of the research group VLCG. Her research interests include grammaticalization processes in the history of English, with special reference to the development of the aspectual system, intensifiers, and youth language.

Javier Pérez-Guerra is Professor of English at the University of Vigo, where he coordinates the 'Language Variation and Textual Categorisation' team. His research focuses on word order in the history of English, information packaging, multidimensional register variation and performance preferences.

Christina Prömer is a doctoral student at the Department of English and American Studies at Vienna University. In her PhD she focuses on voiced suffixes in Modern English, in which she integrates findings from the ECCE research group.

Nikolaus Ritt is Professor of English Historical Linguistics at Vienna University. His research focuses on Early Middle English vowel quantity and, more recently, on co-adaptive relations between competence constituents.

Ole Schützler is Associate Professor of English at the University of Bamberg. He is interested in phonological and grammatical variation and change in varieties of English, with a focus on Scottish English. In his research he combines acoustic analysis, corpus-linguistic methods, sociolinguistics, and construction grammar.

Gunnel Tottie was Professor at the University of Zürich until 2002. With a longstanding commitment to corpus linguistics, she has published on topics in syntax, especially negation and relativization, and more recently, pragmatics.

An Van linden is Assistant Professor of English Language and Linguistics at the University of Liège and affiliated researcher at the University of Leuven. She works on the analysis of mood and modality, complex sentences and grammaticalization, from diachronic and synchronic perspectives.

Gregory Ward is Professor of Linguistics, Gender and Sexuality Studies and Philosophy at Northwestern University. His work is in the general area of discourse/pragmatics, with specific research interests in pragmatic theory, information structure, and reference/anaphora.

Valentin Werner is Assistant Professor of English and Historical Linguistics at the University of Bamberg. The main focus of his work is in applied and variational linguistics, focusing on the language of pop culture, the corpus-based analysis of learner language, and the corpus- and questionnaire-based study of varieties of English.

Debra Ziegeler is Professor at Paris 3 – Sorbonne Nouvelle University. She has worked on constructional issues in Singapore English, aspect, modality, grammaticalization and negation in contexts of linguistic contact.

Preface

Crossing Linguistic Boundaries presents a collection of eleven chapters that focus on variation in areas of intersection between linguistic domains – from prosody to grammar, semantics and pragmatics – doing so from synchronic, diachronic and diatopic perspectives. This project has been possible, first of all, thanks to the expertise and efforts of those eighteen specialists who have generously contributed their work; without them, *Crossing Linguistic Boundaries* would have never come into existence.

We are also immensely grateful to those colleagues who have acted as anonymous external reviewers and whose feedback and insightful comments have contributed significantly to the quality of the volume: Karin Aijmer, Sabine Arndt-Lappe, Marta Carretero, Claudia Claridge, Francis Cornish, María Teresa Espinal, Dolores González, Yoko Iyeiri, Mikko Laitinen, Ursula Lenker, Lucía Loureiro, Javier Martín Arista, Montserrat Martínez, Esperanza Rama, Malte Rosemeyer, Agnes Schneider, Edgar Schneider, Mario Serrano, Irma Taavitsainen, David Tizón, Bertus Van Rooy and Tim Waller.

Our most sincere thanks also go to Andrew Wardell, Helen Saunders and Becky Holland at Bloomsbury Publishing, for their unfailing commitment to the project, their generous and useful advice, as well as their incredible patience and continuous help and support throughout this long journey. It has been extremely gratifying to work with all three of them.

For generous financial support we are grateful to the Spanish Ministry of Science, Innovation and Universities (grants FFI2016-77018-P and FFI2017-86884-P), the Regional Government of Galicia (grants ED431B 2017/12, ED431C 2017/50 and ED431D 2017/09) and the European Regional Development Fund.

This volume is not simply another collective work. Rather, it has a very special meaning for all the editors and contributors involved. The book is dedicated to Teresa Fanego, Professor of English Linguistics at the University of Santiago de Compostela. Back in the 1990s, she founded the *Research Unit Variation, Linguistic Change and Grammaticalization* with a number of her PhD students, among them all four of us. Since then, VLCG has been the fertile soil in which several generations of scholars have grown academically, as well as providing the original source and inspiration for various research groups in other Spanish universities, as members moved away after completing their PhDs. Under Teresa's leadership, and over the almost three decades of its existence, the VLCG Research Unit has become a reference point for English linguistics, both in Spain and abroad, and has fostered fruitful scientific exchanges with many colleagues and research groups across the international academic community. May this publication serve as a tribute to Teresa, one which celebrates a life devoted to teaching and research, and as a token of our deep gratitude and appreciation for her inspiring work and academic excellence.

Introduction

Paloma Núñez-Pertejo, María José López-Couso, Belén Méndez-Naya
University of Santiago de Compostela

Javier Pérez-Guerra
University of Vigo

1. A polyhedral gaze on variation

Traditional descriptive accounts of the linguistic system of the English language are commonly based on a rigid division of academic disciplines into, among others, phonetics/phonology, morphology, syntax, semantics, and pragmatics. Through its eleven chapters, *Crossing Linguistic Boundaries: Systemic, Synchronic and Diachronic Variation in English* considers tensions in various language interfaces by focusing on controversial and recurrent topics in some of the above-mentioned areas: on the grammar/semantics(-pragmatics) interface with a focus on grammaticalization, on marked instances of the correlation between syntax and semantic categories such as verbal mood and aspect, and on pronominal co-reference, all of these in relation to overcoming temporal and geographical limits in the language.

Such a wealth of theoretical perspectives is matched by a concern for methodological rigour. In all these studies, the authors, reputed scholars in English linguistics, demonstrate how theoretically-informed corpus-based approaches can be used to describe and quantify linguistic variation and change in an array of varieties and periods from the history of English. Most contributions are based on large synchronic and diachronic electronic databases and corpora of written and spoken English, with several other studies providing their own data, including bespoke corpora and questionnaires, as a means of exploring lexical variation or diachronic change.

Crossing Linguistic Boundaries is organized around two parts: 'Tensioning the system' and 'Synchronic and diachronic variation', whose contributions are summarized in the following sections.

2. Tensioning the system

Two of the chapters in the first part of *Crossing Linguistic Boundaries* deal with the relation between segmental and suprasegmental phonology and other parts of the linguistic system. Thus, Hickey explores the various semantic and syntactic implications of the different prosodic patterns present in English idioms, while Tottie looks at the way in which vocalizations like *uh* and *um* can become words. The other five chapters in this part revolve around the grammar/semantics-pragmatics interface as the locus of processes such as grammaticalization. With a focus on noun phrases, Doran and Ward investigate certain non-deictic uses of English demonstratives, accounting for these by extending the notion of familiarity to include cultural co-presence. From a diachronic perspective, Ritt, Baumann and Prömer address the history of English *any* as one of continuity and stasis. Davidse and Van linden investigate compositionality of form and meaning in constructions traditionally analysed as instances of subject extraposition, and suggest a common historical source with a specific syntactic design (matrix clause plus complement *that*-clause) conveying a particular interpretation (cognitive/emotional process). In his chapter, Cornillie ventures into the domain of cross-linguistic historical semantics and examines the auxiliation of subjective *threaten* (English) and Spanish *amenazar*. According to his data, the English *threaten* + infinitive construction emerged later than its Spanish counterpart, but both expanded in scenarios where new national languages were developing mechanisms of syntactic elaboration and clearly competing with Latin and its cultural heritage. Finally, in Lewis' contribution, which raises tensions between grammar and pragmatics, we move outside the clause to consider the evolution of the adverb *still*, and the correlation between position, scope and meaning in the development of the discourse functions of English adverbs. In what follows we provide more details about the contributions in this part of the volume.

Idioms in English have been explored in depth from syntactic, semantic and/or lexicographical perspectives. In 'Prosodic templates in English idioms and fixed expressions', Raymond Hickey investigates the prosodic patterning of idioms and fixed expressions on the basis of the distribution of their metrical feet and the position of stressed and unstressed syllables in these structures. His contribution 'crosses' the linguistic boundaries between semantics and prosody in that its ultimate goal is to determine whether the meaning of a fixed expression can or cannot be conditioned by the prosodic pattern. As regards their semantics, prototypical 'rigid' fixed expressions evince (relative) conventionality, opacity and form/meaning compositionality. In terms of prosody, on the one hand, such semantic characteristics are reflected in the fact that fixed expressions do not tolerate contrastive stress on their constituents. On the other hand, fixed expressions in English commonly consist of two, three or (rarely) four feet, that is, they have two, three or four stressed syllables with a variable number of unstressed syllables. Hickey provides examples of stable correlations between prosodic templates and conceptual structure. He argues, first, that two-foot structures (for example, *bread and butter*) imply semantic relatedness; second, that three-foot patterns (as in the prosodic template strong-strong-weak-strong-weak in *signed, sealed and delivered*) convey a sense of completeness; and finally, that four-foot patterns tend to express consequences (e.g., *live by the sword, die by the sword*).

Tottie's chapter, 'Word-search as word-formation? The case of *uh* and *um*', focuses on the transition of forms, such as *uh* and *um* (also *er* and *erm* in non-rhotic variants of English) from fillers used as involuntary planning signals in speech to stance adverbs, that is, to full-fledged words used in writing. While their status as words has been called into question, Tottie considers them as 'nascent' or 'emergent' words in speech on the basis that both spoken *uh* and *um* (UHM) can be used intentionally in writing (written EHM). According to the author, this is a rare case of coinage or root creation, i.e. lexicalization occurring without any kind of prior traditional word-formation process taking place. Apparently, this specific use as stance adverbs was already attested in American journalistic prose in the 1960s, and reached a peak in the 1990s and the twenty-first century. Whereas sentence-initial use of written EHM can easily be modelled on spoken language, it is more difficult to account for written EHM in medial position based on uses of spoken UHM. Here Tottie claims that its use during word-search is the probable spoken model, while she also acknowledges the key role played by longer turn-planning. By conducting a quantitative study based on the Santa Barbara Corpus of Spoken American English (SBC), the author sheds light on the particular role of UHM in word-search, which she describes as 'lexical retrieval' (when only one correct choice is possible, typically a technical term, or the name of a person or place) and 'lexical selection' (when several possible choices exist, but only one is considered by the speaker to be the best). Results show that less than eight per cent of the tokens of UHM retrieved from the SBC corpus marked word-search efforts, *uh* being more frequent than *um*. Conversations including long narrative sections spoken by older people had high overall UHM frequencies, which is not surprising, given that age is a determining factor when it comes to word-search, that is, the UHM ratio increases with age. Her study shows that the so-called 'tongue-in-cheek' function, dominant in written EHM, is almost non-existent in the spoken SBC material. Tottie concludes that word-search is a salient phenomenon because it focuses on content words (especially nouns and adjectives), which would account for its subsequent adoption in writing. As for the almost complete absence of 'tongue-in-cheek' uses in speech, the author attributes this to the friendly, interactive nature of the conversations included. It is claimed that lexicalization of UHM may occur in speech, particularly in sensitive contexts, and that the word-search function of UHM can therefore be regarded as a stage in the word-formation process.

'Demonstratives licensed by cultural co-presence', by Ryan B. Doran and Gregory Ward, deals with two uses of demonstratives in English which imply the effect of familiarity. The chapter intersperses the grammatical characterization of a specific category with its non-linguistic versatility resulting from interpretations implicitly shared by speakers and hearers. 'Familiarity', as understood in this study, is based on the speaker's belief that the hearer is part of a (private, small or large) community where the entity determined by the demonstrative is sufficiently shared by the members of that community. The constructions examined by Doran and Ward contain noun phrases introduced by demonstratives in which the latter are *per se* responsible for triggering this effect of familiarity. The description of the familiarity uses of demonstratives is carried out in this corpus-based qualitative investigation through detailed accounts of almost forty utterances retrieved from their corpus. In particular, the authors describe the so-called referential and predicative uses of *this* and *that* (and their plural counterparts) in a corpus of contemporary naturally-occurring data. Such uses are distinguished from other more prototypical deictic (*this pen on the table*), identificational (*I bought this pen*), (unfamiliar) indefinitive (*I saw this scary hamster at the pet shop*) and degree-modifier (*The hamster was this big*) roles. On the one hand, in the referential use, as in *I'm not fit until I've had that first cup of coffee*, the demonstrative alludes to a fact presumed to be familiar either privately (between speaker and hearer) or, canonically, in the immediate spatio-temporal context. This referential type includes examples in which the demonstrative noun phrase is used as a complete utterance, as in *That moment when someone sneezes on you*, for example, where the speaker is treating the 'getting-sneezed-on' scenario as familiar to speaker and hearer. On the other hand, Doran and Ward identify a second familiarity type of demonstrative, that is, the predicative one, illustrated in *I'm this Jewish girl from New York City* – this predicative interpretation is only possible with the proximal demonstrative *this* and is disallowed with the distal one (*that*). This type of demonstrative (prototypically) predicates a discourse-new property of the relevant referent in the utterance and, what is important here, the kind associated with the property is also presumed to be familiar to the hearer. Doran and Ward's study is an excellent depiction of how a grammatical constituent may achieve a marked pragmatic effect (familiarity) not supported by other linguistic items or phenomena, and thus provides a scenario in which grammatical, semantic and pragmatic realms are closely intertwined.

The chapter by Ritt, Baumann and Prömer, 'The fall and rise of English *any*', addresses the history of English *any* (< OE *ænig*) as one of functional continuity and stasis, were it not for the decline it underwent during the Early Middle English period (*ca.* 1050–1250), a fact that has often been overlooked in the literature. Old English *ænig* and Modern English *any* share a number of similarities, therefore suggesting continuity, in terms of frequency, word-class, occurrence (in singular noun phrases and non-affirmative clauses) and meaning. Both carry the same semantic features of indefiniteness, individualization and non-exclusiveness, which differentiate them from other determinatives, such as *one* or *a(n)*, although there are contexts in which any of these can be used interchangeably. Given their functional overlap, competition between *any*, *one* and *a(n)* is not unexpected, and it is precisely through the interaction between these three determinatives that the authors account for the rise and fall in the frequency of *any* during the Early Middle English period. The decline in the frequency of *any* coincides with a rise in the frequency of *one/a(n)*, which may actually have caused the decrease in use of *any*. Both *one* and *a(n)* were variants of Old English *án*, whose core function was that of a numeral, although it already had other functions that resembled those of the indefinite article. As *án* grammaticalized, it increasingly came to be used in the same contexts as *any*. In the resulting competition it was *one/a(n)* that took the lead, causing *any* to decline in Early Middle English. As the grammaticalization of Old English *án* progressed, however, its lineage branched to yield the numeral *one* and the indefinite article *a(n)* as two independent descendants, and neither of these competed with *any* in its core functions any longer. Thus, the latter was re-established in usage and attained once more the frequency that its ancestor had enjoyed in Old English. The authors conclude that the historical evolution of individual linguistic constituents often depends on the constituents with which it co-evolves, and may appear puzzling if studied in isolation.

The consequences which compositionality has in the traditional dichotomy 'form' (syntax) and 'meaning' (interpretation) for the categorization of syntactic expressions are tackled from the perspective of Construction Grammar by Kristin Davidse and An Van linden in their chapter 'Revisiting '*it*-extraposition': The historical development of constructions with matrices *(it)/(there) be* + NP followed by a complement clause'. Their study focuses on constructions consisting of [*it/there/that*] + [*be*] + [noun phrases headed by *wonder* or *doubt*] + [*that*-clauses], as in *It was a wonder that I did this* or in *There is no doubt that I did this*. Using data from well-known historical corpora (the York-Toronto-Helsinki Parsed Corpus of Old English Prose, the Penn-Helsinki Parsed Corpus of Middle English, the Penn-Helsinki Parsed Corpus of Early Modern English and the Corpus of Late Modern English Texts) and WordBanks*Online* for Present-day English, they trace the evolution of the constructions from Old English to the present. In their study, the authors pay attention to, among other variables, the (categorizing versus existential) interpretation of the two constructions, variation in their syntactic design over time, the degree of dependence between the matrix and *that*-clauses, the referential load of the grammatical subjects of *be*, and the type of modifiers attested in the examples. On the one hand, Davidse and Van linden conclude that both types, that is, the so-called predicative *be-wonder* and the existential *be-doubt* patterns, can be explained as members of a macro-construction formally consisting of a matrix clause and a complement (*that*-)clause, and semantically conveying or depicting a specific cognitive/emotional process (matrix clause) and the proposition presupposed by such a process (complement clause). They contend that their claim is supported by the fact that in Old English both constructions allowed the same configurational variants, for example, in parenthetical *as*-clauses and in juxtaposed independent expressions like *It is no wonder*, ... On the other hand, at the meso-constructional level, the predicative (*be-wonder*) and the existential (*be-doubt*) types diverge as regards the preference for pronominal subjects (*it* versus *there*) in the modern and contemporary periods, and with respect to the cognitive/emotional process conveyed by the matrix clause and presupposed by the complement clause ((un)expectedness with *wonder* versus certainty with *doubt*). Finally, the macro-constructional syntactic analysis of 'matrix (*be*) clause' plus 'complement (*that*-)clause' invalidates the traditional analysis of subject extraposition which had been applied specifically to the predicative pattern in the literature.

In 'On grammatical change and discourse environments', Bert Cornillie explores how grammatical change and its actualization are influenced by Discourse Traditions (DTs), that is, normative structures which impose rules of conduct to those authors who follow them. Cornillie proposes that the prestige of specific DTs may have had a direct influence on the success of particular cases of linguistic change, and more specifically, that the interaction between prestigious texts may be the locus for Labovian 'change from above' in the past. The chapter offers a contrastive study of a particular case of syntactic elaboration in English and Spanish: the auxiliation of subjective *threaten* and *amenazar*, which both indicate a prediction on the part of the speaker on the basis of some kind of evidence (e.g., *an annoying rain threatened to soak the Scouts*, COCA). Comparing his previous findings on Spanish with new data from English extracted from EEBO (1470–1690) and CLMET (1710–1920), the author shows that Latinate DTs associated with humanist writings of the Renaissance play a determining role in the emergence and spread of subjective 'threaten'-auxiliaries in both languages.

Subjective *amenazar* and *threaten* are calqued from a Latin construction with a nominal complement indicating fall, ruin and the like (*minari ruinam* > *amenazar con ruina / threaten ruin*) in Latin DTs such as dictionaries and translations. In Spanish the innovation *amenazar* + infinitive occurs first in translations (fifteenth century) and spreads to non-translated texts in the late sixteenth century, specifically with infinitives denoting fall (e.g., *amenazar de se caer* 'threaten to fall'). The emergence of the construction in English takes place from the eighteenth century onwards, that is, later than in Spanish, and should be seen as a case of syntactic elaboration emerging in the scenario of the competition between the new national languages with the Latin cultural heritage. It is only when authors are culturally confident that they are more prone to introduce conscious innovations in the language, that is, changes from above. This momentous period took place for Spanish at the end of the fifteenth century, while English had a later expansion, perhaps due to the political and cultural instability of the seventeenth century. This would explain the different chronologies of Spanish and English when it comes to the origin and actualization of the subjective *threaten*-construction.

In line with studies that have addressed the tendency for adverbs to undergo scope increase by successive reanalyses of the type verb phrase adverb > sentence adverb > connective and/or discourse marker, the chapter by Lewis, 'Grammaticalizing adverbs of English: the case of *still*', explores recent functional splits of the polysemous lexeme *still* which have resulted in emerging uses of the adverb (counter-expectational, concessive-connective, discourse-marking and evaluative) alongside older ones (spatial and temporal). Unlike 'backward-looking' approaches that seek the origin of Present-day discourse markers and study them separately from other evolving adverbs, Lewis adopts a more 'forward-looking' perspective and concentrates on the mechanisms involved in semantic change, rather than on the origin and output of such changes. By combining Modern and Present-day British English data, the author traces the evolution of *still* as a means of comparing the ways in which the splits emerged and to examine whether and how position, scope and meaning became correlated over time. The history of *still* is one of successive extension(s) of meaning and scope. Old English 'spatial' *still* had extended to 'temporal' meaning in durative contexts by Middle English, a typical pathway of semantic change whose transition is typically long. The comparative sense, involving a reanalysis from 'further in time' to 'further in degree', i.e. a shift from one scale to another, developed from the temporal 'ever' sense. In turn, the counter-expectational sense could have begun as an extension of the durative sense while concurrently gaining contrastive implicatures and opening up the probability of an extension from counter-expectation to contrast (contrastive concession), similar to that of *yet*. In addition, more recent developments such as 'discourse-marking' uses are also characterized as extensions of meaning, in this case as extensions of the concessive function or sense. Perhaps due in part to its high frequency, *still* has retained most of its older range of senses while continuing to give rise to new polysemies. The findings also suggest that peripheral position and discourse function did not develop simultaneously; it was the latter that developed first. The existing patterning of an adverb can be expected to be resistant to analogical regularization for some time after new functions emerge, which is indicative of both structural and semantic persistence.

Medial position, for example, characteristic of the temporal adverb, remains common for the newer concessive use, in addition to the newer left-peripheral position, which emerges as a result of the 'modalization' of the lexeme and the strengthening of its connective function. *Still* starts to be attested at left periphery from the mid-nineteenth century onwards, forming a separate information unit. From a diachronic standpoint, the order in which positions occupied by *still* are commonly found is: post-verbal and clause-final > pre-verbal > clause-initial > left-periphery > isolate. The author refers to the history of *still* as showing 'bleaching', or semantic abstraction, and subjectification, typically associated with grammaticalization. Lewis also suggests that analogy with other adverbs, such as *yet*, *surely* or *anyway* may have played a role in the evolution of *still*: *yet* followed a similar pathway of development some two centuries earlier than *still*, while the 'modal' turn showed by *still* in its most recent history could have been modelled on the development of *surely* or *anyway*. The evolution of *still*, then, represents a typical shift from the physical, spatial domain towards more abstract senses; from objective towards more subjective, speaker-attitudinal meanings; from the relatively open class of temporal adverbs towards the more restricted class category of connectives, typical of grammaticalizing expressions. In fact, according to Lewis, *still* is becoming intersubjective, in that it expresses speaker attitude, and more specifically, weakly positive evaluation and mitigation.

3. Synchronic and diachronic variation

The second part of this volume opens with two chapters that address variation in 'daughter' varieties of English vis-à-vis their respective bases in the context of a globalized world. Thus, Krug, Schützler and Werner focus on lexical variation in Gibraltar, British and American English as illustrative of tendencies such as Britishization, but also towards Americanization and globalization, while Loureiro-Porto investigates the spread of *they* with singular antecedent and underspecified gender in Hong Kong, India and Singapore English, varieties with a British-English base and a gender-neutral pronoun in their substrates. The chapters by Hundt and Ziegeler and Lenoble share with the preceding papers an interest in diatopic varieties of English, but focus on verb-centred choices: the variation between the present subjunctive and *should* in subordinate *that*-clauses (*I contend that this (should) be studied in detail*), and co-occurrence restrictions affecting stative verbs with progressive aspect, with particular reference to Indian and Singapore English, respectively. Ziegeler and Lenoble's chapter also introduces a historical angle to this part in that they argue that not only substrate factors but also the diachronic development of English play a role in the extension of contexts accepting stative verbs with progressive aspect.

In more detail, the chapter by Krug, Schützler and Werner, 'How British is Gibraltar English?', focuses on Gibraltar English and its position relative to the two reference L1 varieties of English (British and American English). More particularly, they focus their attention on the linguistic choices Gibraltarians make regarding referentially synonymous expressions such as *lorry/truck* or *parcel/package*, which are said to have differed in usage between British and American English in the late twentieth century.

The strong link between Gibraltar English and British English is more than apparent historically, politically and socio-linguistically, and this is reflected in language use. Nevertheless, it emerges that the lexical binaries that are investigated have to be treated as individual categories, both in terms of their likely diachronic behaviour and their synchronic position on the continuum between British and American English. Individual patterns may show stability or change, sometimes towards a more British orientation, and sometimes towards a more American one. By means of a written questionnaire including almost 70 item pairs, the authors investigate lexical variation in the three varieties of English involved. In order to scrutinize the structure of the different datasets, explorative aggregative data analysis is applied, and two methods of quantification, rater means and item means, are employed to highlight different aspects of the same dataset. The findings confirm the general tendency of Gibraltar English to pattern like, and be more closely associated with, British English. However, the results also reveal that certain lexical items show a more American orientation (e.g., American English *to license, sports, sick* or *for rent* rather than the conservative British English *to licence, sport, ill* and *to let*), and some display similar patterns of development in many regions of the world, thus pointing to globalization in the guise of Americanization. Informants were categorized according to age, gender and language background. While older Gibraltarians are more likely to conform in their usage to the main contact variety, British English, younger speakers display stronger tendencies towards Americanization and globalization. Despite the fact that gender does not seem to be a strong factor in the data, it is apparently the male speakers who are leading the trend towards a less-rigidly British-oriented usage, which constitutes a rather unexpected finding, given that it is usually females who are in the vanguard of linguistic change. Moreover, if the linguistic background is taken into consideration, it is shown that when there is a mixture of English and Spanish, speakers show a more Americanized, even globalized use of the lexical items under study, but when only one of them is spoken, the model adopted is more British than American. In sum, although Americanizing tendencies seem to outweigh trends towards more British forms, and although individual items behave exceptionally, the authors conclude that it is tempting to refer to Present-day Gibraltar English as Gibraltar British English, at least on the lexical level.

In 'Singular *they* in Asian Englishes. A case of linguistic democratization', Lucía Loureiro-Porto explores the factors determining the distribution of singular *they* in Hong Kong English, Indian English and Singapore English. This linguistic feature, which goes back at least to the late fourteenth century, has been shown to be sensitive to both structural factors – more specifically, the type of antecedent – and to extralinguistic determinants such as prescriptivism and democratization. Prescription is responsible for the avoidance of epicene *they* in the written language. Democratization, that is, the tendency to avoid linguistic usages which perpetuate social inequalities and asymmetries, among them sexist language, explains the late twentieth-century spread of this linguistic feature. Using the ICE corpora, Loureiro-Porto extracts *ca.* 300 instances of epicene *they* from some 30,000 potential examples, and explores the relevance of (i) stage of development of the varieties under study, (ii) substrate languages, (iii) text-type, (iv) age and gender of the speaker (only HKE and IND, for which demographic data are available), and (v) type of antecedent. She shows that the incidence of singular *they* is not as high in these Outer circle varieties as in British English, with HKE showing the highest frequency, followed by SIN and IND. In her view, the proximity that HKE shows towards British English cannot be attributed to its less advanced stage of development, since the second wave of feminism, which seems to be pivotal in the rise of frequency of singular *they* in British English, took place after HKE entered phase 3 in Schneider's (2007) model. As to language contact, the substrates of HKE and SIN have a way of referring to an epicene antecedent, and hence would be expected to behave similarly and to show a higher frequency of singular *they*. Tamil, the substrate language of IND, has a gender-marked pronoun, which would anticipate a lower frequency of singular *they* in IND. However, Loureiro-Porto's analysis reveals that the three varieties under study present differences which cannot be interpreted on the basis of the substrate, thus discounting language contact as a conditioning factor. As in the previous literature here, text-type is shown to be highly relevant: in all three Asian varieties singular *they* proves to be a clearly oral feature whose frequency decreases as spontaneity is reduced. Concerning the type of antecedent, the incidence of both indefinite and definite noun-phrase antecedents (i.e. those which indicate avoidance of sexism, and hence democratization) is particularly high in HKE, which suggests a more advanced stage in democratization than the other two varieties. HKE English also shows a marked divide depending on the age of the speaker, with the younger generations (below 40) favouring the feature. In both HKE and IND women use singular *they* far more frequently than men, but it is only in IND that this rise is linked to indefinite and definite noun-phrase antecedents, which suggests that in IND women are taking the lead in this case of linguistic democratization. Given that HKE also ranks high in other democratic features (e.g., use of modals), the author suggests that democratization is more relevant in this variety than in IND and SIN.

Marianne Hundt's contribution, 'It is important that mandatives *(should) be studied* across different World Englishes and from a Construction Grammar perspective', deals with an area of grammar currently undergoing change: variation between the subjunctive and the *should*-periphrasis in mandative constructions, and the expansion of the former to the detriment of the latter. With a focus on different varieties of English, and using evidence from ten ICE corpora and GloWbE, Hundt investigates the relative importance of a number of determining factors which have already been identified in the literature for the selection of the subjunctive and *should*. The chapter offers two complementary studies. The first of these carefully defines the envelope of variation and pays attention to the impact of two external factors (variety and medium/register) and six contextual factors (the lexical trigger, the trigger types – verb, adjective or noun –, the grammatical subject of the subordinate clause, the verb in the subordinate clause, negation, and the presence/absence of the complementizer *that* in the subordinate clause), using ten different ICE corpora, these representing five ENL varieties, four ESL varieties and one ESD variety. The data are subjected to a very rigorous statistical study, using random forest analysis, which allows the author to model the overall importance of factors, and conditional-tree analysis, which helps identify significant predictors for the subjunctive. The second study uses GloWbE for a detailed analysis of the impact of the lexical trigger, exploring nine different items (the verbs *demand, insist, order, propose, recommend, request* and *suggest*; and the adjectives *imperative* and *important*) in six different varieties (British English, American English, Philippine English, Singapore English, Indian English and Hong Kong English). The results of both studies confirm the relevance of language variety for variation: six varieties clearly favour the subjunctive (Canadian English, New Zealand English, Australian English, Philippine English, Singapore English and Jamaican English), three prefer the *should*-periphrasis (British English, Indian English and Hong Kong English), and one shows no clear preference (Irish English). Random forest analysis shows lexical trigger to be the most significant predictor for the selection of the subjunctive vis-à-vis *should* across all varieties of English, alongside other minor predictors such as third person subjects, the verb *be* and affirmative contexts. Finally, Hundt takes a Construction Grammar approach to model this particular case of variation in World Englishes, seeing the subjunctive and the *should*-periphrasis as two constructional variants or alloconstructions of the mandative constructeme (i.e. a construction at a high level of abstraction). She contends that while the underlying mandative constructeme is the same across World Englishes, the frequency patterns emerging from the corpus data reveal that there are region-specific effects at the alloconstructional level, with interaction effects between trigger, variety and negation.

The main aim of 'The stative progressive in Singapore English: A panchronic perspective', by Debra Ziegeler and Christophe Lenoble, is to reconcile two problematical areas relating to the progressive construction in English: its diachronic development and its synchronic dispersal in today's postcolonial heritage. While a broader range of uses may be found in the development of English varieties internationally, the functional range in the older varieties of English has narrowed over time. The study questions the need to use grammaticalization theory to elucidate the diachronic development of the English progressive, given the absence of evidence of a lexical source in the earliest occurrences of the construction in Old English times. It is argued that the pathway of development may be that of a secondary grammaticalization, and one that involves reanalysis, both processes occurring gradually over an extended period of time. Likewise, the authors claim that the synchronic dispersal of the progressive in international varieties of English is not constrained by lexical retention, given that not only dynamic but also stative verbs are likely to occur in the *be + -ing* form. Stative uses of the progressive are well attested in the history of English and in international contact dialects today, such as Singapore, Indian, Papua New Guinean, East and West African English. The co-occurrence of the progressive with stative verbs can either be considered a universal feature of international Englishes or related to contact features in particular substratum languages. Ziegeler and Lenoble argue that there are no substrate-related reasons for the emergence of stative progressives in Singapore English, the variety under close examination here. An additional factor that needs to be considered, so as to account for the occurrence of progressive *have* in Singapore English, is its relatively frequent appearance in semantic adversative contexts. Such contexts are closely examined to determine whether there is a numerical preference for *be + having* occurring in them, and whether or not this may be affecting the so-called stative progressive in international or new dialects of English. The results show that *have* supplies the most frequent usage of stative progressives, perhaps due to its highest frequency as a light verb, while *be having* is also relatively frequent in adversative contexts. In fact, the majority of Singlish uses of progressive *have* come mainly from adversative contexts, and this is similar to what happens in L1 varieties of English. The situation of international (new) dialects of English may therefore be one of replication, that is, when certain forms do not replicate patterns of usage in the substrate model languages, they will replicate the diachronic developmental patterns of their lexifiers; in other words, diachronic reanalysis may also invite replication in new language varieties. In the case of Singapore English, there may be an interaction with a certain semantic domain, that of adversity, and this may interfere with the generalization of the replication hypothesis.

Crossing Linguistic Boundaries has been informed and shaped by the goal of exploring specific cases which are not easily addressed within the framework of traditional linguistic domains and boundaries. The broad spread of topics herein, covering the spectrum of English linguistics from a pioneering variationist perspective, makes the book a source of inspiration for anyone interested in linguistic variation and change in English.

Part One

Tensioning the System

Prosodic Templates in English Idioms and Fixed Expressions

Raymond Hickey
University of Duisburg-Essen

1. Introduction[1]

The status of idioms within the structure of a language has been the subject of many investigations and analyses by syntacticians and semanticists over the past few decades (Makkai 1972; Cacciari and Glucksberg 1991; Cacciari and Tabossi 1993; Everaert et al. 1995). Specifically, the position of idioms within a broadly generative grammatical framework has been the subject of many studies (Fraser 1970; Katz 1973; Newmeyer 1974; Machonis 1985; O'Grady 1998; McGinnis 2002). Other works have appeared which are not bound to a single theory but nonetheless examine idioms from a structural perspective (Nunberg, Sag and Wasow 1994; Schenk 1995; Titone and Conine 1999; Horn 2003; Mateu and Espinal 2007). There is also a practical aspect to idioms and many works concerned with foreign language teaching or of a general lexicographical nature deal with this area of language (Leaney 2005; Ayto 2009). Practically no studies have involved themselves with the prosodic structure of idioms: Ashby (2006), and to a lesser extent, Shiobara (2010), are exceptions here. It is the aim of the current chapter to view idioms from the perspective of their prosody, in particular the patterns of stressed and unstressed syllables which occur in idioms. This chapter is exploratory in nature, but hopefully arrives at valid generalizations concerning idioms.

Definitions of idioms appeal to the fixed nature of the words they contain. For instance, *The New Shorter Oxford English Dictionary* sees an idiom (in the sense used in this chapter) as a 'phrase etc. which is understood by speakers of a particular language despite its meaning's not being predictable from that of the separate words'. The essential part of this definition is that the meaning of an idiom cannot be predicted from that of the individual words it contains. This has led to idioms being structurally invariant. However, one is dealing with gradience rather binarity here and the border between idioms and collocations, the frequent co-occurrence of lexical items, e.g., *a fair trial, inclement weather*, is often difficult to draw with certainty.

The relatively fixed nature of idioms applies on the semantic level but also in the formal expression of idioms, which has a direct consequence for the prosodic structure which correlates with the syntactic elements idioms consist of. Beginning with the semantics of idioms, Nunberg, Sag and Wasow (1994: 498) list three essential features of idioms which are helpful in delimiting these structures:

1. Relative conventionality:
   'the discrepancy between the idiomatic phrasal meaning and the meaning we would predict for the collocation if we were to consult only the rules that determine the meanings of the constituents in isolation'.
2. Opacity (or transparency):
   'the ease with which the motivation for the use (or some plausible motivation – it need not be etymologically correct) can be recovered'.
3. Compositionality:
   'the degree to which the phrasal meaning, once known, can be analysed in terms of the contributions of the idiom parts'.

Relative conventionality can be illustrated by common idioms such as *to kick the bucket* 'to die', where knowledge of the semantics of the individual words in the idiom does not help in deriving the composite meaning. Nunberg, Sag and Wasow (1994: 496–7) furthermore distinguish here between 'idiomatically combining expressions' (ICEs) and 'idiomatic phrases' (IPs). The former refer to those expressions where there is a certain semantic connection between the semantic interpretation as a whole and the elements of which the idiom consists. Their example is *spill the beans*, where *spill* correlates with 'divulge' and *beans* with 'information'. With idiomatic phrases there is no such correlation, e.g., the elements of *kick the bucket* in no way relate to the composite meaning of 'to die'.[2]

Generally, idioms cannot be altered in their structure without excluding their interpretation as idioms. Consider the examples in (1) and (2):

(1) a. He spilled the beans.
     b. *He spilled the green/tasty/large-sized beans.
(2) a. His uncle kicked the bucket.
     b. *His uncle kicked the pale blue/plastic/tiny bucket.

The use of adjectives, such as *plastic* and *tiny*, diverts the attention of the hearer away from the idiom to the literal meaning of the qualifier which automatically excludes an interpretation of the structure as an idiom. This helps to grasp why qualifiers like *proverbial, god-damn* or *bloody*, as in (3), are permissible within an idiom. Here the interpretation as idiom is maintained.

(3) a. His uncle kicked the proverbial bucket.
     b. They let the bloody cat out of the bag.

For similar reasons, it is not possible to have contrastive stress on one of the elements in an idiom, as in (4) below. Again, this would draw attention to the literal meaning of the stressed element and so cause the idiom to misfire.

(4) It was raining 'cats and 'dogs.

Nonetheless, a certain amount of modification of idioms is allowed when contextualized appropriately. Once more, this is permissible if it strengthens the interpretation of an idiom, but does not cause the hearer to deconstruct the idiom lexically. The exchange in (5) between speaker A and speaker B, which involves the use of a quantifier *several* before the first element of the idiom in speaker B's turn, was judged acceptable by a number of native speakers asked for their assessment.

(5) A: I must say, your cousin has a chip on his shoulder.
    B: Well, if you ask me, he has several chips on his shoulder.

The opacity of an idiom is dependent on whether it can be interpreted by present-day speakers in some metaphorical way. This is the case with an idiom like *part and parcel*, e.g., *The health insurance is part and parcel of the deal*, where the interpretation 'an integral element of a deal' suggests itself. Opacity can increase where the user/hearer of an idiom is not aware of its derivation, e.g., *to throw in the towel* (throwing a towel into a ring originally indicated defeat).[3]

1.1. Idioms and fixed expressions

The co-occurrence of words together in phrases can show varying degrees of inflexibility in their internal structure, as discussed above. It is clear that one is dealing with a cline here, from completely rigid series of words to more flexible arrangements where speakers have a certain leeway in the formation of a given expression. The lower end of this cline is represented by collocations as indicated in the previous section. Thus, two words like *pointless exercise* have a high probability of co-occurrence, but other combinations can, and do, occur, e.g., *futile exercise*. At the high end of the inflexibility cline are sequences which are non-compositional and allow for no variation, e.g., *Tom, Dick and Harry*, so that a sequence like *Tom, Michael and Harry* is not a semantic equivalent to the first one.

The issue of inflexibility is not of concern in the present chapter. Here the focus is on the prosodic structure of fixed expressions. Whether all such structures are classified as idioms is a matter of linguistic stance. For instance, binomials, commonly occurring sequences of two elements linked by a conjunction, e.g., *fun and games, give and take, flesh and blood*, share with conventional idioms, like *kick the bucket*, that the elements they consist of do not allow of variation. Thus, sequences like *entertainment and games, handing over and take, meat and blood* are not semantic equivalents to the forms given above. It is the lack of variation in the internal structure of expressions which renders them 'fixed' and this fixedness is connected, in the view of the present author, to specific prosodic patterns. For this reason, the term 'fixed expression', rather than 'idiom', will be used in the remainder of this article.

2. Prosody in English

As a stressed-timed language, English can exploit stress contrasts for semantic purposes, as can be seen with many verb-noun pairs, all of French origin, e.g., 'record (noun) # re'cord (verb), 'convert (noun) # con'vert (verb). The option of having two consecutive syllables with approximately the same degree of stress yields the pattern of equal stress, which can then contrast with initial stress, cf. 'York Street versus 'York 'Square.[4] Here the subscript stroke indicates a reduced amount of stress in comparison with a syllable with a superscript stroke. While phonetically varying degrees of stress can be identified, for semantically contrastive stress in present-day English only two degrees are recognized: full stress ['] and reduced stress [ˌ]. These two stress types are the only two used in the present chapter, as this distinction is sufficient for the analysis of prosody in fixed expressions, just as it is for the analysis of those noun-verb pairs which are distinguished solely by stress. In metrical phonology (Liberman and Prince 1977; Hayes 1995; Kager 1995) a metrical grid can be used which can accommodate between one and three stress distinctions. For instance, in the word *distribution*, the first syllable would have a value of two, the third syllable would show a value of three, while the remaining two syllables would have single values for stress. The phonetic correlates of stress have to do with prominence and can be realized via loudness, pitch and/or duration.

```
(6)            x
        x      x
        x   x  x   x
        dis tri bu  tion
```

However, in the present chapter full stress will be termed 'strong' and abbreviated to 'S' (uppercase), while reduced stress will be termed 'weak' and abbreviated to 'w' (lowercase).

2.1. The concept of foot

In a stress-timed language, every syllable can be classified as either strong or weak, the former displaying acoustic prominence which can be realized by an increase in pitch, length or loudness, or combinations of these parameters in some instances. Sequences of syllables can be classified as constituting feet. The concept of 'foot', from metrical phonology, refers to a sequence consisting of a strongly stressed syllable followed by any sequence of weak syllables, e.g., *do!* [S], *doing* [S – w], *doable* [S – w – w]. Within a word, a foot can exhibit a strong syllable preceded by a weak syllable, e.g., *undoable* [w – S – w – w], see also (7b) below.[5] Three contrastive patterns emerge from the four logically possible combinations of strong and weak stress, as illustrated in (7).

(7) Metrical pattern   Example
     a. S – w   record (noun)
     b. w – S   record (verb)

c. S – S   Hong Kong (two feet)
    S – S – S   First World War (three feet)
d. w – w   – – –

The type shown in (7c) can consist of two or three stressed syllables and is most common in English in proper names, as in the examples shown. Furthermore, there can be a weak syllable between the strong ones, e.g., *Regent Street* [S – w – S] or *Second World War* [S – w – S – S]. Type (7d), as a complete foot, i.e. w – w, is not possible in English.

The semantic exploitation of stress contrasts is not confined to Romance-derived noun-verb pairs but can, for instance, be found with combinations of verb + preposition. In such cases the instance in which the preposition is stressed, as in (8b), can be treated as lexicalized, as the preposition cannot take an object, whereas it must take an object if it is unstressed, see (8a).

(8) a.   S   w
       live on   Some whales, despite their size, 'live on ˌplankton.
       S   S
    b. live on   Marlow died young, but his memory still 'lives 'on his plays.

3. A taxonomy of prosodic templates

In terms of metrical feet, English fixed expressions tend to consist of either two or three feet, i.e. have either two or three stressed syllables (9a, b); occasionally a fixed expression may consist of four stressed syllables (9c).

(9) a. S   S
       cheap and nasty
    b. S   S   S
       eyes in the back of one's head
    c. S   S   S   S
       out of the frying pan, into the fire

When considering the prosodic structure of these fixed expressions, the number of unstressed, weak syllables ('w' in the present notation) is irrelevant. In the last example above there are two weak syllables after each strong one, bar the final syllable: [S – w – w – S – w – w – S – w – w – S]. This means that the first three feet in this fixed expression have the structure [S – w – w], as in (9b), which is perfectly permissible in English.

3.1. Two-foot patterns: binomials

A prosodic pattern with two strongly stressed syllables is the preferred type for binomials (Mollin 2012, 2017). By and large such fixed expressions consist of two elements which are semantically related and usually linked by *and*, though other conjunctions like *or* and *but* are possible. The elements generally belong to the same word class, either as synonyms or as two words which refer to contents frequently associated with each other; in some cases the fixed expressions are now at least partially opaque, e.g., the word *hue* (see example (10f) below) is from Anglo-Norman *hu* ('outcry').

(10) a. rich and famous   b. down and out
     c. cheap and nasty   d. fun and games
     e. push and shove   f. hue and cry
     g. flesh and blood   h. give and take
     i. dead and buried   j. alive and kicking
     k. cut and dried   l. cut and thrust
     m. (to fight) tooth and nail   n. (be all) fingers and thumbs
     o. by trial and error   p. over and done with
     q. (in every) nook and cranny

Some binomials have alternatives which vary in the number of syllables. However, the additional syllables are unstressed, e.g., *alive and well ~ alive and kicking*. The number of syllables in a fixed expression can vary if one of its parts is a verb which can appear in various forms. In example (10m) above one can have *they fought tooth and nail ~ they were fighting tooth and nail*. But again, as in the instance just discussed, it is the number of unstressed, weak syllables which varies.

The relatedness of the words in a binomial pair is normally highlighted by *and* but also by phonetic means, viz. the use of rhyming or alliterating elements.

3.1.1. Rhyming binomials

Some examples of rhyming binomials are given in (11):

(11) a. town and gown   b. doom and gloom
     c. high and dry   d. wear and tear
     e. hustle and bustle   f. by hook or crook
     g. nitty gritty   h. culture vulture
     i. easy peasy

3.1.2. Alliterating binomials

This class of fixed expressions can be subdivided into various semantic classes. The one with the greatest degree of semantic cohesion shows a strongly related meaning between elements and frequently the words in the binomial are synonyms, as in (12a, b) below. Some of the alliterative binomials are partially opaque as they often rely on an element which is no longer current, see (12m) below, or have a realization which is no longer found, e.g., *rack* in *rack and ruin* is from *wreck* with lowering of the /e/ vowel in the environment of /r/ (Hickey 2014).

(i) Similar or related meanings:

(12) a. tried and tested   b. out of house and home
     c. part and parcel   d. footloose and fancy-free
     e. hale and hearty   f. bread and butter
     g. bed and breakfast   h. safe and sound
     i. head over heels   j. done and dusted
     k. spick and span   l. the world and his wife
     m. kith and kin   n. rack and ruin
     o. at sixes and sevens

(ii) Opposites:

(13) a. chalk and cheese   b. feast or famine
     c. wax and wane   d. neither fish nor fowl
     e. through thick and thin

(iii) Comparisons:

Not all fixed expressions of this type involve alliteration, e.g., *plain as daylight, clean as a whistle, happy as a sand-boy, old as the hills, swift as an arrow, light as a feather.*

(14) a. fit as a fiddle   b. dry as dust
     c. dull as dishwater   d. like two peas in a pod
     e. dead as a doornail   f. right as rain
     g. blind as a bat   h. as cool as a cucumber
     i. bright as a button   j. wet one's whistle
     k. as cute as a kitten   l. as soft as silk

(iv) Descriptors and modifiers:

The classification of the following items as fixed expressions is motivated by the alliteration between the elements. If this is not present, then what one finds is more of a collocation and any number of word pairs could be cited, e.g., *fair trial, clear statement, wide awake, fast asleep, squeaky clean.*

(15) a. crystal clear   b. cold comfort
     c. silver surfer   d. pride of place
     e. down in the dumps   f. meet your match
     g. set in stone   h. at death's door
     i. on the back burner   j. below the belt
     k. bite the bullet   l. tricks of the trade
     m. bolt from the blue   n. close call
     o. thick as thieves   p. worse for wear
     q. done to death   r. fair weather friend
     s. gift of the gab   t. great guns
     u. hope in hell   v. labour of love
     w. larger than life   x. short shrift
     y. to wait in the wings

(v) Linked actions, course or development:

(16) a. mix and match   b. cash and carry
     c. aid and abet   d. from pillar to post
     e. from rags to riches   f. from plough to plate
     g. play ducks and drakes with   h. make a mountain out of a molehill

(vi) Container:

(17) a. a pig in a poke   b. a bee in one's bonnet

There is a subset of alliterating two-foot fixed expressions which involve vowel alternations while the remainder of both words remain identical. This often results in words only one of which actually exists independently in the English lexicon. In fact, in many cases neither word occurs independently and the binomial has a certain phonaesthetic component (Zingler 2016) which depends on the occurrence of one of the following vowel alterations.

(18) a. /ɪ –æ/   zig zag, dribs and drabs, KitKat, spick and span
     b. /ɪ – ɔ/   bits and bobs, criss cross,[6] ping pong, flip-flop, hip-hop, ding dong, see-saw[7]
     c. /ɔ – ɜ:/ topsy turvy

3.2. Three-foot fixed expressions

The number of fixed expressions with three feet is smaller than those with two but nonetheless they represent a clear type with identifiable features in form and content. With three syllables, the first one is often a verb which may consist of a single strong syllable or a sequence of strong and weak, depending on the form of the verb in question. Three-foot fixed expressions can also end in either two consecutive strong syllables or have one or more unstressed syllables between these.

(19) Prosodic template: [S – (w) – (w) – S – S]
     a. be all ears   b. paint the town red
     c. money for old rope   d. out of thin air
     e. all in a day's work   f. all the time in the world
     g. for all the tea in China[8]

(20) Prosodic template: [(w) – S – (w) – S – w – (w) – S]
     a. beat around the bush   b. rain cats and dogs
     c. cost an arm and a leg   d. if push comes to shove

3.2.1. The link of form and meaning: three-item lists

Among the three-foot fixed expressions is one type in which there is a clear connection between prosodic structure and meaning. The prosodic template found here is [S – S – w – S – w] and the fixed expressions in question are all found in phrase- or sentence-final position. An example would be: *hook, line and sinker*. This and all fixed expressions with this prosodic pattern imply completeness, entirety, every member of a group, and thus seem to reflect conceptual structure as well (Keysar and Bly 1999). They furthermore typically occur at the end of a sentence or phrase adding to this sense of completeness. For want of a better term, this type is dubbed a three-item list in this chapter.

(21) Prosodic template: [S – S – w – S – w]
 a. Tom, Dick and Harry   b. hook, line and sinker
 c. lock, stock and barrel   d. bell, book and candle
 e. rag, tag and bobtail   f. hung, drawn and quartered
 g. born, bred and buttered   h. cool, calm and collected
 i. signed, sealed and delivered j. high, wide and handsome
 k. up, up and away

Example (21a) is from an eighteenth-century song 'Farewell, Tom, Dick and Harry, Farewell, Moll, Nell and Sue' (Ayto 2009: 358). This means that the expression was extracted from this source and came to be used as it is currently found (a three-item list). (21d) stems from the rite of excommunication: 'Do to the book, quench the candle, ring the bell' (Ayto 2009: 25). Note that the sequence of elements was altered from book, candle and bell to bell, book and candle, perhaps to yield the prosodic structure of a three-item list.

There are instances where these structures are dated, e.g., *hatches, matches and despatches* 'the births, marriages and deaths columns in a newspaper' (Ayto 2009: 166), but which previously carried similar semantics.

The number and position of the unstressed syllables in three-item lists can vary if the words they contain dictate this. In the examples in (22) the final words consist of a single strongly stressed syllable.

(22) Prosodic template: [S – S – w – S]
 a. morning, noon and night   b. blood, sweat and tears
 c. head, heart and soul

In the ensuing examples the middle word is in each case disyllabic and the final word is monosyllabic. The order of words two and three could have been reversed to yield the prosodic structure [S – S – w – S – w]. However, in the first instance the sequence is first adults and then children, while in the second the sequence is one of a descending size of currency units.

(23) Prosodic template: [S – S – w – w – S]
 a. (every) man, woman and child
 b. pounds, shillings and pence

A few other variants with three-item lists occur. In (24a) the phrase *for nothing* is used to obtain a list of three items, all implying 'without any cost'. In (24b) the professions are all polysyllabic words. Note that in both examples the last two syllables are [S – w], thus conforming to the majority pattern for three-item lists.

(24) a. free, gratis and for nothing
     b. butcher, baker, candlestick maker

The instances of three-item lists quoted thus far are all established in English and so it is not easy to test for the productivity of this pattern. However, the following might offer some indirect evidence. An Italian-directed western film from 1966 used a three-item list in its title referring to all the members of the group portrayed in the film: *The Good, the Bad and the Ugly*,[9] which conforms to the prosodic pattern [3S + 1w#].

3.3. Four-foot fixed expressions

As a rule of thumb, the greater the number of feet, the fewer fixed expressions are found. This would seem to hold for present-day English and the number of those fixed expressions which consist of four metrical feet is fairly limited. These expressions usually consist of two juxtaposed parts,[10] each one containing two feet. The two parts of the fixed expression are semantically related, with the second half often being a consequence of the first.

(25) [S   S   –   S   S]
     a. finders keepers, losers weepers
     b. nothing ventured, nothing gained
     c. live by the sword, die by the sword
     d. out of sight, out of mind
     e. in for a penny, in for a pound
     f. here today, gone tomorrow
     g. first come, first served
     h. once bitten, twice shy

A miscellaneous set of four-foot fixed expressions can be found which do not segment into two juxtaposed halves. Some of the prosodic patterns are uncommon, depending on the syntax and lexis of the fixed expression, as in the last example below with [S – S – S – w – w – S – w].

(26) a. the be all and end all
     b. A stitch in time saves nine.
     c. His bark is worse than his bite.
     d. Where there's a will, there's a way.
     e. When the cat's away, the mice will play.
     f. Leave no stone unturned.

4. Conclusion

This chapter has attempted to show that there is a relationship between the meanings of many fixed expressions and the number and distribution of stressed and unstressed syllables as well as their frequent rhyming or alliterative nature. Thus, prosodic structure, rhyme and alliteration help to weld together the semantically related elements of fixed expressions on a phonetic level. Furthermore, there is a basic distinction in the semantic implications of at least three types of fixed expressions, determined by the number of feet they contain, and which can be formulated as follows:

Metrical structure	Semantic implications
two-foot	binomials with high degree of semantic relatedness
three-foot	three-item lists expressing completeness, entirety
four-foot	juxtaposed halves expressing consequence

Notes

1 While this contribution does not lie within the core research areas of Teresa Fanego I hope that she might find time in her well-earned retirement to muse on the matters presented here.
2 For a critique of these notions, see Espinal and Mateu (2010).
3 This distinction is reminiscent of that between idiomatically combining expressions (ICEs) and idiomatic phrases (IPs) by Nunberg, Sag and Wasow (1994) referred to above.
4 In the terminology of poetic metrics these patterns are called trochee and spondee, respectively. An iamb consists of a weak syllable followed by a strong one, e.g., ˌaˈbout.
5 The domain of the foot is also a matter of theoretical interpretation. In the metrical trees found in Liberman and Prince (1977), for instance, a word like *metricality* consists of two feet *metri + cality*, the first weak and the second strong (in relative terms). The first weak foot, however, consists of a strong and a weak syllable, as *me-* has greater acoustic prominence than *-tri-*.
6 This expression derives from *Christ cross* in the seventeenth century, but was later altered phonetically to give the vowel-alternating binomial which exists today.
7 The vowels in this example are long, as English does not have open syllables ending in either /-ɪ/ or /-ɔ/.
8 This type of prosodic template [S – S – w – S – w] exists in other Germanic languages, cf., Swedish *för allt smör i Småland* ('for all the butter in Småland').
9 The Italian title is *Il buono, il brutto, il cattivo* ('The good, the ugly, the bad'), with three disyllabic nouns in a list but with the second and third nouns in reverse order compared to the English original.
10 Occasionally, juxtaposed elements of an idiom may only involve two strong syllables, as in *waste not, want not; the more, the merrier.*

References

Ashby, Michael (2006), 'Prosody and Idioms in English', *Journal of Pragmatics*, 38 (10): 1580–97.
Ayto, John, ed (2009), *Oxford Dictionary of English Idioms*, 3rd edn, Oxford: Oxford University Press.

Brown, Lesley, ed (1993), *The New Shorter Oxford English Dictionary on Historical Principles*, 4th edn, Oxford: Clarendon Press.

Cacciari, Cristina and Sam Glucksberg (1991), 'Understanding Idiomatic Expressions: The Contribution of Word Meanings', in Geoffrey B. Simpson (ed), *Understanding Word and Sentence*, 217–40, Amsterdam: Elsevier.

Cacciari, Cristina and Patrizia Tabossi, eds (1993), *Idioms: Processing, Structure, and Interpretation*, Hillsdale, NJ: Lawrence Erlbaum.

Espinal, M. Teresa and Jaume Mateu (2010), 'On Classes of Idioms and their Interpretation', *Journal of Pragmatics*, 42 (5): 1397–411.

Everaert, Martin, Erik-Jan van der Linden, André Schenk and Rob Schreuder, eds (1995), *Idioms: Structural and Psychological Perspectives*, Hillsdale NJ: Lawrence Erlbaum Associates.

Fraser, Bruce (1970), 'Idioms within a Transformational Grammar', *Foundations of Language*, 6: 22–42.

Hayes, Bruce (1995), *Metrical Stress Theory: Principles and Case Studies*, Chicago: University of Chicago Press.

Hickey, Raymond (2014), 'Vowels before /r/ in the History of English', in Daniel Schreier, Olga Timofeeva, Anne Gardner, Alpo Honkapoja and Simone Pfenninger (eds), *Contact, Variation and Change in the History of English*, 95–110, Amsterdam: Benjamins.

Horn, George M. (2003), 'Idioms, Metaphors and Syntactic Mobility', *Journal of Linguistics*, 39: 245–73.

Kager, René (1995), 'The Metrical Theory of Word Stress', in John Goldsmith (ed), *The Handbook of Phonology*, 1st edn, 367–402, Oxford: Blackwell.

Katz, Jerrold J. (1973), 'Compositionality, Idiomaticity, and Lexical Substitution', in Stephen R. Anderson and Paul Kiparsky (eds), *A Festschrift for Morris Halle*, 357–76, New York: Holt, Rinehart and Winston.

Keysar, Boaz and Bridget Martin Bly (1999), 'Swimming Against the Current: Do Idioms Reflect Conceptual Structure?', *Journal of Pragmatics*, 31(12): 1559–78.

Leaney, Cindy (2005), *In the Know: Understanding and Using Idioms*, Cambridge: Cambridge University Press.

Liberman, Mark and Alan Prince (1977), 'On Stress and Linguistic Rhythm', *Linguistic Inquiry*, 8: 249–336.

Machonis, Peter (1985), 'Transformations of Verb Phrase Idioms: Passivization, Particle Movement, Dative Shift', *American Speech*, 60: 291–308.

Makkai, Adam (1972), *Idiom Structure in English*, The Hague: De Gruyter.

Mateu, Jaume and M. Teresa Espinal (2007), 'Argument Structure and Compositionality in Idiomatic Constructions', *The Linguistic Review*, 24 (1): 33–59.

McGinnis, Martha (2002), 'On the Systematic Aspect of Idioms', *Linguistic Inquiry*, 33 (4): 665–72.

Mollin, Sandra (2012), 'Revisiting Binomial Order in English. Ordering Constraints and Reversibility', *English Language and Linguistics*, 16 (1): 81–103.

Mollin, Sandra (2017), 'Developments in the Frequency of English Binomials, 1600–2000', in Joanna Kopaczyk and Hans Sauer (eds), *Binomials in the History of English. Fixed and Flexible*, 279–95, Cambridge: Cambridge University Press.

Newmeyer, Frederick (1974), 'The Regularity of Idiom Behavior', *Lingua*, 34: 327–42.

Nunberg, Geoffrey, Ivan A. Sag, and Thomas Wasow (1994), 'Idioms', *Language*, 70: 491–538.

O'Grady, William (1998), 'The Syntax of Idioms', *Natural Language and Linguistic Theory*, 16: 79–312.

Schenk, André (1995), 'The Syntactic Behavior of Idioms', in Martin Everaert, Erik-Jan van der Linden, André Schenk and Rob Schreuder (eds), *Idioms: Structural and Psychological Perspectives*, 253–72. Hillsdale, NJ: Lawrence Erlbaum.

Shiobara, Kayono (2010) 'A Prosodic Approach to Ditransitive Idioms', *MIT Working Papers in Linguistics*, 64 (*Proceedings of the Fifth Formal Approaches to Japanese Linguistics Conference*): 241–50.

Titone, Debra A. and Cynthia M. Conine (1999), 'On the Compositional and Noncompositional Nature of Idiomatic Expressions', *Journal of Pragmatics*, 31 (12): 1655–74.

Zingler, Tim (2016), 'Evidence against the Morpheme: The History of English Phonaesthemes', *Language Sciences*, 62: 76–90.

2

Word-search as Word-formation?
The Case of *uh* and *um*[1]

Gunnel Tottie

University of Zurich

1. Introduction

The vocalizations [ə(:)] and [ə(:)m], usually transcribed *uh* and *um* (or *er* and *erm* in non-rhotic varieties of English), are a characteristic feature of impromptu spoken English. They have been called filled pauses, fillers, hesitations, pragmatic markers (and denounced as 'slips', 'stumbles' and 'blunders' in the popular literature; cf., Erard 2007). Their status as words has been debated (Shillcock et al. 2001; Clark and Fox Tree 2002; O'Connell and Kowal 2005; Tottie 2017). Tottie (2017) regards them as 'nascent' or 'emergent' words in speech (cf., Grieve, Nini and Guo 2017), and suggests that this is one of the rare cases of word-formation called coinage or root creation, i.e. lexicalization occurring without any kind of prior traditional word-formation process taking place (McArthur 1992: 876–7; Brinton and Traugott 2005: 43). The classification as words is definitely justified when *uh* and *um* are used intentionally in writing (other than uses that are mimetic of speech), as in (1)–(4):[2]

(1) Obama is more, *um, seasoned.* [His] hair appears to be increasingly gray. (*Washington Post* 2008)

(2) An ode to opera's, *uh, operation.* [P]eople wonder about the castrati – the emasculated singers (*L.A. Times* 2005)

(3) [The actor Ben Affleck goes to sleep during a performance of Shakespeare. He] seemed to be, *um* – how can we put this delicately? – *meditating* during most of the first act. (*Boston Globe* 1999)

(4) Senator Richard Shelby . . . claimed that '[t]he market will view these firms as . . . implicitly backed by the government'. *Um, senator,* the market already views those firms as having implicit government backing, because they do (Paul Krugman, Op-Ed Column, *The New York Times* 2010)

Based on the TIME Magazine Corpus and the Corpus of Contemporary American English (COCA), Tottie (2017) shows that this type of use has become current in

Table 2.1 The aggregate distribution of *uh*, *um* and *er* (EHM) in the TIME Corpus and COCA from the 1960s to the 2000s and frequencies per million words of text

	TIME CORPUS			COCA		
	N EHM	**N words**	**Freq. pmw**	**N EHM**	**N words**	**Freq. pmw**
1960s	3	15,653,909	0.2	–		
1970s	10	12,518,793	0.8	–		
1980s	23	11,053,333	2.1	–		
1990s	79	9,425,993	8.4	199	82,916,667	2.4
2000s	51	6,754,797	7.5	326	83,589,744	3.9
	166			525		

American journalistic prose since the 1960s, reaching high levels from the 1990s into the twenty-first century, as shown in Table 2.1. In addition to *uh* and *um*, the form *er* is – somewhat surprisingly – used in American journalistic prose; these written forms will be subsumed as EHM in the present chapter.

The different proportions in the TIME Corpus and COCA can, at least in part, be explained by the fact that COCA contains both newspapers and magazines.[3] Although newspapers have been classified wholesale as an 'agile' text type (Hundt and Mair 1999), they comprise different subtypes: thus, e.g., news reporting is much less likely to contain expressions of writers' attitudes than, e.g., opinion columns and reviews.

The functions of EHM can be divided into two main types, depending on use in sentence-initial position, as in (5) and (6), or in sentence-medial position, as in (7) and (8). Henceforth, written examples are all from COCA; italics have been added throughout.

(5) This year's unit was supposed to be the school's most talented since ... 1992. *Uh, that's hogwash.* (COCA, 1997, Sporting News, MAG)

(6) it's tempting to believe it will be easy. *Um ... reality check time.* [ellipsis in the original] (COCA, 1994, Outdoor Life, MAG)

(7) happy hour at your neighbor's makes your speech, *er, unrecognizable* (COCA, 2001, Chicago, NEWS)

(8) former boxing champ ... Holyfield agreed to show his dancing, *um, skills.* (COCA, 2007, USA Today, NEWS)

In either position, EHM functions as a stance adverb. Initial EHM usually focuses on a clause and expresses a (usually negative) comment on an earlier proposition, as in (5) and (6) above. Sentence-medial EHM focuses on a following word or word phrase, usually a noun (phrase) or an adjective. Its function is usually 'tongue in cheek', showing the writer's humorous, ironic or euphemistic attitude, as shown by examples (7) and (8) above.[4]

It is easy to find a model in spoken language for the sentence-initial use of EHM. Spoken *uh* and *um*, henceforth subsumed as UHM, are frequently used in answers to questions, especially when the responder needs time to ponder or qualify the question asked, as in (9), where a teacher asks a student about her parents' attitude to the Vietnam War (Tottie 2015a). All spoken examples are from the Santa Barbara Corpus of Spoken American English (SBC), with transcription and soundtrack available online.[5]

(9) MONTOYA: . . . How about your parents.
    CAROLYN: . . . *U=m,*
        . . . well my dad was drafted.
    MONTOYA: . . . He was in Vietnam?
    CAROLYN: . . . *U=m,*
        . . . long story,
        he didn't make it to Vietnam but, (12 *American Democracy is Dying*)

It is more difficult to explain the typical use of written EHM in medial position based on uses of UHM in speech. Like Rühlemann and Hilpert (2017), who discuss the origin of *well* as a discourse marker in written English, Tottie (2017) suggested use for word-search as the likely spoken model, based on examples like (7) and (8) above, and further pointed out that in writing, it is a make-believe word-search.

Although this explanation is plausible, there seem to be no previous studies of the use of UHM for word-search in conversation. Earlier studies of spoken English from the SBC (Tottie 2014, 2015b) have indicated that the typical use of UHM in speech is for planning of longer turns, as shown in example (10) from that corpus.[6] However, neither *such a tiny apartment* nor *our neighborhood* can be characterized as instances of word-search, but are part of the general online planning process.

(10) FRAN: For one thing,
      I had *uh,*
      such a tiny apartment.
      . . . *u=m,*
      . . . when we . . . went back to New York,
      . . . *u=m,*
      . . . I had . . . <X kept X> a studio there.
      . . . And . . . of course,
      that was small and,
      . . . and then,
      we found another studio,
      . . . in *uh,*
      in . . . our neighborhood, (51 *New Yorkers Anonymous*)

In order to assess the importance of the frequency of UHM used for word-search in spoken English, I decided to carry out a quantitative study based on the SBC. It is well suited for that work as it dates from around 1990, the time period when EHM reached high frequency levels in journalistic prose from TIME, and it is the results of this work that I will present and discuss here. Note that my purpose is to throw light on the particular role of UHM in word-search, not to cover all types of word-search, which can be signalled in many ways: by silent pauses or pragmatic markers such as *you know, I mean, like,* etc.

2. The Santa Barbara Corpus study

2.1. Material

The present study of word-search flagged by UHM in the SBC is based on a sub-corpus of 40 recorded and transcribed conversations selected from the SBC total of 60 texts. This sub-corpus comprises about 175,000 words and includes only what can be considered typical speech, i.e. impromptu face-to-face interactive conversations, leaving out prepared texts such as lectures, sermons or guided tours, and telephone conversations.

2.2. Defining word-search

Word-search needs to be carefully defined and operationalized before being made an object of study.[7] It is not a standard technical term in linguistics, where 'lexical retrieval' and 'lexical selection' are used, particularly in psycholinguistics.[8] I shall use those terms as follows: I will use 'lexical retrieval' about the search for a target word where there is only one 'correct' choice, as in (11) and (12). This target word is often a technical term or the name of a person or a place:

    (11) BAILIFF: Are you X --
                     Are you the *uh . . . plaintiff*? (53 *I Will Appeal*)
    (12) GARY: . . . All I . . . I know where it is.
                     . . . It's over near *uh,*
                     . . . (THROAT)
                     . . . (H) *Palo Alto.* (56 *What is a Brand Inspection*)

I use 'lexical selection' where there can be several possible choices but a particular one is considered by the speaker to be the best choice, the *mot juste,* as in (13):

    (13) ALAN: You know they got a,
                   (H) they got a,
                   they got a,
                   uh,
                   . . . *a class= situation,* (60 *Shaggy Dog Story*)

There is likely a cognitive difference between the two types, but that is a topic that is beyond my present aims. I include both types in my search; their relative proportions will be reported but not analysed.

2.3. Method

As word-search is just one of many functions of UHM, automated retrieval would have very low precision and recall, and I therefore decided to carry out my search manually. Establishing formal criteria for classifying UHM tokens as instances of word-search is obviously dependent on the transcription system used in the corpus investigated, in this case the SBC. The SBC makes a four-way distinction between nasal and non-nasal, long and short variants of UHM, viz. *uh* and *uh=*, *um* and *u=m* or *um=*. It seemed reasonable to include not only the lengthened variants, but also short ones if they were accompanied by a preceding and/or following pause marked with three dots, thus exceeding 0,3 seconds. However, in a few cases context was the only indicator of word-search.

An easy case was (14), where UHM appears as *uh=* and is preceded by a pause:

(14) MONTOYA: ...(H) Categorizing,
                 ...*uh=*,
                 the Soviet Union, (12 *American Democracy is Dying*)

However, such uncomplicated cases are rare, and formal criteria can often be difficult to apply. For instance, UHM, three-dot ellipses and the target word can be separated by chunks of transcription including other speakers, as in (15):

(15) LUCY: You know that...archway between the living room and the dining
                room-?
                And [the *um*],
     LINDA: [(SNIFF)]
     DAN: Yeah.
     LUCY: ...*hall?* (49 *Noise Pollution*)

Simultaneous speech, marked by square brackets in the SBC, is another hurdle. In (16) the target word (phrase) is more difficult to find. It has an abundance of simultaneous speech (matched by numbered square brackets) and co-text is necessary to track Lucy's search for a word describing the colour she is thinking of. Moreover, the noun phrase is prefaced by the pragmatic marker *like*.[9]

(16) LUCY: *they p2]ainted the inside the wrong color.*
                We had [3ordered this3] --
     LINDA: [3Well you got it on3] ~Jo=hn.
     LUCY: ... *[4U=m4],*
     ALLEN: [4@Well4],
     JOHN: [4@@4]@[5@@5]
     LUCY: *[5 like an5] eggshell color.* (49 *Noise pollution*)

Cases of unsuccessful retrieval, where no target word appears in the text, must also be accounted for. An example of failed word-search is given in (17). Lynne, a

young girl learning to take care of horses, is trying to tell her listeners that she is
not a real *farrier*, but she fails to find the word, which only comes up later in the
conversation.

> (17) LYNNE: I mean I trim horses=,
> and stuff like that,
> but I mean,
> I'm not like,
> (H) . . . <@ I'm no=t *uh*= @>,
> @
> *(H) I don't know how to say it.*
> But you know,
> they do it for a living. (1 *Blacksmithing*)

The manual search for tokens of UHM was thus not a technically demanding
enterprise but a time-consuming one, as pauses are often located at a considerable
distance from UHM tokens in the transcriptions and because it was sometimes
necessary to look for pauses by checking the timeline (supplied in the margin in the
SBC, but shown here only in example (22)) to find pauses that were not indicated by
three-dot ellipses.

Since I was the only researcher, the only safeguard against subjectivity was two
consecutive passes, separated by a couple of months. My principle was to include rather
than reject doubtful cases; in spite of this policy, the proportion of word-search cases
was unexpectedly low. However, even if I missed some cases, the number would have
been very low, and my aim is not to provide exact figures here but a sense of proportions.

2.4. Results

There were altogether 2,220 tokens of UHM in the partial SBC corpus used for this
project, but fewer than 170 – less than 8 per cent – marked word-search efforts. They
occurred in a total of 145 cases of word-search; this is because there were a few
instances with more than one token of UHM, as in (18), which has five UHM tokens.
This is an extreme number; the great majority of examples contained only one UHM
token and only a few two.

> (18) TOM2: (H) But she was a real ship,
> a two-hatch ship,
> (H) based in *uh*,
> *in,*
> . . . *in uh,*
> *(H) uh==,*
> *in um,*
> . . . % % = % % *uh=,*
> *West Africa.* (32 *Handshakes All Around*)

Table 2.2 Cases of word-search with UHM in the SBC sub-corpus

	Non-nasalized		Nasalized		
	uh	*uh=*	*um*	*um=*	**UHM**
N	68	40	20	17	145
%	47%	28%	14%	12%	
	108		37		145

As demonstrated by (18), both nasalized and non-nasalized tokens were used in the word-search process; *uh* was more frequent than *um*, with *uh* accounting for two-thirds and *um* one-third of the examples. Table 2.2 shows the totals of UHM in word-search examples and the proportions of long and short tokens of *uh* and *um*.[10]

The majority of UHM tokens were used in searches for nouns or noun phrases, 118/145 (81 per cent). Twenty-six of these were proper nouns and ninety-two were common nouns. Thirty-one of the common nouns were cases of lexical retrieval of terms like *plaintiff* in (11) above. Lexical selection accounted for seventy-four cases, as in (19). Adjectives were the targets in eight cases, as in (20), and a verb only in a single case, (21). The remaining target words were an assortment of count nouns, adverbs or zeroes, i.e. unsuccessful searches. The most typical examples are thus of the types shown in (19) and (20):

(19) REED: (H) chances are (Hx),
               . . . you've uh hurt that,
               . . . *uh ligament* in the back too. (46 *Flumpity-Bump Down the Hill*)
(20) MARIE: Fevers are like,
               . . . *um*,
               . . . (H) . . . *good* for babies like,
               when they're i- b- getting sick,
               because they help . . . the immune system fight harder.
               (36 *Judgmental on People*)
(21) SUE: at the wedding,
               see,
               is when Helen=,
               . . . *uh=*,
               . . . *conceived*, (23 *Howards End*)

Most texts contained only the odd instance of UHM used for word-search, and some of them had no instances at all. The conversations that showed higher numbers were those that had high overall UHM frequencies, especially the ones that contained long narrative sections spoken by older people. In (18) above, from *Handshakes All Around*, Tom2, aged 72, produces five tokens of UHM to reach the target word, and in (13) above, from *Shaggy Dog Story*, Alan, 66, searches for an expression to characterize a particular ethnic group. In (22) below it takes Doris, 83, three and a half seconds to come up with the word for her medication, *diuretic*, as is clear from the timeline in the left margin.[11]

(22)	1036.75	1037.69	DORIS:	. . . He said uh,
	1037.69	1040.35		take %% . . . the *uh*,
	1040.35	1041.82	SAM:	. . . (H)
	1041.82	1042.60	DORIS:	what do you call it?
	1042.60	1043.99		. . . The water pill.
	1043.99	1045.66		. . . (H) Diarrhetic.[12]

(11 *This Retirement Bit*)

It is hardly surprising that older speakers produced more examples of word-search than younger speakers – cf., earlier research by, e.g., Tottie (2011) that shows a higher UHM ratio with age. What is more noteworthy is that the 'tongue-in-cheek' use of UHM for delicacy, euphemism or irony, which is dominant in writing, first seemed to be non-existent in the SBC material (Tottie 2017). However, subsequent re-examination of larger chunks of context led to my identifying two possible candidates for classification as instances of delicacy or irony, viz. (23) and (24) below.

The context of (23) is that Lisbeth and Jennifer (mother and daughter) have had a disagreement about what happened earlier in the day. Bill (Lisbeth's husband and Jennifer's father) searches for a word to describe his wife and daughter's communication problem by calling them, somewhat hesitantly, *hyper . . . uh sensitive to one another's language*. This could be a politer way of saying that they are very touchy, always quarrelling, etc.

(23) BILL: [5~J=5]ennifer and ~Lisbeth are *hyper . . . uh*[6= *sensitive6*],
     MARY: [6Like I told you twenty ti6]=mes.
     BILL: to one another's language.
               . . . So,
               [if ~Jenni]fer says,
     MARY: [XXX].
     BILL: . . . uh Mo=m,
               . . . ~Lisbeth hears,
               . . . a lot more [into it] . . . than Mom. (33 *Guilt*)

The conversation in (24) – the same as (21) above with a wider context – takes place at a book club discussion between middle-class women aged 46–85, at a meeting where the topic is E.M. Forster's novel *Howards End*. The book's character Helen becomes pregnant without being married (the wedding mentioned in the text is somebody else's) and she leaves England to bear the child. The speaker, Sue, chooses a technical and stylistically marked term, *conceive*, instead of *become pregnant* or something more graphic, and she clearly has to search for that word.

(24) SUE: [Well --
    LINDA: Tibby wasn't there.
    SUE: When . . . when he- they- --
                at the wedding,
                see,
                is when Helen=,
                . . . *uh=,*
                . . . *conceived,*
                and so then,
                shortly thereafter,
                she me- went away.
                She went to like,
                . . . Ger[many], (23 *Howards End*)

With a possible two out of 145 cases of UHM conveying delicacy or euphemism, the SBC offers slender evidence of transit from filled pause to word in spoken language (more specifically a stance adverb), but it deserves to be considered.

3. Discussion

Some questions are raised by the data presented above. First of all, how could the infrequent use of word-search UHM in speech – about 8 per cent of the total number of UHM tokens – lead to lexicalization and word status in written language? My suggestion is that word-search is a salient phenomenon because it focuses on content words – we have seen that most SBC tokens involve nouns and adjectives. Word-search UHM highlights elements that are important in the context of interaction, and this makes this type more noticeable, more salient in speakers' minds, than other uses of UHM. This could explain its subsequent adoption in writing. Secondly, how could the least frequent type, i.e. the 'tongue-in-cheek' use of UHM for delicacy, euphemism or irony have become the chosen one in writing? And thirdly, where did lexicalization occur, in speech or in writing? My suggestion here is that the near-absence of 'tongue-in-cheek' uses of UHM in the SBC sub-corpus is most likely due to the friendly, interactive nature of the conversations included. Irony and euphemism are stylistic devices more germane to (journalistic) writing than to amicable face-to-face interaction, but some situations require careful handling of language. In (23) and (24) above, speaking is private but guarded. In (23) Bill does not want to cause more friction than there already is between his wife and daughter, and in (24) Sue is careful not to mention passion or illegitimate babies. Both are well-educated, middle-aged speakers: Bill is a fifty-two-year-old professor and Sue is a fifty-three-year-old accountant with a master's degree; both can be assumed to be highly literate and aware of their choice of words. All this indicates that there is a case for assuming that lexicalization of UHM can occur in speech, in particular in sensitive contexts. Comparing wholesale categories like speech and writing is thus not enough – situation and context are of prime importance.

A different corpus than the SBC sub-corpus used for this study might have yielded different results, e.g., one consisting of political debates. This is suggested by (25)–(27) below, spoken examples culled from the web:[13]

> (25) Um we realize this is a very *um difficult* area and it's one that we did inherit, the skills crisis from the Howard government (Transcript of interview with Justine Elliot, Minister for Ageing; http://www.abc.net.au/4corners/content/2009/s2586025.htm)
>
> (26) We were in the middle of this, *um, difficult* situation between Venezuela, Colombia and Ecuador ... (US Institute of Peace interview; https://www.usip.org/public-education/educators/juanes-building-peace-through-music-transcript)
>
> (27) What was your boss like? Heather: Well she wasn't er wasn't very easy ..., she was *a bit er difficult very difficult* to get on with ... (The London Bubble Theatre; http://www.londonbubble.org.uk/page/stories/)

Note the choice of *difficult* in (25)–(27). *Difficult* is a cover-up term both in the two political examples and in the speaker's public characterization of her boss in (27). One has the sense that the speakers would have said something much more critical and less guarded if they had been speaking in a non-public situation. Using *difficult*, and showing that this is a thoughtful word-choice by means of UHM, is a convenient way out for the speakers. However, these examples are of recent date, and the use of *uh/er* and *um/erm* in emails, chats and blogs has contributed to erase the borders between speech and writing (cf., Clark and Fox Tree (2002: 105, fn.10) and, especially, Rose (2011)). The 1990s examples from the SBC are therefore better evidence for lexicalization of UHM in speech than the ones taken from the web, as today's speakers may also have been influenced by examples seen in printed material with tokens of EHM as stance adverbs.

I conclude that the word-search function of UHM can thus be a stage in the word-formation process. Note also that in this process, there is a subtle change in the meaning of *hesitation*. The OED gloss of *hesitate* (s.v.1a) is in fact contradictory between 'hold back in indecision' and its opposite, 'to scruple', which has nothing to do with indecision but with reluctance:

> To hold back in doubt or indecision; to show, or speak with, indecision; to find difficulty in deciding; to scruple.

The OED gives no examples of the 'scruple' meaning under *hesitate*, but the entry of *scruple* (s.v. 5) provides a suitable gloss:[14]

> To hesitate or be reluctant (*to do* something), esp. on conscientious grounds, or out of regard for what is fit and proper.

It is precisely being reluctant 'out of regard for what is fit and proper' – or at least pretending to be – that is indicated by medial EHM in journalistic writing (Tottie

2017), and it is the regard for what is fit and proper that motivates the speakers who select the words *hypersensitive* and *conceive* rather than less polite alternatives.

Appendix

Transcription conventions in the Santa Barbara Corpus; from Du Bois et al. (1992).

Units	
Intonation unit	[carriage return]
Truncated intonation unit	- -
Truncated word	-
Transitional continuity	
Final	.
Continuing	,
Appeal (seeking a validating response from listener)	?
Speakers	
Speech overlap (numbers inside brackets index overlaps)	[ ]
Accent and lengthening	
Primary accent (prominent pitch movement carrying intonational meaning)	^
Secondary accent	'
Unaccented	
Lengthening	=
Pause	
Long and medium	. . .
Short (brief break in speech rhythm)	. .
Latching	(0)
Vocal noises	
e.g., (TSK), (SNIFF), (YAWN), (DRINK)	
Glottal stop	%
Exhalation	(Hx)
Inhalation	(H)
Laughter (one pulse)	@
Quality	
Loudness	
Forte: loud	<F F>
Piano: soft	<P P>
Pitch	
Higher pitch level	<HI H>
Lowered pitch level	<LO LO>
Parenthetical prosody	<PAR PAR>
Tempo and rhythm	
Allegro: rapid speech	<A A>
Lento: slow speech	<L L>
Marcato: each word distinct and emphasized	<MRC MRC>
Arrhythmic: halting speech	<ARH ARH>
Voice quality	
Whispered	<WH>
Breathy	
Creaky	<%>
Crying	<CRY>

Yawning	<YWN>
Quotation quality	<Q>
Transcriber's perspective	
Uncertain hearing	<X X>

Notes

1   For Teresa Fanego, brilliant scholar, invaluable colleague and friend. I thank Sebastian Hoffmann and two helpful reviewers for constructive criticism of an earlier version of this chapter.
2   Examples (1)–(4) are taken from incidental reading.
3   For details, see Tottie (2017).
4   For further discussion of subtypes of EHM as stance adverbs, see Tottie (2017).
5   Line breaks mark intonation units, commas continuing intonation and periods final intonation. The symbol '=' denotes lengthening of a preceding vowel, 'X' denotes unclear words, two dots a pause shorter than 0.3 seconds and three dots longer pauses. Brief simultaneous speech – usually indicated by square brackets – has been removed in (9) for clarity. Names of numbered source texts from SBC are given in italics. For an overview of SBC transcription symbols, see the Appendix.
6   On the planning function of UHM, see e.g., Biber et al. (1999); Carter and McCarthy (2006); Jucker (2015).
7   The OED only defines *word search* as 'a puzzle in which the object is to find hidden words, typically within a grid of apparently jumbled letters'. (i) is one of the examples listed:

   (i) Word searches, quizzes, and crosswords were added. (1978 *Eng. Jrnl.* Apr. 79/2)

8   'Lexical retrieval' is common in 'tip-of-the-tongue' studies, as in e.g., Drevets and Lickley (2017).
9   In this example, I have italicized Lucy's name and the target words to facilitate following her contribution.
10 When examples contained more than one token of UHM, the token closest to the target word or phrase was used for the statistics in Table 2.2.
11 In this case, the token would have been spotted anyway because of the three-dot pauses preceding it, but the timeline gives an exact measure.
12 The transcriber's version of the word.
13 I am grateful to Philip Shaw for supplying these examples from the internet. Unfortunately, (27) is no longer available online.
14 The only dictionary (out of a large number examined) that explicitly includes 'reluctance' under *hesitate* is Roget's Thesaurus (2001).

Corpora

COCA = Davies, Mark (2008–), *The Corpus of Contemporary American English (COCA): 560 million words, 1990-present*. Available online: https://corpus.byu. edu/coca/.

SBC = *Santa Barbara Corpus of Spoken American English*. Available online: http://www.linguistics.ucsb.edu/research/santa-barbara.corpus.
TIME = Davies, Mark. (2007–), *TIME Magazine Corpus: 100 million words, 1920s-2000s*. Available online: https://corpus.byu.edu/time/.

References

Biber, Douglas, Stig Johansson, Geoffrey Leech, Susan Conrad and Edward Finegan (1999), *Longman Grammar of Spoken and Written English*, London: Longman.

Brinton, Laurel and Elizabeth C. Traugott (2005), *Lexicalization and Language Change*, Cambridge: Cambridge University Press.

Carter, Ronald and Michael McCarthy (2006), *The Cambridge Grammar of English. A Comprehensive Guide. Spoken and Written English Grammar and Usage*, Cambridge: Cambridge University Press.

Clark, Herbert H. and Jean E. Fox Tree (2002), 'Using *Uh and Um* in Spontaneous Speaking', *Cognition*, 84 (1): 73–111.

Drevets, Megan and Robin Lickley (2017), 'A Psycholinguistic Exploration of Disfluency Behaviour during the Tip-of-the-Tongue Phenomenon', in Robert Eklund and Ralph Rose (eds), *Proceedings of DiSS 2017, The 8th Workshop on Disfluency in Spontaneous Speech*, 21–4, Stockholm: Royal Institute of Technology.

Du Bois, John W., Susanna Cumming, Stephan Schuetze-Coburn and Danae Paolino (1992), *Discourse Transcription*, Santa Barbara: The University of California.

Erard, Michael (2007), *Um . . . Slips, Stumbles, and Verbal Blunders, and What They Mean*. New York: Pantheon Books.

Grieve, Jack, Andrea Nini and Diansheng Guo (2017), 'Analyzing Lexical Emergence in Modern American English Online', *English Language and Linguistics*, 21 (1): 99–127.

Hundt, Marianne and Christian Mair (1999), '"Agile" and "Uptight" Genres: The Corpus-based Approach to Language Change in Progress', *International Journal of Corpus Linguistics*, 4 (2), 221–42.

Jucker, Andreas (2015), '*Uh* and *Um* as Planners in the Corpus of Historical American English', in Irma Taavitsainen, Merja Kytö, Claudia Claridge and Jeremy Smith (eds), *Developments in English: Expanding Electronic Evidence*, 162–77, Cambridge: Cambridge University Press.

McArthur, Tom (1992), *The Oxford Companion to the English Language*, Oxford and New York: Oxford University Press.

O'Connell, Daniel C. and Sabine Kowal (2005), '*Uh* and *Um* Revisited: Are they Interjections for Signaling Delay?', *Journal of Psycholinguistic Research*, 34 (6): 555–76.

OED = *Oxford English Dictionary Online*. Available online: http://www.oed.com/.

Roget's International Thesaurus 6th edn. (2001), ed. Barbara Ann Kipfer, New York: Harper Resource.

Rose, Ralph (2011), 'Filled Pauses in Writing: What Can They Teach Us about Speech?', Poster presented at the Production and Comprehension of Conversational Speech Workshop, Nijmegen.

Rühlemann, Christoph and Martin Hilpert (2017), 'Colloquialization in Journalistic Writing: The Case of Inserts with a Focus on *Well*', *Journal of Historical Pragmatics*, 18 (1): 104–35.

Shillcock, Richard, Simon Kirby, Scott McDonald and Chris Brew (2001), 'Filled Pauses and their Status in the Mental Lexicon', in *DiSS'01, Disfluency in Spontaneous Speech*, ISCA Tutorial and Research Workshop (ITRW), 53–6; ISCA Archive, http://www.isca-speech.org/archive/diss_01.

Tottie, Gunnel (2011), '*Uh* and *Um* as Sociolinguistic Markers in British English', *The International Journal of Corpus Linguistics*, 16 (2): 173–96.

Tottie, Gunnel (2014), 'On the Use of *Uh* and *Um* in American English', *Functions of Language*, 21 (1): 6–29.

Tottie, Gunnel (2015a), 'Turn Management and 'Filled Pauses', *Uh* and *Um*', in Karin Aijmer and Christoph Rühlemann (eds), *Corpus Pragmatics. A Handbook*, 448–93, Cambridge: Cambridge University Press.

Tottie, Gunnel (2015b), '*Uh* and *Um* in British and American English: Are They Words? Evidence from Co-occurrence with Pauses', in Nathalie Dion, André Lapierre and Rena Torres Cacoullos (eds), *Linguistic Variation: Confronting Fact and Theory*, 38–54. New York: Routledge.

Tottie, Gunnel (2017), 'From Pause to Word. *Uh, Um* and *Er* in Written American English', *English Language and Linguistics*, 21 (1): 1–26.

3

Demonstratives Licensed by Cultural Co-presence[1]

Ryan B. Doran
University of Regina

Gregory Ward
Northwestern University

1. Introduction

In this chapter, we investigate two uses of English demonstrative noun phrases (NPs) – one referential and one predicative – in which the demonstrative is licensed by socio-cultural knowledge that the speaker assumes is part of the common ground. While the previous literature has examined uses of demonstratives that involve reference to entities that are assumed to be familiar to a specific speaker/hearer dyad, the role of more general socio-cultural knowledge in the use of demonstratives has not received the same attention.

The first use of the demonstrative that we describe involves reference to entities or kinds of entities that are presumed to be familiar on the basis of shared cultural knowledge of scenarios involving such kinds, as seen in (1):

(1) That's how we've always moved this country forward. By all of us coming together on behalf of our children. Folks who volunteer to coach *that team*, to teach *that Sunday School class*. Because they know it takes a village [corpus][2]

Here the speaker is assuming that the hearer is familiar with scenarios involving volunteering for activities related to children.

In the second use that we consider, the demonstrative is not being used to refer to a specific entity or kind of entity, but rather to predicate a property of the referent in question. Moreover, this predicate is presumed to convey additional information in virtue of stereotypes associated with the property, as seen in (2):

(2) She [Supreme Court Justice Elena Kagan] said 'no' each time to a series of questions from Congress members that went something like: Have you ever hunted? Does anybody in your family hunt? Do any of your friends hunt? 'It

was pretty pathetic, really', Kagan joked. 'I'm *this Jewish girl from New York City*, and this is really not what we did on the weekends'. [corpus]

Here the speaker is not referring to any entity with the demonstrative. Rather, she is predicating of herself the property of 'being a Jewish girl from New York City', which is a property assumed to be rich with culturally-familiar stereotypes.

While these two uses of demonstrative NPs are subject to distinct constraints, they nonetheless share the feature of drawing on socio-cultural knowledge which the speaker assumes will be familiar to the hearer. In this way, the felicitous use of both of these uses of the demonstrative requires shared socio-cultural knowledge or, in the terminology of Clark and Marshall (1981), the speaker must have grounds for assuming that she and her hearer are CO-PRESENT within the relevant social community. Thus, we see that, as with other uses of demonstratives, the felicitous use of the demonstrative requires that a certain sort of knowledge be (treated as) shared by the speaker and hearer. However, in the case of the two uses that are the subject of this chapter, the basis for this assumption is general socio-cultural knowledge, rather than knowledge that is specific to the discourse context and to a particular speaker-hearer dyad.

In Section 2 we begin with the use of the demonstrative that is licensed by shared cultural scenarios, as in (1) above. We first discuss previous literature on demonstratives and show how this use is distinct, before turning to examine the basis for familiarity that licenses its use. In Section 3 we examine the predicative use, as shown in (2) above. Likewise, we first show how this use is distinct from other uses of the demonstrative before turning to set out the felicity conditions for predicative use. Finally, Section 4 concludes our discussion of these uses.

2. Demonstratives licensed by shared cultural scenarios

In the first use of demonstratives that we consider in this chapter, the speaker is using a demonstrative NP, typically but not necessarily the distal variant, to refer to an entity whose assumed familiarity is based on the existence of a shared cultural scenario, as illustrated in (3):

(3)   a. Megan shared her story of the realities of a military wife, and how she felt the day she got *that knock on the door*. [corpus]
      b. I'm not really fit to talk in the morning until I've had *that first cup of coffee*. [corpus]

Our claim is that this use is licensed when the speaker has grounds for presuming the hearer's familiarity with a particular cultural SCENARIO (Fillmore 1982) – a structured event of cultural import. This scenario is relevant in context and can be specified directly by the demonstrative itself or evoked by an entity stereotypically associated with that scenario. In (3a), for example, the speaker is assuming familiarity with the culturally-shared scenario in which a door knock stands proxy for the event of learning of a military family member's death. Likewise, in (3b), the speaker presumes that the hearer is familiar with the morning routine scenario involving the consumption of (one or more cups of) coffee.[3]

This use thus shares certain features with other uses of the distal demonstrative that presume familiarity; however, the basis for the familiarity that licenses this particular use is distinct. Specifically, we argue that the presumed familiarity that licenses this use is grounded in COMMUNITY CO-PRESENCE (Clark and Marshall 1981). That is, community members, in virtue of their membership, can be assumed to be familiar with the relevant scenario and, even in the absence of actual membership, community co-presence may be inferred.

In the canonical use of the distal demonstrative, as in (4), the speaker refers ostensively to a specific entity in the immediate spatio-temporal context (Kaplan 1989; Diessel 1999, *inter alia*).

(4) I spilled *that cup of coffee*. [pointing to a cup of coffee]

Here, the intended referent of the demonstrative is a particular cup of coffee in the immediate perceptual environment that is being indicated by the speaker's demonstration. Another related use of the distal demonstrative is to refer to specific entities that are assumed to be known to the hearer on the basis of private shared knowledge (Joshi 1982; Gundel, Hedberg and Zacharski 1993; Levinson 2004, *inter alia*), as in (5):

(5) *That dog* (next door) kept me awake. [= Gundel et al. 1993, example (5)]

Here, the speaker is referring to a particular dog, which is assumed to be already familiar to the hearer. On the intended interpretation, the relevant dog is not present in the context of utterance, but is instead presumed to be familiar on the basis of some shared experience, e.g., a previous conversation. The familiarity required for the felicity of the demonstrative in (5) is satisfied by the (presumed) shared knowledge that is specific to this particular speaker-hearer dyad, rather than general knowledge that any hearer can plausibly be assumed to share with the speaker.

Similarly, our previous work (2015) argued that such socio-cultural knowledge can license a distributed interpretation of demonstratives. Such uses are distinct from the use that we are concerned with here because the demonstrative receives a variable interpretation, but they nevertheless are licensed by shared cultural knowledge, as in (6):

(6) a. Quicklimos Wedding Limousine Services. Every bride looks forward to *this day*.[4] [= Doran and Ward 2015, #7a]
     b. Getting a puppy is exciting for everyone, but *those first few weeks at home* can shape the dog he will grow to be. [= Doran and Ward 2015, #7b]

In (6a), for example, the demonstrative is interpreted distributively rather than referentially. Here, the demonstrative NP specifies the wedding day of each individual bride, which is licensed by the culturally-based and presumably shared knowledge that brides have a particular wedding day associated with them.

The use of the demonstrative that we are concerned with here shares features with the examples in (5) and (6): a sensitivity to information with which the hearer is assumed to be familiar and a sensitivity to the socio-cultural context of the utterance. Consider the examples in (3), repeated below in (7):

(7) a. Megan shared her story of the realities of a military wife, and how she felt the day she got *that knock on the door*. [corpus]
     b. I'm not really fit to talk in the morning until I've had *that first cup of coffee*. [corpus]

Recall that this use of the distal demonstrative is licensed when the speaker has a basis for presuming familiarity with a culturally-familiar scenario, which the speaker evokes by means of the demonstrative NP. This use is thus distinct from the 'private shared knowledge' use of the distal demonstrative in which reference is made to a specific discourse entity that is familiar, as in (5) above.

In support of this claim, we note that in the absence of a relevant culturally-familiar scenario, infelicity results (on the intended interpretation). Consider (8):

(8) a. Ready to buy *that house/that car/that puppy*? [corpus]
     b. #Ready to buy *that vacuum cleaner/that garden hose/that sport coat*?

In (8a–b), deictic and anaphoric interpretations are available for all of the demonstrative NPs. However, the demonstratives in (8a) license an additional interpretation, given that there is a culturally-familiar scenario associated with buying these kinds of entities. For example, buying a house stereotypically involves house viewings, real estate agents, securing a mortgage and so forth. However, this interpretation is not available for the demonstratives in (8b), as there is no appropriately familiar culturally-based scenario associated with these kinds; there is, for example, no routine that one stereotypically goes through in order to purchase a vacuum cleaner. Thus, it is the availability of culture-based scenarios that licenses the demonstratives in (8a), but not those in (8b), on the intended interpretations.

As mentioned above, with the use being considered here, we find that the demonstrative can either specify a culturally-familiar scenario directly or can specify an entity that stands proxy for an event or property within the relevant scenario. Consider (9):

(9) a. Why you absolutely need to take *that vacation*. [corpus]
     b. New Car vs. Used Car. Advantages of buying new … It has no history, no past, and it has *that new car smell*, too! [corpus]

In (9a), the vacation scenario is evoked directly through the use of the demonstrative NP and is licensed by the presumed cultural familiarity of this scenario. In (9b), however, the relevant culturally-familiar scenario is that of buying a new car. Here, it is the smell of a new car – stereotypically representative of a new car – that the speaker is referring to with the demonstrative. In this way, the relevant scenario may be specified by proxy, in which an element of the scenario stands in for the whole scenario.

Note that when the scenario is evoked by a proxy relationship, this relationship holds between the scenario and elements which are considered to be characteristic or emblematic of that scenario. Consider (10):

(10) a. Looking forward to *that beer at the end of the day*. [corpus]
    b. #Looking forward to *that tea at the end of the day*.

Here, the demonstrative in (10a) is felicitous given that a beer stands proxy for the 'relaxing-after-work' scenario. This scenario is evoked by the activity of drinking beer, which is a characteristic element of that scenario.[5] In (10b), however, while drinking tea can certainly be part of one's routine of relaxing after work, it is not stereotypically characteristic of that scenario in a North American cultural setting.[6] Thus, this demonstrative NP fails to evoke the relevant 'relaxing-after-work' scenario and its use is infelicitous without further information about the hearer's typical relaxing-after-work routine. What is essential for the felicity of the demonstrative on this interpretation is that the proxy element be stereotypically emblematic of the relevant scenario.

We propose that the relevant notion of familiarity that licenses this use of demonstratives is that of community membership (Clark and Marshall 1981). That is, the speaker must have a plausible basis for believing that the hearer is a member of a certain social community and will thus be sufficiently familiar with the relevant scenario in virtue of their community membership. Consider (11):

(11) But most Americans have other things on their minds right now. Paying the bills. Finally taking *that vacation*. Baseball. They're not really paying a lot of attention to the campaign. [corpus]

Here, the writer is assuming that it is sufficiently familiar to a general American readership that taking a vacation is among the set of routine summer activities. Note that there is no one particular vacation being specified by the demonstrative; rather, taking a vacation is emblematic of typical summer activities for the relevant audience. In the context of this example, the writer seeks to evoke this particular scenario in making the point that the American electorate does not pay much attention to politics during the summer. Note further that the demonstrative could have also been felicitous in place of the definite article in another familiar activity, namely paying the bills. However, the use of the demonstrative with *bills* would have suggested a different scenario. Such a scenario would be typical of routine life activities in general, rather than typical summer activities, and thus would not be consistent with the overall point that the writer is making in this passage.

Within a more specialized community, the presumed familiarity with the relevant scenario will be correspondingly limited to that community, as illustrated in (12).

(12) Most hunters cherish *that permit*. [corpus]

For us, cultural scenarios involving hunting are not particularly familiar. But we nevertheless can infer that the speaker here is evoking a scenario in which, for the community of hunters, the permit stands proxy for the process of obtaining a hunting permit. Despite the fact that we are not co-present with the relevant community (in the sense of Clark and Marshall 1981), we can see that the demonstrative here is felicitous because the speaker is assuming that there is a scenario associated with getting a hunting permit and that this scenario will be familiar to those members of the hunting community.

Our account of this use also provides an explanation for the observation that a demonstrative NP may receive a distributed interpretation (King 2001; Elbourne 2008), as shown earlier in (6) and below in (13):

(13) a. Most avid snow skiers remember *that first black diamond run they attempted to ski.* [= King 2001, Ch 1 #5]
    b. Every father dreads *that moment when his oldest child leaves home.* [= King 2001, Ch 1 #4]

In these examples, the demonstrative NPs can receive an interpretation in which their value co-varies with the preceding quantified NP. In (13a), for example, the relevant black diamond hill is the first one attempted by each avid snow skier and in (13b) the relevant moment is the one that each father dreads when his oldest child leaves home.

However, as we have previously argued (Doran and Ward 2015), the distributed interpretation of the demonstrative may be available even in the absence of a quantified expression, as in (14):

(14) Here are 3 steps to help getting you to take *that first plunge underwater* as a certified Scuba Diver. [corpus]

Here, the value of the demonstrative co-varies with whoever it is that is reading the webpage, rather than being interpreted under the scope of a quantified expression. Hence, the distributed interpretation is not wholly explained by the presence of a quantified expression.

Our analysis provides a straightforward account of the felicity of the demonstrative NPs in these examples. Note that in the examples with a distributed interpretation, a culturally-shared scenario is available to license the relevant interpretation, e.g., a skier's first black diamond run (13a), the first child to leave home (13b) or a scuba diver's first dive (14). Our analysis predicts that the demonstratives in these examples will be felicitous provided that the speaker has a basis for presuming that the hearer will be familiar with the relevant scenarios. Thus, we can provide a unified account of the distributed interpretation: one that involves culturally-familiar scenarios and community co-presence.

Finally, our analysis can be straightforwardly extended to explain a popular meme in social media. In this meme, the demonstrative NP is presented as a complete utterance – itself a marked, non-standard usage – appearing frequently as text over an appropriate image with humorous intent. Consider (15):

(15) a. *That moment when you step on a LEGO.* [corpus]
    b. *That moment when someone sneezes on you.* [corpus]

In both of these examples, the demonstrative evokes a scenario; in (15a), the 'step-on-a-pointy-toy' scenario is presumably familiar to an audience of parents and the demonstrative is correspondingly felicitous. However, in (15b), the speaker is treating the 'getting-sneezed-on' scenario as familiar in order to implicate that the audience can relate to such situations, without it actually constituting a pre-existing culturally-familiar scenario. That is, while there is currently no culturally-shared stereotypical scenario of getting sneezed on, the use of the demonstrative here signals that the speaker is treating the relevant scenario as if it were a familiar one. In doing so, the use of the demonstrative in this meme allows the speaker to introduce a situation with which the audience may in fact be familiar, but in so doing the speaker is able to treat it as though it already constituted a culturally-shared scenario. The comic effect of the meme results from treating an unfamiliar situation as if it were in fact one that is well known.

3. Predicative use of proximal demonstratives

In the second use of English demonstrative NPs that we consider in this chapter, the demonstrative NP receives a property-denoting interpretation and not a referential one, as shown in (16):

(16) a. Megan bought me the scariest thing alive!! It's *this hamster* and it makes noise and is voice activated and its cheeks light up and it moves around and follows commands!!!! [corpus]

     b. Look, the dealers are the popular kids, but they're not normal popular. They're *these crunchy granola dudes that have convinced everyone that they're cool.* [corpus]

In (16a–b), the demonstrative NPs are not being used by the speaker to refer to any particular entity; rather, they are being used to predicate a property of the referent. On the intended interpretation of (16a), the speaker is not using the demonstrative NP to refer to a specific entity in the context; rather, the demonstrative NP here is being used to predicate a property of the referent introduced in the first sentence. We argue that, in this use, the demonstrative NP functions to classify the referent with respect to a discourse-new property; moreover, this use of the demonstrative indicates that the speaker is conveying additional information about the referent beyond mere category membership. We will first set out the features of this use, showing how it is distinct from other uses of demonstratives, and then we turn to reviewing the data that support our analysis.

In the examples in (16), the speakers are using the demonstratives to attribute properties ('being-a-hamster' and 'being-crunchy-granola-dudes', respectively) to the referents in question and are not referring to any particular individuals. The property-denoting interpretation is, however, restricted only to the proximal demonstrative form; the distal form is disallowed on the intended interpretation, as shown in (17):

(17) a. Griselda is the wife of one of Kevin's law school classmates and she is
          awesome. She's *{#that/this} amazing little spitfire*, full of so much life and
          energy. [corpus]
     b. I was on tour with the Red Hot Chili Peppers, and they brought along a
          vegan chef. Everyone thinks they're *{#those/these} insane party animals*.
          But after the show, we'd hang out, meditate a little and then have really
          great vegan food together. [corpus]

Given that these proximal demonstrative NPs receive a property-denoting
interpretation, the predicative use is distinct from other well-known uses of
demonstratives. For example, consider the deictic use, the identificational use and the
degree modifier use of the demonstratives, shown in (18a–c), respectively:

(18) a. *This hamster right here* is the scariest thing alive. [pointing at a hamster]
     b. The dealers are *these guys in the photograph*. [speaker looking at a picture]
     c. The hamster was *this big*. [gesture indicating size]

In (18a), the demonstrative is used by the speaker to refer to an entity in the immediate
perceptual surroundings, possibly accompanied by an ostensive gesture. In (18b),
the demonstrative appears in predicate position, but it is nevertheless being used
referentially, with the speaker referring to the relevant individuals indicated in
the photograph. The demonstrative here is not being used predicatively, as the
demonstrative NP could also appear in subject position. In (18c), the demonstrative
likewise appears in predicate position, but here it is being used to specify a degree or an
amount of a property that is in turn being predicated of the referent, i.e. the
demonstrative is being used to specify how big the relevant hamster was. Thus, each of
these uses (along with other uses) are distinct from the property-denoting interpretation
that we are concerned with here. Furthermore, note that in each of (18a–c), the distal
demonstrative form would be felicitous given an appropriate context, which is not the
case for the property-denoting use, as was shown in (17). Similarly, the proximal
demonstratives in (18a–c) may receive a contrastive pitch accent when the speaker is
distinguishing the referent in question from among a set of contrasting alternatives;
but such an interpretation is unavailable with the property-denoting interpretations
given in (16).

The property-denoting use of the proximal demonstrative is also distinct from the
so-called 'indefinite-*this*' interpretation, which is similarly restricted to the proximal
form (Prince 1981; Wald 1981; Maclaran 1980, 1982). With the indefinite-*this* use, the
speaker uses the demonstrative to introduce a hearer-new entity into the discourse that
represents a new discourse topic, as shown in (19):

(19) I saw *this scary hamster* at the pet store.

The demonstrative here is being used referentially, but it is distinct from other
referential uses of the demonstrative in that the referent is presumed by the speaker to
be unfamiliar to the hearer. While the referential use of indefinite *this* is distinct from

the predicative proximal demonstrative, the two uses do share the feature of being restricted to informal/colloquial contexts, as illustrated in (20):

(20) a. [Context: news report] Yesterday, police identified a suspect in the Rolling Meadows murder-for-hire case, 43-year-old Jeremy Griffin. He's *{#this/an}* *executive at Motorola.*

     b. [Context: informal conversation] Hey, do you know Jeremy Griffin? He's *{this/an}* *executive at Motorola.*

In the context of a news report, the property-denoting use of the demonstrative in (20a) is infelicitous, whereas in the informal context of (20b), it is fully felicitous.

More generally, the property-denoting use of proximal demonstratives shares with the indefinite-*this* use the feature of being truth-conditionally equivalent to the use of the corresponding indefinite NP. However, in neither instance is the speaker's choice of the demonstrative pragmatically equivalent to the use of the corresponding indefinite NP. Consider (21):

(21) a. Okay, so now everyone thinks I'm *this great big lezzer*, and all my lesbian mates think I'm one of the sisterhood now. [corpus]

     b. Okay, so now everyone thinks I'm *a great big lezzer*.

In (21a), the truth-conditional contribution of the demonstrative NP does not differ from the truth-conditional contribution of the indefinite NP in (21b). In general, whenever the predicative use of a proximal demonstrative NP is felicitous, the corresponding indefinite NP will also be felicitous. It follows that the speaker's use of the demonstrative conveys additional pragmatic information.

Previous accounts of the pragmatic contribution conveyed by non-deictic uses of demonstratives have appealed to the notion of SPEAKER AFFECT (Lakoff 1974; Bowdle and Ward 1995; Wolter 2006; Davis and Potts 2010; Potts and Schwarz 2010; Acton and Potts 2014). According to this notion, certain uses of demonstratives have been shown to convey 'complex multidimensional social meanings involving exclamativity' or 'presumptions about shared attitudes and perspectives' (Acton and Potts 2014: 3).[7] Consider example (22) in which the speaker presumes a shared attitude – specifically one of contempt – with his addressee towards the referent:

(22) *That asshole Cheney* is trying to fuck over the Obamas. [corpus]

In analysing our corpus of naturally-occurring data, we find that all predicative uses of proximal demonstrative NPs involve predicates that either license an exclamative interpretation or denote properties associated with social/cultural stereotypes.

However the notion of speaker affect is characterized, the felicitous use of a predicative proximal demonstrative does not require that the attribute expressed by the speaker be positively or negatively valenced (Doran and Ward 2013, 2015). As evidence, consider example (23), in which the predicative demonstrative NP is felicitous even in the absence of an explicitly positive or negative attitude expressed by the speaker:

(23) A: What's your hotel room like?
    B: I don't know what to think about it. It's *this square-shaped room with beige carpeting*. [*gratia* Jon Stevens, p.c.]

In (23), the speaker expresses his uncertainty about whether he has a positive or negative attitude towards the room in question, thereby presupposing that with further reflection he will have one or the other.

In addition to considerations of speaker affect, there are further pragmatic conditions that license the predicative use of a proximal demonstrative NP. We claim that the following conditions must be met for the predicative proximal demonstrative to be felicitous:

Conditions for felicitous use of predicative proximal demonstratives
(i)   There must be a salient open proposition (OP) in discourse of the form '*r* is an *x*' whose instantiated variable classifies the referent.
(ii)   The OP must be instantiated with a discourse-new property.
(iii) The kind associated with this property must be presumed to be familiar to the hearer.
(iv) The classification of the referent must be sufficient to convey additional information beyond mere category membership, including additional information about the speaker's attitude towards the referent.

Under this analysis, the speaker conveys additional information about the referent, either through an exclamative interpretation or through assumed mutual knowledge about the kind in question. As was the case with the use licensed by shared cultural scenarios (examined in Section 2), the basis for the presumed familiarity in the predicative use of proximal demonstrative NPs is cultural co-presence (Clark and Marshall 1981). The speaker assumes that the hearer will share certain stereotypical information regarding the relevant property in virtue of being co-members of a particular social community. We turn now to take up each aspect of this analysis in turn.

According to condition (i) above, the felicitous use of a predicative demonstrative NP requires a salient OP of the form '*r* is an *x*', where *r* is the referent and *x* is the category that classifies the referent, as shown in (24):

(24) A: Who's Joan? [e.g., What does Joan do?, What's Joan like?]
    B: She's *this lawyer*.

Here, B's response instantiates the variable of the OP by classifying the referent, Joan, as being a member of the category of lawyers. In asking speaker B to provide a category that classifies the referent, speaker A evokes the appropriate OP. When speaker A's question evokes a different OP – one in which the classification of the referent is not at issue – the proximal demonstrative is infelicitous:

(25) A: Who's a lawyer?
    B: Joan's *a/#this lawyer*. [cp. Joan's a lawyer.]

In (25), speaker A's question does not evoke the appropriate OP, i.e. one of asking speaker B to provide a category that classifies the referent; rather, speaker A evokes a different OP. Here, the speaker is asking for a member of the category and the relevant OP is instantiated by the referent, rather than the category. Thus, the use of the proximal demonstrative is infelicitous in (25) because the discourse does not provide a salient OP of the appropriate form.[8]

According to condition (ii), in addition to instantiating an appropriate OP, the property that classifies the referent must be discourse-new, in the sense of Prince (1992). When the relevant property has been previously evoked, infelicity results, as shown in (26a):

(26) a. A: My cousin Bob is coming over today. He's *this fashion model*.
   B: What a coincidence! Have you met my cousin Sam? He's #*this fashion model*, too.
   b. A: My cousin Bob is coming over today. He's *this fashion model*.
   B: Have you met my cousin Sam? He's *a fashion model*, too.
   c. A: My cousin Bob is coming over today. He's *this fashion model*.
   B: Have you met my cousin Sam? He's *this interior designer*.

In (26a), speaker B's use of the demonstrative is infelicitous because the property of 'being-a-fashion-model' has already been evoked by speaker A. The discourse-old property can of course be repeated by speaker B, as in (26b), but only if the indefinite is used rather than the demonstrative. Furthermore, the infelicity of the demonstrative in (26a) must be due to the relevant property being discourse-old, rather than speaker A's previous use of the demonstrative. In (26c), speaker B can felicitously use the proximal demonstrative even after speaker A's previous use of the same construction, provided that the property speaker B predicates of the referent is discourse-new in her utterance. Thus, (26c) shows that the issue with speaker B's use of the demonstrative in (26a) is not that speaker A has already used the proximal demonstrative, but that the relevant property in B's utterance needs to be discourse-new.

There is, however, one kind of exception to the generalization that a discourse-new property is required. In cases in which the property has been previously evoked, the proximal demonstrative can nonetheless be felicitous as a form of ECHOIC MENTION (Wilson 2006), provided that is it interpretable as a continued reference to the evoked property attributable to the same individual. Consider (27):

(27) A: My cousin Bob is cooking dinner tonight. He's *this gourmet chef*.
   B: Well, if he's *this gourmet chef*, then we will be eating well tonight!

In (27), speaker B's use of the demonstrative is felicitous in her reply because she can be interpreted as continuing to attribute the property evoked by A – 'being a gourmet chef' – to Bob. In this sense, the property in question retains its discourse-new status.

Condition (iii) above requires that with the felicitous use of predicative proximal demonstrative NPs, the speaker assumes that the hearer is familiar with the relevant category and, moreover, assumes that the hearer is familiar with what is typical or expected for members of that category. In (28), the demonstrative is infelicitous without the assumption that the kind in question is familiar to both speaker and hearer.

(28) There's a rare bird hanging out in the Smith's backyard. It's #*this piping plover*.

The kind 'piping plover' is not, at least for us, sufficiently familiar to license the demonstrative here. While it may be known that the referent is a kind of bird, what the members of this kind are typically like is not sufficiently familiar for the demonstrative to be felicitous for us.[9]

The final condition for the felicitous use of predicative proximal demonstrative NPs (iv) is that the speaker must provide additional information about the referent in one of two ways. The first way is for the speaker's classification of the referent to provide additional information with respect to stereotypes that are assumed to be familiar, thus licensing additional inferences about the referent. The second way in which the condition can be satisfied is for the speaker's classification of the referent to include a modifier that expresses an evaluative attitude. We take up these two ways in turn.

First, the classification of the referent with respect to familiar kinds can serve to convey additional information about the referent (not explicitly said by the speaker) in virtue of familiar stereotypes about the relevant category and about what is typical for its members. Consider (29):

(29) a. Everyone thinks I'm *this New Yorker*.
     b. Everyone thinks I'm #*this South Dakotan*.

In (29a), membership in the category 'New Yorker' is sufficient to convey additional information about the referent (the speaker) because the kind is associated with various cultural stereotypes about what people from New York are like. Thus, classifying someone as a New Yorker conveys information beyond the mere fact that the person is from New York. In contrast, in (29b), the category 'South Dakotan', for us at least, does not convey any further information about the referent; classifying someone as a South Dakotan implies nothing more than the fact that the person is from South Dakota, thereby rendering the demonstrative in (29b) infelicitous, at least for individuals (such as us) that do not have any particular stereotypes associated with people from South Dakota.

The condition that the speaker conveys additional extra-classificatory information about the referent via stereotypes can be satisfied in various ways. In example (29a), it is satisfied by the stereotypes that attach to being from a certain geographical area. Stereotypes such as this one arise from the conventional associations attached to social and cultural categories, as shown further in (30):

(30) I only met her a few nights ago at a birthday bash, but holy fuck she is perfect. She's *this hippy (sic), Buddhist, zen type*. [corpus]

Here, the social identities of 'hippie', 'Buddhist' and 'zen-type' convey to the hearer information about the referent over and above simple membership in the category. That is, the hearer can infer more about the referent than simply the fact that she is a Buddhist.

In addition to social kinds, certain natural kinds can also have stereotypical associations regarding what the members are typically like. Consider the examples in (31):

(31) a.   A: John just got a new pet. Do you know what it is?
          B: It's *this ferret.*
    b.   A: John just got a new pet. Do you know what it is?
          B: It's *#this dog.*
    c.   A: John just got a new pet. Do you know what it is?
          B: It's *this Chihuahua.*

In (31a), the kind 'ferret' provides additional information about the referent in that members of the category are assumed to be sufficiently alike to make generalizations about members of the category (e.g., the speaker believes that they are unappealing pets). The speaker's use of the demonstrative is thus felicitous here as the classification provides the hearer with information beyond mere membership in the kind. In contrast, in (31b), the kind 'dog' is too heterogeneous to provide any extra-classificatory information about the referent; there are simply too many different breeds of dogs for the demonstrative in (31b) to be conveying any additional relevant information. In (31c), however, where the pet is classified as a specific breed, the demonstrative is felicitous. Members of the kind 'Chihuahua' are assumed to be sufficiently alike and thus this classification does suffice to convey additional information about the referent, e.g., its mannerisms, size and general behaviour.

The second way in which the final condition can be satisfied is for the speaker's classification of the referent to include an expressive modifier. While conventionally associated stereotypes suffice to convey additional information about the referent that licenses the felicitous use of the proximal demonstrative, reference to kinds that do not in and of themselves have any stereotypical associations are also possible. Such kinds are felicitous when the speaker includes a modifier that expresses an evaluative attitude towards the referent through its classification. Consider, for example, artifact kinds. These kinds are typically infelicitous with the proximal demonstrative on the intended interpretation, as they do not, on their own, provide a basis for extra-classificatory information. Consider (32):

(32) a.   A: I heard your sister gave you something strange for your birthday. What was it?
          B: It's *#this pencil.*
    b.   A: I heard your sister gave you something strange for your birthday. What was it?
          B: It's *this{amazing/fucking/stupid/awesome/wicked} pencil*!

Kinds such as 'pencil' typically do not allow for the proximal demonstrative, as in (32a), because such a simple classification for an artifact does not license any further inferences; knowing that an object is a pencil does not put one in a position to know any additional information about the entity given the lack of conventional stereotypes about pencils. However, the inclusion of any of the affect-laden modifiers illustrated in (32b) allows the proximal demonstrative to be used felicitously.[10]

The additional information conveyed, either via conventional stereotypes or the inclusion of expressive modifiers, needs only to provide information about the referent beyond mere category membership; it does not need to make the referent uniquely identifiable. In example (33), the proximal demonstrative is felicitous, but the relevant cultural stereotypes do not in any way put the speaker in a position to distinguish the referent from other members of the relevant categories.

(33) The inspector himself was excellent. We used him for our current house, four years ago. He's *this short guy with very little hair and a pronounced working-class English accent*. It was like having Phil Collins inspect your house. [corpus]

The demonstrative here is felicitous because the kind 'short guy with very little hair and a pronounced working-class English accent' is rich with associations and thus the speaker is able to convey much more than simple kind membership with the classification provided. However, as the second sentence indicates, the same classification is equally true of Phil Collins and so the description contained within the demonstrative does not make the referent uniquely identifiable.

The preceding examples have shown how the conditions enumerated above must be satisfied in order for a proximal demonstrative NP to be felicitous on the property-denoting interpretation. Our analysis has shown further that the expression of an evaluative attitude by the speaker may be present in many cases, but such an attitude is not required for this use of the demonstrative to be felicitous. For example, in (29a), the speaker may have either a positive or a negative attitude towards New Yorkers, but the felicity of the demonstrative is not because the speaker is expressing an attitude. Rather, it is felicitous because of the extra-classificatory information provided by the various stereotypes associated with the kind 'New Yorker'. Properties with conventional associations, such as social categories and cultural stereotypes, will generally be felicitous with the demonstrative and may additionally convey the speaker's attitude about the kind in question. But on the explanation offered here, speaker affect is often the result of – but not necessarily a condition of – felicitous use.

Finally, note that the predicative use of proximal demonstratives may be accompanied by minimizers, e.g., *only, simply, just*, as evidenced in (34):

(34) a. Well, basically, I'm just *this small town girl who lives in [a] not so perfect world*. [corpus]
   b. He was *this muscular, tough looking kid*, you would imagine him being a bully when he's only *this sweet little boy*. [corpus]

In these examples, the speaker is treating the relevant property as a value on a partially-ordered set (Hirschberg 1991) and denies that higher values obtain. So, in (34a), the speaker is asserting that, for the purposes of self-classification, the referent of the demonstrative is only a small town girl – and denies the applicability of higher values with respect to the relevant property under discussion; that is, she is not well-traveled, complicated, sophisticated, urbane, etc. In (34b), which features two tokens of the proximal demonstrative, we see that the first instance serves to classify the referent based on shared stereotypes, while the occurrence of the minimizer *only* before the second instance of the demonstrative denies higher values on the relevant partially-ordered set.

Further, we see that some predicates which, by themselves, would be infelicitous with the proximal demonstrative are nonetheless felicitous with a minimizer. Both examples in (35) are felicitous with the minimizer *just*, but would be infelicitous without the use of the minimizer:

(35) a. If I see my child start to go very quickly for a dog, I say 'hold on'. [She might then say:] 'It's #(just) *this dog*'. [To which I would respond:] 'Yeah, but we don't know anything about that dog right there for a second'. [corpus]

   b. 'I think a lot of people in the artistic community have this misconception that it's #(just) *this pen and ink*', Csernak said. 'I'm trying to reverse the impression of comics'. [corpus]

In (35a), the use of the minimizer *just* evokes a partially-ordered set, in which a set of relevant entities is ranked according to a feature of the set members. Here, the set of {animals} is ordered with respect to degrees of possible danger they represent, and alternative values ranked higher on the scale, e.g., raccoon, wolf, lion, etc., are asserted not to hold. That is, the speaker is conveying that the dogs in general correspond to a low level of danger in the relevant partially-ordered set. Without the minimizer, such an interpretation is unavailable and the demonstrative is infelicitous (cf. 31b). Similarly, in (35b), the minimizer evokes a set of alternatives that people in the artistic community fail to appreciate; thus, the speaker is rejecting the implication that comics have limited impact.

4. Conclusion

In this chapter, we have examined two uses of demonstratives that are distinct from other, more well-known functions of demonstratives. As with other non-deictic uses of demonstratives, the functions examined in this chapter are subject to a familiarity condition; however, the speaker's use of the demonstrative considered here is licensed by familiarity with socio-cultural knowledge. Rather than being licensed by knowledge specific to the particular speaker-hearer dyad, the speaker presumes that the hearer will share the relevant knowledge in virtue of sharing certain aspects of cultural knowledge. Thus, we see that the familiarity condition on demonstratives is realized differently across the various uses, depending upon particular features of the discourse context.

Notes

1 This chapter is an expanded and revised version of our previous work on this topic. We are grateful to the audiences at LSA 2013, 2014 and 2017, BLS 2015, CLS 2015 and AMPRA 2016 for many useful comments and suggestions. A special note of thanks goes to Larry Horn, Craige Roberts, Alex Djalali, Line Mikkelsen, Chris Potts, Jon Stevens, Michael Franke and Tim Leffel. All errors remain our own.

2 All example utterances marked with '[corpus]' are from our corpus of naturally-occurring data, drawn from a wide range of sources – primarily from web pages. Within each example, we italicize the relevant demonstrative NP(s) that illustrate(s) the use in question.

3 While it is true that in most of our examples the demonstrative NP appears as a direct object, this is not a necessary feature of this use, as illustrated in (i):

  (i) *That first cup of coffee* makes every morning a good morning!! [corpus]

4 Note the use of the proximate demonstrative in this example; as mentioned above, most – but clearly not all – of our examples of this usage of the demonstrative involved the distal variant.

5 Note that *Looking forward to <u>that glass of wine at the end of the day</u>* would also work in the same way.

6 While typically infelicitous in a North American cultural context, we acknowledge that example (10b) may be felicitous in a different cultural context, e.g. Britain. This observation in fact illustrates our point: whether the use of the demonstrative is felicitous will depend on shared cultural knowledge, and which cultural scenarios can be presumed to be familiar will depend on the discourse context.

7 A precise characterization of exclamativity is beyond the scope of the chapter, but cf. Martens (2016).

8 The OP requirement explains why most of the examples in our corpus are of the form PRONOUN + BE (present tense) + (proximal demonstrative) NP, as this form allows for a direct instantiation of the relevant OP. However, neither a pronoun nor the present tense is required for this use, e.g., *Joan's this lawyer* or *She was this lawyer I met last year*.

9 Of course, when used in a context in which the discourse participants could be assumed to be sufficiently familiar with the relevant kind (e.g., a conversation between ornithologists), the demonstrative could be felicitous.

10 While the example cited in (32b) has the modifiers prenominally, post-nominal modifiers are also possible, as in (33) below, and subsequent discourse can provide additional information too, as in (16a) above.

References

Acton, Eric K. and Christopher Potts (2014), 'That Straight Talk: Sarah Palin and the Sociolinguistics of Demonstratives', *Journal of Sociolinguistics*, 18 (1): 3–31.
Bowdle, Brian and Gregory Ward (1995), 'Generic Demonstratives', *BLS*, 21: 32–43.
Clark, Herbert H. and Catherine R. Marshall (1981), 'Definite Reference and Mutual Knowledge', in Aravind K. Joshi, Bonnie L. Webber and Ivan A. Sag (eds), *Elements of Discourse Understanding*, 10–63, Cambridge: Cambridge University Press.

Davis, Christopher and Christopher Potts (2010), 'Affective Demonstratives and the Division of Pragmatic Labor', in Maria Aloni, Herald Bastiaanse, Tikitu de Jager and Katrin Schulz (eds), *Logic, Language, and Meaning: 17th Amsterdam Colloquium Revised Selected Papers*, 42–52, Berlin: Springer.

Diessel, Holger (1999), *Demonstratives: Form, Function, and Grammaticalization*, Amsterdam: Benjamins.

Doran, Ryan and Gregory Ward (2013), 'Speaker Affect and Proximal Demonstratives in Predicate NPs'. Paper presented at the 87th Annual Meeting of the Linguistic Society of America, Boston MA.

Doran, Ryan and Gregory Ward (2015), 'Demonstratives with Distributed Interpretations', *CLS*, 51: 129–36.

Elbourne, Paul (2008), 'Demonstratives as Individual Concepts', *Linguistics and Philosophy*, 31 (4): 409–66.

Fillmore, Charles J. (1982), 'Frame Semantics', in The Linguistic Society of Korea (ed), *Linguistics in the Morning Calm. Selected Papers from SICOL-1981*, 111–37, Seoul: Hanshin.

Gundel, Jeanette K., Nancy Hedberg and Ron Zacharski (1993), 'Cognitive Status and the Form of Referring Expressions in Discourse', *Language*, 69: 274–307.

Hirschberg, Julia (1991), *A Theory of Scalar Implicature*, New York: Garland Press.

Joshi, Aravind K. (1982), 'Mutual Beliefs in Question-Answer Systems', in Neil Smith (ed), *Mutual Knowledge*, 181–97, New York: Academic Press.

Kaplan, David (1989), 'Demonstratives', in Joseph Almog, John Perry and Howard Wettstein (eds), *Themes from Kaplan*, 481–563, Oxford: Oxford University Press.

King, Jeffrey C. (2001), *Complex Demonstratives*, Cambridge, MA: MIT Press.

Lakoff, Robin (1974), 'Remarks on *This* and *That*', *CLS*, 10: 345–56.

Levinson, Stephen C. (2004), 'Deixis', in Laurence R. Horn and Gregory Ward (eds), *Handbook of Pragmatics*, 97–121, Oxford: Blackwell.

Maclaran, Rose (1980), 'On the two Asymmetric Uses of English Demonstratives', *Linguistics*, 18: 803–20.

Maclaran, Rose (1982), 'The Semantics and Pragmatics of the English Demonstratives', PhD diss., Cornell University.

Martens, Gouming (2016), 'Dutch Particle Exclamatives', MA diss., University of Leiden.

Potts, Christopher and Florian Schwarz (2010), 'Affective "This"', *Linguistic Issues in Language Technology*, 3 (5): 1–30.

Prince, Ellen F. (1981), 'On the Inferencing of Indefinite-*this* NPs', in Aravind K. Joshi, Bonnie L. Webber and Ivan A. Sag (eds), *Elements of Discourse Understanding*, 231–50, Cambridge: Cambridge University Press.

Prince, Ellen F. (1992), 'The ZPG Letter: Subjects, Definiteness, and Information-status', in William C. Mann and Sandra A. Thompson (eds), *Discourse Description: Diverse Analyses of a Fund-raising Text*, 295–325, Amsterdam: Benjamins.

Wald, Benji (1981), 'Referents and Topic within and across Discourse Units: Observations from Current Vernacular English', in Flora Klein-Andreu (ed), *Discourse Perspectives on Syntax*, 91–116, New York: Academic Press.

Wilson, Deirdre (2006), 'The Pragmatics of Verbal Irony: Echo or Pretence?', *Lingua*, 116: 1722–43.

Wolter, Lynsey (2006), 'That's *That*: The Semantics and Pragmatics of Demonstrative Noun Phrases', PhD diss., University of California – Santa Cruz.

4

The Fall and Rise of English *any*

Nikolaus Ritt, Andreas Baumann and Christina Prömer
University of Vienna

1. Introduction

Most extant research on the history of English *any* has focussed on its role as a negative polarity item (*I have* some *money* vs. *I do not have* any *money*). Its development has mostly been studied in the context of negation strategies, and particularly with regard to the decline of double negation (see, for example, Fischer 1992: 280–5; Iyeiri 1999, 2002, 2010; Tottie, Tieken-Boon van Ostade and van der Wurff 1999; Hoeksema 2012). Therefore, most studies have been concerned with the Middle and the Early Modern English periods, and have shown that the frequency of *any* began to rise significantly at the beginning of the fourteenth century, reaching a peak towards the end of Early Modern English.

What has received rather less attention in the literature is the fact that before the frequency of *any* began to rise during the later Middle English period, it had first undergone a decline in the twelfth and the first half of the thirteenth centuries. A rough impression of that decline is conveyed in Table 4.1 and Figure 4.1. They are based on normalized frequencies of *any* (or any of its many historical spelling variants; cf. OED s.v. *any*, adj., pron., and n., and adv.) in nine of the eleven subperiods in the *Helsinki Corpus of English Texts* (Rissanen et al. 1991; henceforth HC), i.e. from before 850 to 1570.[1] It also becomes evident from a cluster analysis of the diachronic development (Figure 4.2), in which the turn-around period (1050–1350) forms a separate cluster.

This chapter addresses the questions (a) why the frequency of *any* first fell after the Old English period and (b) why it rebounded again afterwards. It proposes that the fate of *any* can only be understood in the context of the grammaticalization of the Old English numeral *án* 'one' and the emergence of the indefinite article. During one stage

Table 4.1 Normalized frequency of *any* per century (<850 to 1570; data derived from the HC)

Period	pre 850	850–950	950–1050	1050–1150	1150–1250	1250–1350	1350–1420	1420–1500	1500–1570
any per million	913	587	1,264	772	230	462	2,030	1,557	3,118

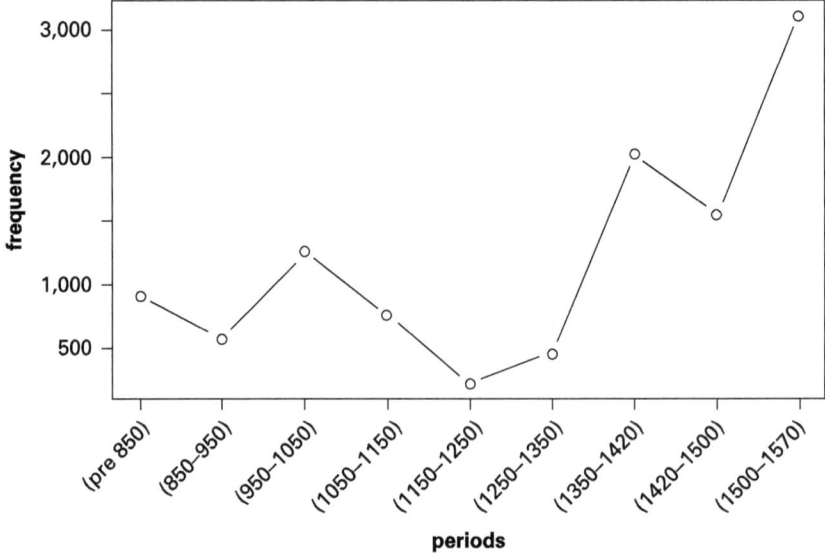

Figure 4.1 Frequency trajectory of *any* (normalized per million words).

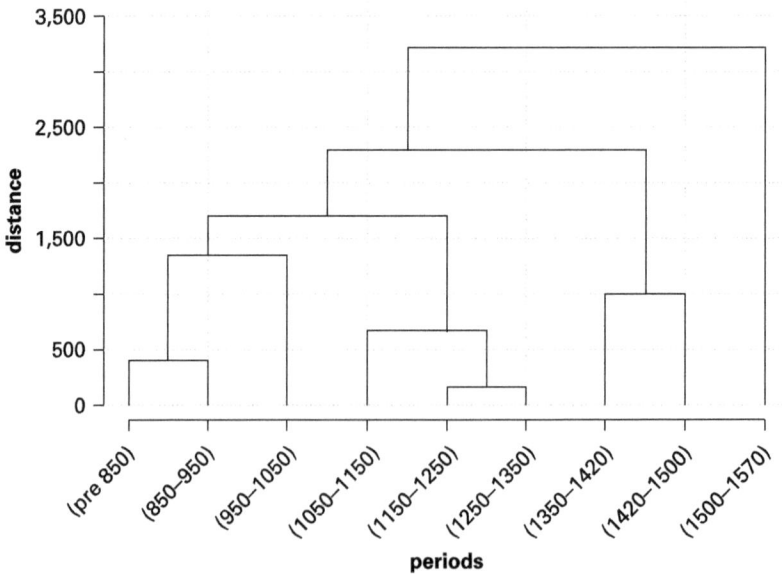

Figure 4.2 Variability-based neighbour clustering (VNC) of all periods (computed with an R-script by Gries and Hilpert 2008).

in that process, *one/a(n)* came to be used in ways that were similar to that of *any*. This created a competition between the determinatives and *one/a(n)* gained the upper hand. As the indefinite article emerged, however, it diverged from the numeral and became a separate lexical item. While it became increasingly unspecific with regard to the reference relations it encoded, the numeral reassumed its more restricted original functions. This renewed the usefulness of *any*, which had retained its ability to indicate a distinct, non-exclusive subtype of indefinite reference. Thus, it failed to disappear, but re-established itself instead.

2. Any in Old and Modern English

If one did not know that *any* was rare during the Early Middle English period, a comparison of Modern English *any* and its Old English ancestor *ænig* would convey a strange impression of historical stasis. The two are similar in many respects. Let us look at frequency first: in the Old English sections of the HC (up to 1050), the various forms of *ænig* occur at a rate of 1.081 per million words, which is hardly less than the 1.174 occurrences of *any* per million words that the *Corpus of Historical American English* (COHA) returns for the last century (1910–2010). It certainly is not a difference to write home about.[2]

As far as word-class membership is concerned, not much seems to have changed either. The only innovation is that *any* has come to develop adverbial uses in which it pre-modifies mostly comparatives as in (1):

(1) Knowing you coped with mother too doesn't make me feel *any* better. (OED, K. Ferrier *Let.* 30 Jan. 1951)

Such uses are not attested in Old English,[3] but also in Modern English they represent a small minority, amounting to less than two percent of the occurrences COHA returns for the last hundred years.

By far the most frequent uses of *any* in Contemporary English are as a determinative (2), or as a pronoun (3):

(2) a. Do you have *any* reason to think that your seed is capable of begetting a male child? (OED, A. Ghosh *River of Smoke*, iv. 104, 2011)
     b. Mom never wore *any* form of make up. (OED, C. C. E. Vermaak *Confessions of Dyslexic Virgin*, 194, 2006)
     c. There are strategies that *any* company can use to cultivate customer engagement. (OED, *1to1 Mag.* Oct. 20/2, 2005)
(3) a. He'd love to meet more of the natives. Especially if *any* were like that Lucile Raoul. (COHA, 1957, Atlantic Monthly)
     b. Maybe he should talk to a priest? He didn't know *any*. (OED, A. Atwater-Rhodes *Token of Darkness*, i. 8, 2010)
     c. I had always ambled through life, never suffering from *any* of the ills the urban mind is prey to. (OED, *Independent*, 24 Feb. 15/1, 2011)

Old English *ænig* is attested in more or less the same roles: (4) illustrates determinative uses, (5) pronominal ones.

(4) a. nænigum   ricum   men   æfre   *ænig*   feoh   sellan   wolde.
       to no   rich   men   ever   *any*   cattle   sell   would
       'He would not sell any cattle to rich men'.

                    (YCOE, Bede, *History of the English Church*, O2, ninth century)

    b. Ge   cnapan,   hæbbe   ge   *ænige*   syflinge   begyten?
       you   children   have   you   *any*   food   received
       'Have you been given anything to eat, children?'

                    (OED, Ælfric *Catholic Homilies*: 2nd Ser. (Cambr. Gg.3.28)
                                        xvi. 164, tenth century)

    c. Þa   namen hi   þa   men   þe   hi   wenden ðat   *ani*   god   hefden.
       then   took   they   the men   who they thought that   *any*   property   had
       'Then they took the men who they thought owned anything'.

                    (OED, *Anglo-Saxon Chron.* (Laud) (Peterborough contin.)
                                    anno 1137, *ca.* 1160)

(5) a. Ne   sege   þu   heononforð þæt   *ænig*   sy   his   gelica
       not   say   thou   henceforth   that   *any*   is   his   like
       'Do not say anymore that anything can be compared to him'.

                    (YCOE, Ælfric, *Lives of Saints*, O3, eleventh century)

    b. For þon þe   þu   eart   blind,   þu   ne   gesihst   *ænigne*   of
              Godes   þam   halgum.
       because you are   blind   you not see   *any* of God's the   saints
       'Because you are blind, you don't see any of God's Saints'.

                    (OED, *St. Andrew* (Corpus Cambr.) in F. G. Cassidy and
                    R. N. Ringler *Bright's Old Eng. Gram. & Reader*, OE)

Like Modern English *any*, its Old English ancestor occurred mostly in singular noun phrases. Plurals amount to only 1.5 per cent of all Old English occurrences in the HC. Contemporary English has higher numbers, but they reflect a fairly recent development. At the beginning of the nineteenth century, plural noun phrases still represented only about 5 per cent of all occurrences (1810: 93/1,664, 1820: 620/12,491; source: COHA).[4]

Another property that Modern English *any* and Old English *ænig* share is that the majority of them occur in non-affirmative clauses, such as negations, questions, conditionals, or in comparatives of the type 'x *is greater than any y*', which are implicitly negative as well (they imply '*There is no y that is as great as* x'). Old English examples of each type are given in (6) to (9). The fact that their Modern English translations all contain *any* as well highlights the similarity.

(6) Question:
    Cweðe   ge   þæt   ic   eow   dide   æfre   *ænigne* unþang?
    say   you that   I   you   did   ever   *any*   ungratefulness
    'Do you say that I have ever shown you any ingratitude?'

                    (HC, *Old English Appolonius of Tyre*, O3, eleventh century)

(7) Negation:

Ne	gyrn	ðu	on unriht	*æniges*	þinges	þe	oðer	man	age.
not	covet	you	unjustly	*any*	thing	that	another man		owns.

'Do not covet anything that another man owns'.

(HC, Wulfstan's *Homilies*, O3, eleventh century)

(8) Conditional:

He	nære	na	ælmihtig,	gif	him	*ænig*	gefadung	earfoðe	wære
he	not-were	not	almighty,	if	him	*any*	arrangement	difficult	were

'He would not be almighty, if anything were difficult for him'

(HC, Ælfric's *De temporibus anni*, O3, eleventh century)

(9) Comparative:

ðæt	lead	ðonne	is	hefigre	ðonne	*ænig*	oðer	andweorc.
the	lead	then	is	heavier	than	*any*	other	metal.

'Lead, then, is heavier than any other metal'

(HC, Alfred's *Cura Pastoralis*, O2, ninth century)

In both Old and Modern English, however, *any* does also occur in affirmatives, where it has come to be referred to as 'free choice *any*' (Vendler 1967; Ladusaw 1979). (10) is an Old English example of such an use.

(10)

Forþy	bið	*ænig*	þing	full	þe	sum	bið	wana.
therefore	are	*any*	things	ful	because	some	are	empty.

'The reason why anything can be full is that some things are empty'.

(HC, Alfred's *Boethius*, O2, tenth century)

Finally, the parallels between Old and Modern English are striking also in terms of semantic and pragmatic functions. The following discussion intends to demonstrate this, but will have to rely on some simplification. A large body of literature on the semantics and pragmatics of *any* has been produced in fields such as logic or formal truth conditional semantics, and there is no way in which this contribution can do justice to the complexity of the issues that *any* raises from a philosophical and theoretical perspective. Since the focus of this chapter is on the history of *any*, and particularly on its relation to the history of *one* and the indefinite article *a(n)*, the most important question for our purposes is to identify the ways in which *any* differs from other determinatives. This is a time-honoured method in structural linguistics that has proved highly productive in historical research (see particularly Rissanen 1967, 1988, 1997a, 1997b).

Let us establish the Modern English facts first. As a determinative, *any* serves primarily to specify the way in which a noun phrase refers to external reality. So what kind of reference relation does *any* establish and how does it differ from other determinatives? One obvious difference is between *any* and determinatives such as *the, this, that* or possessives such as *my, your, their*, etc. The latter refer to entities whose specific identity is either established already or getting established when the determinatives are used. They are definite determiners; *any* is not. Like the indefinite article *a*, the determinative *some* or the numeral *one*, *any* establishes reference to entities whose identity is either irrelevant or unknown to either all interlocutors or at least to the addressee. Thus, *any* belongs to the class of indefinite determinatives which are used when 'the reference of X is not uniquely identifiable in the shared knowledge of speaker and hearer' (Quirk et al. 1985: 272). Other members in that class are *some, a* and *one*. What distinguishes *any* from them?

First, consider the difference between *any* and *some*. It is – to a considerable extent – distributional: the two determinatives tend to occur in different environments. *Some* typically occurs in positive declaratives, such as (11), while *any* is more typical of negative contexts or questions, such as (12):

(11) There were *some* students in my lecture.
(12) a. There were not *any* students in my lecture.
     b. Were there *any* students in your lecture?

To the extent that *some* and *any* are in complementary distribution, the semantic contrast between them is difficult to pin down. It becomes more obvious, however, in contexts where both can occur, as in (13):

(13) a. You could see *some* doctor.
     b. You could see *any* doctor.

In both (13a) and (13b), the noun phrase headed by *doctor* refers to an unidentified doctor, so reference is indeed indefinite in both cases. However, (13b) indicates more than just that. Specifically, it indicates that the individual being referred to is a randomly chosen one from a plurality (or even from the complete set) of doctors that may be around. It also signals that the choice of any specific doctor would not rule out the choice of another one. Thus, *any* does various things at once. First, it establishes that doctors represent a class with an unspecified number of members. Secondly, it profiles the individuals in that class and casts them as alternatives. Finally, it expresses that there is no criterion that would suggest the choice of a specific doctor at the exclusion of any of the others.[5] *Some*, on the other hand, indicates less than that. Most importantly, it does not inherently signal a plurality of possible referents, and although it does obviously refer to a single individual, the fact that it does not evoke the whole class as a conceptual background also reduces its individualizing force in comparison to that of *any*.[6]

It is important, at this point, to recall that there is a difference between interpretations that are pragmatically possible, or even plausible, in a given utterance context and the meanings conventionally encoded by specific lexical items. Thus, the difference between *any* and *some* that has just been described needs to be thought of as semantic. It is a difference between the meanings that are conventionally associated with the lexical representations of the two items,[7] and these meanings are more specific than the meanings that may come to be conveyed or constructed, pragmatically, in actual discourse situations. Thus, pragmatically speaking, much of the meaning that *any* indicates by virtue of its inherent semantics may also be inferable – or presupposed – in utterances where *some* is used. For example, it is clearly common knowledge that there are many doctors, and it follows logically that the specific one referred to by *some* doctor must be a single member of that class. Also, it may be a default assumption shared by the interlocutors that there will be various equally good choices among the doctors that there are. The point is that *any* signals these aspects inherently, by virtue of its lexical semantics, while *some* does not.[8,9]

For the purposes of this discussion, then, the conventionalized, semantic meaning of *any* will be defined as both 'individualizing'[10] (since reference is typically to an unidentified, but particular individual) and 'non-unique' or 'non-exclusive' (since simultaneous reference to any alternative individual in the whole class is explicitly not ruled out). Graphically, the reference relations it establishes can be represented as in (14):

(14)   *any* x

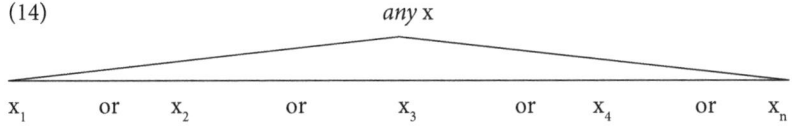

x_1 or x_2 or x_3 or x_4 or x_n

The specific reference relations established by *any* become even more noticeable when one compares them to those established by the numeral *one* and the indefinite article (*a*)*n*, although it is important to keep in mind that *one* and *a*(*n*) do not always express reference. They do not do so, for instance, in examples (15) and (16).

(15) Do I have to decide if I want to be *a* teacher or *a* doctor or *a* lawyer? (COCA, 1993, Bk:DarkestHour, FIC)

(16) Nearly all teachers and medical doctors have more than *one* job. (COCA, AmerStudies, ACAD)

When *one* and *a*(*n*) do refer, however, they do so in different ways than *any* does. Consider in this respect the examples in (17).

(17) a. You are free to see *any* doctor who accepts Medicare. (COCA, 2014, NYTimes, NEWS)

b. You are free to see *one* doctor who accepts Medicare.

c. You are free to see *a* doctor who accepts Medicare.

Like that of *any*, the reference expressed by *one* is to an unidentified individual. Thus, it is also indefinite and individualizing. In contrast to that of *any*, however, the reference expressed by *one* is exclusive or unique. Like *any*, it implies that there may be many doctors, but only one of them can be chosen and once the choice is made, visits to any of the other doctors are ruled out. Obviously, *one* cannot determine nouns in the plural, while *any* can, albeit it does so only rarely and practically never in affirmatives (see above). Thus, a central function of the numeral *one* is to indicate a 'contrast with a higher number of items' (Rissanen 1997a: 88). Graphically, the reference relations expressed by the numeral *one* can be represented as in (18).

(18)

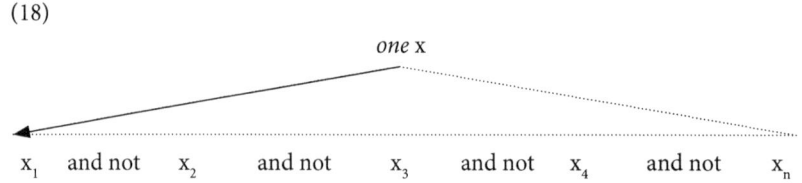

one x

x₁   and not   x₂   and not   x₃   and not   x₄   and not   xₙ

The reference expressed by *a*, finally, is the vaguest of them all. While it is also indefinite, it is open to a variety of interpretations and does not signal any of them inherently. Instead, which of them gets instantiated in any specific utterance depends mostly on the context. Consider (17c) and the examples in (19).

(19) a. There is *a* doctor who lives next door.
     b. *A* doctor is bound by the Hippocratic oath.

In (17c) above, reference is clearly indefinite. It is also individualizing, and most likely it is also non-exclusive, i.e. it does not imply that only a single doctor may be seen. In (19a), reference is also indefinite, as the doctor is not identified. Like in (17c), it is to an individual, but most likely it is exclusive, as the plural would have been used if the doctor next door was not the only doctor who lived there. Crucially, however, the adequate interpretation of the reference relations obtaining in (17c) and (19a) relies mostly on world knowledge, and is not inherently signalled by the use of *a*. This is because *a* can also be used in contexts where generic reference to all members of a class is intended, as in (15), or in contexts where no reference relation is established at all, as in (19b).

The vagueness of the reference relations inherently expressed by the indefinite article *a(n)* reflects that it is highly grammatical and syntactically conditioned. It has come to serve as the default item to be used when the grammar requires a determinative slot to be filled, as it does in noun phrases headed by common count nouns in the singular, and when the noun phrase does not refer to an object or individual that is known to the interlocutors. So, all that *(a)n* signals inherently and by convention is indefiniteness. Any of the more specific reference relations that obtain in individual utterances can, and need to be, inferred.

Thus, the features that distinguish *any* from other determinatives are (a) indefiniteness, (b) individualization and (c) non-exclusiveness or uniqueness. Table 4.2 expresses this in terms of a feature matrix. It includes only *any*, *one* and *(a)n*, since the

Table 4.2 Feature matrix

Semantic dimension	*any*	*one*	*a(n)*
Definiteness	−	−	−
Individualization	+	+	/
Exclusiveness (Uniqueness)	−	+	/

rise and fall in the frequency of *any* during the Early Middle English period results from an interaction between the three of them.[11]

Before turning to that chapter in the history of *any*, however, note first how the reference relations expressed by its Old English ancestor *ænig* seem to have been practically equivalent. This is demonstrated in examples (20) to (22).

(20) Swa oft   swa him *ænig* munuc to com, þonne lædde he hine into his huse.
    as often as him *any* monk to came then led   he him into his house.
    'Whenever *any* monk came by, he led him into his house'.
                                (YCOE, *Saint Euphrosyne*, OE, prob. eleventh century)

(21) Wenað we, hwæþer þes æðele wer ær   *ænigne* lareow   hæfde?
    know we if   this noble man ever *any*   teacher had
    'Do we know if this noble man had ever had any teacher?'
                                (YCOE, *Gregory's Dialogues*, OE24, eleventh century)

(22) Worhton þa mææstan yfel þe   æfre *ænig* here don   meahte
    did.PL the most   evil that ever *any* army do   might
    'They inflicted the greatest harm that ever any army might do'.
                                (YCOE, *Anglo-Saxon Chronicle*, OE twelfth century)

Example (20) is the most straightforward one of the three. Reference is made to a plurality of monks, indeed to all of the monks that ever came by. The reference is indefinite, as their identities are unknown and irrelevant. At the same time each individual monk in the set is profiled as the one that gets asked in at each of the separate occasions. The reference is therefore not just indefinite, but also individualizing and non-exclusive. The same reading makes equal sense in the two other cases. (21) refers to the class of teachers, and the question is if any one of them happened to be the teacher of the noble person that the sentence is about. Reference is indefinite, because the identity of the teacher is unknown, it is individualizing, but at the same time no single one of a plurality of potential teachers is ruled out. So, the reference is non-exclusive as well. Finally, (22) refers indefinitely to the set of all imaginable armies. Reference is clearly individualizing, because the focus is on the damage that a single one of them could do, not all of them together. And it is clearly non-exclusive because every single one of all imaginable armies qualifies as a candidate for the hypothetical comparison. Thus, examples (20) to (22) show quite clearly that Old English *ænig* carried the same semantic features as its Modern English descendant *any*. And the same applies, by the way, to examples (6) to (10) above.

We can now draw the interim conclusion that there is indeed a very strong similarity between Modern English *any* and its Old English predecessor *ænig*. Both are about equally frequent, both are most frequently used as determinatives or pronouns, both occur in the same range of sentence types and both convey the same semantic (or conventionalized pragmatic) meaning. This similarity suggests continuity and makes it quite surprising that the history of *any* should have been interrupted by a phase in which it declined significantly. Section 3 will investigate possible reasons for that decline and its subsequent reversal.

3. Why the frequency of *any* declined but rose again during the Early Middle English period

3.1. Competition and changes in the relative frequencies of *any*, *one* and *a(n)*

Let us start with an observation on Modern English. As we have seen, Modern English *any* is semantically distinct from, but nevertheless quite similar to, the numeral *one* and to the indefinite article *a(n)*. Thus, there are contexts in which any of them can be used without changing the meaning drastically. Consider the examples in (23) to (25). In each of them, the first sentence (a) is an actual occurrence attested in COCA, while the other two (b and c) are variants created for the present purpose.

> (23) a. Now if you can give me *any* reason why I should not teach her along with you, say it. (COCA, 2008, Read, FIC)
> b. Now if you can give me *one* reason why I should not teach her along with you, say it.
> c. Now if you can give me *a* reason why I should not teach her along with you, say it.
> (24) a. Give me *one* reason why you can't do that. (COCA, 1999, ABC_20/20, SPOK)
> b. Give me *any* reason why you can't do that.
> c. Give me *a* reason why you can't do that.
> (25) a. Give me *a* reason why a mother would kill her own child. (COCA, 1997, CBS_SatMorn, SPOK)
> b. Give me *one* reason why a mother would kill her own child.
> c. Give me *any* reason why a mother would kill her own child.

In each of the three examples, replacing any of the three determinatives with any of the other two hardly changes the meaning. In all of them, the presupposition seems to be that the reason asked for will be hard to find. In (25a) this is clear from the context, since infanticide counts as an abominable and hardly forgivable act. In (24a), the speaker implies that even a single reason will be difficult to come by, let alone more, and in (23a) the construal is that there may be a large number of reasons to be thought of, but not a single one of them will be adequate. But those are nuances. The general thrust of each of the utterances remains the same, no matter which of the three determinatives is actually used. This shows that there are contexts where *any*, *one* and *a(n)* can all occur and do similar jobs, even though their lexical meanings can be clearly distinguished.

Bearing that in mind, consider Table 4.3 and Figure 4.3, which compare the development of the frequency of *any* to that of *one* and *a(n)* put together.

Figure 4.3 shows that the decline in the frequency of *any* coincides with a rise in the frequency of *one*/*a(n)*. We have already established that they are semantically similar and that all three of them are frequently used as determinatives. *Any* and *one* both occur as pronouns as well. Obviously, items with so much functional overlap are likely to come into competition. Thus, the rise in the frequency of *one* and *a(n)* may not just correlate with the decline of *any*, but may have actually caused it.

At the same time, evidence from the Early Modern English period onwards shows all three determinatives to have stably co-existed, and they still do so, of course. If, therefore, the decline in the frequency of *any* was due to competition from *one* and *a(n)*, that competition must have been resolved in some way, or *any* would not have made a comeback.

3.2. The gradual grammaticalization of *one* and its effects on *any*

In contrast to that of *any*, the historical development of *one* and *(a)n* has seen significant changes not only in terms of frequency, but also semantically, syntactically and phonologically. There is much research on them (see e.g. Christophersen 1939; Rissanen 1967, 1997b; Ringe and Taylor 2014; Sommerer 2018) and we can use it to recapitulate the story of *one* and *a(n)*, illustrate it with examples and demonstrate its relevance for the history of *any*.

Table 4.3 Normalized frequencies of *any* and *one/a(n)* per million words (<850 to 1570; data derived from the HC)

Period	pre 850	850–950	950–1050	1050–1150	1150–1250	1250–1350	1350–1420	1420–1500	1500–1570
any	913	587	1,264	772	230	462	2,030	1,557	3,118
one/a(n)	2,740	2,640	2,718	4,170	7,663	10,330	12,387	12,757	15,419

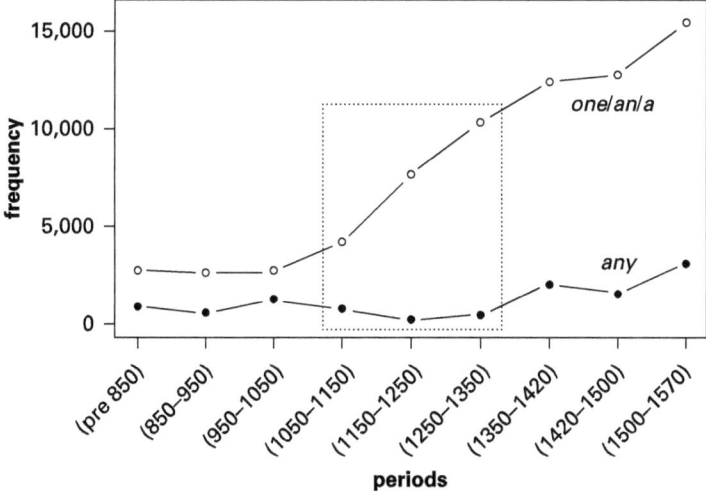

Figure 4.3 Developments of *any* (solid dots) and *one/an/a* (open dots). Frequencies normalized per million words. The dashed box denotes the turn-around period.

Most importantly, there was no clear distinction yet in Old English between *one* and *a(n)*. Both were variants of *án*, from which *(a)n* developed through a classical grammaticalization process that involved rising frequency, semantic bleaching, loss of syntactic mobility and phonological reduction (for grammaticalization paths leading to article emergence, see Himmelmann 2001). The core function of Old English *án* was that of a numeral. Syntactically, it could serve as a determinative and as a pronoun, just like its Modern English descendant. In both functions it could express reference. (26) and (27) show what reference relations *án* established when it was used as a numeral and did refer. They were indefinite, individualizing and exclusive (or unique), just as those of the modern numeral.

> (26) Ða   cwæð   se   hælend   *an*   þing   þe   is   wana
>   then   said   the   saviour   *one*   thing   to-you is   lacking
>   'Then Jesus said, "There is one thing you lack".'
>   (OED, *West Saxon Gospels*: Luke 18:22, OE)
> (27) Þa   lægdon hi   fyr on, &   forbærndon eall þa tun   buton *ane* huse.
>   then laid   they fire on and burned   all the town but   *one* house
>   'Then, they set fire and burned down the whole town, except for one house'.
>   (OED, *Anglo-Saxon Chronicle*. (Laud) (Peterborough interpolation) anno
>   1070, lOE)

They fully match Rissanen's (1967: 5) description of the strictly numerical use of *án* as establishing a contrast to a plurality.

Another type of use that Rissanen (1967) attributes to *one* is individualizing. In such uses, *one* singles an unidentified referent out from a larger group. Example (28) illustrates that kind of use, and the translation shows how well it corresponds to its modern analogue.

> (28) He wæs *an* þara ealdra of ðam yldostum witum   Iudeisces folces
>   he was *one* of the elders of the oldest   sages   of Jewish people
>   'He was one of the elders from among the oldest wise men of the Jews'.
>   (YCOE, Ælfric, *Supplemental Homilies*, O3, eleventh century)

Another similarity to Modern English *one*, is that Old English *án* could be used non-referentially, as in (29) and (30), where it establishes a contrast to higher numerals.

> (29) Se   wer   mot   habban   butan   *an*   wif.
>   the   man   must   have   but   *one* wife
>   'A man may have only one wife'.
>   (OED, *Regula Canonicorum* (Corpus Cambr. 191) lxv.305, OE)
> (30) Þa   heold Seaxburg his cuen *an* gear þæt rice   æfter him.
>   then held Seaxburg his queen *one* year that realm after him
>   'Seaxburg's Queen governed the realm for one year after his death'.
>   (OED, *Anglo-Saxon Chronicle*, Parker, eOE)

Even though Old English *án* resembled its Modern English descendant in many of its uses, however, it also had others already, which 'more or less resembl[ed] that of the indefinite article' (Rissanen 1967: 267). Some examples are:

(31) Ðær   wearð   Alexander   þurhscoten   mid   *anre*   flan
      there   was   Alexander   pierced   with   *an*   arrow
      'There Alexander was pierced by an arrow'.

(YCOE, Orosius, O2)

(32) Her   is   cumen   *an*   draca   þe   me   sceal   forswelgan
      here   is   come   *a*   dragon   which   me   will   devour
      'A dragon has come here, which will devour me'.

(YCOE, Ælfric, Catholic Homilies I, O3, eleventh century)

As Sommerer (2018: 87) points out, however, 'in all the examples, *an* is compatible with a numerical reading'. They represent the numeral in an article-like use, but not an article as such yet. In such uses, some of the inherent features of the numeral are redundant, because the context already implies them. That Alexander was hit by a single specific arrow and that the dragon that had arrived was a specific one follows from world knowledge. The exclusiveness of the reference does not require to be signalled, but that it was signalled by *án* did not disturb either.

There are already Old English examples, however, in which an exclusive interpretation of reference does not make sense anymore. In (33), for example, it is clear that not any transgression (of all imaginable ones) is tolerated, and in (34) reference is clearly made to all and any of the cows or pigs that might have been – but were not actually – missed.

(33) He   þe   ne   þoleð   and   forbereð   noht   *a*   misbode.
      he   you   not   allows   and   suffers   not   *one*   wrongdoing.
      'He does not allow you or suffer a single transgression'.

(OED, Old Eng. Homilies, 2nd Ser. 79, a1225)

(34) Ne *an* cu, ne *an* swin næs belyfon   þæt næs   gesæt on his gewrite
      not *one* cow not *one* pig was   remaining that was not put   in his record
      'Not a single cow or pig failed to be recorded'.

(YCOE, Anglo Saxon Chronicle, ca. 1160)

Thus, the grammaticalization of what was once a numeral had clearly started in Old English already, and in that process uses became increasingly frequent where the inherent lexical meaning associated with *án* was bleached, so that it gradually lost its conventional association to the semantic features that described its lexical content. As to the order in which they were lost, the most likely (if not the only) possibility is that the most specific one will have gone first, and that was exclusiveness or uniqueness, as the examples above illustrate. Since exclusiveness defines a subtype of individualizing reference, it makes no sense to signal it if individualization is not signalled, or at least implied, at the same time. Thus, an item cannot really cease to refer to individuals without also ceasing to refer exclusively, so that *one* – as it began to bleach – must have lost the meaning of exclusiveness before that of individualization.[12] In that phase, it is obvious that it will indeed have become a strong competitor to *any*, because it was in terms of exclusiveness alone that the two items contrasted. Since the progressing grammaticalization of *án* went hand in hand with the expectable rise in frequency, the pressure on *any* must have risen, and is likely to have caused its decline during the Early Middle English period. This also seems corroborated by Middle English descendant forms of Old English *án* that were phonetically reduced and appeared in contexts where *any* would have worked equally well.

(35) da eifulle dieulen bied swa ladliche and swo grislich an to lokin, dat
     the evil devils are so   horrible and so hideous at to look that
     gif *a* mann iseiȝe ne   anne, he scolde sone bien ut of his iwitte.
     if   *a* man saw only one he would soon be out of his wit.
     'Those evil devils were so horribly hideous that if a (any) man saw only one, he
     would go mad'.
                                                      (HC, *Vices and Virtues, ca.* 1200)

(36) Ne   fel   neuere *a* reynes droppe for-to destourbi a mannes mod.
     not fell   never *a* rain's drop for-to disturb a man's mood.
     'There never fell a (one/any) drop of rain, that might lower one's spirits'.
                                                  (HC, *Lives of Saints*, twelfth century)

(37) We ne   moȝe naȝt *ane* time of þe daye þolye þe asaylinges of
     we not can   not *one* time of the day bear the attacks of
     þe dyeule wyþ-oute þe help of oure lhorde.
     the devil without the help of our Lord.
     'Without the help of God, we could not withstand the attacks of the devil at
     any time of the day'.
                                              (HC, *Ayenbite of Inwit*, fourteenth century)

In these examples, *a(n)* expresses indefinite and individualizing, but not exclusive reference, and does exactly what *any* might have done instead. The increasing grammaticalization of the numeral must therefore have at least contributed strongly to the marginalization of *any* to which the data from the first half of the Middle English period testify.

The question that remains to be addressed, then, is why *any* was not ousted from the language completely as the grammaticalization of *one* progressed and the frequency of its reduced form *a(n)* continued to increase. As will be demonstrated, the answer is in fact already implied in what has been established so far. Thus, we know from Modern English evidence that the grammaticalization of Old English *án* did not simply produce a bleached variant of it, but resulted in divergence (Hopper 1991: 24): when the indefinite article emerged in its fully developed form, its use was syntactically conditioned and its form so reduced that it was no longer a variant of the numeral. Instead, the lineage of Old English *án* had branched and given rise to two separate items: the numeral *one*, which reverted to signalling the highly specific referential relations of its Old English ancestor, and the indefinite article *a(n)*. Ever since that divergence, *one* and *a*(*n*) have remained neatly distinct, and in Modern English they can clearly not be considered as two allomorphs of a single polysemous morpheme anymore.

What makes this relevant for the history of *any* is easy to see. In contrast to some of the bleached variants of Early Middle English *one*/*a*(*n*), neither of the two morphemes that emerged after the branching were serious competitors of *any* anymore. With *one*, it once again contrasted on the dimension of exclusiveness, just as Old English *ænig* had contrasted with *án*. The new *a*(*n*), on the other hand, was semantically so vague that all it inherently signalled was a lack of definiteness. Thus, its rising frequency ceased to threaten *any*, which became useful once again, was re-established in usage, and reassumed the relative frequency its ancestor had in Old English. Figure 4.4 visualizes the three phases in the development.

4. Conclusion

What we have shown is that the history of *any* is indeed one of functional continuity. We have also seen that what seems like an interruption in an otherwise straightforward story of faithful transmission can be explained quite naturally if one considers developments that affected the systemic environment of *any*, and in particular its close neighbour, the numeral *one*. What can be learnt from this on a more general level is that the history of any single item can hardly ever be fully understood if one studies it in isolation from the rest of the language to which it belongs, because languages are indeed organic systems in which all parts hang together, and some of them very closely indeed.

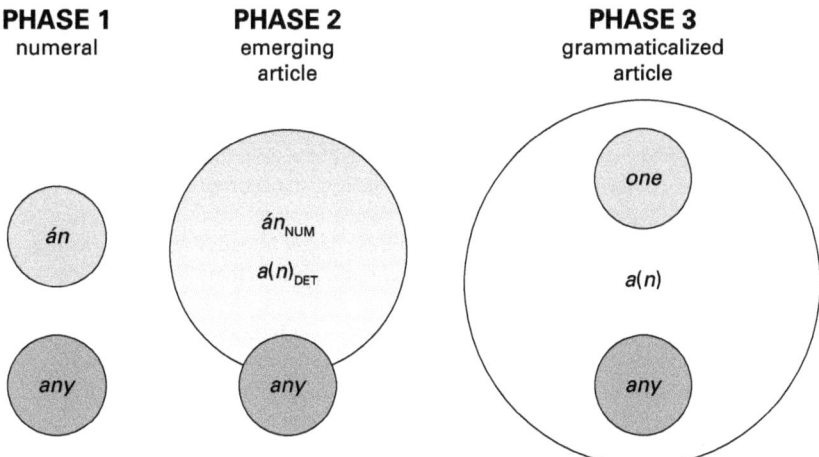

Figure 4.4 Effects of the grammaticalization of *one* on its relation to *any*.

Notes

1 While it is likely that the HC data convey an exaggerated impression of the Early
  Middle English dip, the picture changes only in degree but not in quality if one
  searches corpora that have become available more recently, such as the *Early English
  Books Online* corpus (EEBO; https://corpus.byu.edu/eebo) or the *Penn-Helsinki Parsed
  Corpus of Middle English* (PPCME2; Kroch and Taylor 2000; https://www.ling.upenn.
  edu/hist-corpora/PPCME2-RELEASE-4/index.html). The picture that emerges from
  these two corpora has the normalized frequency of *any* at between 724 per million
  words for the period between 1050 and 1150 (PPCME2). For the next period
  (1250–1350), the evidence is sparse and difficult to assess. If one considers only texts
  which can be placed in that period on the basis of both their composition and the date
  of the manuscript, the frequency of *any* drops once again radically to less than 200 per
  million words. If one includes texts with a later manuscript date as well, on the other
  hand, it rises slightly, to 968 per million words. Afterwards the rise continues. The
  PPCME returns 1,231 per million words for 1350–1450. For the period 1480–1590,
  EEBO returns 1,293 per million words, and 2,287 per million words for 1600–1690.
  Towards the end of the seventeenth century (the 1690s in EEBO), the frequency
  climbs to about 2,500 per million words. From 1800 to 2000, evidence from Corpus of
  Contemporary American English (COHA) suggests a gradual decline from about
  1,800 per million words towards less than 1,000.
2 This comparison neglects occurrences of *any* in complex pronouns such as *anybody*,
  anyone or *anything*, which emerged only in the Middle English period.
3 The OED quotes a first attestation from about 1300, a verse from a legend about the
  childhood of Jesus, dated about 1300 (MS Laud 137; Horstmann 1881: 7):

   (i) Withoute *ani* more   lette Þat treo ful   sone upriȝht him   sette.
       without   *any* further delay the tree very soon upright itself set.
       'Immediately, the tree stood straight'.

   The syntactic status of *any* in this sentence is at least ambivalent, however. While
   it is of course possible to analyse it as an adverb that premodifies *more*, i.e. [[[any]$_{adv}$
   [more]$_{adj}$]$_{adj}$[lette]$_n$]$_{np}$, it is not less plausible to read it as a determinative, i.e. as [[any]$_{det}$
   [[more]$_{adj}$[lette]$_n$]$_{np}$]$_{np}$. Thus, the occurrence is probably best considered as representing
   a bridging context that only first motivated neoanalysis (cf., Traugott 2015: 65) of
   any as an adverb. Unambiguously adverbial uses do not seem to be attested until later.
4 Plural noun phrases have not risen much above 8 per cent in the 2000s either
  (2,234/24,030; source: COCA). Among Middle English occurrences in the HC, they
  represent about 4 per cent. While the recent increase is interesting, it is too recent to
  be a relevant factor in the development that this chapter intends to explain. During
  the periods on which we focus, the few plural noun phrases that contain *any* are
  negligible.
5 Thus, *any* refers simultaneously to a whole class and to the individual members in it. This
  dual nature has given rise to a debate in the literature about whether *any* should be
  regarded as an indefinite determinative or as a universal quantifier (see e.g., Dayal 2005;
  Heim 1982 [2011]; Vlachou 2006). As pointed out, however, the focus of this
  contribution is on the history of *any*. Therefore, it cannot go into the intricacies of that
  debate.
6 In noun phrases headed by non-count nouns (typically referring to aggregates or
  substances), *any* serves more or less the same functions, except that the reference it

indexes can of course not be individualizing in the narrow sense. Instead, fractions, subtypes, instantiations or occurrences become conceptual analogues of individuals. Thus, in an example like (ii) the use of *any* construes an individual occurrence of water as a potential referent. Since the occurrence is not realized, reference necessarily remains indefinite. It is also non-exclusive: any potential occurrence of water would be as good as any other. In (iii), on the other hand, non-exclusive and indefinite reference is made to different subtypes of food.

(ii)   'I don't see *any* water', replied the man, 'nothing but a rock and a woman'. (COHA, Judd, Sylvester. *Margaret: A Tale of the Real and Ideal*, Blight and Bloom, 1845)

(iii) We think that *any* food that has ... fructose ... in it is a safe food to eat. (COCA, Spoken Component. *The fallacies of fat*, 2013)

Reference is also individualizing, as emerges from the fact that any food is taken up anaphorically by the rather uncommon singular noun phrase *a food*. This highlights that reference is to each type of food individually, rather than generically to the whole class of fructose-containing foods.

7   Readers who regard reference as a pragmatic phenomenon by definition are invited to think of the difference as pertaining to the level of conventionalized as opposed to situationally constructed pragmatic meaning.

8   That *any* has a stronger individualizing force than *some* is also reflected in the fact that *some* is much more likely to appear in plural noun phrases (more than 44 per cent of all cases in the spoken component of COCA) than *any* (less than 20 per cent).

9   This does not mean, of course, that noun phrases headed by *some* may not be interpreted, pragmatically, as referring in a similar way as noun phrases headed by *any*. The meaning of *some* is simply wider than that of *any* and allows more room for interpretation.

10 We are aware that this terminological choice might be considered idiosyncratic, but there are good arguments for it. In contrast to possible alternatives such as 'particularizing', or even 'specific', 'individualizing reference' does not imply reference to a unique individual and allows one to treat uniqueness as a separate property. This makes it possible to distinguish *any* neatly from *one*, whose reference is also to an individual, but to a specific one, at the exclusion of others. 'Specific reference', which is a commonly used term, conflates individualization and uniqueness, and is, on top of that, sometimes confused with definite reference, even though it is of course possible to make indefinite reference to a specific individual, if that individual is unidentified.

11 Note at this point that the expression of individualizing but at the same time non-exclusive reference makes little sense in statements that report actual, specific events. It is questionable, for example, what kind of rational interpretation a statement such as *Yesterday I saw any doctor who accepts Medicare* could get. Thus, it is hardly surprising that *any* is used to refer to potential participants in counterfactual or hypothetical events and that it occurs most frequently in questions or negations. The main reason why an affirmative example has been chosen to illustrate the differences between *any*, *one* and *a(n)* is simply that it brings them out more clearly. In the context of questions and negations, some of them are neutralized and, as we shall see below, this may have increased the competition between the three determinatives.

12 You cannot refer exclusively to something, unless it is also distinguished from the things that are excluded. Exclusive reference to everything is an oxymoron.

Corpora

COCA = Davies, Mark (2008–), *The Corpus of Contemporary American English (COCA): 560 million words, 1990–present.* Available online: https://corpus.byu.edu/coca/.

COHA = Davies, Mark (2010–), *The Corpus of Historical American English (COHA): 400 million words, 1810–2009.* Available online: https://corpus.byu.edu/coha/.

EEBO = Davies, Mark (2017), *Early English Books Online.* Part of the SAMUELS project. Available online: https://corpus.byu.edu/eebo/.

HC = *The Helsinki Corpus of English Texts* (1991), Department of Modern Languages, University of Helsinki. Compiled by Matti Rissanen (Project leader), Merja Kytö (Project secretary); Leena Kahlas-Tarkka, Matti Kilpiö (Old English); Saara Nevanlinna, Irma Taavitsainen (Middle English); Terttu Nevalainen, Helena Raumolin-Brunberg (Early Modern English).

PPCME2 = Kroch, Anthony and Ann Taylor (2000), *Penn-Helsinki Parsed Corpus of Middle English*, 2nd edn. Available online: http://www.ling.upenn.edu/hist-corpora/PPCME2-RELEASE-4.

YCOE = Taylor, Ann, Anthony Warner, Susan Pintzuk and Frank Beths (2003), *The York-Toronto-Helsinki Parsed Corpus of Old English Prose.* Electronic texts and manuals available from the *Oxford Text Archive.* http://www-users.york.ac.uk/~lang22/YCOE/YcoeHome.htm.

References

Christophersen, Paul (1939), *The Articles: A Study of their Theory and Use in English*, Copenhagen: Munksgaard.

Dayal, Veneeta (2005), 'The Universal Force of Free Choice *any*', *Linguistic Variation Yearbook* 4: 5–40.

Fischer, Olga (1992), 'Syntax', in Norman Blake (ed), *The Cambridge History of the English Language. Vol. 2: 1066–1476*, 207–408, Cambridge: Cambridge University Press.

Gries, Stefan T. and Martin Hilpert (2008), 'The Identification of Stages in Diachronic Data: Variability-based Neighbor Clustering', *Corpora* 3: 59–81.

Heim, Irene R. (1982 [2011]), 'The Semantics of Definite and Indefinite Noun Phrases', PhD diss., University of Massachusetts Amherst.

Himmelmann, Nikolaus (2001), 'Articles', in Martin Haspelmath, Ekkehard König, Wulf Oesterreicher and Wolfgang Raible (eds), *Language Typology and Language Universals*, 831–41, Berlin: De Gruyter Mouton.

Hoeksema, Jack (2012), 'On the Natural History of Negative Polarity Items', *Linguistic Analysis*, 38 (1–2): 3–35.

Hopper, Paul (1991), 'On Some Principles of Grammaticalization', in Elizabeth C. Traugott and Bernd Heine (eds), *Approaches to Grammaticalization. Vol. 1*, 17–35, Amsterdam: Benjamins.

Horstmann, Carl, ed. (1881), *Altenglische Legenden.* Heilbronn: Gebrüder Henninger.

Iyeiri, Yoko (1999), 'Multiple Negation in Middle English Verse', in Gunnel Tottie, Ingrid Tieken-Boon van Ostade and Wim van der Wurff (eds), *Negation in the History of English*, 121–46, Berlin: De Gruyter Mouton.

Iyeiri, Yoko (2002), 'Development of *Any* from Middle English to Early Modern English: A Study Using the *Helsinki Corpus of English Texts*', in Shunji Yamazaki, Junsaku Nakamura and Toshio Saito (eds), *English Corpus Linguistics in Japan*, 211–23, Leiden: Brill.

Iyeiri, Yoko (2010), *Verbs of Implicit Negation and their Complements in the History of English*, Amsterdam: Benjamins.

Ladusaw, William A. (1979), 'Polarity Sensitivity as Inherent Scope Relations', PhD diss., University of Texas at Austin.

OED = *Oxford English Dictionary Online*. Available online: http://www.oed.com/.

Quirk, Randolph, Sidney Greenbaum, Geoffrey Leech and Jan Svartvik (1985), *A Comprehensive Grammar of the English Language*, London: Longman.

Ringe, Donald A. and Ann Taylor (2014), *The Development of Old English*, Oxford: Oxford University Press.

Rissanen, Matti (1967), *The Uses of 'One' in Old and Early Middle English*, Helsinki: Société Néophilologique.

Rissanen, Matti (1988), 'Where Philology and Linguistics Meet: Reference, (In) Definiteness and Old English *Sum*', in Dieter Kastovsky and Gero Bauer (eds), *Luick Revisited: Papers Read at the Luick-Symposium at Schloß Liechtenstein, 15.–18.9.1985*, 295–310, Tübingen: Narr.

Rissanen, Matti (1997a), 'The Pronominalization of *One*', in Matti Rissanen, Merja Kytö and Kirsi Heikkonen (eds), *Grammaticalization at Work: Studies of Long-term Developments in English*, 87–143, Berlin: De Gruyter Mouton.

Rissanen, Matti (1997b), 'Whatever Happened to the Middle English Indefinite Pronouns?', in Jacek Fisiak (ed), *Studies in Middle English Linguistics*, 523–9, Berlin: De Gruyter Mouton.

Sommerer, Lotte (2018), *Article Emergence in Old English: A Constructionalist Perspective*, Berlin: De Gruyter Mouton.

Tottie, Gunnel, Ingrid Tieken-Boon van Ostade and Wim van der Wurff (eds) (1999), *Negation in the History of English*, Berlin: De Gruyter Mouton.

Traugott, Elizabeth C. (2015), 'Toward a Coherent Account of Grammatical Constructionalization', in Jóhanna Barðdal, Elena Smirnova, Lotte Sommerer and Spike Gildea (eds), *Diachronic Construction Grammar*, 51–80, Amsterdam: Benjamins.

Vlachou, Evangelina (2006), 'Definite and Indefinite Free Choice Items: Evidence from English, French and Greek', in Pascal Denis, Eric McCeardy, Alexis Plamer and Brian Reese (eds), *Proceedings of the 2004 Texas Linguistics Society Conference: Issues at the Semantics-Pragmatics Interface*, 150–9, Somerville, Mass.: Cascadilla Proceedings Project.

Vendler, Zeno (1967), *Linguistics in Philosophy*, Ithaca: Cornell University Press.

5

Revisiting 'it-extraposition': The Historical Development of Constructions with Matrices (it)/(there) be + Noun Phrase followed by a Complement Clause[1]

Kristin Davidse
KU Leuven

An Van linden
KU Leuven/Université de Liège

1. Introduction

In this article, we examine the historical development of complementation constructions whose matrix is a predicative or existential clause containing one full noun phrase (NP), followed by a complement clause, as illustrated by (1) and 2). We will give arguments for viewing them as one 'macro-construction', i.e. as a form-meaning pairing defined by a highly schematic structure and corresponding functions (Traugott 2008: 236).

(1) My kids got to see that my out-of-home life was far more complex and intense than they thought. *It was a wonder to them* that I get to do all this stuff. (https://our-story-begins.com/2015/08/)
(2) such preparations are used in certain cases of anaemia and even by some people who believe (though it isn't proven) that it will prevent their hair from greying. *There is no doubt* that fluoride is necessary for the healthy formation and growth of bones and teeth (WB)[2]

Theoretically, we situate ourselves within the tradition of semiotically-based, functional-structural construction grammars such as Langacker (1987, 1991, 2002), Halliday (1994) and McGregor (1997). They all seek to identify which precise units are involved in conceptually motivated structural relations and they recognize the role played by different types of structural relations, such as modification versus complementation, in the way form codes meaning.

In a nutshell, our functional-structural analysis is as follows. The primary structural units are the matrix and the complement clause. On a lexical reading, the matrices convey a specific emotional or cognitive state. The *that*-clause represents the proposition presupposed in the emotion process or created by the cognition process depicted by the matrix. In other words, on their lexical reading, they are factive or reporting complementation constructions. In (1) the matrix *it was a wonder to them* conveys that the speaker's children are very surprised. The *that*-clause contains the presupposed factive proposition that they are surprised about. In (2), the matrix *there is no doubt* conveys that scientists know for sure *that fluoride is necessary for healthy bones and teeth* as opposed to some people believing without proof that fluoride prevents their hair from going grey. The complex sentence with *there is no doubt* is thus a construction of reported thought.

Importantly, the two matrix types can, through grammaticalization and subjectification, acquire a speaker-related meaning, conveying mirative, evidential or modal qualifications, which scope over the proposition in the complement clause (McGregor 1997: 64–73). In (3), *it's no wonder* comments on the proposition in terms of its (un)expectedness, i.e. mirativity (DeLancey 2001). Its meaning can be paraphrased by an expectation adverb such as *of course* (Simon-Vandenbergen and Aijmer 2007: 172). The speaker's lack of surprise about the proposition *Norwegians hunt whale* is justified by the following clause, *There's nothing else left to catch*. In (4), *there is no doubt* expresses the speaker's modal qualification by a high degree of certainty of the proposition that the racehorse Petite Margot will prove to be a winner. The use of epistemic modal *may* in the preceding sentence supports this reading, as it is another instance of the speaker modally qualifying his assessment of Petite Margot.

(3) *It's no wonder* Norwegians hunt whale. There's nothing else left to catch. (WB)
(4) SHE may never match her full-brother Ollie Magern but *there is no doubt* PETITE MARGOT has a big race in her. (WB)

There is no *syntactic* difference between the lexically- (1)–(2) and grammatically-used (3)–(4) complementation constructions. Both consist of a matrix and a subordinated complement clause. However, as pointed out by Boye and Harder (2007: 584–9) for examples with a matrix like *I think*, different *discursive* uses are involved, in which either the matrix or the complement clause is discourse primary. This can be brought out by textual follow-ups such as questions or reactions like *really?* which pick out the unit that is primary in the discourse context. In many actual contexts, the distinction, which is of its nature cline-like (Hopper and Traugott 2003: 6), remains underspecified, but it can be illustrated for clear cases. With a clear lexical example like (1), *It was a wonder to them that I get to do all this stuff*, following questions and exclamations clearly pick up on the matrix: *Was it a wonder to them? Really?* By contrast, an example with a miratively-used matrix, as in (3), would not be queried by an open-ended polar interrogative *Is it a wonder?* and *Really?* would be felt to apply to the whole complex sentence in its meaning 'of course, Norwegians hunt whale'.

The comprehensive account proposed here goes against the mainstream position, which analyses examples with a predicative matrix differently from those with an existential matrix. More specifically, the examples with *it* + *be* + predicative complement are set apart as a construction in its own right involving *it*-extraposition (Quirk et al. 1985: 1391; Huddleston and Pullum 2002: 1403). On this analysis (often credited to Rosenbaum 1967), the *that*-clause in (1) is said to be extraposed from the subject position, which is filled by *it*. The 'extraposition construction' in (1) is thus viewed as deriving from the non-extraposed structure, *That I get to do all this stuff was a wonder to them*. Consequently, the clause in final position is analysed as 'semantically ... stand[ing] in the same relation to the verb (or verb + predicative complement)' (Huddleston and Pullum 2002: 1403) as in the non-extraposed variant, i.e. as a subject clause. In other words, the *that*-clause is viewed as the 'predicand' to which the predicate phrase relates, e.g., *is a wonder* in (1). The extraposition analysis of examples with a predicative matrix has as an important consequence that the examples with an existential matrix are not seen as subtypes of the same overarching construction, since they do not have alternates in which the *that*-clause functions as subject.

In this contribution we set out to show that the historical development of these constructions supports analysing them as one schematic macro-construction, which provides a natural explanation for their similar – lexical and grammatical – meanings. At the same time, we will also do justice to the distinct grammatical semantics of the two matrix types, by analysing them at the meso-constructional level, where sets of similarly behaving more specific constructions can be distinguished (Traugott 2008: 236). We will trace the development of the complementation constructions whose matrices contain the nouns *wonder* and *tweo/doubt* from Old to Present-day English. Because the noun *doubt* entered English from French only at around 1225, we will investigate the data with Germanic *tweo* ('doubt') for the Old English period. Throughout their history, these nouns have featured in matrices with *be*, either predicative (1) or existential (2), which we will analyse as subtypes, or more specific meso-constructions (Traugott 2008: 236), of the very schematic complementation structure we posit at the macro-level.

In Section 2 we describe the extraction and compilation of the corpus data on which our study is based. We reconstruct the historical development of the complementation constructions in two main temporal stages, Old English (Section 3) and Middle to Present-day English (Section 4). As we will show, the greatest changes took place between these two periods, with the constructions studied remaining relatively stable from Middle English onwards. In Section 5, we spell out the main consequences of our alternative account in comparison with the traditional extraposition account.

2. Extraction and compilation of corpus datasets

2.1. Datasets with complementation constructions whose matrix contains *be* + NP with *wonder*

Since the *Oxford English Dictionary* (OED) puts the first occurrence of the noun *wonder* at *c.* 700, it was possible to collect data from Old English on. Diachronic data

Table 5.1 Historical data: Complementation constructions with matrices (*it*)/(*there*) *be* + *wonder*

Period	Corpus	N of words (millions)	N of relevant tokens	Normalized frequency (/1,000,000)	Subperiod	N of relevant tokens
Old English: 750–1150	YCOE	1.45	64	44.1	750–950	15
					950–1150	49
Middle English: 1150–1500	PPCME2	1.16	38	32.8	1150–1350	24
					1350–1500	14
Early Modern English: 1500–1710	PPCEME	1.79	14	7.8		
Late Modern English: 1710–1920	CLMETEV	15.01	92	6.1		

were extracted from the following corpora: the York-Toronto-Helsinki Parsed Corpus of Old English Prose (YCOE) for the period 750–1150, the Penn-Helsinki Parsed Corpus of Middle English (PPCME2) for 1150–1500, the Penn-Helsinki Parsed Corpus of Early Modern English (PPCEME) for 1500–1710 and the Corpus of Late Modern English Texts (CLMETEV) for 1710–1920. Exhaustive extractions were made on the noun *wonder*, including all spelling variants attested in the OED as well as all morphological variants. This yielded 2,017 hits in total. From these extractions, we manually selected all instances with a matrix containing a NP with *wonder* as predicate of *be*, followed by a finite complement clause, as in (1) above. Table 5.1 indicates the number of relevant instances retrieved for the three main historical periods and their subperiods.

The synchronic dataset was compiled from WordBanks*Online*. For reasons of comparability with the diachronic data, we extracted data from written British English sources only. We took a random sample of 250 instances of the noun *wonder*. This yielded eighty-nine instances of the complementation constructions in question.

2.2. Datasets with complementation constructions whose matrix contains *be* + NP with *tweo*/*doubt*

For Old English, the YCOE was trawled for examples with the noun *tweo* in all its spelling and morphological variants. From these, instances of the complementation constructions investigated were manually selected, yielding the number of relevant tokens indicated in Table 5.2. No relevant Middle English tokens were retrieved from the PPCME2; the only example of the noun was found in the prepositional phrase *wið-uten alche twene* 'without any doubt' (1150–1250). Out of the seven quotations of the lemma *tweon* in the online Middle English Dictionary, six involve the phrase *buton/ wið-uten tweon* and just one instantiates a construction studied here.[3]

As the noun *doubt* was borrowed from Old French into Middle English around 1225, it was possible to collect diachronic data from Middle English on from the

Table 5.2 Old English data: Complementation constructions with matrices (*it*)/(*there*) + *be* + *tweo*

Period	Corpus	N of words (millions)	N of relevant tokens	Normalized frequency (/1,000,000)	Subperiod	N of relevant tokens
Old English: 750–1150	YCOE	1.45	21	14.5	750–950	9
					950–1150	12

Table 5.3 Historical data: Complementation constructions with matrices (*it*)/(*there*) + *be* + *doubt*

Period	Corpus	N of words (millions)	N of relevant tokens	Normalized frequency (/1,000,000)	Subperiod	N of relevant tokens
Middle English	PPCME2	1.16	9	7.8	Early	1
					Late	8
Early Modern English	PPCEME	1.79	17	9.5		
Late Modern English	CLMETEV	15.01	311	20.7		

PPCME2, the PPCEME and the CLMETEV. Again, all spelling and morphological variants were included in the queries. Table 5.3 lists the number of relevant tokens retained for the two historical periods covered.

The synchronic dataset was compiled from written British English sources of the Wordbanks*Online* corpus. We took a random sample of 250 hits, extracted on the noun *doubt*, which yielded eighty-eight relevant tokens.

3. Complementation constructions with (*it*)/(*there*) *be* + NP in Old English

In this section we first survey the main descriptive lines set out in historical reference works and studies for the complementation constructions with (*it*)/(*there*) *be* + NP in Old English (Section 3.1). As we will see, these historical studies deviate already on a number of points from the traditional approach to *it*-extraposition found in synchronic reference works such as Quirk et al. (1985) and Huddleston and Pullum (2002). Firstly, it is generally assumed that the so-called 'extraposed' form is historically prior and should be seen as the default (e.g., Visser 1963–1973; Los 2015; Ramhöj 2016). Secondly, a number of authors tacitly or explicitly include examples with existential matrices as instances of the same complementation construction. Finally, considerable attention has gone to the early forms of predicative and existential matrices without *it* and *there*, and to the precursor of *it*-extraposition featuring the demonstrative *that*. In Section 3.2 we will propose our own account of the Old English data, which explicitly delineates the macro-construction more broadly as subsuming predicative and existential matrices.

3.1. The literature on the development of *it*-extraposition in Old English

It is generally assumed that the earliest variant, or the source construction, of *it*-extraposition is formed by examples whose matrix consists of *be* + NP only, as in (5). Such matrices have been referred to as 'subjectless' (e.g., Visser 1963–1973) or 'impersonal' (e.g., Visser 1963–1973; Traugott 1992).

(5) *Micele mare wundor is* þæt he wolde beon mann on þisum life. (YCOE, 950–1050)
     'Much greater wonder (it) is that he wanted to be a human in this life'.

Intriguingly, a number of authors, when they discuss precursors of *it*-extraposition such as (5), include existential examples such as (6).[4] For the latter, the term 'subjectless' seems inappropriate, as, on at least some analyses, *nan tweo*, which denotes the entity (not) existing, is the subject in this clause. However, both (5) and (6) can be called 'impersonal' in the sense that they do not explicitly code any personal participants in the process (who may nevertheless be involved in their contextualized interpretation).

(6) forþon *nis nan tweo* þæt forgifnesse syllan nelle. (Traugott 1992: 271, 850–1050)
     'therefore there is no (lit. 'not-is no') doubt that he will give forgiveness'.

Some authors seem to tacitly interpret the latter as predicative structures (Méndez-Naya, p.c.). This is also how they tend to be parsed in the YCOE.[5] Others, like Visser (1963–1973: 19–20), Traugott (1992: 271), Williams (2000: 179–80) and Pfenninger (2009: 54), translate examples like (6) into Present-day English existential clauses, but do not comment on this in their description.

In a similar way, examples with an existential matrix with subject *it* have been included in discussions of *it*-extraposition. Because the distinction between noun and adjective was not clear in Old English (and early Middle English) in a number of cases (see Van linden 2012: 132), some of these examples are, strictly speaking, ambiguous between an existential and a predicative reading, as in (7). However, the possibility of the existential reading is sometimes overlooked.

(7) But Jhesus . . . he knewe alle men; and for *it was not nede* to hym, that ony man schulde bere witnessyng (1380, *The New Testament in English* according to the version by John Wycliffe; cited in Loureiro-Porto 2010: 374)
     'Jesus . . . he knew them all, so it was not necessary [lit. 'there was no need to him'; our translation] that anyone gave testimony on them . . .'

When no predicative reading is possible, it is mostly noted that *it* is an alternative of existential *there*, as does Mitchell (1985, I: 625) with regard to example (8).

(8) *Is hit lytel tweo* þæt . . . (Mitchell 1985, I: 625, our translation)
     'Is there little doubt that . . .?'

The largely tacit inclusion of examples with existential matrices under the heading of extraposition constructions seems to be caused by the surface similarity between the so-called 'expletiveless' predicative (5) and existential matrices (6), and between predicative (1) and existential matrices (8) with subject *it*. To our knowledge, no proposals have been made to consciously subsume the subtypes with predicative and existential matrix under the same macro-construction and present structural and semantic arguments for this.

A second precursor of *it*-extraposition pointed out in the literature is formed by examples with matrices with the demonstrative *that* as subject, as in (9).

(9) *þæt is wundor*, þæt ðu swa ræðe forhæfdnisse & swa hearde habban wilt.
    (YCOE, 850–950)
    'that is wonder, that you want to have fierce and harsh abstinence'.

Examples of this type are generally ascribed the same structure (e.g., Mitchell 1985, I: 18–19) as, but different discourse semantics than, *it*-extraposition. According to Möhlig-Falke (2012: 176), for instance, the demonstrative subject *that* 'claims ... the audience's attention and anticipates that something of high information value follows in the appositional clause'. Interestingly, Méndez-Naya (1995) advocates a different structural analysis for examples like (9), according to which the *that*-clause is in an appositional relation to the demonstrative subject *that*. Her main arguments for this are the following. Firstly, in Old English the default was to have no explicit subject in impersonal predicative matrices, but *if* the subject was explicitly coded, it was more commonly demonstrative *that* than *it*. The choice for *that* was always motivated by contextual emphasis (Méndez-Naya 1995: 31). Secondly, Méndez-Naya (1995: 28) argues that the emphasis on subject *that* went together with a strong tendency to have punctuation, indicative of a syntactic/intonational boundary, after the matrix. As punctuation in historical texts may have been inserted by the text editors, it has to be noted that this is a tenuous argument.[6]

3.2. The development of complementation constructions with *be* + *wundor* and *be* + *tweo* in Old English

In this section, we present a description of the complementation constructions with *wundor* and *tweo* in our Old English datasets, distinguishing the meso-constructional level (Section 3.2.1) from the macro-constructional level (Section 3.2.2). At the meso-constructional level, we show that the complementation constructions with *be* + *wundor* have a predicative matrix and those with *be* + *tweo* an existential one. By way of grammatical argumentation for this (see McGregor 1994: 305), we adduce the different syntactic paradigms formed by the matrix variants with *wundor* and *tweo*. We also propose that the predicative and existential matrices code – subtle – semantic differences. At the macro-constructional level, we argue that the different meso-constructions share the same schematic structural and functional components. We argue that their primary structural units are the matrix and the complement clause. In support of this, we point out that the matrices, in their grammatical uses, which qualify the proposition in the complement clause, have the same paradigmatic variants, viz., parentheticals and independent sentences juxtaposed to the proposition they relate to. We then show how these structural units correlate with the main functional units of the lexical and grammatical readings, as set out for examples (1)–(2) and (3)–(4) in Section 1 above.

3.2.1. *Predicative* be + wundor *versus existential* be + tweo

Our grammatical argumentation to distinguish between predicative and existential matrices of complement constructions in Old English rests on the different matrix variants observed with *wundor* and *tweo*. Tables 5.4 and 5.5 categorize the different matrix types attested in the Old English data in terms of the absence or presence of the pronouns *it* and *there*, and the presence of demonstrative *that* referring forward to the proposition in the complement clause.

Table 5.4, which summarizes the *wundor* data, presents the variants of the predicative matrix recognized in historical studies (see Section 3.1). They can have no overt subject (10), subject *that* (11) or subject *it* (12), and the predicative complement with *wundor* appears in the nominative case. The analysis of all these types as construing a predicative relation is uncontroversial.

(10) *Micele mare wundor is þæt he wolde beon mann on þisum life* (YCOE, 950–1050)
    'Much greater wonder (it) is that he wanted to be a human in this life'
(11) *þæt is wundor, þæt ðu swa ræðe forhæfdnisse & swa hearde habban wilt.* (YCOE, 850–950)
    'that is wonder, that you want to have such fierce and harsh abstinence'.
(12) *Full mycel wundor hit wæs þæt þæt mæden gebær cild.* (YCOE, 1050–1150)
    'Very great wonder it was that that maiden bore a child'.

The sample is really too small to formulate reliable quantitative generalizations but it offers some support for the idea that the variants without overt subject and with subject *that* are older than the matrix with *it*, because the latter is the least frequent in the Old English dataset.[7]

Table 5.5 summarizes our classification of the matrix types with *tweo* in our Old English dataset. It is immediately clear that we are dealing with a different syntactic paradigm than that of the predicative matrices in Table 5.4.

Table 5.4 Classification of matrix types with *be* + *wundor* in the Old English dataset

OE subperiods	Ø *be wundor*	*þæt be wundor*	*hit be wundor*	Total
850–950	2	9	4	15
950–1050	13	7	2	22
1050–1150	8	14	5	27
Total	23	30	11	64

Table 5.5 Classification of matrix types with *be* + *tweo* in the Old English dataset

OE subperiods	Ø *be tweo*	*þæs be tweo*	*hit be tweo*	*þær be tweo*	Total
850–950	5	3	1	0	9
950–1050	3	0	0	0	3
1050–1150	4	1	3	1	9
Total	12	4	4	1	21

Most strikingly, the variant with existential *there*, e.g., (16), is part of this paradigm, which is not attested in the *wundor* dataset. This very fact reveals that in the variant with *it* in examples like (8) above and (15) below, we are dealing with existential *it* (Breivik 1983: 257; López-Couso 2006, 2011, p.c.). Indeed, when Mitchell (1985, I: 625) discusses *it* as a more common alternative of expletive *þær*, he illustrates this precisely with the Old English example *Is hit lytel tweo þæt...* quoted as example (8) above. The late occurrence of existential *þær* in our dataset is in accordance with the chronology of its appearance registered in the literature. Traugott (1992: 217–19) notes that *þær* became more frequent – yet by no means obligatory – in Late Old English only. Moreover, it has been observed that negative existentials (such as (13)–(16) below) lagged behind affirmative ones in adopting existential *there* (e.g., Breivik 1983; López-Couso 2006: 182, 2011: 96).

The variant which contains only *be* and a NP with *tweo*, e.g., (13), is likewise an existential clause.[8] As pointed out by, amongst others, Breivik (1983: 278, 319, 1989: 50), Traugott (1992: 217–19) and López-Couso (2006: 182), this variant was the most common type of existential in Old English, which it also is in the small dataset surveyed in Table 5.5.

The variant that has received least attention and that we would like to draw particular attention to is the one with the genitive of the demonstrative *that*, *ðæs* 'about that', e.g., (14). The referential function of *ðæs* in the existential matrix is wholly equivalent to that of subject *þæt* in the predicative matrix (11): they both realize emphatic cataphoric reference to the upcoming *that*-clause. The fact that this cataphoric reference to the *that*-clause in apposition is realized by a genitive, shows that the matrix in (14) does not have a predicative structure because the demonstrative would have been in the nominative then. It is precisely because the matrix is existential that its subject position cannot be used to point forward to the complement clause.

(13) *nan twio næs* þæt he þurh þone sceolde cuman to hefegum martyrdome. (YCOE, 850–950)
'no doubt (there) was (lit. 'not-was') that he should come to grievous martyrdom through it'.
(14) *Nis ðæs* ðonne *nan tweo*, gif suelc eaðmodnes bið mid oðrum godum ðeawum begyrded, ðæt ðæt bið beforan Godes eagum soð eaðmodnes, (YCOE, 850–950)
'(There) is (lit. 'not-is') about that no doubt then, if such humility is encompassed with other good virtues, that that is true humility before God's eyes'

(15) ða cwæð he: Forðæm *hit is nan tweo* þæt ða goodan beoð symle waldende, & þa yflan nabbað nænne anwald; (YCOE, 850–950)
'Then he said: Therefore there is no doubt that the good ones are always powerful, and the evil ones do not have any power;'

(16) Mid þy þa seo gesomnung eall gehyrde swa openlice þa stefne, þa *næs þær nænig tweo*, þæt hit nealæhte þara forðfore, þe þær gecigde wæron. (YCOE, 1050–1150)
'Since the whole congregation then heard the voice so openly, there was no doubt then that it drew near to the death of them who were named there'.

The analysis we propose for the distinct syntactic paradigms associated with the predicative and existential matrix in Old English is summarized in Table 5.6 in terms of the presence or absence of clitic or demonstrative pronouns. This table can also be read as the predictions we formulate about the distribution of these elements in predicative and existential matrices, whereby we not only specify possible but also impossible elements and combinations. Table 5.7 gives the quantitative attestation of the subtypes in the *wundor* and *tweo* datasets.

With regard to the pronouns that can occur as subjects, it is generally accepted that predicative clauses can have *it* or *that* (not both together), but not *there*. *It* or *that* simply make explicit the person and number marking associated with the finite verb in the matrices without an overt subject. Existentials in Old English could have *it* or *there* (not both) as subject, and not *that*. These generalizations are borne out by the *wundor* and *tweo* data.

The presence of *it* and *there* in the existential matrices can be related to the distribution of pronouns surveyed by Larsson (2014) for weather expressions and

Table 5.6 The distribution of matrix types in Old English complementation constructions

Matrix	Predicative	Existential
no clitic pronoun	Ø BE *wundor* / *wundor* Ø BE	(Ø) BE *tweo* / *tweo* (Ø) BE
(h)it	(h)it BE *wundor* / *wundor* (h)it BE	(h)it BE *tweo* / *tweo* (h)it BE
there	Excluded (*þær BE *wundor*)	þær BE *tweo*
demonstrative pronoun referring to complement	þæt (NOM case) BE *wundor*	þæs (GEN case) BE *tweo*
excluded combinations	*þæt (h)it BE *wundor*	*þær (h)it BE *tweo*

Table 5.7 The distribution of matrix types in complementation constructions with *wundor* and *tweo* in the Old English datasets

Matrix + post-verbal complement	Predicative: *wundor*	Existential: *tweo*
no clitic pronoun	23 (36%)	12 (57%)
(h)it	11 (17%)	4 (19%)
there	0	1 (5%)
demonstrative pronoun referring to complement	30 (47%)	4 (19%)
Total	64 (100%)	21 (100%)

existentials in Germanic languages: these pronouns include (the counterparts of) *it*, *there* and in some Germanic languages *here*, but never *that*. This distribution is suggestive of the semantics which, in accordance with our cognitive-functional theoretical position, we ascribe to the clitic subjects of existentials (see e.g., Langacker 1991: 352ff). Rather than viewing them as semantically empty, we propose to extend the 'ambient' meaning that Bolinger (1973: 261–4) ascribes to *it* in weather expressions to existential *it* and *there*, which likewise index the environment to which the semantics of the relation between *be* and the existent NP is related (see below).

Subjects *that* and *it* in the predicative matrices, by contrast, refer, in our view, to the proposition in the complement clause. In Old English complementation constructions with predicative matrices, this pronominal link was not an inherent part of the construction: the matrix could have no pronominal subject (36 per cent of the *wundor* data). The link between matrix and complement clause is already coded by the complementation construction as such and by the complementizer, if one is present. Any pronominal coding is in addition to this. That the demonstrative *that* refers forward to the proposition is generally accepted. In the *wundor* data, the option of using the emphatic cataphoric demonstrative is the most common one (47 per cent). The other option is the use of clitic subject *it*. As surveyed by Kaltenböck (2003), the question has been hotly debated if *it* is a place-filler or has some meaning, and if the latter, whether or not it is referential. We side with Kaltenböck's (2003: 244–52) arguments for viewing *it* as weakly cataphoric: in an example like (12) *it* indicates that 'something' was 'very great wonder', and its identity is then provided by the following *that*-clause.

The existential matrices can also contain a pronoun referring to the proposition, which in Old English was always the demonstrative. As the subject position is not available for this, the cataphoric demonstrative appears in the genitive, which functions as an adjunct 'about that'. In our dataset *ðæs* occurs only in the variant without *it* or *there* (14).[9] The option of a pronoun referring to the proposition is chosen in 19 per cent of the Old English data. It should be borne in mind that the link between the matrix and the proposition is in any case expressed by the complementation construction as such.

Having established that *wundor* is systematically used in predicative matrices and *tweo* in existential ones, the next question is what different grammatical semantics they code.

Predicative clauses are generally ascribed a 'categorizing' meaning: they put the entity referred to by the subject into a specific type or category. In complementation constructions with predicative matrices, the covert or overt subject is what Lyons (1977: 443) refers to as a 'third order entity', 'such abstract entities as propositions, which are outside time and space' of the situation represented in the matrix. For the grammatical semantics of a predicative complement realized by a full NP, we follow Langacker's (1991: 68) elucidation: the full NP 'conjures up' an instance conception for the purposes of making a type attribution. As Langacker (1991: 68) puts it, in such predicative clauses, a categorization relation is implied by the coded correspondence relation between instances. In the *wundor* data, the predicative complement can include premodifiers such as *micele mare* (10) or *full mycel* (12) that describe the size of the instance of wonder involved. In other words, in an example like (12), *Full mycel wundor hit wæs þæt þæt mæden gebær cild*, the third-order entity designated by the subject of the matrix (the birth of Jesus from a virgin) is said to correspond to, to be an instance of, 'a real great wonder', which implies that it is categorized as 'very wondrous'. The context of (12) suggests that the implied assessor is the speaker/preacher, who involves his audience into this assessment. In the Present-day English example (1), *It was a wonder to them that I get to do all this stuff*, the addition of *to them* explicitly identifies the speaker's children as the experiencers of the wonder at their father's professional activities. In example (3), *It's no wonder Norwegians hunt whale*, *it's no wonder* is more likely to be interpreted as a purely speaker-related, subjective mirative qualification of the following proposition.

In sum, matrices with predicate phrases such as *be a/much/no wonder* allow the language user to set up a correspondence relation between an emotional reaction to, or a subjective assessment of, the proposition, whereby the premodifiers of the predicative NP can convey degree modification of the emotion or evaluation. The very fact that the predicative matrix is impersonal and typically does not code any experiencers[10] allows for both lexical and grammatical interpretations. In the former, experiencers are contextually inferred, while in the latter, the impersonal coding squares with the Langackerian (2002) notion of subjectivity, according to which the speaker remains 'offstage' in a subjective construal.

What then are the grammatical semantics of the existential matrices? In Davidse (1992, 1999) the existent NP was argued to code the quantified instantiation of a type of entity which is set within a specific spatio-temporal domain by the information coded or implied by the whole existential clause. Example (16) suggests a lexical contextualization of *næs ðær nænig tweo*, in which it is the congregation that knew for sure 'that it drew near to the death of them who were named there'. The matrices of examples such as (14) and (15) convey speaker-related, 'subjective', meanings: the domain of instantiation is the here and now of the speaker's assessment, within which 'no doubt' (14)–(15) exists. The matter which the speaker qualifies with great certainty is the proposition in the complement clause, explicitly referred to by *ðæs* in (14). Thus, these existential matrices convey cognition states such as 'not doubt/know' or modal qualifications such as 'certainty', which are related to the proposition contained in what is structurally the complement clause. The premodification of the existent NP can convey degree modification of the emotion or cognition process, and of the modal evaluation. Again, we note that the impersonal nature of the existential matrix allows for both lexical readings, in which cognizants are contextually inferred, and grammatical interpretations. Both lexical and grammatical readings are attested from the earliest period on.

Whilst the impersonal predicative and existential structures code, strictly speaking, different grammatical semantics, the above discussion has shown that they can be used to evoke very comparable meanings. In the next section we turn to the shared structural and functional features of the two types of complementation constructions.

3.2.2. *The macro-level: Constructions with matrices* (it)/(there) be + NP *followed by a complement clause*

In Section 1, we have already indicated that the primary structural assembly relation in these complementation constructions is between the matrix (irrespective of whether it is predicative or existential) and the complement clause. In other words, we reject the extraposition analysis of the subtype with predicative matrix according to which the *that*-clause stands in a subject relation to verb and predicative complement, yielding a structural analysis with three basic constituents (e.g., Huddleston and Pullum 2002: 1403). In our view, it is only in the so-called 'non-extraposed' variant, as in (17), that the complement clause is the subject of the construction.

(17) he knew such an antidote for it ... *That the snakes did not do him any harm was no wonder*, but how he managed it with the vipers ... I know not. (WB)

Following Halliday (1994) and Langacker (1991), we analyse the *that*-clause functioning as subject in examples like (17) as a nominalized clause. *That the snakes did not do him any harm* is reclassified as a nominal both externally, allowing it to function in the nominal subject slot, and internally, as it discharges all the basic functions of nominals, i.e. type specification, instantiation, quantification and grounding to the deictic centre. The 'proposition conveyed by the nominalized clause can be regarded as a detailed type specification for the resulting noun.... The specified type ... has only a single instance, with the consequence that the derived noun is inherently definite' (Langacker 1991: 148–9).[11]

Our position is that complementation constructions with impersonal predicative and existential matrices consist of two primary constituents, the matrix and the complement clause. The Old English data provide formal support for this analysis in that, irrespective of the matrix type, the same two variants of the complex sentence structure are attested. In the first variant, the clause corresponding to the matrix appears as an independent sentence discursively 'juxtaposed' to the preceding sentence, which contains the proposition it relates to, as in (18) and (19). In (19), the juxtaposed sentence *Nis þæs nan tweo* contains the demonstrative *that* in the genitive case, which refers back to the preceding proposition about which there is no doubt. The second variant is a parenthetical clause, which comments on the proposition it interrupts, like the parenthetical *swa*-clause in (20).[12] As argued by Brinton (2008: 124–7, 154–7, 235–7), *as*-clauses can be viewed as parenthetical comment clauses: they function in the same way as adverbial disjuncts (Quirk et al. 1985: 612ff) to express a speaker comment applying to the proposition. Importantly, the so-called 'non-extraposed' variants, as illustrated in (17), are not attested in the Old English data. The syntactic paradigms of the complex sentences with predicative and existential matrices are thus fully identical. This supports a structural analysis of the macro complementation construction in terms of the two clauses, matrix and complement clause, as main building blocks.

(18) Þanon he welt þam gewealdleðerum ealle gesceaftu. *Nis nan wundor*, forþam ðe he is cyning & dryhten & æwelm & fruma & æ & wisdom rihtwis dema (YCOE 850–950)
'Henceforth he rules all creation with reins. It is no wonder (lit. 'not is no wonder'), for he is the king, the lord, the beginning, the creator, the law, wisdom and the righteous ruler'

(19) þa cwæð he: Genog rihte þu hit ongitst, nu þu ongitst þæt þa good ealle sint
<þæt> ilce þæt gesælð is, & sio gesælð is ðæt <hehste> good, & þæt hehste
good is God, & se <God> is semle on anum untodæled. ða cwæð ic: *Nis þæs*
nan tweo; ac ic wolde nu þæt ðu me sædest hwæthwugu uncuðes. (YCOE
850–950)

'Then he said: You understand it correctly enough, now that you realize that
all the good things are the same as happiness is, and the happiness is the
highest good, and the highest good is God, and the God is always one alone
undivided. Then I said: There is no doubt about that; and now I would like you
to tell me something unknown'.

(20) Wæs he gefeonde, *swa hit nænig wundor is*, denunge fota ðara ðe he swa
micelre tide benumen wæs (YCOE, 850–950)

'Was he rejoicing, as it is no wonder (lit. 'as it not any wonder is'), at the service
of the feet, which he was deprived of for such a long time'.

Building on our analysis of the lexical and grammatical readings of the predicative
and existential matrices (Section 3.2.1), we can conceptually motivate why the matrix
and the complement clause are the basic structural components of the macro-
construction and why a syntactic paradigm of juxtaposed and parenthetical structures
is associated with it.

Let us start with the lexical, representational, reading of the complementation
construction. As we saw in 3.2.1, both the predicative and the existential matrix allow
the *inference* of an emotional state (e.g., 'proposition surprised X') or cognitive state
(e.g., 'X knows proposition') and its – implied – experiencers or cognizants. The
complement clause represents either the factive proposition or the content of the
knowing. On these readings, the whole construction is interpreted as a factive or
reporting construction. Importantly, for the data with matrices containing *be* + the
nouns *wonder* and *tweo/doubt*, the factive and reporting readings seem to need the
complex sentence structure in which the complement clause is structurally subordinated
to the matrix clause. If this assumption is correct, then, we would expect that lexical
readings will be possible of the 'non-extraposed' variants, when they appear much later
in the piece (see Section 4).

By contrast, the speaker-related readings of the impersonal clauses as mirative,
evidential or modal qualifications are associated with both the complex sentence
structures, e.g., (14)–(15), and the juxtaposed (18)–(19) or parenthetical (20) variants.
It appears, indeed, that the impersonal clauses are a 'natural' coding means of subjective
qualifications in which the speaker remains off-stage (cf. Langacker 2002: 9). That such
qualifications are often conveyed by juxtaposed and parenthetical clauses is well-
known. But due to discursive foregrounding of complement clauses, structural matrices
can function as grammatical qualifiers too (Boye and Harder 2007: 584–9).

In conclusion, in this section we have set out our description of the complementation
constructions with *wundor* and *tweo* in our Old English datasets. We have shown, that
at the meso-constructional level, all the forms of (*it/that*) + *be* + *wundor* can be
analysed as historical variants of a predicative matrix and those with (*of that*) +
(*it/there*) + *be* + *tweo* as historical variants of an existential clause. We have set out

cognitive-functional analyses of their semantics, which bring out differences as well as functional similarities. We have, then, at the macro-constructional level, posited one schematic complementation construction whose primary structural units are the impersonal matrix and the complement clause. We have elucidated its lexical as well as its grammatical readings.

4. The development of complementation constructions with *it be wonder* and *there be doubt* from Middle to Present-day English

In this section we trace the further development of the complementation constructions from Middle to Present-day English for the *wonder*-data and for the data extracted on *be + doubt*, which complement the Old English *tweo*-data.

Table 5.8 summarizes how the variants of the matrix with *be + wonder* developed from Middle English up to the present. In contrast with Old English, it was the predicative matrix with *it* that predominated, by and large, from Early Middle English on. The frequency of matrices with cataphoric *that* declined strongly. This variant is not attested in our Modern and Present-day datasets, even though it is still very infrequently found, as illustrated by the internet example quoted in endnote 6. Subjectless matrices disappeared in Late Middle English, when the subject became an obligatory element of clause structure (Van linden 2012: 133–4). The picture is thus one of crystallization towards the form with a predicative *it*-matrix. This confirms the stability and entrenchment of the predicative matrix with *wonder* in complementation constructions.

Yet, we witness the emergence in Late Modern English (more specifically in the subperiod 1710–1780) of the existential variant *there is no wonder*, which we illustrate with the later example (21). Our Present-day dataset contains only one such example, which suggests that it is a very marginal variant, which may disappear again. What are we to make of the recent appearance of an existential variant, however marginal, in the construction in which the predicative matrix had hitherto been so stable? We suggest that it has arisen as the result of confusion between predicative and existential matrices, but as 'motivated' confusion so to speak. As argued in Section 3.2.1, the inferred representational meanings of impersonal predicative and existential matrices are very

Table 5.8 The distribution of matrix types in complementation constructions with *be + wonder* in Middle English to Present-day English datasets

Matrix	1150–1500 ME		1500–1710 EModE		1710–1920 LModE		1993–PDE	
	n	%	n	%	n	%	n	%
Ø is (no) wonder	13	34.2	0	0	0	0.0	0	0.0
that is (no) wonder	2	5.3	0	0	0	0.0	0	0.0
it is (no) wonder	23	60.5	14	100	90	97.8	88	98.9
there is (no) wonder	0	0.0	0	0	2	2.2	1	1.1
Total	38	100	14	100	92	100	89	100

similar. Hence, in (21) the matrix is readily understood as [that the king ...] 'shouldn't surprise us', with the speaker/writer involving his readers in this emotional reaction. We propose that it is precisely because of the structural and semantic similarity of the routinized patterns with predicative and existential matrices that there is this marginal confusion of the two.

(21) That the king of Kandy did not reside at Newera Ellia *there is little wonder*, as a monarch delighting in a temperature of 85 Fahrenheit would have regarded the climate of a mean temperature. (CLMETEV, 1850–1920)

When we consider the syntactic paradigm of the whole complementation construction, it can be noted that the juxtaposed variant, illustrated with the Old English example (18), continues to be the main multi-clausal alternate, even though its frequency declines throughout this whole period (for detailed discussion, see Gentens et al. 2016). The 'non-extraposed' variant, e.g., (22), appears only in Late Modern English, in the subperiod 1780–1850, and remains very infrequent.

(22) That you should possess such varieties of taste *is no wonder*, considering what an abundance of intellectual honours you inherit. (CLMETEV, 1780–1850)

Example (22) illustrates the structure in which the *that*-clause functions as a nominalized subject clause (see Section 3.2.2), which is treated as the 'basic' variant in the traditional extraposition approach. One of its well-known information structure features is that the 'fronted' *that*-clause contains given information while the main clause predicate presents new, focal information (Kaltenböck 2000: 162–5). Interestingly, example (21) with an existential matrix has the same basic word order with the same information structure. Syntactically, of course, the *that*-clause cannot function as subject in the existential clause in (21).

Table 5.9, then, summarizes how the variants of the matrix with *be* + *doubt* developed through time. The existential clause without subject clitic is still common in Middle English, where it accounts for 36.5 per cent, but it disappears at the end of Middle English. (23) is an interesting example because it contains the Middle English counterpart of *þæs*, viz. *therof*. This is an adverbial compound consisting of preposition *of* and the pronominal use of *there* realizing entity-deixis, which is glossed in the *OED* as 'of that'; it is counted as an example without subject clitic in Table 5.9 below.

(23) for *therof is no doubt*, that it is deedly synne in consentynge. (PPCME2, *c.* 1405 Chaucer *CT.Pars.* (Elsm) 295.C2)
'for of that (there) is no doubt, that there is deadly sin in consenting [to evil]'.

Existentials with *it* virtually disappeared after 1570, when they generally ceased being used in negative existentials, where they had held out longest (López-Couso 2011: 96). In Present-day English, the existential matrix with *there* is the only form attested in the Wordbanks data. However, it is interesting to note that on the internet examples with *it's/is no doubt* can be found, of which at least some seem to be produced

Table 5.9 The distribution of matrix types in complementation constructions with *be + doubt* in the Middle English to Present-day English datasets

Matrix	1150–1500 ME		1500–1710 EModE		1710–1920 LModE		1993–PDE	
	n	%	n	%	n	%	n	%
Ø *is (no) doubt*	3	33.3	0	0	0	0	0	0
it is (no) doubt	4	44.4	5	29	1	0.3	0	0
there is (no) doubt	2	22.2	12	71	310	99.7	88	100
Total	9	100	17	100	311	100	88	100

by native speakers, such as (24). In other words, just as we saw a marginal existential variant, as in (21), emerge of predicative *it be (no) wonder* in recent corpus data, we see that a marginal predicative variant of existential *there be (no) doubt* is cropping up in internet data. In our view, this suggests that language users are aware of the fact that the inferred representational and grammatical meanings of existential matrices are very similar to those of predicative matrices and are routinizing the two constructions as subtypes of one macro-construction.

(24) *It's no doubt* that we have a talented team here at Old City Web Services. (http://oldcitywebservices.com/finding-meaning-mission-work/)

Turning to the syntactic alternates of the complementation construction (see Davidse et al. 2015), we find that the parenthetical variant is the only one in Middle and Early Modern English, e.g., (25). The first example with a fronted subordinated complement clause (26) occurs only in the period 1710–1780 in our data. It is structurally fully analogous with example (21) with *there is little wonder*, with the complement clause and impersonal matrix as the two primary structural units.

(25) The especes that sourden of Pride, soothly whan they sourden of malice ymagined, avised, and forncast, or elles of usage, been deedly synnes, *it is no doute*. (PPCME2, *c.* 1405 Chaucer *CT.Pars.* (Elsm) 302.C1)
    'The types [of sin] that originate in pride, truly when they originate in imagined, devised and planned malice or else in habitual action, are deadly sins, it is no doubt'.

(26) That he was a lover of the muses, *there is not the least doubt*, as we find him patronizing the poets so warmly. (CLMETEV, 1753 Cibber, *The lives of the poets of Great Britain and Ireland*)

In sum, the complementation constructions with *wonder* and *doubt* show a parallel development from Middle English to Present-day English. The association with respectively predicative and existential clauses is stable in them, yet with both, the other matrix type has recently cropped up as a marginal variant. Equally stable are the juxtaposed and parenthetical alternates, whereas the non-extraposed structure in the strict sense is a late and marked variant in the *wonder*-data. This distribution supports our claim that the complementation constructions with predicative and existential matrix form a macro-construction with shared structural features and the same schematic semantic functions.

5. Conclusion

In this chapter we have described from a diachronic point of view complementation constructions with predicative and existential matrices followed by a complement clause. More specifically, we have reconstructed, on the one hand, the development from Old to Present-day English of such constructions with matrices containing *be* + NP with *wonder*, whose main variant has been *it's a/no wonder that* ... from Middle English on, i.e. the construction traditionally viewed as *it*-extraposition. On the other hand, we have traced the development through Old English of such constructions with *be* + *tweo* and from Middle to Present-day English of constructions with *be* + NP with *doubt*. We have proposed a comprehensive analysis of them at two levels of generality.

At the highest level of generality, we have given arguments for viewing complementation constructions with impersonal predicative and existential matrices as one macro-construction. This entails a rejection of the *it*-extraposition account in its strict form. We have argued that the two impersonal matrix types allow the inference of lexical readings (as specific emotional or cognitive states) and are also natural coders of their grammatical readings as modal, mirative or evidential qualifications. Historically, these two readings are present from the start. The proposed analysis of matrix and complement clause as the primary structural units explains the parenthetical and juxtaposed alternates that are attested throughout their history. By contrast, the 'non-extraposed' form in which the nominalized *that*-clause appears as subject of the predicative matrix is a late and informationally marked development, which cannot plausibly be posited as the basic form defining the structure and meaning of the constructions with an impersonal matrix.

At a lower level of generality, the meso-constructional level, we found that the variants of the matrices with *wonder* and *tweo/doubt* show a diachronically stable persistence of predicative matrices in the former and of existential ones in the latter, with, however, some recent intermingling of the two. We discussed the different grammatical semantics coded by the two matrix types, while also noting the presence of very similar functional elements, such as the quantification and degree modification afforded by the full NP in both. This, in turn, feeds back into the proposed macro-analysis, as these functional-structural resources code the intensification of both the lexical readings (emotion and cognition states) and the grammatical readings (interpersonal qualifications) of the matrix.

With the diachronic case studies presented here we have launched our case for the macro- and meso-constructional analysis of complementation constructions with predicative and existential matrices proposed here. We are aware of the fact that case studies such as these may show quirks specific to the nouns studied. Clearly, the investigation will have to be extended to other lexical types such as *It is a* *fact/mystery/puzzle/*etc. *that* and *there is no question/chance/*etc. *that.* More cases will have to be studied to further verify, refine or modify the proposed analyses and to formulate robust quantitative generalizations.

Notes

1   We dedicate this article to Teresa Fanego in warm appreciation for all that she has done and continues to do in support of true scholarship of the English language, in particular, the functional-cognitive study of English historical syntax. We salute Teresa for her remarkable achievements as researcher, teacher, supervisor, editor and network builder. A researcher *pur sang*, Teresa has in all her other academic roles made very many good things happen through her integrity and generosity. She has always steered clear of personal acclaim and has focused in every venture on the (joint) work and the people involved. For all these reasons we are delighted to have been invited to contribute a study to this *Liber Amicorum* as a token, on behalf of the whole Leuven 'Functional and Cognitive Grammar' research unit, of our gratitude to Teresa. We thank the two anonymous referees for their careful reading of an earlier version of this article and for their very helpful suggestions for revision. We also gratefully acknowledge the following research grants, which supported work on this article: (i) 'Beyond the clause: encoding and inference in clause combining' (C14/18/034) (promotor: Jean-Christophe Verstraete; co-promotors: Bert Cornillie, Kristin Davidse and Elwys De Stefani), granted by the research council of the University of Leuven; (ii) 'Negation and grammaticalization. The development of modal, polar and mirative meanings by expressions with 'no' *need*, 'no' *wonder*, 'no' *chance*, 'no' *way*', awarded to An Van linden by the research council of the University of Liège.

2   The examples marked with (WB) were extracted from Wordbanks*Online* and are reproduced with the permission of HarperCollins. For examples found on the internet with Google, the URL is given.

3   This is (i) below:

   (i) *Nis nan twyn þæt* eow ne beo forgolden ælc þære stæpe þe ge to Godes huse steppeð, ebnben [read: emben] eower sawle þearfe. (a1150(OE) *Vsp.D.Hom.* (Vsp D.14))
   'There is no (lit. 'not-is no') doubt that you will be recompensed for each step that you take towards God's house with regard to your soul's need'.

4   In a sense, this generalization over examples with predicative matrices like (5) and existential ones like (6) is entailed by the notion of 'null subjects' in the formal tradition, which refers to the presence of a syntactic position for expletives, which are left unexpressed, be they *it* or *there* (e.g., Hulk and van Kemenade 1993; Williams 2000).

5   Out of the twelve 'subjectless' matrices with *tweo* in YCOE (see Table 5.5 below), ten have the existent NP tagged as predicative NP (NP-NOM-PRD), as in (ii) below. In the other two instances, the NPs are tagged as NP-NOM.

   (ii) ((IP-MAT-SPE (NP-NOM-x *exp*) (ADVP (ADV For+d+am)) (NEG+BEPI *nis*) (NP-NOM-PRD (NEG+Q^N *nan*) (N^N *tweo*)) (CP-THT-SPE-x (C +t+at) þes andwearda wela myrð & let þa men þe bioð <atehte> to þam soðum gesælðum.)) (YCOE 850–950)

'Therefore there is no doubt that this present wealth hinders and impedes the men that are attracted to the true felicities'

6 It is interesting to note that examples of such appositional relations between cataphoric *that* and a *that*-clause are still – infrequently – found in Present-day English, as in (iii). In this example, the comma between matrix and complement clause suggests that the complex sentence would naturally be uttered with two tone groups (marked by //), which correspond to two information units (Halliday and Matthiessen 2004: 88): *he says that's no wonder // that the wedding had been postponed //*.

> (iii)   He says *that's no wonder*, that the wedding had been postponed.
> (http://tvmegasite.net/updates/passions/2005/pass-01-31-05.shtml)

7 In terms of strict chronology of appearance, matrices with subjects *hit* and *that* and without overt subject are found in the same texts, e.g., in Boethius' *The Consolation of Philosophy*, Gregory's *Pastoral Care* and *Orosius*.

8 We will not enter into the different analyses that have been proposed in the literature for this syntagmatic pattern in Old English. In the tradition represented by an author such as Breivik (1983, 1989), *nan twio* in (13) would probably be analysed as the subject NP and no covert expletive would be posited. By contrast, in the tradition represented by Hulk and van Kemenade (1993) and Williams (2000) the picture is more complex. On the one hand, they hold that some Old English existentials, such as (13), contain a syntactic position for enclitic *it* or *there* but leave the expletive subject unpronounced, which is why they speak of a null-subject. On the other hand, some existentials are considered not to have such a syntactic position and to be expletiveless, i.e. without a null subject. We will not go further into this discussion as our focus is on the semantic and discursive contrasts between predicative and existential clauses.

9 There does not seem to be any grammatical principle against *þæs* occurring in existentials with subject *it* or *there*, but the juxtaposition of two pronouns, one salient and one clitic, may generally have been avoided. *Þæs* is found in personal matrices with *habban tweo* ('have doubt'), as illustrated in (iv), where it points forward to the *that*-clause, realizing the discontinuous appositional relation discussed by Méndez-Naya (1995).

> (iv)   Hwylc geleaffullra manna is þæt *þæs ænigne tweon* an his mode *hæbbe*, þæt heofon ontyned sie to ðære stemne þæs sacerdes <on> þa tid þære halgan onsægdnesse, (YCOE 950–999 HomM 11 (ScraggVerc 14) 80)
> 'Who of believing men is (one) that about that has any doubt in his mind, that heaven will be opened to the voice of the priest at the moment of the holy offering'

10 Unless they are coded by an adjunct, as in (1) *It was a wonder to them*.

11 For detailed argumentation for the nominalized status of such *that*-clauses, see Heyvaert (2003).

12 As these variants do not constitute complement constructions, they are not included in Tables 5.4 to 5.7 above.

Corpora

CLMETEV = De Smet, Hendrik (2006), *The Corpus of Late Modern English Texts (Extended Version)*. Department of Linguistics, University of Leuven.

PPCME2 = Kroch, Anthony and Ann Taylor (2000), *Penn-Helsinki Parsed Corpus of Middle English*, 2nd edn. Available online: http://www.ling.upenn.edu/hist-corpora/PPCME2-RELEASE-4.

PPCEME = Kroch, Anthony, Beatrice Santorini and Lauren Delfs (2004), *The Penn-Helsinki Parsed Corpus of Early Modern English*. Department of Linguistics, University of Pennsylvania. CD-ROM, 1st edn, release 3. Available online: http://www.ling.upenn.edu/ppche/ppche-release-2016/PPCEME-RELEASE-3.

WB = *Wordbanks Online*. Available online: www.wordbanks.harpercollins.co.uk

YCOE = Taylor, Ann, Anthony Warner, Susan Pintzuk and Frank Beths (2003), *The York-Toronto-Helsinki Parsed Corpus of Old English Prose*. Electronic texts and manuals available from the Oxford Text Archive; http://www-users.york.ac.uk/~lang22/YCOE/YcoeHome.htm.

References

Bolinger, Dwight (1973), 'Ambient *It* Is Meaningful too!', *Journal of Linguistics*, 9: 261–70.

Boye, Kasper and Peter Harder (2007), 'Complement-taking Predicates: Usage and Linguistic Structure', *Studies in Language*, 31: 569–606.

Breivik, Leiv E. (1983), *Existential There. A Synchronic and Diachronic Study*, Bergen: University of Bergen.

Breivik, Leiv E. (1989), 'On the Causes of Syntactic Change in English', in Leiv E. Breivik and Ernst Håkon Jahr (eds), *Language Change: Contributions to the Study of its Causes*, 29–70, Berlin: De Gruyter Mouton.

Brinton, Laurel (2008), *The Comment Clause in English. Syntactic Origins and Pragmatic Development*, Cambridge: Cambridge University Press.

Davidse, Kristin (1992), 'Existential Constructions: A Systemic Perspective', *Leuvense Bijdragen*, 81: 71–99.

Davidse, Kristin (1999), 'The Semantics of Cardinal versus Enumerative Existential Constructions', *Cognitive Linguistics*, 10 (3): 203–50.

Davidse, Kristin, Simon De Wolf and An Van linden (2015), 'The Development of the Modal and Discourse Marker Uses of *(there/it is/I have) no doubt*', *Journal of Historical Pragmatics*, 16 (1): 25–58.

DeLancey, Scott (2001), 'The Mirative and Evidentiality', *Journal of Pragmatics*, 33 (3): 369–82.

Gentens Caroline, Ditte Kimps, Gilles Jacobs, Kristine Davidse, An Van linden and Lot Brems (2016), 'Mirativity and Rhetorical Structure: The Development and Prosody of Disjunct and Anaphoric Adverbials with *No Wonder*', in Gunther Kaltenböck, Evelien Keizer and Arne Lohmann (eds), *Outside the Clause*, 125–56, Amsterdam: Benjamins.

Halliday, M. A. K. (1994), *An Introduction to Functional Grammar*. 2nd edn, London: Arnold.

Halliday, M. A. K. and C. M. I. M. Matthiessen (2004), *An Introduction to Functional Grammar*, 3rd edn, London: Arnold.

Heyvaert, Lisbet (2003), *A Cognitive-Functional Approach to Nominalization in English*, Berlin: De Gruyter Mouton.

Hopper, Paul and Elizabeth C. Traugott (2003), *Grammaticalization*, 2nd edn, Cambridge: Cambridge University Press.

Huddleston, Rodney and Geoffrey K. Pullum (2002), *The Cambridge Grammar of the English Language*, Cambridge: Cambridge University Press.

Hulk, Aafke and Ans van Kemenade (1993), 'Subjects, Nominative Case, Agreement, and Functional Heads', *Lingua*, 89: 181–215.

Kaltenböck, Gunther (2000), '*It*-extraposition and Non-extraposition in English Discourse', in Christian Mair and Marianne Hundt (eds), *Corpus Linguistics and Linguistic Theory*, 157–75, Amsterdam: Rodopi.

Kaltenböck, Gunther (2003), 'On the Syntactic and Semantic Status of Anticipatory *It*', *English Language and Linguistics*, 7: 235–55.

Langacker, Ronald W. (1987), *Foundations of Cognitive Grammar 1: Theoretical Preliminaries*, Stanford: Stanford University Press.

Langacker, Ronald W. (1991), *Foundations of Cognitive Grammar 2: Descriptive Application*, Stanford: Stanford University Press.

Langacker, Ronald W. (2002), 'Deixis and Subjectivity', in Frank Brisard (ed), *Grounding: The Epistemic Footing of Deixis and Reference*, 373–97, Berlin: De Gruyter Mouton.

Larsson, Ida (2014), 'Choice of Non-referential Subject in Existential Constructions and with Weather-Verbs', *Nordic Atlas of Language Structures*, 1: 55–71.

López-Couso, María José (2006), 'On Negative Existentials in Early English', in Leiv E. Breivik, Sandra Halverson and Kari E. Haugland (eds), *'These things write I vnto thee . . .': Essays in Honour of Björg Bækken*, 175–87, Oslo: Novus Press.

López-Couso, María José (2011), 'Developmental Parallels in Diachronic and Ontogenetic Grammaticalization: Existential *There* as a Test Case', *Folia Linguistica* 45 (1): 81–102.

Los, Bettelou (2015), *Historical Syntax of English*, Edinburgh: Edinburgh University Press.

Loureiro-Porto, Lucía (2010), 'Verbo-nominal Constructions of Necessity with *þearf* n. and *Need* n.: Competition and Grammaticalization from OE to eModE', *English Language and Linguistics*, 14 (3): 373–97.

Lyons, John (1977), *Semantics. Vol. 1*, Cambridge: Cambridge University Press.

McGregor, William B. (1994), 'Review of P. Hopper and E.C. Traugott (1993), *Grammaticalization*', *Functions of Language*, 1 (2): 304–7.

McGregor, William B. (1997), *Semiotic Grammar*. Oxford: Clarendon Press.

MED = *Middle English Dictionary*. Available online: https://quod.lib.umich.edu/m/med/.

Méndez-Naya, Belén (1995), '*Hit* and *þæt* Anticipating Subject Clauses in OE: True Syntactic Equivalents?', *Neuphilologische Mitteilungen*, XCVI: 23–37.

Mitchell, Bruce (1985), *Old English Syntax*, 2 vols., Oxford: Clarendon Press.

Möhlig-Falke, Ruth (2012), *The Early English Impersonal Construction: An Analysis of Verbal and Constructional Meaning*, Oxford: Oxford University Press.

OED = *Oxford English Dictionary Online*. Available online: http://www.oed.com/.

Pfenninger, Simone E. (2009), *Grammaticalization Paths of English and High German Existential Constructions: A Corpus-based Study*, Bern: Peter Lang.

Quirk, Randolph, Sidney Greenbaum, Geoffrey Leech and Jan Svartvik (1985), *A Comprehensive Grammar of the English Language*. London: Longman.

Ramhöj, Rickard (2016), 'On Clausal Subjects and Extraposition in the History of English', PhD diss., University of Gothenburg.

Rosenbaum, Peter S. (1967), *The Grammar of English Predicate Complement Constructions*, Cambridge, Mass: M.I.T. Press.

Simon-Vandenbergen, Anne-Marie and Karin Aijmer (2007), *The Semantic Field of Modal Certainty. A Corpus-based Study of English Adverbs*, Berlin: De Gruyter Mouton.

Traugott, Elizabeth C. (1992), 'Syntax', in Richard M. Hogg (ed), *The Cambridge History of the English Language. Vol. I: The beginnings to 1066*, 168–229, Cambridge: Cambridge University Press.

Traugott, Elizabeth C. (2008), 'Grammaticalization, Constructions and the Incremental Development of Language: Suggestions from the Development of Degree Modifiers in English', in Regine Eckardt, Gerhard Jäger and Tonjes Veenstra (eds), *Variation, Selection, Development: Probing the Evolutionary Model of Language Change*, 219–50, Berlin: De Gruyter Mouton.

Van linden, An (2012), *Modal Adjectives: English Deontic and Evaluative Constructions in Diachrony and Synchrony*, Berlin: De Gruyter Mouton.

Visser, Fredericus Th. (1963–1973), *An Historical Syntax of the English Language*, Leiden: E. J. Brill.

Williams, Alexander (2000), 'Null Subjects in Middle English Existentials', in Susan Pintzuk, George Tsoulas and Anthony Warner (eds), *Diachronic Syntax: Models and Mechanisms*, 164–87, Oxford: Oxford University Press.

6

On Grammatical Change and Discourse Environments[1]

Bert Cornillie
KU Leuven

1. Introduction[2]

In this chapter I present an inquiry into the role of discourse environments in language change. Discourse environments refer to both the micro-level (the linguistic organization of the utterance) and the macro-level (Discourse Traditions (DTs), cultural settings, socio-historical context, societal debate). The aim is to discuss the different roles that discourse environments play in historical-linguistic accounts. Discourse is a broad concept, and is currently used in many (sub)disciplines of the humanities and social sciences, including linguistic pragmatics, literary studies, communication sciences and sociology, to name just a few. The concept of discourse environment itself requires an in-depth discussion if it is to be used as a means of accounting for specific instances of language change. Hence, my approach here will adopt three perspectives: (i) I first deal with discourse in terms of textual traditions. Concepts such as Communicative Immediacy and Distance will be discussed and related to discourse genres and traditions; (ii) I focus on the specific discourse environments in which language change occurs. With reference to this, I present Petré's (2014) findings on the relationship between presence or absence of sentence particles and word order in Old English; (iii) finally, I expand the notion of discourse environments to include the cultural settings and the socio-historical context in which a community of speakers produces their utterances. More specifically, I use this approach to account for the process of syntactic elaboration observed in the auxiliaries *amenazar* and *threaten*, which arose in the realms of Spanish and English Humanism, respectively, due to contact with Latin DTs, and can thus be seen as instances of 'change from above'.

The structure of the chapter is as follows. In Section 2 I discuss the value of DTs for historical linguistics. Section 3 is concerned with specific discourse environments in Old and Middle English. In Section 4, I examine how grammar can undergo changes due to changing cultural settings, looking particularly to the auxiliation of Spanish *amenazar* and English *threaten*. Finally, in Section 5 I present the conclusions.

2. Historical Linguistics and Discourse Traditions

Historical linguists face a number of challenges in terms of the status of the data they use. Despite the existence of large diachronic corpora, historical linguists often lack crucial information about the broader social context in which linguistic production took place. When we talk about change in context, the notion of context is often difficult to delineate accurately. How does the context relate to the community of speakers? How can we define such a community from the past on the basis of the available data? On addressing such questions, it soon becomes evident that access to the past is irrevocably limited. Yet, it is a challenge that linguists engaged in historical-linguistic analysis face continually. As Labov (1994: 11) notes, 'historical linguistics is the art of making the best use of bad data'.

An alternative approach is to forget about speakers of the past and to focus on texts that speak for the past. If texts and textual traditions are themselves taken to be the informants, it is imperative for historical linguists to focus on the locus of change in specific DTs that belong to a community. According to Oesterreicher's (1997: 20) seminal definition, DTs are 'conventionalized normative frames that guide the transmission of meaning by means of linguistic elements both in its production and its reception' (my translation).[3] Hence, DTs are normative structures which impose a series of rules of conduct on authors who seek to belong to them. Some DTs are more prestigious than others and authors are often attracted to linguistic fashions. For example, constructions and words typical of an educated or highbrow DT may subsequently be found in other more popular DTs through a process of imitation. Thus, the spread and success of new constructions has to do with the prestige of specific DTs.[4]

The DT model can also serve as an empirical approach for identifying the local discourse environments on a continuum between Communicative Immediacy (i.e. spoken – and written – interaction) and Communicative Distance (i.e. lack of interaction) (Koch and Oesterreicher 1985). Although DTs can be situated on the continuum between these two poles, they should not automatically be seen as existing on a continuum from spoken language to written language. As Koch and Oesterreicher (2011: 34) argue, spoken language DTs such as a scientific lecture or a sermon are closer to the Communicative Distance end of the continuum than a private letter or SMS messages, while legal texts are clearly more proximate to the Communicative Distance pole.

Categorial problems notwithstanding, historical linguistics can benefit substantially from the Orality vs Scripturality continuum. Clear boundaries are never easy to draw, though. Epic poems (e.g., *Cantar de mio Cid*, twelfth or thirteenth century), for instance, are a written version of what was originally a spoken genre to be performed before an audience. By contrast, Renaissance dialogues, at first sight a spoken genre, are in fact structured as questions and answers from manuals and guides. Moreover, genres vary over the centuries. So, whereas dialogues are commonly found in the modern novel today, they have not always been so widespread in fiction.

The model of DTs also allows us to reinforce Labov's (2007) opposition between 'change from below' and 'change from above'. Reinterpreted in historical-linguistic terms, change from below is located in the speaker-hearer interaction and is often related to the conventionalization of pragmatic implicatures, which leads to semantic change (Traugott and Dasher 2002; Fanego 2010). In this type of change from below, we observe the grammaticalization of existing forms, involving decategorialization, as in the case of the epistemic adverbial phrases *a lo mejor* ('perhaps') and *tal vez* ('perhaps'), which acquire their new modal meaning in spoken interaction (Cornillie 2016a). By contrast, change from above has to be situated within the dynamic interaction between prestigious texts, these often belonging to the Communicative Distance. Language contact through the translation of prestigious texts, for instance, may bring about change from above. The prestige of a certain DT favours the spread of new forms via different DTs. Moreover, change from above can be combined with change from below. The calques and loanwords present in a certain DT can lead to change in the linguistic system in a specific period of history (change from above) and then undergo adaptation through interaction between speakers (change from below). Thus, calques can also undergo further grammatical change in their process of adaptation into the target language.

In Section 3, I show that the grammaticalization of Spanish *amenazar* ('threaten') follows a clear path: the Spanish calque of Latin *minari* ('threaten') evolves into an auxiliary verb + infinitive simultaneously with the conventionalization of the new subjective reading of *amenazar*-constructions in Spanish. This is not, however, the case with English *threaten*. It is also observed that the new forms that started in the language of Distance shift to the language of Immediacy. Thus, a DT approach also sheds new light to the process of 'actualization' of the grammaticalized form. Traditionally, actualization has been defined as 'the gradual mapping out of the consequences of the reanalysis' (Timberlake 1977: 141), whereas De Smet (2012) sees it as the spread of the new grammatical form so as to fit into increasingly more combinatorial possibilities. Similarly, in this study, actualization is understood as the spread of new constructions to new linguistic environments. From a DT point of view, (the actualization of) grammatical change cannot be accounted for without examining DTs from the double perspective of change from above and change from below.

3. Discourse organization and the verb in English and Spanish

As we know, specific discourse environments, that is, specific combinations of words organizing and structuring the discourse, may favour the use of specific linguistic forms and constructions. The influence of DTs on the type of clause combining cannot be underestimated: medieval texts, for instance, rely heavily on parataxis and coordination, whereas Renaissance texts exhibit elaborate subordination patterns; humanist authors use an increasingly refined set of connectives and subordinate clauses. Thus, linguists should approach grammatical variation by taking into account specific discourse settings, discourse environments and DTs. Following this approach, Petré (2014) shows how the Old English copular verb *weorðan* ('become') disappears due to its association with inversion and with the adverb *þa* ('then'). Thus, these two discourse phenomena not only changed the shape of the English sentence, but also affected the grammatical paradigm of copular verbs. Example (1) shows how *þa* is accompanied by the inversion of the subject and the verb.

(1) Hit gelamp sume dæige, þæt se halge were … his salmsanges on þan wætere
     hnacodan leomen adreah, swa his gewune wæs. *þa geherde he* færinge ridenda
     menige.(c 1150. LS (Neot): 58–61)
     'It happened someday, that the holy man … was singing his psalms in the
     water naked, as was his habit. Then *heard he* suddenly many horsemen'.

Van Kemenade and Los (2006) and Los (2012) present the following formula for this linguistic change: XVS –> (X)SV. Originally, the adverb goes together with a postposed subject, but when the adverb disappears, the inverse order is no longer necessary. Petré (2014) also argues that this change is probably due to language contact with the Danish invaders who conquered the Eastern coast of Britain in the ninth century. Contact between Danes and Anglo-Saxons may have led to language change, in that the SV word order is assumed to be more likely to effect successful communication than the more complex VS word order. If this is the case, the incipient loss of subject inversion in Old English is an instance of change from below. Interestingly, Petré's (2014: 16) account also hints at changing discourse genres: 'the decline of XVS and the emergence of alternatives … led to a reshaping of the whole narrative genre'. Hence, the pathways of changes in discourse environments are bidirectional: (i) an evolution from change in spoken or written interaction (discourse, communicative needs) to a change in the grammar; and (ii) an evolution from a change in the grammar to a change in the discourse genre. These changes led to hybrid genres with different DTs: subject inversion was not excluded from Early Modern English argumentative texts, but due to the changing word order, speakers stopped using certain collocations and began to use new ones.

In a similar vein, an analysis of changing discourse patterns may yield interesting results when we look at other language families, such as the Romance languages. It is known that copular conjunctions, particles and adverbs in sentence-initial position were common in the European medieval narrative, which, as noted above, was characterized by parataxis and coordination. Against this background, it is highly probable that specific discourse structures determined the grammatical structure of the clause. With regard to Romance, several studies address the order of verb and subject, but also account for clitics in relation to the discourse structure (Davies 1997; Penny 2002; Poole 2013; Mackenzie 2017). The so-called Tobler-Mussafia law, for instance, posits that preverbal clitic placement in Old Spanish (and Modern European Portuguese) is restricted to non-sentence-initial position, as in the examples in (2):

(2) a. Vio*lo* mio Cid Ruy Díaz el castellano. (*Cantar de mio Cid.* Verse 749)
         'My Sir Ruy Díaz 'the Castilian' saw him'.
     b. Et fizieron *les* y luego en valladolit las bodas. (*Estoria de España II*, fol. 289 v.)
         'And they held the wedding for them there in Valladolid'.

In Old Spanish, postposition of dative or accusative clitics was most common when the verb is in sentence-initial position (2a) or when following connectives such as *e(t)* ('and')

(2b). It took several centuries for the present-day preverbal position of the clitic pronoun (e.g., *lo vió, les hicieron*) to become the default option, with the exception of specific verb forms such as finite verb forms of the imperative and the non-finite verb forms of the gerund and the infinitive. The change in the textual traditions of the modern era is related to this grammatical change. In fact, contemporary Spanish still allows postposition in certain formulaic expressions. In (3), a military announcement is expressed in an archaic way, by means of a finite verb and an unusually postposed reflexive pronoun.

(3)   Ello determinó que aquella misma autoridad militar ordenase, el 12 de marzo
      de 1993, la incoación de expediente disciplinario por falta grave, y, con
      carácter preventivo, *decretose* el arresto por tiempo de un mes.
      (*Boletín Oficial del Estado*. España. núm. 89, de 14 de abril de 1999)
      'this caused that the same military authority requested, on March 12th 1993,
      the start of a disciplinary inquiry because of serious mistakes, and, on a
      preventive basis, the arrest during one month was declared'.

Both the Spanish and the English examples of discourse environments suggest that the decline of disappearing forms is rather gradual and that it is linked to varying discourse genres and traditions. From a radical discourse perspective, the link between discourse and grammar can be seen as a straightforward one; in line with Kabatek (2006, 2013), it can even be claimed that different DTs have different grammars. The respective interaction between competing lexemes/constructions and the (discourse) environment in which they arise is a challenging line of research, as the nature of these environments remains understudied in historical linguistics (but see De Smet 2013; Petré 2014).

4. Syntactic elaboration processes in Spanish and English

In this section, I focus on the role of Latin in the syntactic elaboration processes observed in Spanish and English as a specific case of change from above. Syntactic elaboration refers to the process of enriching the syntactic combinatorial possibilities of a language at a certain point of its history. The notion is inspired by Kloss's (1978) German notion of *Ausbau*, which is used for the expansion of a language towards new functions, and by Kabatek's (2006) application to the lexicon of the Alfonsí era. It is commonly acknowledged that the elaboration of the written syntax of most European languages, as opposed to their spoken counterparts, is heavily indebted to Latinate DTs (see Blatt 1957). However, the extent to which particular constructions are loan constructions or vernacular innovations is still a matter for discussion. My main claim here will be that Latin borrowing and vernacular syntactic elaboration go hand in hand (see Cornillie 2014; Cornillie and Octavio de Toledo y Huerta 2015). Below I present evidence from both Spanish and English.

Threaten/amenazar and *promise/prometer* are new auxiliaries in the languages of Europe, in that they do not belong to the typical set of modal auxiliaries that are seen from the earliest periods. Interestingly, the new auxiliaries emerge in French, Spanish, Portuguese, German, English and other languages at different stages in history. There is a long tradition of research on these verbs. The list below offers an overview of the literature dealing with either the formal or the conceptual side of the two auxiliaries:

- Spanish: Hernanz (1999); Vázquez-Laslop (2001); Cornillie (2004, 2005a, 2005b, 2007, 2014, 2016b); Cornillie and Octavio de Toledo y Huerta (2015)
- French: Ruwet (1972, 1983); Rooryck (1997, 2000)
- Portuguese: Pinto de Lima (2014)
- English: Traugott (1993, 1997); Traugott and Dasher (2002); Kissine (2010)
- Dutch: Verhagen (1995, 1996, 2000); Vliegen (2006); Cornillie (2014)
- German: Askedal (1997); Diewald (2001, 2004); Abraham (2003); Metzger (2003); Heine and Miyashita (2004, 2008); Reis (2004); Heine and Kuteva (2006); Vliegen (2006); Diewald and Smirnova (2010).

Notably, Cornillie (2014, 2016b) and Cornillie and Octavio de Toledo y Huerta (2015) are the only studies that link the origin and evolution of the subjective reading of Spanish *amenazar* and its Dutch counterpart *dreigen* to language contact with Latin. Hence, many accounts have reflected on the auxiliation of *promise* and *threaten* without undertaking a proper textual analysis, which we might see as a serious shortcoming. In this chapter I look into the origin and development of both *amenazar* and *threaten* by comparing and contrasting them.

We turn first to the layering of objective and subjective *amenazar/threaten*. The objective reading of the verb (and the subject) scores high in agentivity and has a clear valency structure, as exemplified in (4).

(4)   El MBL [Movimiento Bolivia Libre] vuelve a *amenazar con dejar* la coalición.
(Notic: Bolivia:ERBOL:06/13/96)
'The MBL once again *threatens* to leave the coalition'.

In the subjective auxiliary reading of *amenazar* in (5) the subject does not bear any agentivity. The speaker makes a prediction on the basis of some kind of evidence (see Cornillie 2007).

(5)   El importante encuentro *amenaza ser ensombrecido* por medidas de presión de varios sectores, por lo que el gobierno dispuso la intervención de las Fuerzas Armadas.
(Notic: Bolivia: ERBOL:04/15/96)
'The important meeting *threatens* to be overshadowed by pressure measures from several sectors, as a consequence of which the government ordered the intervention of the Armed Forces'.

The synchronic coexistence (or layering) of the two readings has led cognitive and functional linguists to account for the subjective reading of *threaten* (and *promise*) on the basis of features belonging to the objective reading. Thus, cognitive mechanisms are considered to play a role in the following ways: metaphorical transfer, i.e. a person threatens with something vs. a situation threatens; force dynamics (attenuation, metonymy and subjectification) (Langacker 1995, 2000; Cornillie 2007); speaker-hearer subjectivity – character subjectivity (Verhagen 2000) and pragmatic inference of futurity (Traugott 1997). Since the conceptual structure of objective *amenazar/threaten+* preposition + infinitive was present in early Spanish texts (see Cornillie and Octavio de Toledo y Huerta 2015 for an overview of the Castilian distribution of *amenazar* and *prometer* in the thirteenth, fourteenth and fifteenth centuries), the question is why it took several hundred years for it to develop a subjective reading. Previous studies have not provided a satisfactory account for this change. Synchronic layering is a risky basis for diachronic research, as other constructions may also have played a role in its emergence (see also Van de Velde, De Smet and Ghesquière 2013 on multiple source constructions). The answer here is that the subjective *amenazar/threaten* + infinitive construction starts from a Latin calque resulting in a construction with a nominal complement in Latinate DTs such as dictionaries and humanist translations. My corpus data indicate that in Spanish the new form arises in the fifteenth century, whereas the English construction emerges in the sixteenth century.

Crucially, the corpus data contain a couple of subjective constructions with prepositional and nominal complements in both Spanish and English. In Spanish, unlike in English, these constructions are found in the same period as the infinitives, i.e. the end of the fifteenth century. There are no separate 'stages of change' (Heine and Kuteva 2006) that can account for the evolution of *amenazar*. Its subjective readings are attested in the Latin-Spanish dictionaries of the late fifteenth century, such as Palencia's dictionary, in (6), and Nebrija's dictionary, in (7) and (8). In all three examples, the prediction semantics and the reference to some kind of epistemological or perceptual basis are clearly present.

(6) monstruum es quasi monestrum: que amonesta auer de venir algo siniestro.
    'that warns that something bad is to happen'
    & prodigium lo antedize: 'and foretells it'
    & portentum lo amenaza: 'and gives a sign of it'
    & ostentum lo muestra: 'and shows it'
    (Alfonso de Palencia. 1490. *Universal vocabulario de latín en romance*. Seville)

(7) Portentum.i. milagro que significa mal 'the miracle that stands for something bad'
    Portentosus. a. um. lo que assi amenaza mal 'what is a bad portent'
    Prodigium. ij. milagro que amenaza mal 'miracle that portends evil'
    Prodigiosus. a. um. por cosa assi milagrosa 'for something miraculous'
    (Antonio de Nebrija. 1492. *Dictionarium latino-hispanicum*. Salamanca)

(8) Amenazar a menudo. minitor .aris 'threaten often. I threaten. you threaten'
    Amenazar caida.LAT. minari ruinam. 'threaten fall LAT. threaten ruin'
    (Antonio de Nebrija. 1492. *Dictionarium latino-hispanicum*. Salamanca)

The example in (8) is particularly revealing, in that it refers to the imminent threat of the potential change-of-state of 'falling' (*amenazar caida* 'threaten fall'). It is especially with this 'fall' semantics that we find the first examples of subjective *amenazar*, which arise in translations from Latin in the same period as Palencia's and Nebrija's dictionaries, that is, in the last decade of the fifteenth century. The *amenazar*-construction in (9) has a prepositional complement in de Gordonio's translation.

(9)   & la crisi[s] siempre sospecharas que siempre *amenaza de recayda*. (Bernardus de Gordonio. 1495. *Prognostica. Las pronósticas*)
      'and the crisis you will always suspect that it always *threatens (with) fall*'.

We cannot underestimate the role of copyists, translators and editors in the textual transmission and any grammatical changes deriving from this. The documents of the Madison corpus in which *amenazar* appears first and most frequently are translations from Latin to Castilian. The verb does not appear in original Castilian works, nor in translations from Arabic, in the case of the Alfonsí texts. All instances of subjective *amenazar* come from texts published in high register DTs that reflect Communicative Distance, far removed from popular genres (for other examples, see Kabatek 2008; Pons Rodríguez 2010).

In Cornillie and Octavio de Toledo y Huerta (2015), we show that Latin *minari* ('threaten')-constructions with nominal complements can be found in all stages of the classical language, including authors such as Cicero and Virgil, as well as in medieval and humanist works in Latin. In our (2015) article, we also give an overview of Middle French, Toscan, Aragonese and Old Castilian. The conclusion is that the *threaten*-construction is relatively entrenched in the vernacular languages used by the respective translators. For example, Enrique de Villena, one of the most notable pre-humanist authors writing in Castilian, translates the Latin verbs *intentare* and *tenere* by means of *amenazar* + nominal complement. The very fact that this verb is chosen to express a prediction about imminent change illustrates the degree to which the subjective reading of *amenazar* is entrenched. Interestingly, the *minari*-construction with the infinitive does not appear in Latin, and in Old Spanish the auxiliary use is not yet part of the Spanish grammatical system. But at the end of the fifteenth century a process of syntactic elaboration of the Spanish language took place and authors started to use new constructions that eventually came to be part of the grammatical system of Spanish. It can be assumed that such elaboration has to do with the competition of the new national languages with the Latin cultural heritage and with the spread of printing (the Gutenberg Revolution), which allowed authors to circulate their writing more widely.

Let us now look at three examples occurring within the timespan of one century to draw clearer conclusions. The first example is the subjective *amenazar de se caer*-construction in (10), which is the only one with an infinitive found in the fifteenth century. This construction is a clear syntactic innovation, in that there is a shift from a main verb with a nominal complement (*amenaza caída* 'threatens fall') to an auxiliary verb with an infinitive (*amenaza de se caer* 'threatens to fall'). Without the *threaten* auxiliary, the main verbs would be '[the tooth] moves and falls'.

(10) desçeca & consume los humores podridos que corrompen las rayzes de los dientes & las enzias. refirma el diente que se anda & *amenaza de se caer*. (Bartholomaeus Anglicus; Vicente de Burgos (translator). 1494. *Liber de*

proprietatibus rerum (1230–1240). *Propiedades de las cosas.* Toulouse) [confortat dentem mobilem *casum conminantem* (*De propietatibus Rerum*, XVII, 136)]) '[this] dissects and depletes the rotten pieces that corrupt the roots of the teeth and molars. Repair the tooth that moves and threatens to fall'.

This is a special kind of borrowing, i.e. it is an instance of semantic borrowing, but is no example of grammatical borrowing. Although the 'fall' semantics is directly borrowed into Spanish, the syntactic pattern is not, since the original Latin form consists of a complex noun phrase with a present participle of the verb *conminari* (*dentem casum conminantem*).

Example (11) is also illustrative of the change under examination. In this sixteenth-century example (1532), Alonso de Virués, a creative (and hence not so meticulous) translator of Erasmus' work, uses the new subjective *amenazar*-construction with the same infinitive, i.e. *caerse* ('to fall'). As shown above, this verb is found in Vicente de Burgos's translation of Anglicus's medieval encyclopaedia some forty years previously.

(11) Si el cuerpo es casa del alma, muchos veo que tienen sus almas muy ruynmente aposentadas.
[JOC.] Assi es; ca las aposentan en casas llenas de goteras, escuras, humosas, ventosas, desportilladas, podridas y que ya *amenazan de caerse* (Alonso de Virués. 1532. *Colloquios de Erasmo*) [Erasmus' original: Sic est, videlicet in aedibus perstillantibus, opacis, ventis omnibus obnoxiis, fumosis, pituitosis, laceris ac ruinosis, denique putribus et infectis.]
'If the body is the home of the soul, I see that many have their souls very badly lodged. [JOC] Indeed. Since they put them up in houses [that are] full of leaks, dark, smoky, windy, nicked, rotten and which already threaten to fall'.

It is important to stress that the original version of Erasmus's text lacks a reference to the verb *minari* ('threaten'), but instead contains the adjective *ruinosus* ('ruinous'). Hence, by translating the adjective by means of an auxiliary, the author/translator looks for a non-literal alternative and, by doing so, shows his syntactic creativity. The fact that other authors do the same suggests that the auxiliary use of *amenazar* is not a hapax and is increasingly entrenched in the linguistic system of Pre-classical Spanish.

Finally, (12) is the first attestation of subjective *amenazar* + infinitive in an original Spanish, i.e. non-translated, text. This example comes from a theatre play by Lope de Vega from the end of the sixteenth century (*Corpus del español*; see Cornillie 2007).

(12) Este tronco anciano, que ya *amenaza a caer* de la muerte en el mar cano (Lope de Vega. 1598. *El vaso de elección San Pablo*)
'This old trunk, which at the moment threatens to fall dead in the grey sea'.

The examples above indicate that the specific subjective conceptualization of *amenazar* is not the result of a century-long evolution, but occurs simultaneously in constructions with a nominal complement and constructions with an infinitival complement. However, there is a drastic syntactic change: Latin *minari* was either part of a nominal complement or had a nominal complement itself, whereas the vernacular Spanish language innovates its syntax by adding an infinitive. *Amenazar* is a case of syntactic innovation from a finite full verb with a nominal complement to an auxiliary verb with a main verb infinitive. Moreover, the subjective reading of *amenazar* has not changed much over the centuries; what has changed is the range of infinitives combining with the verb, which can be seen as an example of host-class expansion (Himmelmann 2004: 32).

Let us now examine whether the same evolutionary path is attested in English. To account for the evolution of English *threaten*,[5] I have analysed data from the Early English Books Online (EEBO, 755 million words, 1470s–1690s, Mark Davies) and the Corpus of Late Modern English Texts (CLMET, 10 million words, 1710–1920, Hendrik De Smet). The results are as follows: in EEBO (prior to the end of the seventeenth century), none of the 2,568 examples contained a clear subjective *threaten* + infinitive construction, whereas in CLMET one third of the cases (55/160) presented subjective readings. This difference between the two periods is quite remarkable and requires further examination.

First, the verb *threaten* (all forms and uses) is attested in EEBO at the beginning of the sixteenth century, but the *Oxford English Dictionary* (OED) mentions early uses of the verb as early as the thirteenth century (*The South English Legendary* and *The Chronicle of Robert of Gloucester*).[6] The first *threaten* + infinitive construction recorded in the EEBO material, reproduced in (13), is found in a translation from a Latin text written by Erasmus and published in 1531. However, this example does not yield a subjective reading, due to the context of destruction. The negative infinitive *destroy* is in combination with the subject *myschewes*, that is, we have a personification reading expressing a real threat.

(13) Howe many be distroyed by lyghtnyng / erth quakes / groude openynges / lakes / floddes of ye see and ryuers / infectous aer / venom / wyld beastis / fallyng of huge thinges, yll phisicios: but no way greatter distruction than through warres? [.] # but all these myscheues *thretten to distroye* but the body: Howe many dagers hange ouer ye soule? fro ye fleshe a houshold enemy / fro the worlde nowe flattryng that it may strangle.
(Gentian Hervet. 1531. *De immensa dei misericordia. A sermon of the excedynge great mercy of god, / made by ye moste famous doctour maister Eras. Rot. Translated out of Latine into Englisshe, at the request of the moste honorable and vertuous lady, the lady Margaret Countese of Salisbury*)

In the same historical period, William Tyndale and Miles Coverdale begin to use the *threaten*-construction with a negative nominal complement, more specifically in their theological texts and Bible translations. Tyndale travelled a lot to Germany and Flanders[7] (Antwerp) to meet humanists, and any linguistic innovation of that period is hence to be situated in the realm of humanism (direct contact with Latin – and Greek) and the Gutenberg Revolution (spread of printing). Miles Coverdale was very much inspired by the Tyndale Bible translation (Pentateuch). It is in this humanist context of Latin (and Greek) translations into English where we find the first examples of *threaten* with negative nominal complements in EEBO. However, in (14), *threaten* does not convey a subjective reading, in that it bears clear agentivity of God, directed to a human entity. In (14a), the passive form of *threaten* is used, whereas in (14b) it is God who threatened.

(14) a. Vnto the disobedient that will not turne / is *threatened wrath / vengeaunce and damnacion* / accordinge to all the terrible curses and fearfull ensamples of the Byble.
(William Tyndale. 1534. *The Newe Testament dylygently corrected and compared with the Greke by Willyam Tindale, and fynesshed in the yere of our Lorde God*)
b. rych are not dismade whan god doth defy vs: and not only proclameth warre, but *threateneth* also *destruccion, abiection and rootynge out.*
(Translated from Latin. Miles Coverdale. 1538. *An exposicion vpon the songe of the blessed virgine Mary*. Author: Martin Luther)

These examples show the syntactic pattern of the verb *threaten* with a deverbal nominal complement (*wrath, vengeaunce and damnacion* in (14a) and *destruccion, abiection* in (14b)) and a gerund (*rootynge out* in (14b)). Let us now look at a series of examples belonging to the second half of the sixteenth century that can be considered bridging contexts between the objective and the subjective constructions, both syntactically and semantically. A crucial role is attributed to the inanimate subject lacking agentivity. The same semantics of the nominal complements described for Spanish above, i.e. with frequent mentions of *ruin(e)* and *fall*, is prototypical. As for the DTs, the first examples are attested in wisdom literature and rhymes and refer to meteorological processes such as rain (15) and thunder (16).

(15) Sharpe is the warre, that teares a house in twaine:
wo worthe those words, that brings in braules by swarms
Darke be those cloudes, that alwaies *threatens raine*:
Curste bee the cause, that breedeth woe and paine,
and dampde in hell, those subtell spirits shalbe
(Thomas Churchyard. 1579. *A generall rehearsall of warres, called Churchyardes choise*)

(16) stir vp a hiue of bees
and of the abundance of vaine mind with words in aire he flees:
as though it were a thunder crack that neuer brings foorth raine
but dailie *threatens ruine and wrack* with ratling rumors vaine:
(Thomas Churchyard. 1595. *A musicall consort of heauenly harmonie*)

As in the Latin examples (*minari ruinam*), destruction and decay frequently combine with English *threaten* at the end of the sixteenth century. In example (17), which stems from a Latin translation, the verb *threaten* is used intransitively: *destruction threatens*, whereas in (18) an ancient building *threatens ruine*.

> (17) but if some god to chuse would me assigne, i all would prayse, but dido should be mine: but hard's my choise, when there the thundering (iove, *destruction threatens* if i disobay: and here my friendly foe, heart-pursuing Loue, by all his powers, coniures my mind to stay.
> (Ovidius translated from Latin to English. 1600. *Remedie of Love*)
>
> (18) Turkie hath very good cause to bewaile his death, for theyr religion like an ancient building, worne with extremity of age, riues, &; *threatens ruine* on euery side, if it be not supported by newe proppes: one of the best meanes the deuill inuented to holde that vppe, was the helpe of thy father, to pull downe all other religions vnder heauen.
> (Thomas Nash. 1589. *A countercuffe giuen to Martin Iunior by the ventruous, hardie, and renowned Pasquill of England caualiero*)

Another important force in the consolidation of the innovative uses of *threaten* is Edward Grimeston, a prolific translator who translated from Spanish and French at the beginning of the seventeenth century. The collocation *threaten (a/one's) ruine* is used in the context of decreasing Christianity (19) and danger (20).

> (19) Christianitie without doubt augments and increaseth, and brings forth daily more fruite among the indian slaves: and contrariwise decreaseth and *threatens a ruine* in other partes, where have beene more happy beginnings: and although the beginnings at the west indies have beene laboursome.
> (Translated from Spanish by Edward Grimeston. 1604. *The naturall and morall historie of the East and West Indies*. Author: José de Acosta)
>
> (20) filling it with such confusion, as shee leaues him neither memory, nor iudgement, nor will, to encounter any danger that *threatens his ruine*.
> (Translated from French by Edward Grimeston. 1621. *A table of humane passions*. Author: N. Coeffeteau)

Importantly, despite the entrenchment of the *threatens ruine*-expression, the examples from Grimeston do not yield any subjective cases of *threaten* + infinitive. In (21), *threaten to ruin* is used agentively, in that the subject is involved in a battle. Hence, there is no syntactic elaboration from *threaten ruin* to *threaten to ruin* in sixteenth century English.

> (21) and seeing that no warning could diuert them from these acts of hostility, they had resolued to present a siege to draw them to their duties: but they grew more insolent, *threatning to ruine* all the protestants houses within the Prouince: Wherupon, they had giuen commandement to the Earle of mandsfelt to presse the siege, that the inhabitants might be forced to vnite themselues with the other towns of bohemia, and to liue in peace.
> (Translated from Spanish. Edward Grimeston. 1623. *The imperiall historie: or The liues of the emperours, from Iulius Caesar, the first founder of the Roman monarchy*. Author: Pedro Mexía, from Seville)

The OED also includes two examples from William Shakespeare, a contemporary of the aforementioned authors. Given the status of Shakespeare as a successful actor, writer and part-owner of a theatre in London, and coming as he did from an important family, the occurrences in (22) and (23) are an indication of the prestige of the *threaten*-expression, both in its transitive (22) and intransitive (23) uses, at the beginning of the seventeenth century (Shakespeare died in 1616).

(22) We have landed in ill time – the skies look grimly.
     And *threaten present blusters.*
     (William Shakespeare. 1610–1611. *A Winter's Tale*)
(23) Though the Seas *threaten* they are mercifull
     (William Shakespeare. 1611. *The Tempest*)

Let us now examine whether the prototypical 'fall'-construction (cf. Latin, Spanish and Dutch) gives rise to the new auxiliary function of *threaten* in English. I will show that the Latin-based *threaten fall* collocation is found with many authors, but that it does not seem to be a triggering force in English, unlike in Spanish and Dutch (see Cornillie 2014). The renowned Bible translator George Joye, a colleague of William Tyndale and Miles Coverdale, is the first author of the corpus who used *threaten* in a non-agentive way with *fall* as a complement, as in (24), an example from 1531.

(24) ieremie in the: 51: chapter: for there ar many thingis that *threten an heuy fall*
     &; change to your popishe kingdome: the lorde of powrs hath decree to
     abate
     (George Joye. d. 1531. *The letters which Iohan Ashwel priour of Newnham Abbey besids Bedforde, sente secretely to the Bishope of Lyncolne in the yeare of our lord M.D.xxvii*)

In the second half of the sixteenth century and the beginning of the seventeenth century, Churchyard, Robert Southwell, Philip Sidney and Cambridge theologian William Perkins all have recourse to the construction as well, as illustrated in (25)–(29). All these authors travelled on a regular basis and wrote and published in Latin as well as in English.

(25) the heat of my good hap is gon, the prime of pompe is past, and as the vvarmth
     forsakes the vvorld, the colde comes on as fast: the spring but *threatens fal of leafe*, all bravrie beggrie brings, he vvepes in vvant, that first in vvelth, and
     toppe of triumph sings
     (Thomas Churchyard. 1578. *A lamentable, and pitifull description, of the wofull warres in Flaunders*)
(26) and on euerie side the ruinous cottage of your faint and feeble flesh,
     threatneth fal
     (Robert Southwell. 1595 (published in 1622). *A short rule of good life*)
(27) he came in like a wild man; but such a wildnes, as shewed his eye-sight had
     tamed him, full of withered leaues, which though they fell not, still *threatned*

falling: his impresa was, a mill-horse still bound to goe in one circle; with this word, data fata sequutus:

(Philip Sidney. 1586 (published in 1590). *The Countesse of Pembrokes Arcadia*)

(28) they send for the most part, all their Clergie immediatly to heauen without let, wheras all the temporality (except martyrs) must passe by purgatory: here are great buildings, but on a sandy foundation, goodly castles, but built in the ayre; if these deuises vvere of god, they would certainly stand, but their long tottring *threatens a suddaine fall*:

(William Perkins. 1602 (published in 1605). *Of the calling of the ministerie two treatises, discribing the duties and dignities of that calling. Delivered publickly in the Vniuersitie of Cambridge, by Maister Perkins*)

(29) the tottering and ruinous cottage of thy faint flesh *threatneth fall*: (William Perkins. 1602 (published in 1628). *Deaths knell*)

Owen Felltham, an English writer born in 1602, was still a teenager when he wrote the compilation of essays *Resolues, diuine, morall, politicall*, which enjoyed great popularity in the day. The fact that both *ruine* and *fall* are the nominal complements of *threaten* in example (30) confirms that the collocation, which was once a borrowing from Latin, was clearly entrenched in the seventeenth-century English of native writers. The same holds for the influential poet Richard Brathwaite (see (31)).

(30) then to haue his seat on the mountains top, where euery blast *threatens both his ruine, and fall*

(Owen Felltham. c 1620. *Resolues, diuine, morall, politicall*)

(31) this house i liue in, like a shaking frame *threatens* each day *a fall*

(Richard Brathwaite. 1619. *A new spring shadovved in sundry pithie poems*)

Despite the evidence with nominal complements, no auxiliary example of *threaten to fall* has been attested in the sixteenth- and seventeenth-century material examined.[8] Moreover, all examples found in the corpus with an infinitive have an agentive reading of *fall* in the construction *fall (up)on somebody* 'attack fiercely or unexpectedly'. So, the specific locus of change for the grammaticalization of *threaten* remains to be accounted for. Since we have no corpus data between 1690 and 1710, the missing link may be found there. Further research will show whether the success of the subjective construction in Late Modern English can be located there.

The frequency distribution in the CLMET is presented in Table 6.1: from the beginning of the eighteenth century to the beginning of the twentieth century there is an increase in the frequency of *threaten* + *to* INF. As for the proportion of texts bearing this construction, it is telling that in the most recent period almost half the texts convey a subjective *threaten*-construction. If we take into account the number of authors represented, the construction turns out to be even more entrenched: in every 1.4 authors there is a subjective use of *threaten* + *to* INF.

A more detailed examination of the distribution of the construction over the two centuries is shown in Table 6.2. After checking the number of texts for the different periods, it reveals an extremely low frequency of this pattern in the first half of the

Table 6.1 General overview of subjective *threaten*

CLMET	No. of authors	No. of documents	No. of words	Subjective *threaten*	x/10,000
1710–1780	15	24	2,096,405	4	0.019
1780–1850	29	39	3,739,657	13	0.034
1850–1920	28	52	3,982,264	38	0.095
TOTAL	72	115	9,818,326	55	

	No. of authors using *threaten*	No. of documents with *threaten*	Subjective *threaten* in every x texts	Subjective *threaten* in every x authors
1710–1780	4	4	6	3.75
1780–1850	6	10	3.90	4.83
1850–1920	20	24	2.17	1.40
TOTAL	30	38		

Table 6.2 Detailed overview of subjective *threaten*

	1710–1733	1733–1766	1766–1800	1800–1833	1833–1866	1866–1900	1900–1920
Number of occurrences	0	2	10	3	10	23	7
Number of documents	0	2	5	3	9	15	4

eighteenth century. Together with the high frequency at the end of the eighteenth century, this suggests that the *threaten*-construction is a linguistic fashion, with a revival from the mid-eighteenth century.

Overall the slow actualization of the *threaten*-construction in English is quite similar to the later evolution of Spanish *amenazar* (Cornillie and Octavio de Toledo y Huerta 2015). Yet, since *threaten to fall/ruine* is not attested in the English data, the specific bridging context for the infinitival construction in the seventeenth century remains to be accounted for. This distribution suggests grammatical change from above, that is, pertaining to Communicative Distance. Further corpus research is needed to unravel this evolution.

The first eighteenth-century example in CLMET is from Horace Walpole's letters and has a copular verb (unlike the change-of-state infinitive, example (32)), where *be an excise or convention* is being modalized by means of the auxiliary *threaten*.

(32) it has been settled that he should go thither on Tuesdays, and Majesty on Saturdays, that they may not meet. The Neutrality (287) begins to break out, and *threatens to be an excise or convention*. The newspapers are full of it, and the press teems. It has already produced three pieces: 'The Groans of Germany' (Horace Walpole. 1735–1748. *Letters* Vol.1)

Henry Fielding (1707–1754) is another original and innovative writer using *threaten* + *to* INF in the first half of the eighteenth century, as in (33).

(33) 'I think I had experience enough of it', answered the other: 'my first mistress
     and my first friend betrayed me in the basest manner, and in matters which
     threatened to be of the worst of consequences-even to bring me to a shameful
     death'. 'But you will pardon me', cries Jones, 'if I desire you to reflect fielding'
     (Henry Fielding. 1749. *The History of Tom Jones*)

Other authors display all kinds of verbs, both copular ones and change-of-state verbs.
It is clear that the construction *threaten + to* INF also benefits from the prestige of
authors such as the Brontës and other distinguished writers present in the CLMET.
The CLMET data lend themselves to further research beyond the limits of this chapter.

5. Conclusions

In this chapter, I have examined the relation between discourse environments and
grammatical change. In Section 2, I discussed the importance of DTs for historical-
linguistics research. Since it is hard to define a speaker community in the past, textual
traditions offer a suitable empirical basis here, allowing for a dynamic view of prestige
and innovation, as well as of disappearance and decline. DTs can serve to identify
the extent to which traditions have an impact on the linguistic system. I have argued
that the continuum from Communicative Immediacy to Communicative Distance is
helpful in accounting for differences between 'change from below' and 'change from
above' and that grammaticalization takes place both in speaker-hearer interaction and
in textual interaction with prestigious authors. Language change is a multifaceted
phenomenon with a strong cultural dimension. Section 3 has illustrated how changes
in the organization of discourse may lead to constructional change. To show this, I
used Petré's (2014) case of the SV word order and the decline of *weorðan* due to the
disappearance of an Old English sentence adverb.

My work on Spanish and English, presented in Section 4, has addressed the origin
and actualization of the subjective *threaten*-construction. Despite arising from the same
basis, clear differences between the evolution of Spanish *amenazar* and that of English
threaten have been detected, which may have an explanation in terms of socio-cultural
settings as macro discourse environments. The new *amenazar*-construction occurs in
a period of cultural and political effervescence in Spain. By the end of the fifteenth
century writers are confident enough to introduce conscious innovations into the
Castilian language, which can be seen as instances of change from above. Moreover,
these authors want to position their national languages on a par with Latin, by means of
fostering the prestige of vernacular syntax. In contemporary terms, they are experiencing
a '"Yes we can"-moment'. Interestingly, the same shift from a nominal *threaten*
complement to an infinitive was observed for Dutch in the first half of the seventeenth
century, i.e. the Dutch Golden Age (Cornillie 2014). In German and English, the
infinitival construction emerges much later. In the case of English, the political turmoil
and instability of the seventeenth century may have had its influence on the literary and
linguistic production of the time. The eighteenth and the nineteenth centuries are then
centuries of expansion and innovation in English culture and language.

If this view also holds for the European languages and their chronologies, we have a sound piece of evidence as to the influence of cultural environments on the syntactic elaboration of a language. When authors feel culturally confident, their constructions undergo more innovations. Such an analysis challenges some aspects of the functional approach to language, in that not change from below, but change from above, as in the case for *amenazar* and *threaten*, may play a crucial role in the coding of grammar. Such a view contrasts with Du Bois's (1985:363) claim that '[g]rammars code best what people do most'. Alternatively, we can claim that the concept of 'interaction' should be broadened to include interaction of cultural practices and Discourse Traditions.

Notes

1   Back in 2005 Teresa Fanego gave a plenary lecture on grammaticalization and discourse at the FITIGRA-conference in Leuven (Fanego 2010). There we met with other people to discuss the future of the Societas Linguistica Europaea. It was an important moment, amongst other things because at that very point colleague Fanego became a candidate to lead the *Folia Linguistica* journal. Also, for both of us it was a starting point of a strong involvement in SLE affairs. Till the end of our terms we have collaborated very well, although we have had arguments once in a while. But is there any other way to make progress? Thank you, Teresa, for all your efforts.
2   I would like to thank the anonymous reviewers and the editors for their valuable and enriching comments and criticisms. All remaining problems are mine.
3   Oesterreicher (1997: 20): 'moldes normativos convencionalizados que guían la transmisión de un sentido mediante elementos lingüísticos tanto en su producción como en su recepción'.
4   Some linguists prefer to use the expression 'discourse genres' instead of DTs, whereas others refer to DTs as different low-level discourse practices within established discourse genres (Kabatek 2013). In her analysis of the Spanish adverbs ending in *–mente*, Company Company (2012) shows that certain discourse genres are inherently hybrid. If we look at historical narrative texts, for instance, some texts present, in addition to the historical account, also wisdom and moral reflections, such as in the thirteenth-century Alfonsí book called *General estoria. Segunda parte* (Company Company 2012), whereas many other historical texts only present the facts without displaying such reflections. The notion of discourse genre proposed by Company Company (2012) may include different DTs: e.g., historical narrative and wisdom reflections.
5   The orthographic variants <threten, thretten, threaten, treten, tretten and threatten> were also considered. In EEBO I found sixty-eight cases of <threten>, thirty-one cases of <thretten>, twenty cases of <threatten>, sixteen cases of <treten>, one case of <treatten> and none of <tretten>.
6   The verb *threaten* was already in use in the Old English period with the meaning 'press, urge, force' (OED s.v. *threaten* v. 1).
7   William Tyndale has another, less positive, Flemish connection: for his Lutheran practices, he was tortured to death and burned in Vilvoorde, a town ten kilometres away from Brussels.
8   There is one *threaten to fall* example that at first sight may be revealing, but in reality belongs to a different type, in that it is a passive construction, which implies that there is always some kind of agent:

(i) i can not determine me, whiche is the beste, or to saye more properly the worste, extreme myserie without the danger of fortune, or extreme prosperitie, that is always *thretened to falle*: in this case to be so extreme i wyl not determin me, sith in the one is a perillous lyfe, and in the other renoume is sure: (John Bourchier Berners. 1537. Translation of Antonio de Guevara's *The golden boke of Marcus Aurelius Emperour and eloquent orator*).

Corpora

CLMET = De Smet, Hendrik (2005), *The Corpus of Late Modern English Texts*. Department of Linguistics, University of Leuven.

CdE = Davies, Mark (2002–), *Corpus del Español: 100 million words, 1200s-1900s*. Available online: http://www.corpusdelespanol.org/hist-gen/. (Historical / Genres)

EEBO = Davies, Mark (2017), *Early English Books Online*. Part of the SAMUELS project. Available online: https://corpus.byu.edu/eebo/.

References

Abraham, Werner (2003), '"Epistemic Creationism": Myths vs. *profunda facie* Explanatory Irrefutables on Modal Verbs in German and in General', in Lars-Olof Delsing, Cecilia Falk, Gunlöf Josefsson and Halldór Á. Sigurðsson (eds), *Grammar in Focus. Festschrif for Christer Platzack. Vol. II*, 1–88, Lund: Lund University.

Askedal, John Ole (1997), '*Drohen* und *versprechen* als sog. 'Modalitätsverben' in der deutschen Gegenwartssprache', *Deutsch als Fremdsprache*, 34: 12–19.

Blatt, Franz (1957), 'Latin Influence on European Syntax', *Travaux du Cercle Linguistique de Copenhague*, 11: 33–69.

Company Company, Concepción (2012), 'Condicionamientos textuales en la evolución de los adverbios en −*mente*', *Revista de Filología Española*, 92 (1): 9–42.

Cornillie, Bert (2004), 'The Shift from Lexical to Subjective Readings in Spanish *Prometer* "to Promise" and *Amenazar* "to Threaten". A Corpus-based Account', *Pragmatics*, 14 (1): 1–30.

Cornillie, Bert (2005a), 'Agentivity and Subjectivity in Spanish *Prometer* and *Amenazar*. A Study of Constructional and Diatopical Variation', *Revista Internacional de Lingüística Iberoamericana*, 5: 171–96.

Cornillie, Bert (2005b), 'A Paradigmatic View of Spanish *Amenazar* "to Threaten" and *Prometer* "to Promise"', *Folia Linguistica*, 39 (3–4): 385–415.

Cornillie, Bert (2007), *Evidentiality and Epistemic Modality in Spanish (Semi-)Auxiliaries. A Cognitive-Functional Approach*, Berlin: De Gruyter Mouton.

Cornillie, Bert (2014), 'Over de Subjectieve Lezing van *Dreigen* in het 16de- en 17de Eeuwse Nederlands. Historische Pragmatiek vs Contact-geïnduceerde Taalverandering', in Freek Van de Velde, Hans Smessaert, Frank Van Eynde and Sara Verbrugge (eds), *Patroon en Argument. Een Dubbelfeestbundel bij het Emeritaat van William Van Belle en Joop van der Horst*, 329–48. Leuven: Leuven University Press.

Cornillie, Bert (2016a), 'Acerca de la locución epistémica *tal vez* en el Siglo de las Luces: Innovación y especialización', in Martha Guzmán Riverón and Daniel M. Sáez Rivera (eds), *Márgenes y centros en el español del siglo XVIII*, 183–99, Valencia: Tirant Humanidades.

Cornillie, Bert (2016b), 'On the Pace of the Grammaticalization of "Threaten" and "Promise" in the Languages of Western Europe'. Paper presented at SLE 2016, University of Naples.

Cornillie, Bert and Álvaro S. Octavio de Toledo y Huerta (2015), 'The Diachrony of Subjective *Amenazar* "Threaten". On Latin-induced Grammaticalization in Spanish', in Andrew D. M. Smith, Graeme Trousdale and Richard Waltereit (eds), *New Directions in Grammaticalization Research*, 187–208, Amsterdam: Benjamins.

Davies, Mark (1997), 'The Evolution of Spanish Clitic Climbing: A Corpus-based Approach', *Studia Neophilologica*, 69 (2): 251–63.

De Smet, Hendrik (2012), 'The Course of Actualization', *Language*, 88 (3): 601–33.

De Smet, Hendrik (2013), *Spreading Patterns: Diffusional Change in the English System of Complementation*, Oxford: Oxford University Press.

Diewald, Gabriele (2001), '*Scheinen*-Probleme: Analogie, Konstruktionsmischung und die Sogwirkung aktiver Grammatikalisierungskanäle', in Reimar Müller and Marga Reis (eds), *Modalität und Modalverben im Deutschen*, 87–110, Hamburg: Buske.

Diewald, Gabriele (2004), 'Faktizität und Evidentialität: Semantische Differenzierungen bei den Modal- und Modalitätsverben im Deutschen', in Oddleif Leirbukt (ed), *Tempus / Temporalität und Modus / Modalität im Sprachenvergleich*, 231–58, Stauffenburg Verlag: Tübingen.

Diewald, Gabriele and Elena Smirnova (2010), *Evidentiality in German. Linguistic Realization and Regularities in Grammaticalization*, Berlin: De Gruyter Mouton.

Du Bois, John W. (1985), 'Competing Motivations', in John Haiman (ed), *Iconicity in Syntax*, 343–65, Amsterdam: Benjamins.

Fanego, Teresa (2010), 'Paths in the Development of Elaborative Discourse Markers: Evidence from Spanish', in Kristin Davidse, Lieven Vandelanotte and Hubert Cuyckens (eds), *Subjectification, Intersubjectification, and Grammaticalization*, 197–237, Berlin: De Gruyter Mouton.

Heine, Bernd and Hiroyuki Miyashita (2004), '*Drohen* und *Versprechen*– zur Genese von Funktionalen Kategorien', *Neue Beiträge zur Germanistik*, 3 (2): 9–33.

Heine, Bernd and Hiroyuki Miyashita (2008), 'Accounting for a Functional Category: German *Drohen* "to Threaten"', *Language Sciences*, 30: 53–101.

Heine, Bernd and Tania Kuteva (2006), *The Changing Languages of Europe*, Oxford: Oxford University Press.

Hernanz, María Luisa (1999), 'El infinitivo', in Ignacio Bosque and Violeta Demonte (eds), *Gramática descriptiva de la lengua española*, 2195–356, Madrid: RAE – Espasa Calpe.

Himmelmann, Nikolaus P. (2004), 'Lexicalization and Grammaticization: Opposite or Orthogonal?', in Walter Bisang, Nikolaus P. Himmelmann and Björn Wiemer (eds), *What Makes Grammaticalization: A Look from its Components and its Fringes*, 21–42. Berlin: De Gruyter Mouton.

Kabatek, Johannes (2006), 'Las tradiciones discursivas del español medieval: Historia de textos e historia de la lengua', *Iberoromania*, 63 (2): 28–43.

Kabatek, Johannes (2013), '¿Es posible una lingüística histórica basada en un corpus representativo?', *Iberoromania*, 77 (1): 8–28.

Kabatek, Johannes, ed. (2008), *Sintaxis histórica del español y cambio lingüístico: Nuevas perspectivas desde las tradiciones discursivas*, Frankfurt/Madrid: Vervuert – Iberoamericana.

Kissine, Mikhail (2010), 'Metaphorical Projection, Subjectification and English Speech Act Verbs', *Folia Linguistica*, 44 (2): 339–70.

Kloss, Heinz (1978), *Die Entwicklung Neuer Germanischer Kultursprachen seit 1800*. 2, Düsseldorf: Schwann.

Koch, Peter and Wulf Oesterreicher (2011), *Gesprochene Sprache in der Romania. Französisch, Italienisch, Spanisch*, 2nd edn, Berlin: De Gruyter Mouton.

Koch, Peter and Wulf Oesterreicher (1985), 'Sprache der Nähe – Sprache der Distanz. Mündlichkeit und Schriftlichkeit im Spannungsfeld von Sprachtheorie und Sprachgeschichte', *Romanistisches Jahrbuch*, 36: 15–43.

Labov, William (1994), *Principles of Linguistic Change. Vol I: Internal Factors*, Oxford: Blackwell.

Labov, William (2007), 'Transmission and Diffusion', *Language*, 83 (2): 344–87.

Langacker, Ronald W. (1995), 'Raising and Transparency', *Language*, 71 (1): 1–62.

Langacker, Ronald W. (2000), 'Subjectification and Grammaticization', in *Grammar and Conceptualization*, 297–315, Berlin: De Gruyter Mouton.

Los, Bettelou (2012), 'The Loss of Verb-Second and the Switch from Bounded to Unbounded Systems', in Anneli Meurman-Solin, María José López-Couso and Bettelou Los (eds), *Information Structure and Syntactic Change in the History of English*, 21–46, Oxford: Oxford University Press.

Mackenzie, Ian (2017), 'The Rise and Fall of Proclisis in Old Spanish Postprepositional Infinitival Clauses: A Quantitative Approach', *Bulletin of Hispanic Studies*, 94 (2): 127–46.

Metzger, Kai (2003), 'Die Lesarten von *Drohen* und *Versprechen* und ihre Konstruktionsarten. Eine Korpusanalytische Untersuchung', Zulassungsarbeit zur Staatsprüfung für das Lehramt an Gymnasien, Universität Tübingen.

OED = *Oxford English Dictionary Online*. Available online: http://www.oed.com/.

Oesterreicher, Wulf (1997), 'Zur Fundierung von Diskurstraditionen', in Barbara Frank, Thomas Haye and Doris Tophinke (eds), *Gattungen Mittelalterlicher Schriftlichkeit*, 19–41, Tübingen: Narr.

Penny, Ralph (2002), *A History of the Spanish Language*. 2nd edn, Cambridge: Cambridge University Press.

Petré, Peter (2014), *Constructions and Environments: Copular, Passive, and Related Constructions in Old and Middle English*, Oxford: Oxford University Press.

Pinto de Lima, José (2014), *Studies on Grammaticalization and Lexicalization. Estudos de Gramaticalização e Lexicalização*, Munich: Lincom Europa.

Pons Rodríguez, Lola (2010), 'La historia de los marcadores discursivos en español', in Óscar Loureda Lamas and Esperanza Acín Villa (eds), *Los estudios sobre marcadores del discurso en español, hoy*, 523–615, Madrid: Arco Libros.

Poole, Geoffrey (2013), 'Interpolation, Verb-Second, and the Low Left Periphery in Old Spanish', *Iberia*, 5 (1): 69–98.

Reis, Marga (2004), 'Modals, So-Called Semi-Modals, and Grammaticalization in German'. Paper presented at Berkeley Germanic Linguistics Roundtable.

Rooryck, Johan (1997), 'On the Interaction between Raising and Focus in Sentential Complementation', *Studia Linguistica*, 51 (1): 1–49.

Rooryck, Johan (2000), *Configurations of Sentential Complementation: Perspectives from Romance Languages*, Routledge: London.

Ruwet, Nicolas (1972), *Théorie Syntaxique et Syntaxe du Français*, Paris: Éditions du Seuil.

Ruwet, Nicolas (1983), 'Montée et Contrôle. Une Question à Revoir', *Revue Romane*, 24: 17–37.

Timberlake, Alan (1977), 'Reanalysis and Actualization in Syntactic Change', In Charles N. Li (ed), *Mechanisms of Syntactic Change*, 141–77, Austin: University of Texas Press.

Traugott, Elizabeth C. (1993), 'The Conflict Promises to Erupt into War', *Proceedings of the Nineteenth Annual Meeting of the Berkeley Linguistics Society*, 348–58.

Traugott, Elizabeth C. (1997), 'Subjectification and the Development of Epistemic Meaning: The Case of *Promise* and *Threaten*', in Toril Swan and Olaf Jansen Westvik (eds), *Modality in Germanic Languages*, 185–210, Berlin: De Gruyter Mouton.

Traugott, Elizabeth C. and Richard B. Dasher (2002), *Regularity in Semantic Change*, Cambridge: Cambridge University Press.

Van de Velde, Freek, Hendrik De Smet and Lobke Ghesquière (2013), 'On Multiple Source Constructions in Language Change', *Studies in Language*, 37: 473–89.

van Kemenade, Ans and Bettelou Los (2006), 'Discourse Adverbs and Clausal Syntax in Old and Middle English', in Ans van Kemenade and Bettelou Los (eds), *The Handbook of the History of English*, 224–48, Oxford: Blackwell.

Vázquez-Laslop, María Eugenia (2001), 'Epistemic *Prometer* and Full Deontic Modal Verbs', *Belgian Journal of Linguistics*, 14: 207–41.

Verhagen, Arie (1995), 'Subjectification, Syntax, and Communication', in Dieter Stein and Susan Wright (eds), *Subjectivity and Subjectivisation in Language*, 103–28, Cambridge: Cambridge University Press.

Verhagen, Arie (1996), 'Sequential Conceptualization and Linear Order', in Eugene H. Casad (ed), *Cognitive Linguistics in the Redwoods: The Expansion of a New Paradigm in Linguistics*, 793–817, Berlin: De Gruyter Mouton.

Verhagen, Arie (2000), '"The Girl that Promised to Become Something": An Exploration into Diachronic Subjectification in Dutch', in Thomas F. Shannon and Johan P. Snapper (eds), *The Berkeley Conference on Dutch Linguistics 1997: The Dutch Language at the Millennium*, 197–208, Lanham MD: University Press of America.

Vliegen, Maurice (2006), 'The Relation between Lexical and Epistemic Readings: The Equivalents of *Promise* and *Threaten* in Dutch and German', in Bert Cornillie and Nicole Delbecque (eds), *Topics in Subjectification and Modalization*, 73–95, Amsterdam: Benjamins.

7

Grammaticalizing Adverbs of English: The Case of *still*

Diana M. Lewis

Aix Marseille University / Laboratoire Parole et Langage

1. Introduction

A particularity of the Present-day English (PDE) adverb is its heterogeneity: adverbs attach to different constituent types, instantiate a wide range of meaning types and span the traditional lexis-grammar divide. In English three main sorts of adverb are traditionally identified according to the constituent modified: 'sentence adverbs', i.e. those that modify the sentence, 'VP adverbs', i.e. those that modify the verb phrase, and 'degree adverbs', i.e. those that modify adjectives or other adverbs. Since Middle English, the type and token frequency of sentence adverbs has increased remarkably (Swan 1988a, 1988b). This has occurred largely through scope expansion of existing adverbs, which have undergone syntactic and semantic re-orientation, resulting *inter alia* in an adverbialization of speaker comment (Swan 1988a: 16). This adverbialization can be seen as one facet of a wider phenomenon of information 'compression' (Biber and Clark 2002: 62–3) or 'densification', especially in written English, but also in spoken language (Leech et al. 2009: 219). At the same time it exemplifies a semantic process of subjectification.[1]

This chapter examines recent functional splits in the English lexeme *still* which have resulted in counter-expectational, concessive-connective, discourse-marking and evaluative uses emerging alongside the older spatial and temporal ones. The aim is to adopt a prospective rather than a retrospective view of the expression, tracing its evolution to compare the ways in which the splits emerged, and to investigate whether and how position, scope and meaning become correlated. The question is also addressed of whether there is evidence that the different polysemies emerge by qualitatively different mechanisms.

Section 2 briefly discusses the background to changes in the English sentence adverb in the Modern English period. This is followed in Section 3 by a look at PDE *still* and in Section 4 by a review of its history. Section 5 sets the findings in the context of current debates on modelling and categorizing these types of change. Section 6 provides a summary and conclusion.

2. The development of English sentence adverbs

Nevalainen (2004: 2) describes adverbs as being a 'weakly codified area in English grammar'. In fact, the English adverb has long been considered an unsatisfactory category (Michael 1970; McCawley 1983), because it encompasses several different syntactic distributions and its boundaries and defining features are vague. The relations between the adverb and what it modifies – verb, verb phrase, adjective, adverb, clause, sentence – are varied and often vague too. Formally, the adverb spans long-established forms conserved by frequency, adverbs derived regularly via *-ly* suffixing and lexicalizations (in the sense of univerbation and loss of compositionality) of phrasal adverbials.

The adverb occupies three main syntactic positions with respect to its host unit: initial, medial (i.e., pre-verbal/post-auxiliary in clauses, including post-*be*) and final. Both sentence adverbs (SAdvs) and VP adverbs (VPAdvs) occur in all three positions, with different syntactic and semantic scopes. Many forms function as both SAdv and VPAdv. They are therefore often distinguished by their semantics rather than by their surface distribution. As Croft points out, 'distributional analysis must take into consideration distributional facts RELATIVE TO THE MEANING of the words and constructions being analysed, or else important linguistic generalizations will be missed' (2001: 73; emphasis in the original). Sentence adverbs thus identified are assumed to be in underlying 'peripheral' or parenthetical syntactic positions. It is therefore convenient to distinguish initial position from left-peripheral position, medial position from parenthetical position and final position from right-peripheral position (see Section 3). However, the precise scope (syntactic or semantic) of a given occurrence of an adverb, and whether it is peripheral or parenthetical or not, can be hard to determine.

In the recent evolution of English adverbs, perhaps the most striking phenomenon has been the great expansion of sentence adverbs over the Late Middle and Early Modern English periods, as highlighted by Swan (1988a, 1991). English has seen successive rises in type frequency of three kinds of sentence adverb (Swan 1988a). First, modal adverbs such as *plainly* and *clearly*, following on from Old English, where similar 'truth intensifiers' were commonplace. After modal adverbs came evaluative adverbs such as *curiously*, subject-oriented adverbs such as *wisely*[2] and, most recently of all, speech-act adverbs such as *frankly*. The similar rise in the number of sentence adverbs marking coherence relations is documented by Lenker (2010). Lenker terms these 'adverbial connectors' and shows that many of those which arose in the early part of the Early Modern English period have been lost, while others emerged only in Late Modern English.

Many studies have addressed the tendency for adverbs to undergo scope increase by successive reanalyses of the type VPAdv > SAdv > connective and/or discourse marker, both in English (e.g., Traugott and Dasher 2002; Brinton 2006) and other languages (e.g., Ramat and Ricca 1998; Fanego 2010). There is little agreement on terminology in this domain, in particular on whether discourse connectives and discourse markers are co-terminous or distinct, or whether connectives are a sub-set of markers. Here we will adopt the third terminological option, whereby 'discourse marker' is a broad term including interpersonal markers, such as *you know*, and expressions of coherence relations (or rhetorical relations), such as *then* or *even so*.

The present study focuses on the evolution of one adverb, *still*, and on whether and how position, scope and meaning become correlated. A further question is whether the emergence of a wide-scope, discourse-marking function of the adverb is qualitatively different from the emergence of other uses. These questions are addressed through a case study, based on historical corpus data, of the evolution[3] and expansion of *still* over the Modern English period.[4]

3. *Still* in Present-day English

Still is the seventeenth most frequent adverb in the British National Corpus at around 718 per million words, just ahead of *even* (figures from Leech, Rayson and Wilson 2001). There is little difference in the frequencies between the spoken (739 pmw) and written (715 pmw) parts of the corpus. The form *still* occurs today as verb, noun, adjective and adverb. It retains much of the sense of 'quiet' and 'motionless' it had in Old English, as well as occurring in a range of ossified expressions such as *the still of the night*, *still-born* and so on. Adverbial *still* evolved into a range of uses, some of which have now fallen into obsolescence or occur only dialectally.

Previous studies of *still* have sought, from within different linguistic frameworks, to account for the semantic range of this adverb in PDE (e.g., König and Traugott 1982; Michaelis 1993, 1996; Ippolito 2004; Crupi 2006; Bell 2010). Most concur that the various PDE adverbial uses are closely linked and can be said to share a common semantic schema that is scalar. Michaelis (1993), for instance, identifies three related 'senses' for adverbial *still*, which she terms 'temporal', 'marginality' (at the margin of a graded category) and 'adversative' (concessive). These are exemplified in (1a), (1c) and (1d), respectively.

(1)   a. The cat is *still* asleep. [temporal, VPAdv]
    b. A university novel is a tricky thing; an Oxford novel *still* trickier [comparative, AdjAdv] (*The Guardian* newspaper, 30/03/2012)
    c. I think south east Asia *still* counts as Asia [temporal / marginal, VPAdv] (*The Guardian* newspaper, 15/05/2014)
    d. My smart school *still* failed me [concessive-connective, SAdv] (*The Guardian* newspaper, 11/09/2004)
    e. I shall have to stop playing golf again … *still* it hasn't stopped me yet [contrastive-concessive connective, SAdv] (BNC KC1)
    f. I don't know what they've done to it to make it spread *but still* [contrastive-evaluative, SAdv] (BNC KBW)
    g. A: 'd'ya think she'll go back to work Kevin?' …
        B: 'no .. I don't think she will to be honest with you'
        A: <sigh>
        B: '*still*'
        A: 'I don't blame her' [evaluative, interjection] (BNC KBC)

The examples in (1) show the range of uses that are common in present-day standard British English. They reflect a typically polysemous lexeme, where occurrences cluster in context types and clear senses can be distinguished, but where outliers make it hard to draw neat boundaries between them. Within the very broad category of adverb, different types occur. The examples in (1) include VP-adverb (VPAdv), adjective-modifying adverb (AdjAdv), sentence adverb (SAdv) and interjection. As outlined in Section 2, SAdv *still* may occur pre-verbally, as in (1d), at left periphery (LP), as in (1e), or as part of the expression *but still*, at right periphery (RP), as in (1f).[5]

(1a) is temporal and the predicate can be glossed as 'continues to sleep'. There is usually an implicature of counter-expectation (the situation lasts longer than expected). The addition of *still* to a clause with a stative or durative predicate serves to emphasise the (unexpectedly long) duration. (1b) is the most clearly scalar example: it requires a gradable predicate (*tricky* in the example). *Still* introduces a higher stretch of scale with regard to some reference point that is already high: a university novel is already high on the scale of difficulty of novel-writing. (1c) is ambiguous between a temporal reading ('continues to count; i.e., has not been changed') and a far more likely marginal-concessive reading ('only just counts / counts despite being peripheral'). (1d) is concessive and counter-expectational[6], as in '[smart schools are not expected to fail their pupils]; despite its being smart, my school failed me'. In (1e) *still* is concessive, marks a contrast (cf., *on the other hand*, *however*, *but*) and at the same time implies speaker's positive evaluation of the idea in its scope: it expresses that being able to continue to play golf produces positive affect. The *but still* of (1f) provides a retrospective speaker comment signalling that the unfavourable situation just expressed is bearable or can be disregarded (cf., *never mind*). So here again *still* involves counter-expectation. There may be an incipient lexicalization ([but] [still] > [but still]). An alternative analysis would be that *but still* is a stand-alone fragment like that in (1g), although there is no pause before it. Finally, (1g) illustrates stand-alone *still* used (very much in the sense of (1f)) to mitigate any negative evaluation of the previous idea by signalling that it is less troubling than might be thought. In (1f) and (1g), then, *still* is becoming intersubjective, bordering on a hedging or politeness function. We suggest that it would be misleading to conceive of the 'uses' of (1e–g) as discrete. Rather, they form a cline of expression of speaker attitude (weakly positive evaluation).

As outlined above, the main types of adverbial *still* in PDE all involve counter-expectation of some sort. We therefore follow Michaelis (1993) in positing that the various uses of *still* share a common schema of counter-expectation. According to Michaelis (1993: 196), each sense of *still* 'involves a particular form of expectation contravention', so that *still* 'has a modal component: it evokes an 'expected outcome' and is scalar. *Still* marks an event or situation as being maintained beyond expectation, on some scale such as time, as in (1b), or affect, as in (1f). While we argue for this common schema across all the different uses, there are no grounds for assuming that any one sense is 'core', or that the earliest sense or the most 'literal' sense is somehow 'basic' in the speaker's lexicon. Moreover, a common schema across members of a polysemous set such as *still* is unlikely to be sufficiently specific to differentiate it from other lexemes.

Michaelis (1996: 181) further argues that '[t]he synchronic meaning links forged . . . will bear no direct relation to any trajectory of semantic change. In the present case,

I argue, the modern speaker has reconciled the senses of *still* by extracting a set of accidental yet salient semantic commonalities from these senses. The resultant generalization provides a schematic semantic structure under whose rubric all of the senses are grouped'. Whether or not speakers in fact make such a generalization, we agree that there is no link between the PDE speaker's representation of *still* and the historical evolution of the lexeme. The abstract schema, then, is posited to represent a potentially perceived commonality across PDE uses of the lexeme. From the diachronic point of view, however, the perception of a common feature may provide a clue to the cognitive mechanisms behind the semantic evolution.

Lexical adverbs like *still* can typically occur in the following positions with respect to the clause: pre-verbal (before the verb, between the auxiliary and the verb, or after the verb *be*), post-verbal (immediately after the verb), clause-final (at the end of the nuclear clause), clause-initial, at left periphery, and at right periphery. *Still* occurs regularly in the data in all but one of these positions: it does not occur at the right periphery (other than in the phrase *but still*), but it does occur, as seen in (1g), as a stand-alone comment on the previous idea.

The next section traces the emergence of the polysemies of *still* over the Modern English period.

4. *Still* over the Modern English period

4.1. Expansion of *still*

Figure 7.1 shows the change in token frequency of *still* over the Modern English period. The data on which Figure 7.1 is based are described in the Appendix. They were extracted from a historical corpus of British English containing informal texts (such as drama, letters and journals) that can be assumed to be as close as we can get to the spoken language of the day. The examples in this section, unless otherwise stated, are

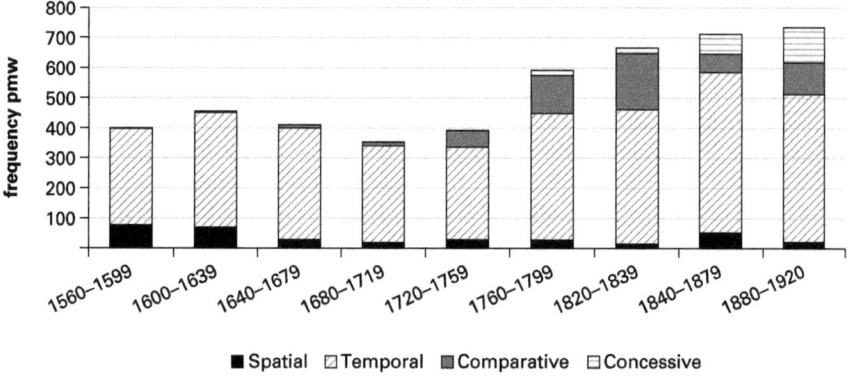

Figure 7.1 Frequency of *still* over the Modern English period.

taken from this corpus, on which the description of the semantic and syntactic changes over Modern English is based. PDE examples are taken from the British National Corpus and from newspaper articles.

It can be seen from Figure 7.1 that, after a relatively stable period during which there may be small fluctuations in the proportions of spatial and temporal uses, the token frequency of *still* starts to climb in the early nineteenth century. An increase in the frequency of comparative *still* occurs first, followed by the appearance and gradual increase of concessive *still*.

From a spatial meaning that dates back to Old English, *still* extended to temporal meaning in durative contexts. The temporal sense itself seems to have expanded to a spectrum of meaning to include the notions of 'continuously', 'constantly', 'always', 'ever'. In our data, the comparative use, which develops out of the temporal 'ever' sense, is seen to increase and then fall off, its peak being in the early nineteenth century. The concessive use emerges from the temporal one by the end of the eighteenth century and increases in frequency over the nineteenth century. The picture is largely one of successive extension of meaning and scope. The most recent developments are the left peripheral and isolate 'discourse-marking' expressions, which can be characterized as extensions of the concessive function.

We will now consider the evolution of *still* from the semantic and syntactic points of view. The method adopted in the semantic categorization is to avoid retrospective over-interpretation of the target item, by assuming that a new reading has semanticized only where the older reading no longer makes sense (cf., Heine's 2002 'switch context' and Diewald's 2002 'isolating context'). Semanticized connective senses often emerge only after long periods of collocation with an existing connective and/or with a particular rhetorical pattern (Lewis 2014b).

The semantic expansion in the adverbial use of *still* can be broadly represented as (2):

(2) spatial > temporal > counter-expectational > contrastive-concessive > evaluative

Figure 7.2 sketches the development of *still* over the Modern English period. *Still* is an interesting case to study because, perhaps due in part to its high frequency, it has continued to give rise to new polysemies while retaining most of its older range of senses.

The evolution overall, from space towards time and then to expectation and contrast, represents a typical shift from the physical, spatial domain towards more abstract senses; from objective towards more subjective, speaker-attitudinal meanings. There is also a shift from the relatively open class category of temporal adverb towards the more restricted class category of connectives. This semantic abstraction (or 'bleaching') and decategorialization are typical of grammaticalizing expressions.

4.2. From spatial to temporal

The emergence of temporal *still* from spatial *still* dates back to Middle English. What we term here for convenience the spatial use of *still* is defined by the *Oxford English*

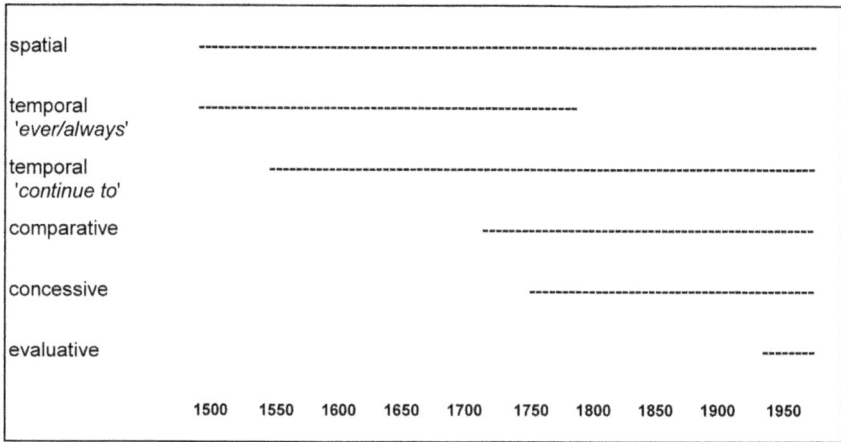

Figure 7.2 Evolution of *still.*

Dictionary as 'at rest; motionless' (OED, s.v. *still* adv. 2). The link between the spatial and temporal notions is clear: it is durative situations and events that can be characterized as motionless. It is a natural inference from 'without motion' to 'without change'. *Still* naturally collocates with stative verbs: in the Paston letters of the late fifteenth century, for instance, the most common verbs with *still* are *be, keep* and *abide*. Commonly found verbs in the sixteenth century are *continue, endure, have, hold, last, lie, maintain, remain, stand* and *tarry*.

By the fourteenth century at least, *still* has purely temporal uses where a spatial interpretation no longer makes sense. Spatial > temporal is, of course, a very typical pathway of semantic change (Heine and Kuteva 2002; Traugott and Dasher 2002). The 'transition' is typically long. In the Early Modern English data, occurrences of *still* with verbs of position can frequently be read as spatial with a temporal implicature, as in (3). There is no ambiguity; rather, the data suggest that both senses obtain, with what Heine and Kuteva (2002: 11) describe as 'conceptual shift' in process.

(3)   stode *still,* and went not away (1560)

With stative verbs expressing situations and states of affairs, there is a gradual shift of meaning from stillness and quietude towards the sense of continuity, of an unchanging situation, both durative, as in (4) ('always'), and iterative, as in (5).

(4)   a. but fooles will be fooles *styll* (*c.* 1575)
       b. . . . is the ready way to goe to Rye? Yes syr: Keepe *still* on the right hand (1586)
       c. to be *still* his drudge while he prowles and purloynes all that I haue (*c.* 1595)
(5)   a. Fie, fie, neuer out of the kitchin, *Still* broyling by the fire. (1602)
       b. He hath beene mooved by dyvers to appeale further, but I have *styll* dyswaded hym from ytt (1623)

This temporal sense of *still* meaning 'always', 'ever', 'constantly' or 'every time' falls into obsolescence by Late Modern English, a semantic narrowing. *Still* develops the more aspectual sense of 'continue to V', where the verb refers to a state or situation. But there is a vagueness across the 'ever' and the 'continue to' senses; the shift is very gradual and for many occurrences both senses can be assumed.

We turn now to the positions occupied by *still*. Overall the diachronic order in which positions are commonly found is shown in (6):

(6)   post-verbal and clause-final > pre-verbal > clause-initial > left-periphery > isolate

The fifteenth-century data show *still* overwhelmingly occurring either immediately after the verb, as in (7a, c), often followed by a prepositional phrase of place, or clause-finally, as in (7b, d).

(7)   a.   I thynke best that they *be styll* wyth yow tyll that I speke wyth yow my-selff (1490s)
      b.   schuld ryde to my lady of Norffolk and *be* wyth hyr *stylle* tyl we haff other tydyngys (1490s)
      c.   and there-fore I *kept stylle* the bestys (1490s)
      d.   that ye your-self *kepe* the goodys *stylle* (1490s)

So-called 'adverb-preposing', whereby the default relative positions of the simplex adverb and the verb changed from verb-adverb to adverb-verb, was consolidating in the late sixteenth century (Breivik and Swan 1994; Rissanen 1999: 268–9). With auxiliary verbs and the copula *be*, however, the order auxiliary–adverb remained. The change to adverb-verb is apparent in the data for *still*. Of the 103 occurrences in the data for 1560–1600 that occur with a full verb, 55/103 (53 per cent) are pre-verb (8a) and 48/103 (47 per cent) are post-verb (8b).

(8)   a.   Yet Hermia *still* loves you (*c.* 1595)
      b.   I frown upon him yet he loves me *still* (*c.* 1595)

The data for the seventeenth century show increasing pre-verbal position amid a good deal of variability (9).

(9)   The sicknes in these parts, thanks be to God, is well abated, though it lurketh *still* in some of our quarters. For the maintenance of those that have been and are *still* infected, wee have been put to lay a sesse upon the countrey, so small were the contributions of the severall parishes throughout all my Diocess, but I have now good hope that ... I shall be able to spare 50=li=. to be sent unto my Lord of London towards the help of those that are infected *still* in that city. (1665)

In PDE, it is the shorter and more frequent manner, time and modal adverbs, like *still*, that are commonly pre-verbal (Quirk et al. 1985: 565–6). Pre-verbal position may carry less informational salience than post-verbal position, but there is no evidence of semantic change correlating with the positional shift over the late sixteenth-century period. The random variation seen in (9) is typical of such a change, before the word order settles into predominantly [aux] – adv – V order, but here it must be taken in the context of the broader word-order change affecting English adverbs. In PDE, the spatial adjective and the aspectual adverb are largely distinguished by word order (*stay still* vs. *still stay*), though not entirely, as final position for the adverb has not yet become obsolete.

4.3. From temporal to comparative

It is the now obsolete sense of 'ever, each time' that develops into the comparative use which is still current today (now somewhat old-fashioned but common in formal language). The earliest example in the data of *still* in a comparative context is (10).

(10) spoonefull by spoonefull: bitterer and bitterer *still* (1599)

From collocation with degree and quantifying expressions – *still more*, 'ever more', as in (11) – there is an extension to degree. The completion of this extension becomes evident where duration no longer figures, as in (12), where the sense is one of degree only.

(11) You do not consider, Lucy, that this way is much more secure and easie, than by injurious Language to exasperate him *still* more, and give occasion of a lasting Quarrel for Life. (*c*. 1696)
(12) Close to this is a *still* more elegant and beautiful monument (1765)

By the mid-eighteenth century the usage of *still* as reinforcing a comparison has already developed. Again, no correlation appears in the data between the position and the sense. And in PDE, degree *still* continues to occur both before (13a) and after (13b) the comparative adjective, depending on the informational salience.

(13) a. So … you, you think there were other facilities arose around about the same time which made the work environment *still* more er *still* better if you like? (BNC GYV)
     b. It's not a question of how good it is to recycle several tons, it would be better *still* not to produce it. (BNC HYJ)

Overall, the reanalysis from 'further in time' to 'further in degree' is a shift from one scale to another and illustrates the scalar nature of *still*.

4.4. Counter-expectation and contrastive-concessive *still*

A different set of contexts results in a counter-expectation sense. *Still* collocates with verbs that already contain the notion of durativity, such as *remain, retain, keep, abide, dwell, last, lie, tarry, continue, dally, endure* and *harp after*. In these contexts *still* can serve to reinforce the durative notion of the verb where the duration of the state of affairs is unexpected, as in (14).

> (14) a. he taryed *still* tyll it was nyght (1565)
>   b. I did within these six days see smoke *still* remaining of the late fire in the City. (1666)

The counter-expectational sense may start, then, as an implicature or an extension of the durative sense. The presence of *still* indicates that the duration is unexpected (14a), but it is a small step from there to inferring that the event itself is unexpected (14b), as the quasi-aspectual *still* and the verb it modifies draw conceptually closer together.

At the same time, *still* gains contrastive implicatures from contrastive contexts. Expression of the situation that renders the duration unexpected results in a contrastive context: two propositions linked by a coherence relation of incongruence or potential incompatibility. Such contexts open up the probability of an extension from counter-expectation to contrast (contrastive concession in this case). This type of contrastive context is illustrated in the examples in (15), where *still* makes sense as 'continue to', but where there is clearly a concessive situation, there being a degree of incompatibility between the two ideas in each case.

> (15) a. A: 'I told him, I lik'd not this Doing, it would not have good end'
>   B: 'Why did you then *still* follow? Why left you him not?' (1571)
>   b. when I speake so faire: wilt *stil* say me nay (1575)
>   c. 'James...I pray yow to leave such talke'. And *still* the said James contynewed in his raidge, bragging and swerynge (c. 1573)

The evolution of *yet* is similar to that of *still*, but earlier, *yet* being already contrastive in Middle English, from the late thirteenth century. *Yet* often occurs in a correlative construction, as in (16a), with *although*. Collocation with *yet* (16b, c) and with contrastive-concessive constructions (17) strengthens the contrastivity of *still*.

> (16) a. *although* our merchantes maie have traffique thither, *yet* he will keape *still* a newtralitie (1586)
>   b. *Yet still* me thinkes the peace of the Church doeth not poize and prevaile with you as it should doe (1601)
>   c. so thou art alwaies asking how shal I do this and that, and *yet* thou remainest *still* ignorant (1610)

By the mid-sixteenth century, the occurrence of *still* in contrastive-concessive constructions (17) suggests a generalized concessive implicature.

> (17) a. Howsoever, doe what I can, I shalbe censur'd *still* (1628)
>   b. Nay, talk as long as you will, I shall *still* be of the same mind. (1679)

Semanticization of *still* as a purely concessive marker can be seen to have taken place once it can felicitously be used in the absence of a reasonable context for continuity, often accompanying a contrastive connective, as in (18), but also in expressions like *still and all* (now restricted to dialectal use).

(18) I am not so insensible of business but that I know you are hurried, *but still* you must admit the necessity (1773)

While the examples in (17) make sense as temporal ('I shall continue to be . . .') with a contrastive contextual implicature, it is difficult to interpret occurrences such as (18) as temporal; *still* here must be interpreted as 'nevertheless'. The inference required before the shift from temporal to concessive can occur is again an expansion: if an event continues to occur, then it continues to be true that the event occurs. That is, continuity of a modal kind is inferred from the more concrete continuity.

It has been argued that scope increase from VPAdv to SAdv is likely to occur (by 'linear modification') as the result of a shift to initial position rather than while the VPAdv is in its prototypical medial position (Fischer 2007: 274–97). However, little support for this hypothesis is found with *still*. There is little evidence, during the long period in which concessive *still* slowly semanticizes, of a correlation between its position and its interpretation. Temporal *still* is found in initial position (19), while concessive interpretations are found in both medial (20) and initial (21) positions. The presence in (21a) of *always* suggests that *still* must be concessive.

(19) I . . . have more engagements on my Hands for a week to come.
      Still my Tutor and I go on extremely well (1805)
(20) the vehicles are not quite so good as in England nor are the Horses, but both are *still* very tolerable (1802)

These observations suggest that position was not a determining factor in facilitating the semanticization of concession and thereby the increase in scope. The examples in (21) suggest wide-scope, left-peripheral *still* has become established by the mid-nineteenth century.[7]

(21) a. There are, perhaps, few places in England, where a gentleman can be comfortably lodged and boarded at a much cheaper rate. *Still* there will *always* be many incidental expenses (1832)
      b. We have had a most splendid spring beginning with February. *Still*, I have been out very seldom, being afraid of treacherous winds (1852)

Temporal *still* continues in PDE to occur in initial position and in collocation with concessive *yet* (22) (cf., example (16b)). The position functions to foreground the notion of continuity beyond expectation.

(22) Mental illness is a result of misery, *yet still* we stigmatise it (*The Guardian* newspaper, 26/02/2016)

With the modalization of *still* ('it continues to be true that . . .') and the strengthening of the connective function, there is a shift leftwards. But medial occurrences that can hardly be interpreted as temporal show that the emergence of concessive *still* did not coincide with initial position or with detachment to the left periphery. In (23) *still* can be given a temporal interpretation (*retain* is a regular collocate) and the concession can be attributed to a (generalized) conversational implicature. By contrast, in (24), where *still* occurs with a non-durative verb and in the correlative pattern *though* X, *still* Y (which starts to replace the earlier *though* X, *yet* Y), a temporal reading is most unlikely (cf., example (18)).

(23) following your advice as to its ornaments only in part. I *still* venture to retain the narrow silver round it (1790s)

(24) though I fear the reputation of my taste and judgment will suffer by the confession. I *still* must confess that I felt far more pleasure than in looking either upon Apollo or the Venus de Medicis. (1814)

Likewise, a temporal reading makes no sense in example (25).

(25) The quadrupeds, whose look, though prone, is *still* well suited to their form and condition (1837; OED)

In PDE, *still* continues to collocate with *but*, and continues to span both temporal and contrastive-concessive meanings (26).

(26) A: 'so that one there is . . . sixes into si . . . thirty-six'
B: 'I know . . . but I *still* don't get what you have to write' (BNC KBJ)

Example (26) is not ambiguous (cf., example (3)); it is a case of dual analysis (Hankamer 1977; see Section 5 below). Its meaning is both temporal and concessive in what is no doubt a reflection of the conceptual contiguity of these two notions. So, while in PDE there are plenty of clearly temporal occurrences and clearly concessive occurrences, there has by no means yet been a clear split.

The historical data on 'marginal' *still* is too sparse to draw any conclusions. But it would make sense as an extension of the epistemic-modal sense.

4.5. Evaluative *still*

In PDE, an evaluative implicature has come to be attached to concessive *still* in particular contexts. From the beginning of the twentieth century, a sub-pattern of the concessive pattern seems to emerge, in which an undesirable, negatively-evaluated event is conceded and a less adverse, mitigating event is then put forward, often containing an explicit speaker stance. Initial-position concessive *still* constructions become correlated with positive affect on the part of the speaker. This sub-pattern is exemplified in (27). This suggests that the *p still q* discourse construction is conventionalizing *q* as positively evaluated by the speaker (similar to evaluative *at least*; see Lewis 2002).

(27) it is always the dregs of the population who show their patriotism by this sort
of behaviour. *Still*, it is refreshing to see someone taking some sort of action.
(1915)

As seen above, the left peripheral position of *still* in (27) is a recent development since the mid-nineteenth century. While the difference between *Still, it is refreshing* and *It is still refreshing* may seem slight, both being concessive and connective, there is perhaps an information structural difference, so that the coherence relation of concession and the connection to the previous idea are less salient in medial position. The fact that the *still*-construction later on can be truncated to stand-alone *still* reveals that initial *still* has gradually become more peripheral, forming a separate information unit.

When *still* occurs alone, in reference to or in response to the previous idea, positive evaluation (and mitigation) is the default interpretation (28).

(28) A: 'what a shame they've missed their walk together'
B: 'yes ... *still* ... you just going back now are you?' (BNC KC9)

This 'stand-alone' *still* again is anaphoric. It is a compact information unit: in a single word, the speaker expresses the idea that although the previously expressed state of affairs is undesirable, it is not (in the speaker's view) as prejudicial or serious as might have been implied (cf., *well, never mind, anyway, not to worry* and other idiomatic forms expressing speaker attitude). It results from the ellipsis (more accurately, the non-expression) of the more positively valued idea that would have followed *still* to mitigate the previous idea. It starts as what Mulder and Thompson (2008) call a 'hanging implication', and conventionalizes to a self-contained speaker comment.

4.6. Discussion

Still in PDE is best analysed as a typical case of polysemy resulting from successive functional splits as more abstract, more grammatical uses of the item emerge. But rather than thinking of the polysemies in terms of discrete 'source' and 'target' fixed notions, and of the expression undergoing reanalyses from one to the other, it may be more accurate to think of the polysemy labels as referring to generalizations across instances that come, through repetition in usage, to cluster in semantic space. The 'semanticizations' of the new polysemies of *still* are best conceived of in terms of this type of clustering.

The history of *still* shows semantic abstraction (or 'bleaching') and subjectification (Traugott 2016: 388 suggests the term 'textual subjectification' for emergent connectives). It shows some decategorialization from the more open-class temporal adverb to the more closed-class connective. *Still* therefore exemplifies changes that are typical of grammaticalization broadly defined. Whether 'grammaticalization' refers primarily to a semantic phenomenon (increasingly grammatical meanings) or to a morphosyntactic one (increased bondedness, scope reduction or decategorialization) is largely a question of definition. The place of *still* in the wider context of differing models of language change will be further discussed in Section 5.

4.7. *Still* in the context of similar adverbs

Several other English adverbs, such as *yet, then, after all, even, anyway, surely, instead, at least* and so on, have likewise evolved a range of polysemies, from more concrete, lexical meanings towards more abstract, grammatical meanings. Such evolutions are well attested for other languages too (Spanish *aún, todavía*; French *encore* (Mosegaard Hansen 2003), *toutefois*; Italian *tuttavia* (Giacalone Ramat and Mauri 2009); see Heine and Kuteva 2002).

For *still*, the obvious comparison to be drawn in English is with *yet*, which evolved a similar pattern of polysemy some two centuries earlier and which has similarly retained older uses alongside later ones, partially retaining older word order too (König and Traugott 1982). *Still* has gradually taken over the contrastive-concessive function of *yet* in the correlative construction *although* X, *yet/still* Y. *Yet* is becoming restricted to its use as 'until now, up until a point in time', especially as a negative polarity item, and to some idiomatized constructions. Analogy with *yet* may therefore have played a role in the evolution of *still*. A comparable case of likely analogical change is the emergence of discourse-marking *in fact* (Schwenter and Traugott 2000; Lewis 2014b) along similar lines to and later than *indeed*. König and Traugott (1982: 177–8) emphasise the longevity of the temporal senses of *yet* and *indeed*: 'the core meanings we have proposed persisted for a considerable period of time (over a thousand years in the case of *yet*) and … have to a large extent constrained subsequent changes, even through several stages of grammaticalization, including the shift to nontemporal, concessive meanings'. We have rejected the notion of core meaning (Section 3), but our data too support the persistence of temporal *still* through the emergence of the concessive construction. It may have to do with the conserving effect of high frequency (Bybee and Thompson 1997; Bybee 2010: 75). Finally, the modal turn of *still*, whereby it implies the truth of the state of affairs it attaches to, is similar to the emergence of modal meanings in adverbs such as *surely, of course, after all* and *anyway*.

5. *Still* and models of language change

There has been some debate over the role of frequency in grammaticalization; in particular over whether frequency increases before or after a semantic shift and/or reanalysis takes place, and, if it increases before, whether it can be considered a cause of semantic change. Traugott (2010: 280), for example, for whom discourse markers and connectives such as concessive *still* emerge through grammaticalization, downplays the role of frequency, suggesting that 'frequency itself appears implausible as a motivation for the onset of grammaticalization'. Some studies claim to show that frequency is a direct cause of semantic change (e.g., Shibasaki 2010: 240). For Bybee (2011: 72), 'frequency or repetition is important to this process of meaning change, not because it causes it, but because only by repetition can the change be implemented'. Clearly change occurs in a particular collocation or context-type, and several grammaticalization theorists have stressed that it is not the token frequency itself, but high relative frequency that can induce a meaning change; that is, the proportion of occurrences that are in the relevant collocation or context for the new meanings (Bybee and Torres Cacoullos 2009). While many studies have centred on collocations of a grammaticalizing item with other linguistic items, cases such as temporal > concessive > evaluative *still* also involve collocation with a particular discourse structure or coherence relation. As mentioned earlier, Figure 7.1 is based on conservative estimates of when the comparative and concessive polysemies semanticize, so that no conclusions can be drawn about the order of frequency increase and the emergence of a new polysemy.

The connective and evaluative uses of *still* are typical 'discourse-marking' functions, expressing textual relations and speaker affect, respectively. Debate on the emergence of discourse markers is sometimes clouded by the instability of the terminology. This is arguably the case for the division of meaning into types. It is often claimed that the meanings expressed by discourse markers are qualitatively different from the meanings of their source expressions: markers are said to have 'pragmatic meanings' (Brinton 2006), 'procedural meaning' (Blakemore 1987; Heine 2013) or 'metacommunicative meaning' (Frank-Job 2006) as opposed to (or in addition to – Moeschler 2016) 'conceptual meaning' or 'propositional meaning'. It is not clear from the literature exactly how the different types of meaning are thought to differ cognitively. But, on the diachronic evidence of *still* and many other similar expressions, the boundary between them is unlikely to be clear-cut, but rather a question of degree. The other side of the 'meaning-type of discourse markers' coin is that some putative conceptual domains, such as coherence relations, politeness and hedging, speaker attitude, some types of modality, etc., are typically (not exclusively) expressed in English by short or idiomatized expressions that occur outside the nuclear clause. The language shows a clear preference for encoding such functions in compact constructions that are tacked on to a clause and are not 'addressable' (Boye and Harder 2007). Speaker attitude and coherence relations thus tend to be 'encapsulated', attaching directly to (and having scope over) the unit expressing the object of the attitude. In the case of *still*, this attachment is seen in both the comparative (AdjAdv) and the concessive (SAdv) uses.

There has been much debate over whether adverbial change from VP-adverb to sentence adverb and adverbial connective or discourse marker can be subsumed under the term 'grammaticalization' or should better be described as 'pragmaticalization' or as something else. This is largely a question of definitions of what counts as 'grammatical', of the role of the sentence in one's grammatical theory and especially of how the semantic/pragmatic border is drawn. This last issue seems crucial. 'Pragmaticalization' implies that the items concerned become more or wholly pragmatic. But to say that discourse markers 'have' pragmatic meaning suggests that such meaning is coded into the entry for the form in the mental lexicon. We prefer to think, in more traditional terms, of semantic meaning as the coded, conventional (including Gricean conventional implicature), non-defeasible meaning and pragmatic meaning as utterance-meaning, i.e. interpretation in the individual situation. In this perspective, all morphemes have coded (semantic) meaning, and pragmatic meaning is generated in a particular utterance on a particular occasion. The interplay between the two types of meaning thus defined plays a key role in the exemplar-based theory of language change (Bybee 2013), which offers a very plausible model of the mechanisms behind the types of gradual change attested for adverbs like *still*. On this view, the (coded) representations of *still* evolve as a function of the myriad pragmatic meanings experienced by the speaker-hearer. We avoid the term 'pragmaticalization', then, on definitional grounds to maintain the traditional semantic/pragmatic distinction. 'Grammaticalization', while not an ideal term, has the advantage of already being an umbrella term that covers a range of language change pending further evidence. A third proposal suggests that items such as connectives that operate at suprasentential level result from instantaneous 'co-optation' of a lexical item which is lifted from 'sentence grammar' and redeployed at the level of 'discourse grammar'. This is the position of Thetical Grammar (Heine, Kaltenböck and Kuteva 2011; Heine 2013; Heine, Kaltenböck, Kuteva and Long 2013), which groups at least some discourse markers and connectives with parentheticals in general. But we have seen that the data on *still* and similar adverbs such as *in fact* (Schwenter and Traugott 2000; Lewis 2014b) and *besides* (Rissanen 2004) suggest that these expressions differ from other parentheticals in that the meaning change, semantic scope expansion and extra-clausal position do not appear to occur simultaneously and suddenly. We therefore avoid the term 'co-optation' for *still* on empirical grounds.

It was suggested above (Section 4.4) that, as constructions with *still* evolve, they become subject to dual analysis by speaker-hearers for extended periods of time, during which, in the relevant contexts, the newer analysis strengthens across occurrences. The notion of dual analysis was put forward by Hankamer (1977: 603) as a means of explanation of what now might be called constructional change: 'The question of the mechanism of syntactic reanalysis – how does a language get from one analysis of a given construction to a quite different one? – is answered almost directly once we grant that the language may have both analyses at once'. In the same vein, Beckner and Bybee (2009: 31) suggest that 'the same word sequence may be characterized by multiple constituent structures', and furthermore 'that constituency may change in a gradual fashion via usage ... and that structural reanalysis need not be abrupt'. This question of abruptness is relevant to our models of scope change. It is the question posed by Fanego (2004: 19): 'when a form belonging to category X is reinterpreted as belonging to category Y, does this involve an abrupt change in the syntactic structure of the corresponding construction or is the change gradual?'. Fanego's (2004: 26) analysis of the development of the English gerund shows that reanalysis depends on 'the speakers' recognition of multiple structural analyses'; the new analyses co-existed with the old ones. This is the case for *still* too. Clearly the emergence in the speaker's representation of her language of a new form-meaning pair, such as the ability to use *still* in a non-temporal, 'mono-analysis' context, is abrupt, but it is a tiny step. Recent work in grammaticalization studies has emphasized the small-step, fine-grained nature of the shift away from the specific and lexical towards the more abstract and grammatical, and the gradual diffusion across context types. These 'micro-changes', according to Traugott and Trousdale (2010: 23–4), 'are discrete and, as conventionalizations, cognitively abrupt (in a tiny way) for individual speakers. However ... changes at the level of the community are not discrete/abrupt'. Corpus data is an inadequate, at best approximate reflection of community-wide change which progresses differently across contexts and sub-communities.

6. Conclusion

Debate on adverbial change has been somewhat hampered by a tendency to examine discourse markers separately from other evolving adverbs and to adopt a 'backwards-looking' approach which seeks the origin of particular present-day discourse markers. The focus has tended to be on the 'output' (the discourse marker, for instance), sometimes referred to as the 'target' or the 'endpoint' of a change (e.g., Diewald 2011: 373). But these metaphors can be misleading, as language is constantly evolving and its direction, rather than being determined by targets, surely 'falls out' from the mental processes of its speakers. It is these processes that are of most interest. Adopting a more 'forward-looking' perspective to internal language change may be more suggestive of the mechanisms involved than an approach that focuses on what look like an 'origin' and an 'output' when viewed retrospectively, but which are in fact ever-evolving (sometimes vanishing) patterns of use in slowly-shifting contexts.

The findings of this study of *still* suggest that peripheral position and discourse function did not develop simultaneously; rather, the discourse function develops first, by 'contagion' with contrastive and counter-expectational contexts and with adversative markers like *but, yet* and *though*. Particular contexts and collocations, including *but still* (frequent from the end of the seventeenth century, and which has arguably lexicalized in PDE, as in example (1f)), would favour the gradual emergence of a concessive reading. The data suggest reanalyses of the type [but] [still p] > [but still] [p] > [still] [p] and [although p] [yet [still q]] > [although p] [yet still] [q]] > [although p] [still q]]. The new analyses exist alongside the older ones, and alongside the dual analysis illustrated in (26).

There is evidence of structural as well as semantic persistence. For instance, the comparative use retains the final position (example (13b)) despite the overwhelming tendency for adjective-modifying adverbs to be in Adv-Adj order. Medial position, typical of the temporal adverb, remains common for the newer concessive use, in addition to the newer left periphery position. Comparable cases also show this kind of persistence. Discourse-connective *instead*, for example, typically in final position before the evolution of the discourse-connective function, retains this position in addition to the newer left-peripheral position (Lewis 2014a). It appears, then, that the existing patterning of an adverb can be resistant to analogical regularization for some time after new functions emerge.

Overall, the evolution of *still* over the Modern English period is compatible with a broad view of grammaticalization as 'extension', but not with the narrower view of grammaticalization as 'increased reduction and dependency' (Traugott 2015: 60). The form runs into a delta of related uses that are seen to be diverging towards various positions on a cline of abstraction. After a period of expansion of use, a new sense settles down as the item consolidates in one or more context types. The scope increase and subjectification of adverbs such as *still* reflect the tendency for speaker attitude to be expressed through operators: to be 'encapsulated', attaching directly to the idea that is the object of the attitude.

Each expression has its own history, which constrains its evolution. Patterns can be sought through the careful observation of shifting collocations and discourse contexts.

This is arguably best done by an approach that takes account of the polysemy as a whole. Too narrow a focus on the emergence of grammaticality or of 'discourse meanings' risks missing generalizations about language change as well as interesting differences.

Appendix: Data for *still*

Period	Source	Words	Total	n	Total	pmw
1560–1599	CED texts	208,200	352,000	89	141	401
	Other drama texts	23,000		8		
	Sermons	21,400		6		
	CEEC texts	104,500		38		
1600–1639	CED texts	213,800	359,800	88	164	456
	Other drama texts	18,000		7		
	CEEC texts	128,000		69		
1640–1679	CED texts	267,000	467,330	92	192	411
	CEEC texts	113,830		71		
	Diaries	86,500		29		
1680–1719	CED texts	304,000	463,520	86	164	354
	Newdigate texts	153,720		69		
	Diary of J. Evelyn	5,800		9		
1720–1759	CED texts	228,140	419,370	60	165	393
	CLMET-3 drama	47,507		30		
	Letters	143,722		75		
1760–1799	CLMET-3 drama	161,620	360,180	76	213	591
	CLMET-3 letters	71,000		55		
	ARCHER letters	38,660		26		
	Other letters	88,900		56		
1800–1839	CLMET-3 drama	76,350	337,650	67	225	666
	CLMET-3 letters	74,500		42		
	Other letters	186,800		116		
1840–1879	Drama	173,400	443,520	103	316	712
	CLMET-3 letters	83,820		86		
	Other letters	186,300		127		
1880–1920	CLMET-3 drama	125,400	520,730	83	383	736
	Other drama texts	117,700		55		
	Journal	11,490		14		
	CLMET-3 letters	86,240		64		
	Other letters	179,900		167		

Notes

1 By subjective is meant the 'way in which natural languages, in their structure and their normal manner of operation, provide for the locutionary agent's expression of himself and his own attitudes and beliefs' (Lyons 1982: 102; cf., Traugott 1989; Visconti 2013).
2 See also González Álvarez (1998) on subject-oriented adverbs in Early Modern English.
3 A referee objects to the use of the word 'evolution'. 'Evolution' is chosen here for the discussions of meaning change in *still* in order to avoid the telic implications that come with terms such as 'development' and to emphasize that semantic shift is ongoing and internal and a by-product of usage. The choice of term also echoes fundamental work on 'the evolution of grammar' (Bybee, Perkins and Pagliuca 1994) and 'the evolution of grammatical categories' (Heine and Kuteva 2002: 6), as well as more specific work on 'the evolution of pragmatic markers' (Brinton 2017).
4 Following the Helsinki corpus convention, we identify Early Modern English as starting around 1500 and lasting until the early eighteenth century (Kytö 1996); Late Modern English is usually dated from the early eighteenth century to the turn of the twentieth century.
5 Issues concerning the syntactic status of peripheral and parenthetical items are beyond the scope of this chapter. We fall back on the traditional division of adverbs into two syntactic categories: VP-adverbs and sentence adverbs, although the distinction is often blurred for adverbs such as *still,* and subsume left- and right-peripheral items under a broad interpretation of sentence adverbial, which may be a misnomer considering that the sentence is not the most appropriate unit of analysis for many of them.
6 Concession is often associated with counter-expectation (e.g., Rossari 2014: 237) due to the incongruity inherent in concession.
7 Punctuation in historical data cannot be used as a guide to either scope or prosody. Moreover, in spoken English, the correlation between expressions regarded as syntactically parenthetical and 'comma intonation' is weak, especially for discourse markers (e.g., Wichmann, Simon-Vandenbergen and Aijmer 2010: 36, whose data 'contradict suggestions that discourse markers tend to be prosodically separate').

Corpora

ARCHER = *A Representative Corpus of Historical English Registers* 3.2. (1990–1993/2002/2007/2010/2013/2016), originally compiled under the supervision of Douglas Biber and Edward Finegan at Northern Arizona University and University of Southern California; modified and expanded by subsequent members of a consortium of universities. Current member universities are Bamberg, Freiburg, Heidelberg, Helsinki, Lancaster, Leicester, Manchester, Michigan, Northern Arizona, Santiago de Compostela, Southern California, Trier, Uppsala, Zurich. Examples of usage taken from ARCHER were obtained under the terms of the ARCHER User Agreement.
BNC = *The British National Corpus,* version 3 (BNC XML Edition) (2007), distributed by Bodleian Libraries, University of Oxford, on behalf of the BNC Consortium. http://www.natcorp.ox.ac.uk/

CED = Kytö, Merja (Uppsala University) and Jonathan Culpeper (Lancaster University) in collaboration with Terry Walker and Dawn Archer (2006), *A Corpus of English Dialogues 1560–1760.*

CEEC = Nevalainen, Terttu, Helena Raumolin-Brunberg, Jukka Keränen, Minna Nevala, Arja Nurmi and Minna Palander-Collin (1998), *Corpus of Early English Correspondence.* Department of Modern Languages, University of Helsinki.

CLMET 3.0 = De Smet, Hendrik, Hans-Jürgen Diller and Jukka Tyrkkö (2013), *A Corpus of Late Modern English Texts (version 3.0).* Department of Linguistics, University of Leuven.

The Newdigate Newsletters, transcribed and edited by Philip Hines, Jr. (1994), Part of the ICAME Corpus Collection.

Additional historical texts (letters and drama)

References

Beckner, Clay and Joan Bybee (2009), 'A Usage-based Account of Constituency and Reanalysis', *Language Learning*, 59: 27–46.

Bell, David M. (2010), '*Nevertheless, Still* and *Yet*: Concessive Cancellative Discourse Markers', *Journal of Pragmatics*, 42 (7): 1912–27.

Biber, Douglas and Victoria Clark (2002), 'Historical Shifts in Modification Patterns with Complex Noun Phrase Structures: How Long Can You Go without a Verb?', in Teresa Fanego, María José López-Couso and Javier Pérez-Guerra (eds), *English Historical Syntax and Morphology*, 43–66, Amsterdam: Benjamins.

Blakemore, Diane (1987), *Semantic Constraints on Relevance*, Oxford: Blackwell.

Boye, Kasper and Peter Harder (2007), 'Complement-taking Predicates: Usage and Linguistic Structure', *Studies in Language*, 31 (3): 569–606.

Breivik, Leiv E. and Toril Swan (1994), 'Initial Adverbials and Word Order in English with Special Reference to the Early Modern English Period', in Dieter Kastovsky (ed), *Studies in Early Modern English*, 11–43, Berlin: De Gruyter Mouton.

Brinton, Laurel J. (2006), 'Pathways in the Development of Pragmatic Markers in English', in Ans van Kemenade and Bettelou Los (eds), *The Handbook of the History of English*, 307–34, Oxford: Blackwell.

Brinton, Laurel J. (2017), *The Evolution of Pragmatic Markers in English. Pathways of Change*, Cambridge: Cambridge University Press.

Bybee, Joan L. (2010), *Language, Usage and Cognition*, Cambridge: Cambridge University Press.

Bybee, Joan L. (2011), 'Usage-based Theory and Grammaticalization', in Heiko Narrog and Bernd Heine (eds), *The Oxford Handbook of Grammaticalization*, 69–78, Oxford: Oxford University Press.

Bybee, Joan L. (2013), 'Usage-based Theory and Exemplar Representations of Constructions', in Thomas Hoffmann and Graeme Trousdale (eds), *The Oxford Handbook of Construction Grammar*, 49–69. Oxford: Oxford University Press.

Bybee, Joan L., Revere Perkins and William Pagliuca (1994), *The Evolution of Grammar: The Grammaticalization of Tense, Aspect, and Modality in the Languages of the World*, Chicago: University of Chicago Press.

Bybee, Joan L. and Sandra A. Thompson (1997), 'Three Frequency Effects in Syntax', in Matthew L. Juge and Jeri L. Moxley (eds), *Proceedings of the Twenty-Third Annual Meeting of the Berkeley Linguistics Society: General Session and Parasession on Pragmatics and Grammatical Structure*, 378–88, Berkeley, CA: Berkeley Linguistic Society.

Bybee, Joan L. and Rena Torres Cacoullos (2009), 'The Role of Prefabs in Grammaticization: How the Particular and the General Interact in Language Change', in Roberta L. Corrigan, Edith A. Moravcsik, Hamid Ouali and Kathleen Wheatley (eds), *Formulaic Language, Vol. 1. Distribution and Historical Change*, 187–217, Amsterdam: Benjamins.

Croft, William C. (2001), *Radical Construction Grammar: Syntactic Theory in Typological Perspective*, Oxford: Oxford University Press.

Crupi, Charlene D. (2006), 'Structuring Cues of Conjunctive *Yet, But* and *Still*: A Monosemic Approach', in Joseph Davis, Radmila J. Gorup and Nancy Stern (eds), *Advances in Functional Linguistics,* 263–81, Amsterdam: Benjamins.

Diewald, Gabriele (2002), 'A Model for Relevant Types of Contexts in Grammaticalization', in Ilse Wischer and Gabriele Diewald (eds), *New Reflections on Grammaticalization*, 103–20. Amsterdam: Benjamins.

Diewald, Gabriele (2011), 'Pragmaticalization (Defined) as Grammaticalization of Discourse Functions', *Linguistics*, 49 (2): 365–90.

Fanego, Teresa (2004), 'On Reanalysis and Actualization in Syntactic Change: The Rise and Development of English Verbal Gerunds', *Diachronica*, 21 (1): 5–55.

Fanego, Teresa (2010), 'Paths in the Development of Elaborative Discourse Markers: Evidence from Spanish', in Kristin Davidse, Lieven Vandelanotte and Hubert Cuyckens (eds), *Subjectification, Intersubjectification and Grammaticalization*, 197–237, Berlin: De Gruyter Mouton.

Fischer, Olga (2007), *Morphosyntactic Change. Functional and Formal Perspectives*, Oxford: Oxford University Press.

Frank-Job, Barbara (2006), 'A Dynamic Interactional Approach to Discourse Markers', in Kerstin Fischer (ed), *Approaches to Discourse Particles*, 395–413, Amsterdam: Elsevier.

Giacalone Ramat, Anna and Caterina Mauri (2009), 'Dalla continuità temporale al contrasto: la grammaticalizzazione di tuttavia come connettivo avversativo', in Angela Ferrari (ed), *Sintassi storica e sincronia dell'italiano: subordinazione, coordinazione, giustapposizione, Vol. 1*, 449–70. Florence: Franco Cesati.

González Álvarez, Dolores (1998), 'Evaluative Subject Modifiers in Early Modern English', *Sederi*, 9: 23–38.

Hankamer, Jorge (1977), 'Multiple Analyses', in Charles N. Li (ed), *Mechanisms of Syntactic Change*, 583–607, Austin: University of Texas Press.

Heine, Bernd (2002), 'On the Role of Context in Grammaticalization', in Ilse Wischer and Gabriele Diewald (eds), *New Reflections on Grammaticalization*, 83–101, Amsterdam: Benjamins.

Heine, Bernd (2013), 'On Discourse Markers: Grammaticalization, Pragmaticalization, or Something Else?', *Linguistics*, 51 (6): 1205–47.

Heine, Bernd, Gunther Kaltenböck and Tania Kuteva (2011), 'On Thetical Grammar', *Studies in Language*, 35 (4): 852–97.

Heine, Bernd, Gunther Kaltenböck, Tania Kuteva and Haiping Long (2013), 'An Outline of Discourse Grammar', in Shannon Bischoff and Carmen Jeny (eds), *Reflections on Functionalism in Linguistics*, 175–233, Berlin: De Gruyter Mouton.

Heine, Bernd and Tania Kuteva, 2002. *World Lexicon of Grammaticalization*, Cambridge: Cambridge University Press.

Ippolito, Michela (2004), 'An Analysis of *Still*', in Robert B. Young (ed), *Proceedings of the 14th Semantics and Linguistic Theory Conference*, 127–44, Ithaca, NJ: Cornell University.

König, Ekkehard and Elizabeth C. Traugott (1982), 'Divergence and Apparent Convergence in the Development of *Yet* and *Still*', in Monica Macaulay et al. (eds), *Proceedings of the Eighth Annual Meeting of the Berkeley Linguistics Society*, 170–79, Berkeley, CA: University of California Berkeley.

Kytö, Merja (1996 [1991]), *Manual to the Diachronic Part of the Helsinki Corpus of English Texts: Coding Conventions and Lists of Source Texts*, 3rd edn, Helsinki: University of Helsinki.

Leech, Geoffrey, Marianne Hundt, Christian Mair and Nicholas Smith (2009), *Change in Contemporary English. A Grammatical Study*, Cambridge: Cambridge University Press.

Leech, Geoffrey, Paul Rayson and Andrew Wilson (2001), *Word Frequencies in Written and Spoken English: Based on the British National Corpus*, London: Longman.

Lenker, Ursula (2010), *Argument and Rhetoric. Adverbial Connectors in the History of English*, Berlin: De Gruyter Mouton.

Lewis, Diana M. (2002), 'Rhetorical Factors in Lexical-Semantic Change: The Case of *At Least*', in Javier E. Díaz Vera (ed), *A Changing World of Words: Studies in English Historical Lexicography, Lexicology and Semantics*, 525–38, Amsterdam: Rodopi.

Lewis, Diana M. (2014a), 'Word Order and the Development of Connective Markers in English', in Laure Sarda, Shirley Carter Thomas, Benjamin Fagard and Michel Charolles (eds), *Adverbials in Use. From Predicative to Discourse Functions*, 229–53, Louvain-la-Neuve: Presses Universitaires de Louvain.

Lewis, Diana M. (2014b), 'The Emergence of Discourse Connectives in Discourse Constructions', in Catherine Bolly and Liesbeth Degand (eds), *Across the Line of Speech and Writing Variation*, 33–49, Louvain-la-Neuve: Presses Universitaires de Louvain.

Lyons, John (1982), 'Deixis and Subjectivity: loquor ergo sum?', in Robert J. Jarvella and Wolfgang Klein (eds), *Speech, Place and Action: Studies in Deixis and Related Topics*, 101–24, Chichester: John Wiley.

McCawley, James D. (1983), 'The Syntax of some English Adverbs', *Chicago Linguistic Society*, 19: 262–82.

Michael, Ian (1970), *English Grammatical Categories and the Tradition to 1800*, Cambridge: Cambridge University Press.

Michaelis, Laura A. (1993), '"Continuity" within Three Scalar Models: The Polysemy of Adverbial *Still*', *Journal of Semantics*, 10: 193–237.

Michaelis, Laura A. (1996), 'Cross-world Continuity, and the Polysemy of Adverbial *Still*?', in Gilles Fauconnier and Eve Sweetser (eds), *Space, Worlds and Grammar*, 179–226, Chicago: The University of Chicago Press.

Moeschler, Jacques (2016), 'Where is Procedural Meaning Located? Evidence from Discourse Connectives and Tenses', *Lingua*, 175/176: 122–38.

Mosegaard Hansen, Maj-Britt (2003), 'From Aspectuality to Discourse Marking. The Case of French *déjà* and *encore*', in Ton van der Wouden, Ad Foolen and Piet Van de Craen (eds), *Particles. Belgian Journal of Linguistics*, 16: 23–51.

Mulder, Jean and Sandra A. Thompson (2008), 'The Grammaticization of *But* as a Final Particle in English Conversation', in Ritva Laury (ed), *Crosslinguistic Studies of Clause Combining: The Multifunctionality of Conjunction*, 179–204, Amsterdam: Benjamins.

Nevalainen, Terttu (2004), 'Three Perspectives on Grammaticalization: Lexico-grammar, Corpora and Historical Sociolinguistics', in Hans Lindqvist and Christian Mair (eds), *Corpus Approaches to Grammaticalization in English*, 1–31, Amsterdam: Benjamins.

OED = *Oxford English Dictionary Online*. http://www.oed.com

Quirk, Randolph, Sidney Greenbaum, Geoffrey Leech and Jan Svartvik (1985), *A Comprehensive Grammar of the English Language*, London: Longman.

Ramat, Paolo and Davide Ricca (1998), 'Sentence Adverbs in the Languages of Europe', in Johan van der Auwera (ed), *Adverbial Constructions in the Languages of Europe*, 187–275, Berlin: De Gruyter Mouton.

Rissanen Matti (1999), 'Syntax', in Roger Lass (ed), *The Cambridge History of the English Language, Vol. III: 1476–1776*, 187–331, Cambridge: Cambridge University Press.

Rissanen, Matti (2004), 'Grammaticalisation from Side to Side: On the Development of *Beside(s)*', in Hans Lindquist and Christian Mair (eds), *Corpus Approaches to Grammaticalization in English*, 151–70, Amsterdam: Benjamins.

Rossari, Corinne (2014), 'How does a Concessive Value Emerge?', in Chiara Ghezzi and Piera Molinelli (eds), *Discourse and Pragmatic Markers from Latin to the Romance Languages*, 237–60, Oxford: Oxford University Press.

Schwenter, Scott A. and Elizabeth C. Traugott (2000), 'Invoking Scalarity: The Development of *In Fact*', *Journal of Historical Pragmatics*, 1 (1): 7–25.

Shibasaki, Reijirou (2010), 'Frequency as a Cause of Semantic Change: With Focus on the Second Person Form *Omae* in Japanese', in An Van linden, Jean-Christophe Verstraete and Kristin Davidse (eds), *Formal Evidence in Grammaticalization Research*, 225–43, Amsterdam: Benjamins.

Swan, Toril (1988a), *Sentence Adverbials in English: A Synchronic and Diachronic Investigation*, Oslo: Novus Forlag.

Swan, Toril (1988b), 'The Development of Sentence Adverbs in English', *Studia Linguistica* 42 (1): 1–17.

Swan, Toril (1991), 'Adverbial Shifts: Evidence from Norwegian and English', in Dieter Kastovsky (ed), *Historical English Syntax*, 409–38, Berlin: De Gruyter Mouton.

Traugott, Elizabeth C. (1989), 'On the Rise of Epistemic Meanings in English: An Example of Subjectification in Semantic Change', *Language*, 65: 31–55.

Traugott, Elizabeth C. (2010), 'Grammaticalization', in Silvia Luraghi and Vit Bubenik (eds), *Continuum Companion to Historical Linguistics*, 269–83. London: Continuum Press.

Traugott, Elizabeth C. (2015), 'Toward a Coherent Account of Grammatical Constructionalization', in Jóhanna Barðdal, Elena Smirnova, Lotte Sommerer and Spike Gildea (eds), *Diachronic Construction Grammar*, 51–79, Amsterdam: Benjamins.

Traugott, Elizabeth C. (2016), 'Identifying Micro-changes: The Case of Subjectification', in Merja Kytö and Päivi Pahta (eds), *The Cambridge Handbook of English Historical Linguistics*, 376–89, Cambridge: Cambridge University Press.

Traugott, Elizabeth C. and Richard B. Dasher (2002), *Regularity in Semantic Change*, Cambridge: Cambridge University Press.

Traugott, Elizabeth C. and Graeme Trousdale (2010), 'Gradience, Gradualness and Grammaticalization: How do they Intersect?', in Elizabeth C. Traugott and Graeme Trousdale (eds), *Gradience, Gradualness and Grammaticalization*, 19–44, Amsterdam: Benjamins.

Visconti, Jacqueline (2013), 'Facets of Subjectification', *Language Sciences*, 36: 7–17.

Wichmann, Anne, Anne-Marie Simon-Vandenbergen and Karin Aijmer (2010), 'How Prosody Reflects Semantic Change: A Synchronic Case Study of *Of Course*', in Kristin Davidse, Lieven Vandelanotte and Hubert Cuyckens (eds), *Subjectification, Intersubjectification and Grammaticalization*, 103–54, Berlin: De Gruyter Mouton.

Part Two

Synchronic and Diachronic Variation

How British is Gibraltar English?[1]

Manfred Krug, Ole Schützler and Valentin Werner
University of Bamberg

1. Introduction

Gibraltar is a British Overseas Territory at the southern tip of Spain which was ceded
to Great Britain by the Treaty of Utrecht in 1713. Today, Gibraltar has a population of
approximately 30,000 and the only official language is English (Levey 2015: 66; Central
Intelligence Agency 2016). Also widely spoken are Spanish and the local Andalusian-
based Spanish variety called Llanito (or Yanito), characterized by extensive code-
switching and lexical borrowing from English (as well as from other languages and
dialects; see Kellermann 2001; Levey 2008). In this linguistic context, the present study
focuses on concepts for which a (traditionally more) British variant and a (traditionally
more) American variant coexist. More precisely, we investigate two referentially
synonymous expressions that are known, or consistently reported in standard reference
works and textbooks, to have differed in usage between British English (BrE) and
American English (AmE) in the late twentieth century (cf., e.g., Algeo 2006; Krug and
Sönning 2017 for web data). On the basis of *n* = 312 questionnaires (i.e. a sample of
roughly one per cent of the population), we investigate what linguistic choices
Gibraltarians make in cases such as *lorry* vs. *truck* or *parcel* vs. *package*. In order to
place Gibraltar with regard to the two major norm-providing varieties of English and
in order to identify patterns of variation and change, we compare questionnaire data
from Great Britain and the US.

The status of Gibraltar English (GibE) is special in a number of ways. Gibraltar has
been labelled an 'unusual British colony' (Weston 2015: 647), and attempts at linguistic
description have been characterized as suffering from a 'mismatch between its colonial
status and sociolinguistic theory' (Weston 2011: 339), for example in terms of
categorizations of GibE within models of World Englishes (such as Kachru's Concentric
Circles Model or Schneider's Dynamic Model of Postcolonial Englishes). While
Spanish-English language contact is omnipresent (Kramer 1998; Suárez-Gómez 2012:
1746–8; see also Table 8.2 below), it is clear that GibE does not epitomize what can be
considered a typical L2 variety for a number of reasons. First, the vast majority of the
current population in Gibraltar speaks English as a first language or can at least be
considered highly fluent (see www.ethnologue.com/language/eng),[2] and our own data

– with a preponderance of younger speakers – seem to reflect the age-grading identified in earlier studies (e.g., Levey 2008: 95, 2015: 53; Weston 2012: 18) in terms of an increasing bias towards English as an L1. Second, *prima facie*, it appears that the political status as British Overseas Territory should lead (as in earlier stages of other colonial contexts) to Gibraltarians perceiving 'themselves as outposts of Britain, deriving their social identity primarily from their common territory of origin and a feeling of culturally belonging there' (Schneider 2007: 37). Interestingly, however, in the sociolinguistic section of our questionnaire, 55 per cent (172/312) of the raters submitted Gibraltar as the country or region with which they identify most, while a mere 12 per cent provided either UK, Britain or England as an answer. For the majority of our raters, therefore, a strong sense of a separate local identity seems to have emerged (*pace* Kellermann 2001: 111; cf., Levey 2015: 51; Weston 2015: 676; Loureiro-Porto and Suárez-Gómez 2017: 96).

Further usage- and domain-related aspects offer important insights. As in all British Overseas Territories, English is the sole official language (and thus also used as medium of instruction; Weston 2011: 359; Levey 2015: 66). English in Gibraltar, then, is not a co-official language, as in other L2 contexts like India or Jamaica. Also, the socio-linguistic information gleaned from our questionnaire supports the view that English is not restricted to official and formal contexts: 56 per cent (175/312) of the raters belong to the category defined as 'English-dominant' based on language use at home (cf. Table 8.2); 71 per cent report to use English at home at least to the same extent as Spanish and a mere 5 per cent report to use no English at all at home (cf. also Loureiro-Porto and Suárez-Gómez 2017: 96–7).[3]

The remainder of this chapter is organized as follows: Section 2 discusses the data and questionnaire structure. Section 3 offers exploratory analyses in the form of distance matrices and identifies broad regional patterns and individual outlier informants, while Section 4 focuses on individual items and rater means. Socio-linguistic factors will be investigated in detail, and apparent-time studies reveal trends of change for individual items as well as recurrent patterns of change in progress in Gibraltar English. Our data suggest that, while Gibraltarians broadly conform in their usage to speakers of the main contact variety, BrE, younger speakers of English in Gibraltar display tendencies of Americanization and globalization in opting less consistently for (conservative) British forms than older Gibraltarians. And while older speakers of both sexes behave conservatively British to the same extent, a gender gap emerges for middle-aged and younger raters: in our Gibraltar data, it is the men who are leading in this trend towards a less rigidly British-oriented usage. Interestingly, however, we also find occasional instances of increasing Britishization for individual items, that is, more consistent usage of traditional British variants among the younger cohorts.

2. Data and questionnaire structure

The questionnaire developed at the University of Bamberg investigates morphosyntactic and lexical variation in varieties of English world-wide (see Krug and Sell 2013 for more detail). The full version takes about sixty minutes to complete and requires high levels of concentration as well as quiet environments, because 138 audio files are played (twice) and rated. For these reasons, it is conducted in educational institutions and larger groups only. The complete questionnaire elicits, *inter alia*, differences between one both medially and conceptually spoken register (a casual conversation among friends) and one semi-formal written register (an email to a former school teacher).

In this contribution, we concentrate on lexical items. In addition to material collected in larger groups and educational contexts, we use material elicited from individuals, mostly in public places (e.g., streets and parks), but also cafés, supermarkets, shops, etc. For this, the lexical part of the Bamberg Questionnaire was used (see Appendix A), which elicits the informants' personal preference in cases where there is a choice between (at least) two (near-)synonyms that are known to differ in British and American usage. For ambiguous terms, the semantic domains are specified. In the pair *lorry vs. truck*, for instance, reference to 'large motor vehicles for carrying goods by road' is made, while for the pair *parcel* vs. *package* a paraphrase 'something you send by mail' is given in the questionnaires.[4]

For each of the 68 lexical binaries[5] (see Appendix A), informants can choose one of five options, or not choose any, that is, opt out. If they choose 'I only use this expression', this translates into a score of +2 if the (more) British variant is chosen; −2 if the (more) American variant is chosen; 'I prefer this expression' translates into +1 if the (more) British variant is chosen; −1 if the (more) American variant is chosen; 'I have no preference' translates into a score of zero. If the informant ticks that he or she uses neither of the two lexical expressions, this item is left out of the calculation. In addition, informants can add brief comments or mention what they would use instead of the two options given.

Informant metadata for this questionnaire study (see Appendix A for detail) include age, gender, nationality, ethnic self-identification, parents' native languages, languages used at home while growing up as well as the informants' educational profile, their current occupation and their parents' highest qualification and (potentially last) occupation. In addition, we ask informants to provide the places of residence for their entire lifespan. In order to test what impact attitudes and identity considerations have on linguistic choices, we also ask informants to provide the region or country they identify with most.

The present study uses questionnaire data from three varieties of English: BrE, AmE and GibE. The vast majority of the data are from Gibraltar (n = 312), while BrE and AmE are represented by much smaller samples (n_{BrE} = 14; n_{AmE} = 25). The main focus of the analysis is therefore on English in Gibraltar, while the latter two varieties are treated as reference points. Data from Gibraltar were collected in 2010; the AmE and BrE data were collected in 2008 and 2010, respectively.

To control for a possible gender bias, the sample was split into male and female raters for the global apparent-time analyses. The GibE data are divided into seven age groups as shown in Table 8.1. Apart from a slight overrepresentation of male raters aged 30–39 (who account for 59 per cent of their cohort), age groups are fairly balanced by gender for raters who are twenty years old and older. The youngest age group (< 20), however, is dominated by female raters, who constitute about two thirds of their cohort,

Table 8.1 Numbers of raters by age group and gender (n_{total} = 312)

	Age group						
	<20	20–29	30–39	40–49	50–59	60–69	>69
Male	51	15	20	13	14	10	11
Female	103	15	14	16	12	8	9
NA	1						
Σ	155	30	34	29	26	18	20

which in turn is due to the fact that large numbers of questionnaires were collected in a girls' school.

For some analyses, we subdivided the GibE sample by raters' language background. The criterion applied was the raters' response to the questionnaire item 'language(s) used at home when growing up'. While alternative language-related parameters could be used (e.g., the native language of raters' mothers or fathers), we consider actual language use during the formative years of childhood and youth to be the best indicator of linguistic background. Responses to this questionnaire item can be placed on the scale shown in the left-hand column of Table 8.2. The extreme poles of this scale are exclusive use of either English (top row) or Spanish (bottom row); in addition, there are three intermediate values.

Two subdivisions can be applied based on this scale, as shown in columns two and three of Table 8.2. One method (Subdivision A) is to decide which of the two languages – English or Spanish – is the dominant one, collapsing 'English (only)' and 'mostly English, some Spanish' into a single category, for example; in this case, only the use of English and Spanish to roughly similar extents remains as an intermediate category. The alternative approach (Subdivision B) is to collapse raters into a single category if they were exposed to both languages while growing up, irrespective of whether English or Spanish was the dominant one. This results in a very large intermediate category and

Table 8.2 Categorization of raters by language background

'Language(s) used at home while growing up'	Subdivision A	Subdivision B
English (only) $n = 65$	English-dominated $n = 175$	English $n = 65$
mostly English, some Spanish $n = 110$		
English and Spanish $n = 48$	English and Spanish $n = 48$	English and Spanish $n = 230$
mostly Spanish, some English $n = 72$	Spanish-dominated $n = 89$	
Spanish (only) $n = 17$		Spanish $n = 17$

smaller groups of raters who were influenced by English or Spanish exclusively. In Section 4 we investigate which of the subdivisions charted in Table 8.2 yield significant results or prompt the most insightful interpretations.

3. Explorative data analysis

As a first step towards describing the structure of large quantitative datasets such as the present one, we rely on explorative aggregative data analysis. This is a hypothesis-generating approach that, in addition to other methods such as multidimensional scaling (MDS; see, e.g., Ruette, Ehret and Szmrecsanyi 2016), has recently proved useful in a number of linguistic studies (see, e.g., Szmrecsanyi and Wolk 2011; McMahon and Maguire 2013; Werner 2014, 2016; Wälchli and Szmrecsanyi 2014; Schützler 2015; Fuchs and Gut 2016). Its aim in the present study is to determine whether data points cluster according to the sociolinguistic variables elicited (such as variety, rater age, gender, language background, etc.), thus both establishing general patterns in the data and highlighting areas that potentially deserve more detailed investigation (e.g., through descriptive and inferential statistics commonly used for hypothesis-testing; see Section 4). At the same time, an analysis of this type may facilitate the establishment of generalized characteristic patterns based on results for individual raters (e.g., association with a reference variety, 'old' vs. 'young' raters, etc.) and may further be used as a tool to identify outliers in the data at a glance.

3.1. Methodological notes

Aggregative analysis has been described as data-driven, that is, it represents a bottom-up approach in not relying on prior assumptions on the structure and distribution of the data. It is aggregative in the sense that it represents a cumulative analysis of multidimensional data (in our case, acceptability ratings of sixty-eight lexical items by different raters from Gibraltar, the UK and the US). Aggregative analysis is a largely visual approach, where graphical representations are eventually used as a means to identify associations and structures in the data (Krug, Schützler and Werner 2016: 37–8). This approach, therefore, exploits that 'humans are very good at seeing things' (Wainer 1992: 15). In other words, the underlying rationale is that visual representations in general (Braithwaite and Goldstone 2013: 1928), and spatial representations (Vessey 1991) like the ones used for the present study in particular, facilitate the comprehension of complex relationships between multiple data points, which would be difficult to process in extended tables, for instance. In concrete terms, in our data we have to compare the values for sixty-eight lexical items across 312 raters of GibE (plus thirty-nine raters from the reference varieties BrE and AmE). It goes without saying that, with such an extended number of dimensions to compare, complexity increases beyond what the human mind can possibly handle.

　　The type of aggregative analysis we use relies on the calculation of distance matrices[6] based on the ratings for sixty-eight lexical items with non-hierarchical phenograms as visual output. We subsequently describe how to arrive at both the former and the latter (see further Krug, Schützler and Werner 2016: 38–41 for a detailed description of procedures and arguments for using non-hierarchical graphical representations).

3.2. Calculating a distance matrix

The distance matrix is calculated with *R* (R Core Team 2016) and quantifies the Euclidean distance (see Szmrecsanyi 2011: 54; Krug, Schützler and Werner 2016: 42) between any two of the 312 raters in the dataset. A spreadsheet containing the transformed raw rating values (on which see below) provides the input for the distance matrix. Note that the sixty-eight lexical items are not internally weighted and thus contribute equally to the calculation.

The computation of distance matrices relies on complete datasets, but in questionnaires there is bound to be missing data (in other words, individual raters may submit fewer than sixty-eight ratings; see Section 2). As a compensating strategy for missing values we decided to apply a method that takes into account average values (i) for the variety as a whole, (ii) for the individual item and (iii) for the individual rater. Thus, missing values are calculated as follows for GibE raters:

$$missing\ value = \frac{average\ across\ all\ raters\ (missing\ item) \times overall\ average\ of\ individual\ rater}{overall\ average\ score\ GibE}$$

These calculations rely on a transformed dataset (with the original scale from −2 to +2 changed to a scale ranging from 1 to 5), in order to avoid multiplication with zero, the potential 'neutral' rating option. Calculated values may have to be manually adjusted so that they observe the upper and lower limits of the transformed scale. This is necessary to avoid nonsensical imputed average values like 0.8 or 5.3, for instance, which would be manually adjusted to 1.0 and 5.0, respectively. Once the missing values are inserted into the spreadsheet, we are able to calculate the Spearman rank correlation between all raters in R, and then use the *dist* method (default settings; Euclidean distance) from the *stats* package to arrive at a distance matrix.

3.3. Visual output

With the help of a purpose-built *R* script called *MakeNex*,[7] we then formally adapt the emerging distance matrix (from CSV spreadsheet format) to a format readable by *SplitsTree* (Huson and Bryant 2006; splitstree.org). This program creates the visual output in the form of phenograms, using the NeighborNet algorithm, and offers different formatting and exporting options for the graphs.[8] For our purposes, we use non-hierarchical 'equal angle' representations that allow a fine-grained view of differences and potential associations between raters (see Figure 8.1). At the same time, this type of display reduces multidimensional complexity in the data, that is, the differences between all possible pairings of categories in an *n*-dimensional space, to a two-dimensional display, which is much more accessible to the human mind (see above).

Note the following (intuitive) properties of the phenograms: (i) the distance between two categories ('nodes', i.e., in our case, raters) consistently is the shortest

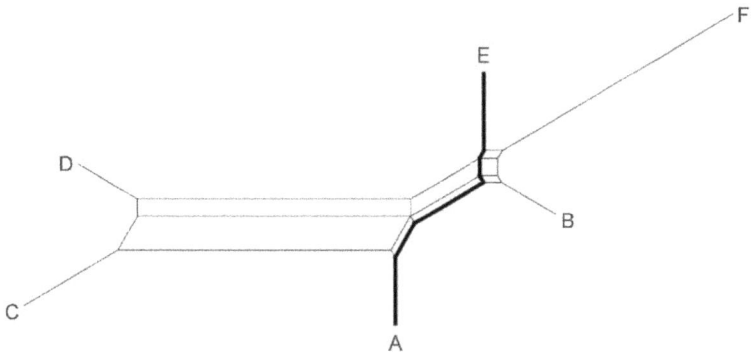

Figure 8.1 Phenogram (NeighborNet) for a simple assumed dataset with six categories (adapted from Krug, Schützler and Werner 2016: 42).

possible way along the edges of the graph and corresponds to the (numerical) Euclidean distance value as represented in the tabular distance matrix (e.g., between categories A and E, highlighted in bold in Figure 8.1); (ii) associations (in our case, in terms of similar rating patterns) exist between neighbouring nodes, for instance between categories C and D in Figure 8.1. Thus, both distances and spatial location play a part in interpreting the graphical output.

3.4. Overall perspective

The overall picture that emerges from a comparison of the ratings of the sixty-eight lexical binaries across 312 raters for GibE, our target variety, is set against the ratings provided by two sets of reference variety raters ($n = 14$ for BrE, $n = 25$ for AmE) in Figure 8.2. The strengths of visual representation are exploited in that nodes for raters receive different shapes (GibE = circles, BrE = grey squares, AmE = black squares). This will facilitate the identification of general structures and potential irregularities in the data.

Two outliers apart (which will be treated shortly), Figure 8.2 provides a clear picture in terms of variety associations. First, it emerges that raters from each variety clearly align with other raters of their variety, which implies that the notion of *variety* is not a mere theoretical sociolinguistic construct, but an empirically valid one when lexical ratings are analysed. More specifically, we find an American cluster towards the left and a British(-influenced) cluster towards the right, with a less densely populated area in the middle, which we interpret as an indication of the relative distance between the two clusters. In other words, Figure 8.2 yields a generalizable clear split (i.e. a large distance) between AmE raters, on the one hand (left), and GibE and BrE raters on the other (right). This finding will receive further support in the other quantitative analyses presented in the remainder of this study.

The robust association between GibE and BrE is plausible from a sociolinguistic and historical point of view, as BrE can be seen as the 'parent' variety of GibE, so that close historical and cultural ties are likely to be reflected in language use.[9] The graphical

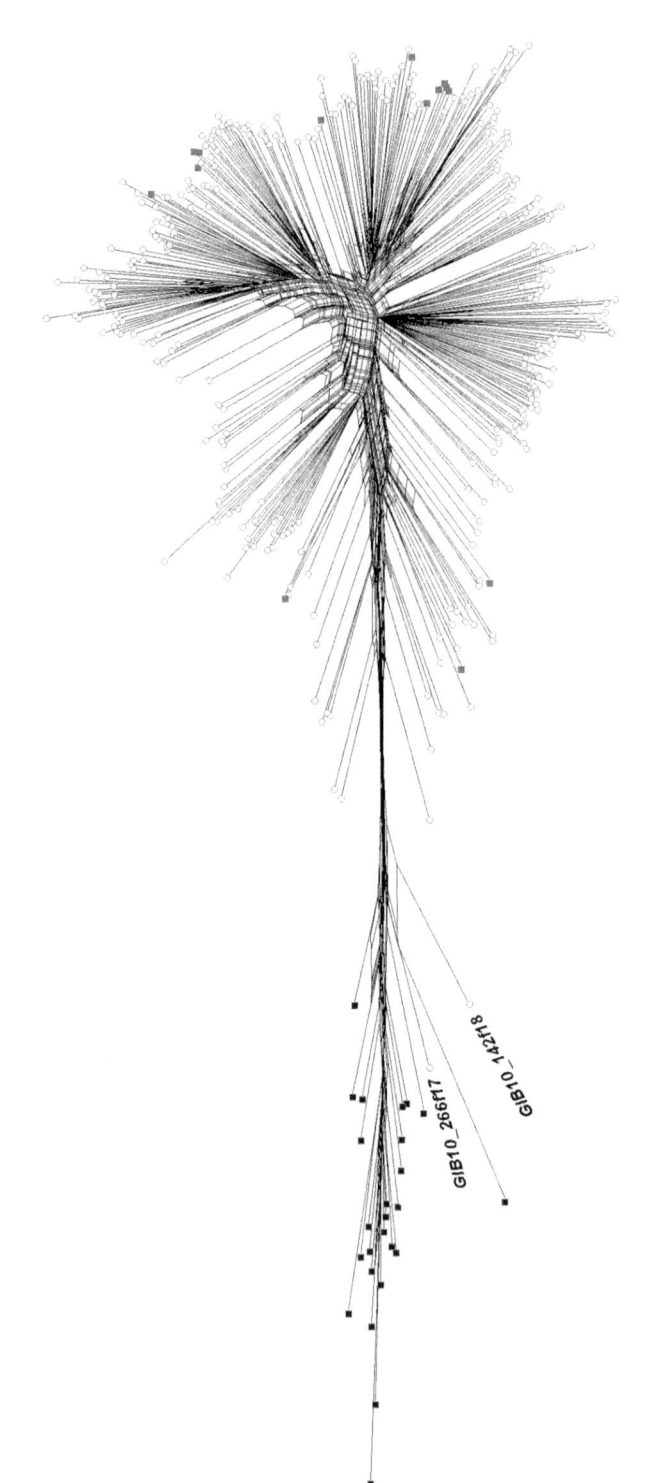

Figure 8.2 Phenogram (NeighborNet) for lexical questionnaire ratings for GibE (all data; BrE (grey squares) and AmE (black squares) as reference varieties; node labels masked).

display suggests that these ties indeed persist in terms of lexical choices when BrE and GibE are compared. An additional inference in terms of Britishness vs. Americanness that we can draw concerns colonial lag, as some of the GibE raters appear even 'more British' (or more traditionally so) than the British themselves. That is, the overall distance between some of the GibE raters to the AmE cluster is bigger than the one observable for some of the BrE raters (on which see further below and Section 4).

As described elsewhere (Krug, Schützler and Werner 2016: 43), one application of our exploratory aggregative analysis is the identification of outliers. With the help of the phenogram shown in Figure 8.2, we are in a position to identify two obvious outliers in terms of associations between GibE and AmE raters at a glance. GibE raters 266 and 142 (labelled nodes in Figure 8.2) cluster with the AmE nodes towards the left of the phenogram. Possible attempts at explaining this surprising association may profit from relating back to the sociolinguistic information elicited by the questionnaire, which, unfortunately, is incomplete for rater 266: the only possible rationale for his AmE-like rating pattern can be found in the reported Irish (hence probably Irish English) language background of the rater's father. Since we have of course no information on the vita of this rater's father, this interpretation remains speculative to a certain extent. Nor can a potentially relevant explanation be provided for rater 142, due to the fact that most sociolinguistic information is actually missing and what is provided (e.g., Spanish-English language background, three years abroad in England as a child) does not enhance our understanding.

We have to accept, then, that for these particular raters, our approach reaches its limits. We nevertheless decided to include the two outliers in the analysis as we have no indication of extended language contact with AmE. Also, due to their minimal relative weight (2/312, i.e. 0.6 per cent of the data), their diverging behaviour will have only a very minor impact on our overall results, as all remaining GibE raters cluster around a common centre (see below). The noise which these two outliers potentially introduce into further analyses (see Section 4) is therefore negligible. Other researchers, depending on their aims, might proceed differently, especially if an extended number of outliers occurs in their data (see Krug, Schützler and Werner 2016: 43–4 for discussion).

3.5. Refining the display

In Figure 8.3, following suggestions developed in Krug, Schützler and Werner (2016: 43), we add three modifications. As the representation in Figure 8.2 is close to being visually overcharged, we decided to present additionally a random sample of fifty GibE raters, which leads to greater clarity of exposition. Furthermore, we introduce nodes for a hypothetical 'average' rater for each variety (labelled AVER_* in Figure 8.3), which represents a meta-category based on average values across all relevant raters for all of the sixty-eight lexical items. Lastly, we adjust the node design for the GibE raters according to gender (female = filled circles, male = unfilled circles) as a test case for identifying potential effects of sociolinguistic factors on the clustering.

First of all, even though the hypothetical average raters for Gibraltar (AVER_GIB) and Britain (AVER_GB) display a similar distance from the American (AVER_US) average rater in Figure 8.3, it is the American and British average raters that emerge as

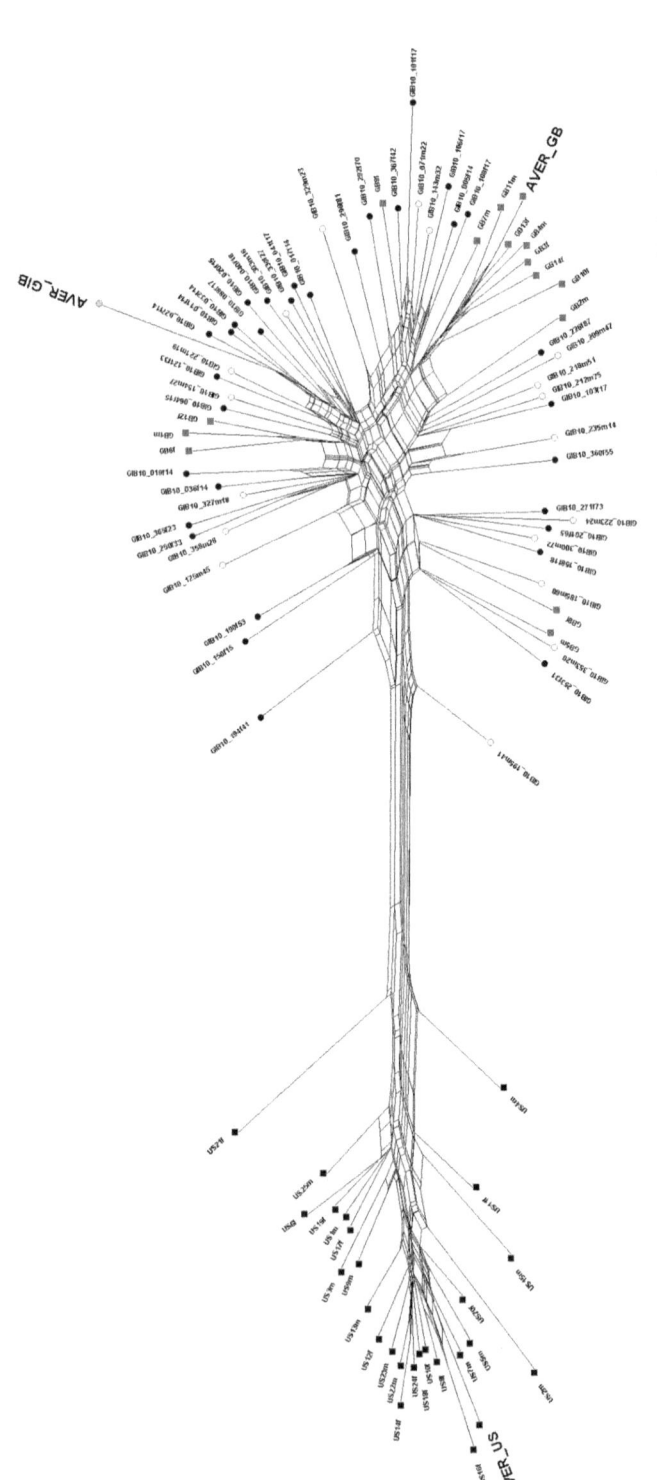

Figure 8.3 Phenogram (NeighborNet) for lexical questionnaire ratings for GibE (sampled data; female = filled circles, male = unfilled circles; BrE (grey squares) and AmE (black squares) as reference varieties). [Node labels appear in the format Variety(Year)_RaterGender(Age), e.g., GIB10_253f31]

poles in the dataset, as they exhibit the maximal distance among the regional averages. AVER_GIB and the majority of GibE raters lie somewhere between these poles, although a few GibE raters are even more distant from AVER_US than AVER_GB is. This result is in line with our earlier hypothesis that 'the average L2 user will figure between the major poles of the average BrE and AmE language users [so that] in graphical representations of large and varied datasets, L2 varieties will typically be found in the space *between* BrE and AmE' (Krug, Schützler and Werner 2016: 45; emphasis added). The hypothesis that (raters of) L2 varieties are influenced by linguistic contact with both BrE and AmE (i.e. one form of linguistic globalization) can therefore be extended to the postcolonial language-contact scenario investigated in the present dataset.

In what follows, we will continue to integrate our present findings into the fourfold typology of linguistic globalization established in Krug, Schützler and Werner (2016: 55), which we repeat here for convenience:

1. Convergence (understood as 'a process of increased or increasing similarity') on (former) British norms.[10]
2. Convergence on (former) American norms.
3. Convergence on free variation between (former) British and American norms.
4. Convergence on a norm that is neither a former (standard) British nor a former (standard) American norm, but potentially originates in a low-prestige dialect or L2 variety.

It has been argued that for socio-cultural reasons English in Gibraltar is used as a 'powerful means of expressing affiliation to Britain and proving an ethnic identity separate from Spain' (Kellermann 2001: 412). On a related note, Kellermann (2001: 414) diagnoses a continuing stigmatization of deviations from the exonormative BrE model. Such input- and usage-related aspects, ultimately traceable to issues of linguistic identity, at least partly serve to explain the very close association between GibE and BrE in our dataset. The same applies to the fact that some GibE raters exceed the 'Britishness' values of the average BrE rater, while most show a globalizing tendency that places them somewhere between the British and American poles in our dataset. On a more general note, our findings suggest that individual (post-)colonial scenarios and their potential linguistic consequences (cf. Schneider 2007) have to be considered when attempting an interpretation of empirical data in terms of nativizing or globalizing tendencies. We will explore this further in Section 4 when we treat individual items. In the present case, the late, comparatively slow and as yet unfinished decolonization of Gibraltar (Kellermann 2001: 140) seems to have led to a persisting linguistic orientation towards BrE, which in all likelihood is motivated essentially by political circumstances (Weston 2011: 365, 2015; Levey 2015: 51, 57).

A secondary finding that emerges from the display in Figure 8.3 relates to the issue of gender as an often-described sociolinguistic factor. The representation in Figure 8.3, with male nodes in unfilled circles and female nodes infilled circles, yields no clear pattern or clustering. This analysis suggests that gender is not an immediately obvious factor in the present study, which may appear surprising at first sight. Note that we arrive at similarly indistinct displays if we (re-)shape the nodes of the GibE raters for language background or age. (We refrain from displaying such non-results here.) In our more fine-grained regression analysis in the following sections, however, we will see that speakers under seventy diverge subtly and that our male raters show stronger tendencies than our female raters of the second globalization type sketched above, in moving slightly away from rigidly British linguistic behaviour into the direction of American behaviour.

4. Rater means, individual items and sociolinguistic factors

This part of the study first re-inspects some issues discussed in the context of the explorative analysis from a slightly different angle, using mean values instead of distance metrics. On this basis, a more fine-grained analysis of individual lexical binaries can be presented. We believe that in complex datasets like the one we are looking at, both approaches – the one presented above (hypothesis-generating) and the one shown in this section (hypothesis-testing) – are not only legitimate but necessary: using explorative aggregative analyses in combination with approaches that are more transparently grounded in the underlying data may reveal different aspects of variation and change. Therefore, the following analyses will refer back to what has been stated above, where appropriate.

4.1. Methodological notes

In what follows, two methods of quantification need to be understood and kept distinct: (i) rater means, which are average values calculated for individual raters from all sixty-eight ratings and (ii) item means, which are average values calculated for individual lexical items across all raters in the respective sociolinguistic subgroup. Whenever item means are plotted, their number will invariably be sixty-eight, while the number of raters varies depending on the subsample inspected. Results based on item means will normally not be in conflict with results based on rater means – rather, both approaches highlight somewhat different aspects of the same dataset. Therefore, in some plots they will be shown in combination. As discussed above, in the explorative aggregative analyses ratings were transformed into a scale with $1 \leq rating \leq 5$ for methodological reasons. In the following paragraphs, ratings are centred round zero, that is, they take values of $-2 \leq rating \leq +2$. This way, values below zero indicate a preference of the lexical variant traditionally associated with AmE (e.g., *truck*), while values above zero indicate a preference of the (traditionally) BrE variant (e.g., *lorry*), which is a more intuitively plausible representation of results. In this case, missing values are not a problem, and we therefore work with the original data and do not make use of imputation for missing values.

4.2. Global comparison of varieties

As a starting point for this part of the analysis, we compare GibE to the two reference varieties (BrE and AmE) at a global level. In Figure 8.4, the horizontal bar in each plot

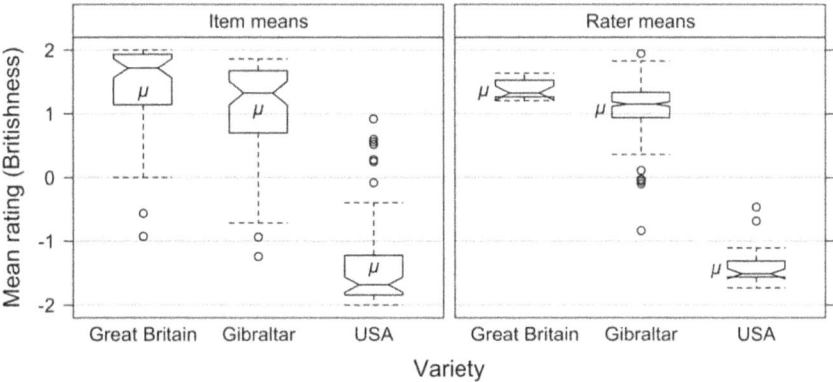

Figure 8.4 Global comparison of GibE, BrE and AmE.

represents the value of the median and the symbol *μ* additionally indicates the position of the arithmetic mean. Each box contains the central 50 per cent of cases and the whiskers embrace the remaining two quartiles, excluding outliers. The notches in each plot can be treated as confidence intervals, indicating a significant difference between groups if they do not overlap.

The left-hand panel of Figure 8.4 shows the sixty-eight item means for all three varieties, with GibE positioned between the major standard dialects. The right-hand panel makes the same comparison based on rater means. Both panels show even more clearly than the distance matrix in Figure 8.3 above the intermediate position of GibE when compared to BrE and AmE. Individual items and individual speakers are not considered here, although important outliers will be discussed briefly below. Two aspects of variation are readily apparent. On the one hand, there is a clear ordering of varieties in terms of their general degree of Britishness, irrespective of which of the two views on the data we adopt: British raters tend to award higher (i.e. more British) values to the lexical items under investigation and American raters on average award the lowest values (close to −2), which indicates that rather clear norms of usage exist with regard to the phenomena under investigation. Secondly, Figure 8.4 confirms what was also evident in the NeighborNets shown in Figures 8.2 and 8.3 above, namely that GibE is very similar to BrE as far as our lexical items are concerned. When we base the analysis on rater means instead (right-hand panel of Figure 8.4), the dispersion of values becomes considerably more compact, but does not change fundamentally otherwise. Importantly, in either panel of Figure 8.4 the notches of the boxes do not overlap, which is interpreted as indicating statistically robust differences between all three varieties. In addition, for both items and raters we can observe that the interquartile ranges (the heights of the boxes) are greatest for GibE. This ties in with a pattern which we have observed before (Krug, Schützler and Werner 2016: 61), *viz.* that our questionnaire data from L2 varieties (and, by concomitance, L2 speakers) are less uniform than those from standard BrE or AmE (and their raters). It was argued above that GibE is not a typical L2 variety of English. Based on the current data, we therefore expand our hypothesis from L2 varieties to postcolonial varieties in the present context of globalization.

A few notable outlier values need to be discussed. In the plot of individual items the two outliers in BrE are *to licence*, whose putative American variant *to license* is in fact preferred (mean rating = −.93), and *compare X to Y*, whose variant *compare X with Y* is preferred (mean rating = −.57). In GibE, the two outliers are *sport*, with a mean rating of −1.24 (i.e. a clear preference of *sports*), and *to let*, with a mean rating of −.94 (reflecting a preference of *for rent*). In AmE, the four most notable outliers are *typical of* (preferred to its supposedly AmE variant *typical for*, with a mean rating of +.92), *subway* (preferred to the allegedly more AmE variant *underpass*; mean rating = +.60), *backwards* (preferred to the variant *backward*; mean rating = +.56) and *a book about chemistry* (preferred to the variant *a book on chemistry*; mean rating = +.52). Those (and other) items are plotted in detail in Figure 8.5 below, which is followed by further discussion. What we learn from such results is that dictionaries, textbooks and style books often simplify or represent an earlier historical state when labelling an item as 'BrE' or 'AmE'.

The panel based on rater means in Figure 8.4 features one outlier rater in GibE with exceptionally low mean ratings; this is the same rater discussed in the context of the explorative analysis in Section 3. Another rater is exceptional in reporting to use only the BrE variant for sixty-two out of sixty-eight items, thus obtaining sixty-two times the rating +2 (while skipping five items and reporting to use only *baked potato*, the more AmE variant), which results in an overall mean of +1.94 for those items that were evaluated. In this case, a closer inspection of his personal information sheet is instructive. This rater is an extremely highly qualified forty-nine-year-old male lawyer holding a PhD. Interestingly, both parents' native language is given as Spanish, while at the same time English was the only language used at home while growing up. Not surprisingly, this rater lived in the UK from age 19 to 29, where in all probability he received his university education and professional training, as there was no tertiary education in Gibraltar at the time. The consistency with which this rater opted for the BrE variants is nevertheless astounding; apparently, he has access to an extremely clear intuition regarding the difference between the two variants that were offered. What probably underpins his linguistic Britishness is that he lived in the UK during the pre-internet 1980s, that is, at a time when the distinction between our 'British' and 'American' variants was still more categorical than in the more globalized, early twenty-first century. Nevertheless, language contact with twentieth-century BrE alone would probably not have effected such categorical usage. More likely, his linguistic sensitivity was further strengthened through subsequent extended periods in international contexts outside Britain: from age 30 to 35 he lived in Hong Kong and the following seven years in Finland. An additional likely factor is that both parents of our informant were teachers. These would belong to a less globalized generation and, on a more speculative note, were probably aware of transatlantic lexical differences and followed (and maybe passed on to their son) a rather traditional British model.

4.3. General behaviour of individual lexical items

In Figure 8.5, the item means of all sixty-eight lexical binaries are shown for the three varieties included in this study. Items are not ordered alphabetically or according to

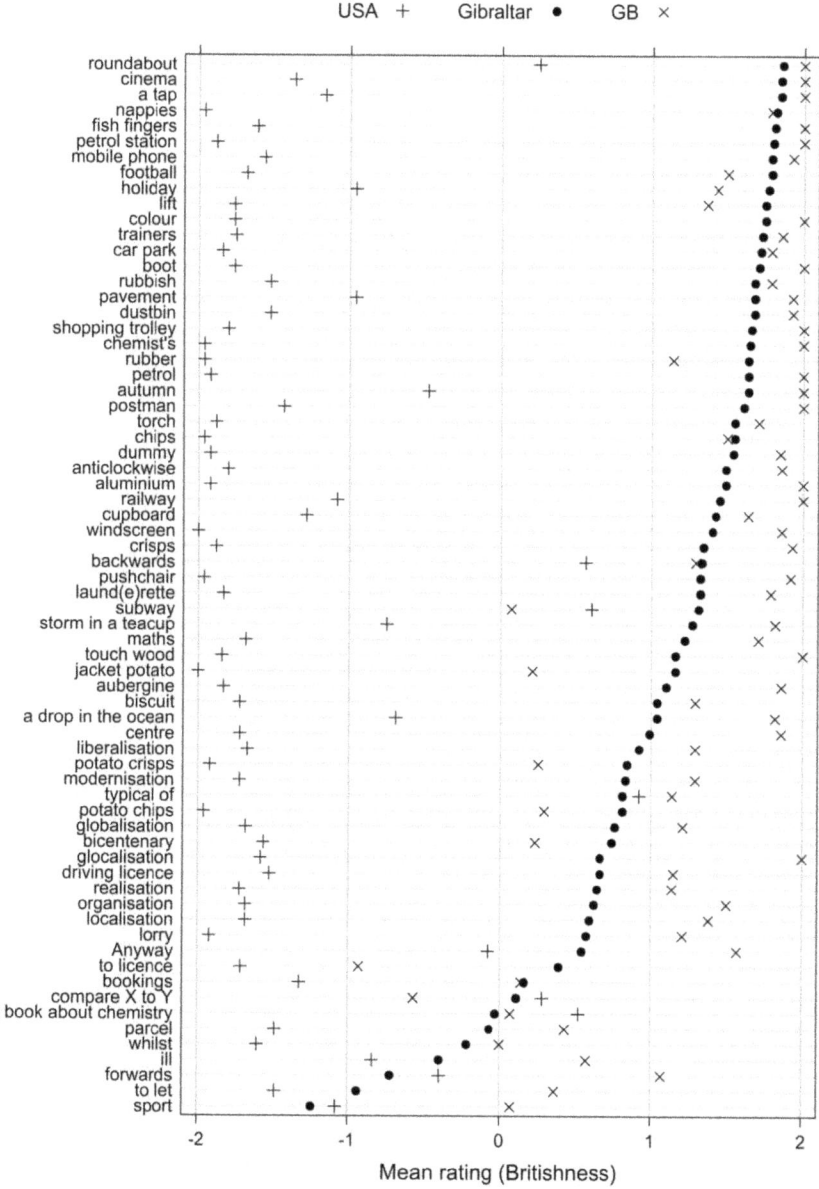

Figure 8.5 Ratings for individual items in AmE, GibE and BrE.

their arrangement in the questionnaire, but by their mean rating in GibE – that is, items appearing at the top of the figure received the highest average rating by GibE raters. The plot is useful for three purposes. First, it provides a vast amount of descriptive detail concerning specific lexical preferences across varieties and items. Second, individual items not in accordance with the generally expected pattern (that is, with ratings in Gibraltar not intermediate between the other two varieties; cf., Figure 8.4) can be quickly identified. And, finally, the figure provides yet another perspective on the relatively close alignment of GibE and BrE, on the one hand, and the rather different preferences in AmE, on the other.

The outlier items that were discussed above can be clearly seen in this display, the additional advantage being that their positions in all three varieties are apparent at a glance. For example, it is evident that the two BrE outliers *to licence* and *compare X to Y* – with ratings of −.93 and −.57, respectively – are positioned relatively far towards the bottom of the plot. This indicates that in GibE those two items are also not very strongly drawn towards the supposedly BrE pole of the scale and that their relatively loose orientation towards the putative BrE norm may be more general. *Compare X to Y* takes intermediate values close to zero in all three varieties and appears to be in fairly free variation, that is without particularly clear preferences of either form. Items that are given ratings below zero in GibE are *sport* (−1.24), *to let* (−.94), *forwards* (−.72), *ill* (−.40), *whilst* (−.22), *parcel* (−.07) and *a book about chemistry* (−.03), that is, the seven items at the bottom of Figure 8.5. If zero is taken as an arbitrary threshold value, those items can be taken as a set that deserves further investigation.

There are fifteen items whose behaviour is exceptional in that they receive clearly higher (i.e. more British) ratings in GibE than in BrE: *football, holiday, lift, rubber, subway, jacket potato, potato crisps, potato chips, bicentenary, to licence, compare X to Y, nappies, chips, backwards* and *bookings*.[11] *Jacket potato* also featured in the context of the outlier rater discussed above, who only made an exception to his otherwise perfectly uniform ratings (+2) for this item. The patterns found for *typical of* and *compare X to Y* are striking: the former is rated lowest in GibE, that is, even our AmE raters tend to prefer the supposedly BrE variant more strongly. It has to be noted, however, that ratings in all three varieties are relatively close together (between +.81 and +1.14). Therefore, the important aspect of the pattern is perhaps not so much the cross-varietal ranking but the fact that *typical of* seems to be generally preferred irrespective of variety.

In contrast, the pattern found for the item *compare X to Y* is truly puzzling, since it is an inversion of what would be expected: ratings are lowest (i.e. least British) among BrE raters and highest among AmE raters, with GibE closer to the latter. There may be other factors at work here, which complicate (or even confound) the analysis of this particular item. For example, the two options that were offered (*compare to* vs. *compare with*) may not be perfect synonyms in all varieties investigated but may involve semantic nuances that made a straightforward decision difficult for raters. There is also *compare X and Y* as a third option, which, although not stated in the questionnaire, may have affected ratings in a way not transparent to the researcher. In any case, which of the three options is truly more British or more American in present-day usage is far from clear and deserves further investigation.

Concerning the global picture, the data shown in Figure 8.5 contribute yet another facet to the explorative analysis presented above. There is a very clear positive correlation between individual items' mean ratings by GibE raters and BrE raters (Pearson's r =. 71; p = .000). In Figure 8.5, this is reflected in the fact that towards the bottom of the plot, ratings given by both GibE and BrE raters clearly tend towards the left-hand (i.e. more AmE) pole of the scale. There is a negative correlation between BrE and AmE ratings, which is also statistically significant but considerably weaker ($r = -.25$; $p = .036$). Finally, the negative correlation between GibE and AmE ratings is of a similar nature as the one between BrE and AmE ratings, but it is weaker and fails to reach statistical significance by a very small margin ($r = -.23$; $p = .056$). Those findings once more confirm the general tendency of GibE to pattern like BrE, but also to be positioned somewhat closer to AmE.

The results presented in Figure 8.5 suggest that the global differences between BrE and GibE on the one hand vs. AmE on the other are a function of clearly patterned preferences associated with specific lexical items. In other words, certain items appear to serve as variety markers by diverging strongly between the two linguistic (and cultural) spheres influenced by Great Britain and the US, respectively, while others do not show this kind of divergence. The former tend to be found nearer the top of Figure 8.5, the latter nearer the bottom. The results for individual items and the correlation measures that were applied not only confirm the global analysis summarized in Figure 8.4 but also corroborate what was revealed in the explorative analyses: there is a much closer association between BrE and GibE, in this case based on specific items.

At a more general level, Figure 8.5 casts serious doubts on standard classifications of certain lexical variants as either 'British' or 'American'. Binary classifications obviously do not work; statistical preferences are the rule rather than the exception. Furthermore, based on our data, some items' label as (more) 'British' or 'American' will even have to be reversed, at least for an adequate description of English(es) in the early twenty-first century.[12]

4.4. Apparent-time trends

The synchronic lexical differences between GibE and the two reference varieties are an important step forward in the description and contextualization of GibE among World Englishes. However, we are also interested in the emergence and (ongoing) development of those differences. The present section focuses on this aspect by inspecting lexical variation in the GibE ratings with the help of apparent-time studies.

Figure 8.6 shows average ratings across seven age groups, again based on item means and rater means (for an identification of individual items see below). The picture that emerges is not suggestive of any strong ongoing process of change. There appears to be an Americanizing trend in apparent time, but this pattern is not very pronounced, and the oldest group of raters does not conform to it.

For a more fine-grained picture, male and female raters were separated. This was also important to control for the gender imbalance among the youngest raters (see Table 8.1 above). Moreover, precise ages, not age groups, were used. In Figure 8.7, rater means of male and female raters are plotted using different symbols; a smoothed local regression line indicates general tendencies within both groups.

Among male raters (see dashed regression line in Figure 8.7), there is a fairly monotonic, if not particularly steep, downward trend towards less British-oriented preferences. Female raters appear to follow this trend only hesitatingly: only young raters are affected, while the generally high preference of BrE variants is rather robust

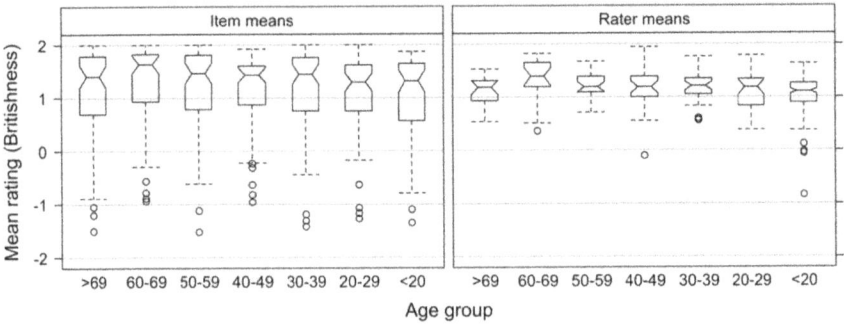

Figure 8.6 Differences according to age groups.

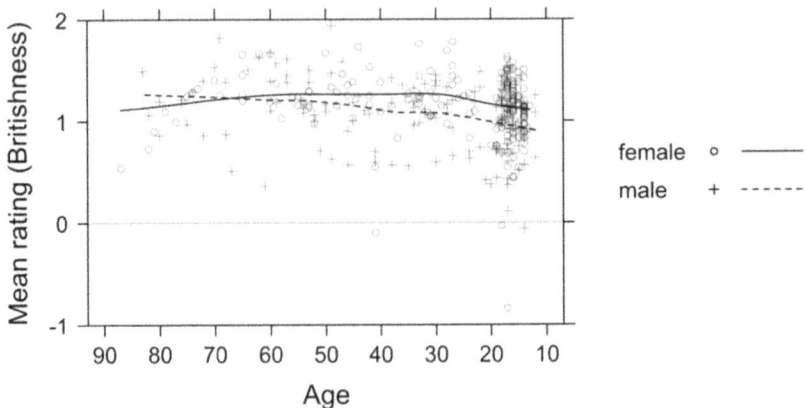

Figure 8.7 Rater means by age and gender; general trends indicated by smoothed regression lines.

for older groups. Female raters over seventy have strikingly low average values, which results in the slope of the smoothed regression line for this portion of the data. However, not too much weight should be placed on this finding, since there are only few data points for the relevant age range. The pattern may be explicable in terms of the amount of formal education that the oldest raters have received: for eight out of nine female raters aged seventy and above – including all those older than eighty – the respective socio-linguistic information ('qualification') is not available (i.e. it was not volunteered). This can be tentatively interpreted as indicating that the respective raters may indeed have undergone less formal education and qualification, resulting in lower linguistic awareness and looser norms of usage.

When seen as an instance of linguistic change, the pattern displayed by the more innovative Gibraltarian males may, *prima facie* at least, appear surprising, considering that it is often females who are in the vanguard of linguistic changes (see, e.g., the synopsis in Labov 1990; or Nevalainen 1996; Raumolin-Brunberg and Nurmi 1997).

What we observe is a particular (and less often described) kind of change: on the increase among males is a competing variant which diverges from the traditional BrE norm and whose status in terms of overt vs. covert prestige is in all likelihood different for different social groups. In this case, therefore, the Gender Paradox as discussed by Labov (1990: 213–15) does not help to explain the pattern. In essence, then, there appears to be a slow-moving general trend towards more globalized (i.e. less rigidly British-oriented) usage, but the older BrE norm is largely intact, and it is the female raters who adhere to it somewhat more strongly. An alternative – or rather complementary – sociolinguistic explanation considers the interaction between social circumstances and age. Speakers between the age of thirty and fifty-five have been shown to peak in the usage of (in our case, BrE) standard variants. This 'sociolectal retrenchment' (Tagliamonte 2012: 49) has been ascribed to increased social pressure during that period, caused, for instance, by starting a family, raising children or career advancement (see also Chambers 2009: 195). Female speakers in our sample (see Figure 8.7) seem to conform to this pattern, while it is less pronounced for the males.

Rater age and rater mean are positively correlated for male raters (Pearson's $r = .31$; $p = .000$). In other words, the older the male raters, the higher (i.e. more British) their average ratings become. A linear regression model (in which the effect of age is naturally also significant) predicts a decrease in average rating of 0.55 over a time span of 100 years for males. For female raters, the correlation of rater age and rater mean fails to reach statistical significance (Pearson's $r = .129$; $p = .087$). Results from a linear regression model suggest that there is a decrease of 0.23 for women over a period of 100 years. In sum, there is a very clear and consistent (if not particularly dramatic) Americanizing tendency among male Gibraltarians at this global level, looking at rater means only; more recently, a similar process seems to affect females as well.

In Figure 8.7, only five female raters over seventy-five with their relatively low average ratings (including a nearly ninety-year-old with particularly low overall means) are responsible for the curvature of the regression line at the highest age values. In addition, among themselves, these five female raters exhibit a trend which is the inverse of the general tendency, that is, the older ones prefer the putatively AmE variants. With only five informants each for raters over seventy-five, sparse data are in fact a problem for both genders in our dataset. If we concentrate in our analysis on speakers aged seventy-five and younger, as displayed in Figure 8.8, developments in apparent time can be interpreted with more confidence.

For raters up to seventy-five, gender-based linear regression models yield statistically significant findings that are also more readily interpretable: if we fit separate models to the data for males and females, the estimated expected rating at age seventy-five is remarkably similar for both groups, namely 1.307 for males and 1.308 for females. This is also clearly reflected in the starting points of the smoothed regression lines for male and female raters in Figure 8.8. The plot also indicates that ratings expected from men and women follow monotonic negative trajectories that gradually diverge from each other as younger speakers are inspected; as in the previous analysis discussed above, the downward (i.e. Americanizing) trend is also somewhat more pronounced among male raters (coefficient = .0061) than among female raters (coefficient = .0034).[13] The

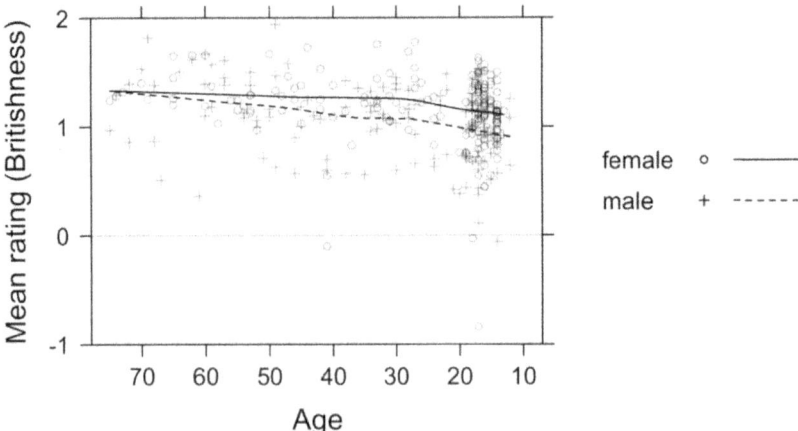

Figure 8.8 Rater means by age and gender; general trends indicated by smoothed regression lines for speakers aged up to seventy-five.

coefficients of the linear regression indicate to what extent average ratings of our lexical items change per year; the yearly decrease for men (from older to younger informants) is about twice that for women. Thus, over an eighty-year span, men's average ratings decrease by 0.49, while women's average ratings decrease by 0.27. As in the previous regression analyses based on the entire dataset, therefore, female raters diverge from the older British norms somewhat more slowly than their male counterparts. And while both analyses converge in suggesting Americanizing (or globalizing) tendencies for all Gibraltarians, the analysis based on the entire dataset and displayed in Figure 8.7 (and the contigent linear regressions) suggests a later onset of Americanization for women by about ten years. Due to the reasons advanced above (first and foremost, data scarcity for over-seventy-five-year-olds), however, we diverge from the usual convention and give preference here to the results obtained through the analysis of the incomplete dataset.

4.5. Language backgrounds

Figure 8.9 displays the distributions of item means (average of all sixty-eight binaries) for each of the six language background groups identified in subdivisions A and B of Table 8.2 above. No significant pattern emerges, irrespective of whether we use Subdivision A or Subdivision B for the categorization of language backgrounds detailed in Table 8.2.

Figure 8.10 displays rater means for each of the six language background groups identified in Table 8.2. Again, no significant pattern emerges if we apply Subdivision A. However, if Subdivision B is applied, the group of raters with mixed language backgrounds (i.e. those whose household usage is not purely English or Spanish) do exhibit some tendency to Americanize when compared to the other two, the picture being somewhat obscured by the presence of outlier values, however. If we trim the sample by omitting all outlier raters seen in the right-hand panel of Figure 8.10, the

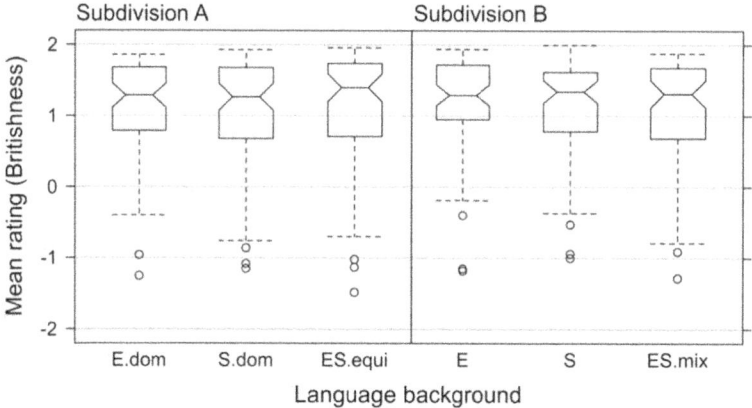

Figure 8.9 Item means (average of all sixty-eight items) by language backgrounds (six groups).

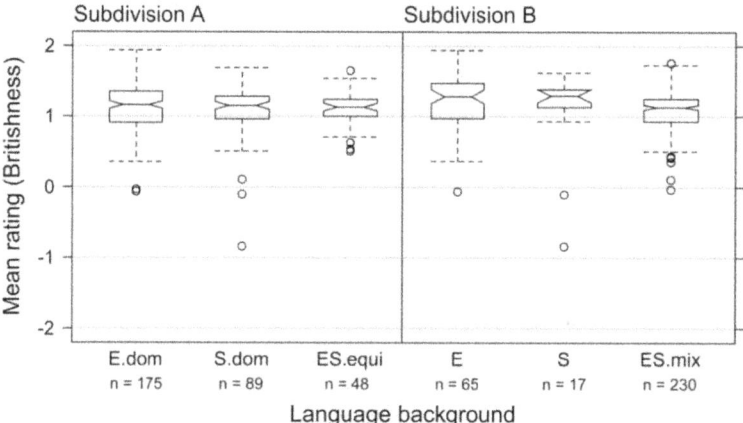

Figure 8.10 Rater means by language backgrounds (six groups).

respective arithmetic mean values for groups are $\mu_E = 1.21$, $\mu_S = 1.30$ and $\mu_{ES.mix} = 1.10$. Two-tailed t-tests applied to the three possible pairings of groups yield the following results: there is no significant difference between groups 'E' (English-only) and 'S' (Spanish-only), with $t(47.6) = 1.55$ and $p = .127$; the difference between groups 'E' and 'ES.mix' is statistically significant, with $t(82.3) = 2.09$ and $p = .040$; and the difference between groups 'S' and 'ES.mix' is also significant, with $t(18.7) = 4.23$ and $p = .000$. What is interesting about these results is that raters of mixed language background do not take a position intermediate between the purely monolingual raters. Whenever there is a mix of English and Spanish spoken at home, speakers exhibit a more globalized usage of our lexical items than in either English-only or Spanish-only familial language contexts. This is somewhat difficult to interpret but seems to suggest that when English or Spanish are the only languages spoken in the home, language contact (or the model adopted) is more exclusively British than when both Spanish and English are spoken at home. In the latter cases, on the basis of our findings, there should be more extensive contact with American and global Englishes.

4.6. Individual lexical items in apparent time

In the final part of our analysis we inspect the likely diachronic behaviour of individual items based on an alternative apparent-time approach: first, the item mean for all sixty-eight items was calculated for each of the seven age groups defined in Table 8.1 above; that is, a total of 476 mean values. For each item, the seven values were correlated with the seven age groups (i.e. the integers 1–7), using Pearson's product-moment coefficient.[14] Items were then ranked and ordered based on the correlation coefficient, as documented in Appendix B. A positive correlation indicates a development towards more British usage, while a negative coefficient indicates Americanization. Most correlations (43/68 = 63 per cent) are negative (i.e. Americanizing), although one needs to bear in mind that many patterns hardly suggest a trend towards more British or more American usage, even if the associated correlation coefficient naturally will be positive or negative. Also note that a high correlation coefficient merely reflects linearity and consistency of a pattern and does not necessarily indicate a strong diachronic effect.

Diachronic developments of all sixty-eight items are plotted in Appendix C. Here we discuss only those twenty-one items whose mean ratings correlated significantly (or nearly significantly) with rater age ($p < .1$). The details for age-related differences of these items are presented in Figure 8.11.

- Items with positive trends (becoming more British) include *jacket potato, maths, subway, whilst, book about chemistry* and *cinema*.
- Items with negative (Americanizing) trends include *to licence, biscuit, Anyway, . . ., storm in a teacup, lorry, parcel, drop in the ocean, nappies, driving licence, dustbin, petrol station, pushchair, postman, shopping trolley* and *railway*.
- NB: The four items *cinema, railway, shopping trolley* and *postman* are merely 'trending' in that the correlation with rater age is marginally non-significant ($.5 \leq p < .1$).

The six items moving towards the BrE pole of the scale can be subdivided into three sets:

- *Jacket potato, maths* and *subway* start from an intermediate value that reflects relatively free variation between the AmE and the BrE variant, and undergo very clear processes of change (*jacket potato*: +.20 → +1.39, with an even slightly higher peak at +1.41; *maths*: +.40 → +1.40, with an even higher peak at +1.50; and *subway*: −.22 → +1.59, peaking at +1.79).
- *Whilst* and *a book about chemistry* move towards the 'middle ground', starting from the American side of the continuum (*whilst*: −.89 → −.04; *book about chemistry*: −.78 → +.12, if we look at the extreme points).
- *Cinema* is already very British-oriented but is further consolidated, with scores between +1.56 and +2.00.

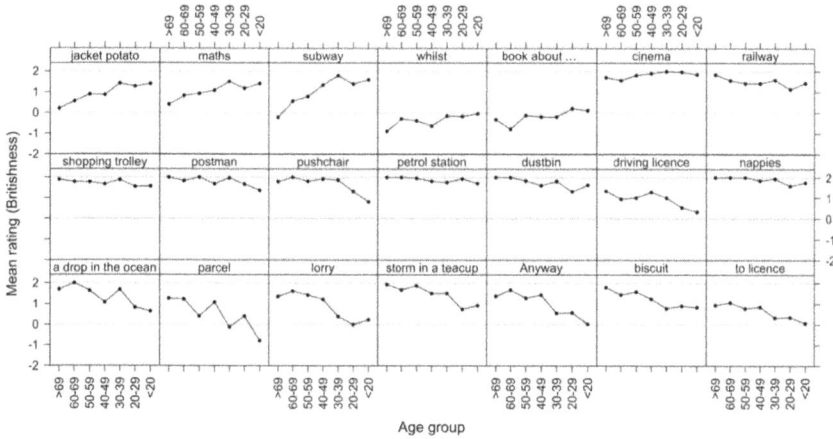

Figure 8.11 Apparent-time trends for selected items in GibE.

On the other hand, those items that become more Americanized over (apparent) time invariably start at rather high levels of Britishness. For some there is only a minor loosening of their orientation towards BrE norms (*railway, shopping trolley, postman, petrol station, nappies*), while others undergo more dramatic changes (e.g., *pushchair, driving licence, parcel, lorry, Anyway, . . .*). The three items *shopping trolley, petrol station* and *nappies* remain clearly oriented towards the BrE norm, but the significant small-scale trends that we detect in them nevertheless indicate that this norm is beginning to weaken. The item *pushchair* has rather stable mean values for older raters, followed by a very rapid change in the two youngest age groups (i.e. raters under thirty), the preference of the BrE variant dropping from a nearly categorical value of +1.87 to +.80. Finally, *parcel* and *lorry* are noteworthy for the particularly strong overall change they undergo, with values dropping from +1.26 to −.79 for *parcel* and from +1.61 to ±0 for *lorry* (if we look at the peak values of the latter).

5. Discussion and aspects of globalization

Questionnaire results reflect individuals' intuitions about language rather than actual performance, which for some linguists working in a usage-based framework casts serious doubts on their validity (cf., Dollinger 2015: ch. 3 for related aspects and ways to counterbalance potential shortcomings of questionnaires). The current project has addressed such issues by collecting large numbers of questionnaires for our contact-varieties (thus de-individualizing the intuitions collected and making the data amenable to sociolinguistic analysis) and by comparing, in an earlier publication, questionnaire-based results with web-based data (see Krug and Sönning 2017). The two approaches yielded highly significant correlations between rank-based hierarchies, which makes global spurious findings for our lexical items rather unlikely. In addition, we have included several control items in the questionnaire, which address issues relating to the reliability of rater responses (e.g., a number of *-isation* spellings spread across the questionnaire).[15]

Furthermore, the consistency with which we find correlations between parent and (post-)colonial varieties (e.g., between British and Maltese English, on the one hand, and American and Puerto Rican English, on the other; see Krug, Schützler and Werner 2016 for details) makes us optimistic as regards the usefulness of questionnaire-based research into lexical (and potentially other types of) variation. The present investigation provides further support for optimism: based on the – unsurprising but hitherto also unexplored – striking similarity between BrE and GibE for lexical binaries, it is tempting to label present-day GibE on the lexical level as Gibraltar British English, or GiBrE, for short (rather than GibE or GibrE, for instance).

What we can conclude from the previous section is that the lexical binaries investigated in this study clearly have to be treated as individual categories, both in terms of their likely diachronic behaviour and their synchronic position on the continuum between BrE and AmE. Against the background of apparent-time analyses of individual items, it is not surprising that the global approach (based on overall rater means) yields less striking results: the apparent stability at a global surface level only smoothes over multiple individual patterns, some stable, others changing in different directions, sometimes towards a more British, more often towards a more American orientation. We found five significant apparent-time trends towards a more BrE usage pattern in our Gibraltar data, most notably so for *jacket potato, maths* and *subway*. These compare with twelve Americanizing items that exceed the 5 per cent significance level, the most obvious ones being *to licence, biscuit, Anyway, . . ., storm in a teacup, lorry* and *parcel*, which are increasingly being replaced by their more American counterparts *to license, cookie, Anyways, . . ., tempest in a teapot, truck* and *package*.

Some items display similar patterns of development in many regions of the world, and can thus be interpreted more confidently as instances of globalization. On the basis of this and previous studies into other traditionally British-oriented varieties of English (in Malta, the Channel Islands and indeed the UK itself; cf., Krug and Rosen 2012; Krug, Schützler and Werner 2016), we can assume globalization in the guise of Americanization (our globalization type 2) for *lorry, parcel* and *to licence*, onto whose territory encroach their American counterparts. Another example is *sport*, which is being superseded by *sports* in many regions of the world, too. In our Gibraltar data, there is only a statistically non-significant apparent-time trend towards *sports* (see Appendices B and C). Significantly from a linguistic perspective, however, all age-groups display solidly negative (i.e. more American) usage ratings for this item. Seen from this perspective, *sports* is in fact the most Americanized item in Gibraltar, together with *for rent* (which is preferred over *to let* in GibE, and which shows strong signs of Americanization in the Channel Islands as well as in Malta). A similar case is *sick*, which seems to be spreading at the expense of the once more British variant *ill* in many English-speaking regions of the world. As with *sport(s)*, the Americanizing apparent-time trend is negligible in GibE but, like *sport*, *ill* belongs to the small group of only six items that have solidly negative ratings overall.[16]

Evidently, therefore, different types of globalization coexist (see our typology developed in Krug, Schützler and Werner 2016: 55, and sketched in Section 3 above), as well as different methods of identifying individual items participating in globalization. Apparent-time approaches are one such method; comparing overall item means represents an alternative (i.e. identifying which traditional British forms have the lowest means in British-oriented varieties). Where the results point in the same direction, and not only in British-oriented but also in American-oriented varieties, we can be most confident. But it would be naïve to assume that evidence will typically converge in all varieties of English around the world. What we may hope to find are regional patterns or parallel patterns of development in disparate regions of the world that can be motivated. What we must expect, however, are also distributions which cannot be motivated, and ever-changing patterns of preference. Charting such complexity, we believe, is nevertheless worth its while. It is, we would in fact argue, indispensable if we want to improve our understanding of the nature of language contact and its relationship with language change.

Appendix A. Gibraltar version of the Bamberg Questionnaire (lexical part only)

Gibraltar English Questionnaire
Informant Information Sheet

Informant ID #
_____

Date
_____

Personal Information

Age
_____

Gender
○ male   ○ female

Nationality
_____

Ethnic Self-Identification
_____

Country or region you identify with most
_____

Language(s) used at home while growing up
○ English
○ mostly Spanish, some English
○ mostly English, some Spanish   ○ Spanish
○ other: _____

Mother's native language(s)
_____

Father's native language(s)
_____

Education Profile

Primary School
○ State
○ Private
○ Church
○ other *(please specify below)*
_____

Secondary School
○ State
○ Private
○ Church
○ other *(please specify below)*
_____

Name and place of secondary school
_____

Qualifications (completed or ongoing)
○ Vocational classes *(please specify below)*
○ Apprenticeship *(please specify below)*
○ Bachelor
○ Master's
○ PhD
○ other *(please specify below)*
_____

Your current occupation
_____

Mother's highest qualification
_____

Mother's (last) occupation
_____

Father's highest qualification
_____

Father's (last) occupation
_____

Partner's highest qualification
_____

Partner's (last) occupation
_____

Location Timeline

Years lived outside Gibraltar
_____

Age	Location lived at from age 0-100 *(please indicate city/town or country, if abroad)*
0	
1	
2	
3	
4	
5	
6	
7	
8	
9	
10	
11	
12	
13	
14	
15	
16	
17	
18	
19	
20	
21	
22	
23	
24	
25	
26	
27	
28	
29	
30	
35	
40	
45	
50	
55	
60	
65	
70	
75	
80	
85	
90	
95	
100	

Rev. 2017-10-17GI

Gibraltar English Questionnaire
Lexical Items

Informant ID #

Date

	I always use this expression	I use this expression more often	I have no preference	I use this expression more often	I always use this expression		I never use either expression	Explanation / Comment
a drop in the ocean	○	○	○	○	○	a drop in the bucket	○	
a faucet	○	○	○	○	○	a tap	○	
aluminum	○	○	○	○	○	aluminium	○	
anticlockwise	○	○	○	○	○	counterclockwise	○	
eggplant	○	○	○	○	○	aubergine	○	*(fruit/vegetable)*
fall	○	○	○	○	○	autumn	○	*(season of the year)*
backward	○	○	○	○	○	backwards	○	
bicentenary	○	○	○	○	○	bicentennial	○	
cookie	○	○	○	○	○	biscuit	○	*(something sweet to eat)*
bookings	○	○	○	○	○	reservations	○	
trunk	○	○	○	○	○	boot	○	*(of a car)*
car park	○	○	○	○	○	parking lot	○	
center	○	○	○	○	○	centre	○	*(spelling)*
chemist's	○	○	○	○	○	drugstore / drug store	○	
ill	○	○	○	○	○	sick	○	
French fries	○	○	○	○	○	potato chips	○	*(warm, sometimes greasy)*
fries	○	○	○	○	○	chips	○	*(warm, sometimes greasy)*
cinema	○	○	○	○	○	movie theater	○	
color	○	○	○	○	○	colour	○	*(spelling)*
cupboard	○	○	○	○	○	closet	○	*(for clothes)*
driver's license	○	○	○	○	○	driving licence	○	
dummy	○	○	○	○	○	pacifier	○	*(for babies)*
trash can	○	○	○	○	○	dustbin	○	
fish fingers	○	○	○	○	○	fish sticks	○	
soccer	○	○	○	○	○	football	○	*(kicking game, only goalkeeper uses hands)*
forwards	○	○	○	○	○	forward	○	
globalization	○	○	○	○	○	globalisation	○	
glocalisation	○	○	○	○	○	glocalization	○	
vacation	○	○	○	○	○	holiday	○	
liberalization	○	○	○	○	○	liberalisation	○	
baked potato	○	○	○	○	○	jacket potato	○	
laund(e)rette	○	○	○	○	○	laundromat	○	
potato crisps	○	○	○	○	○	potato chips	○	*(crunchy, cold)*
crisps	○	○	○	○	○	chips	○	*(crunchy, cold)*

Rev. 2017-10-12v4

Gibraltar English Questionnaire
Lexical Items

Informant ID # _____

Date _____

	I always use this expression	I use this expression more often	I have no preference	I use this expression more often	I always use this expression		I never use either expression	Explanation / Comment
to licence	○	○	○	○	○	to license	○	
elevator	○	○	○	○	○	lift	○	
localisation	○	○	○	○	○	localization	○	
truck	○	○	○	○	○	lorry	○	(large motor vehicle for carrying goods by road)
maths	○	○	○	○	○	math	○	
cell phone	○	○	○	○	○	mobile phone	○	
modernisation	○	○	○	○	○	modernization	○	
diapers	○	○	○	○	○	nappies	○	(for babies)
organisation	○	○	○	○	○	organization	○	
package	○	○	○	○	○	parcel	○	(something you send by mail)
pavement	○	○	○	○	○	sidewalk	○	(for pedestrians, next to street)
gasoline	○	○	○	○	○	petrol	○	
petrol station	○	○	○	○	○	gas station	○	
mailman	○	○	○	○	○	postman	○	
pushchair	○	○	○	○	○	stroller	○	(for toddlers)
railroad	○	○	○	○	○	railway	○	
realisation	○	○	○	○	○	realization	○	
traffic circle	○	○	○	○	○	roundabout	○	(for cars)
rubber	○	○	○	○	○	eraser	○	
trash	○	○	○	○	○	rubbish	○	
shopping trolley	○	○	○	○	○	shopping cart	○	
sports	○	○	○	○	○	sport	○	
storm in a teacup	○	○	○	○	○	tempest in a teapot	○	
underpass	○	○	○	○	○	subway	○	(path for pedestrians under a road)
to let	○	○	○	○	○	for rent	○	
flashlight	○	○	○	○	○	torch	○	(electric lamp)
touch wood	○	○	○	○	○	knock on wood	○	
sneakers	○	○	○	○	○	trainers	○	
whilst	○	○	○	○	○	while	○	
windshield	○	○	○	○	○	windscreen	○	
a book about chemistry	○	○	○	○	○	a book on chemistry	○	
compare X to Y	○	○	○	○	○	compare X with Y	○	
typical of	○	○	○	○	○	typical for	○	
Anyways, ...	○	○	○	○	○	Anyway, ...	○	

Rev. 2017-10-17GJ

Appendix B. Correlations of mean ratings of individual items and seven age groups in GibE: Americanization (negative correlations) vs. Britishization (positive correlations)

lexical item	r	p		lexical item	r	p	
jacket potato	.94	.002	***	petrol	−.32	.487	
maths	.89	.008	**	trainers	−.34	.453	
subway	.89	.007	**	typical of	−.37	.417	
whilst	.78	.040	*	to let	−.39	.389	
book about chemistry	.77	.042	*	car park	−.47	.282	
cinema	.71	.072	.	ill	−.49	.269	
football	.63	.131		laund(e)rette	−.49	.266	
forwards	.60	.151		holiday	−.53	.220	
chips	.55	.200		bicentenary	−.55	.203	
compare X to Y	.47	.286		cupboard	−.56	.190	
mobile phone	.44	.325		windscreen	−.56	.191	
crisps	.38	.399		fish fingers	−.57	.180	
roundabout	.32	.480		aubergine	−.58	.169	
a tap	.30	.516		dummy	−.59	.165	
boot	.30	.510		potato chips	−.60	.157	
bookings	.29	.535		sport	−.60	.154	
autumn	.20	.672		modernisation	−.64	.124	
centre	.18	.696		pavement	−.64	.119	
globalisation	.18	.695		rubbish	−.66	.104	
organisation	.18	.705		railway	−.69	.084	.
colour	.16	.739		shopping trolley	−.73	.060	.
anticlockwise	.14	.759		postman	−.74	.056	.
liberalisation	.14	.771		pushchair	−.76	.046	*
backwards	.05	.917		petrol station	−.78	.038	*
localisation	.01	.980		dustbin	−.79	.035	*
touch wood	−.04	.939		driving licence	−.80	.030	*
glocalisation	−.11	.809		nappies	−.80	.031	*
rubber	−.11	.820		a drop in the ocean	−.82	.023	*
torch	−.11	.807		parcel	−.84	.018	*
lift	−.12	.803		lorry	−.89	.007	**
realisation	−.15	.742		storm in a teacup	−.89	.007	**
potato crisps	−.22	.628		Anyway,...	−.89	.007	**
aluminium	−.29	.529		biscuit	−.92	.003	***
chemist's	−.31	.495		to licence	−.93	.003	***

Appendix C. Americanization vs. Britishization in Gibraltar English: apparent-time trends for all items (ordered by strength and polarity of correlation; seven age groups)

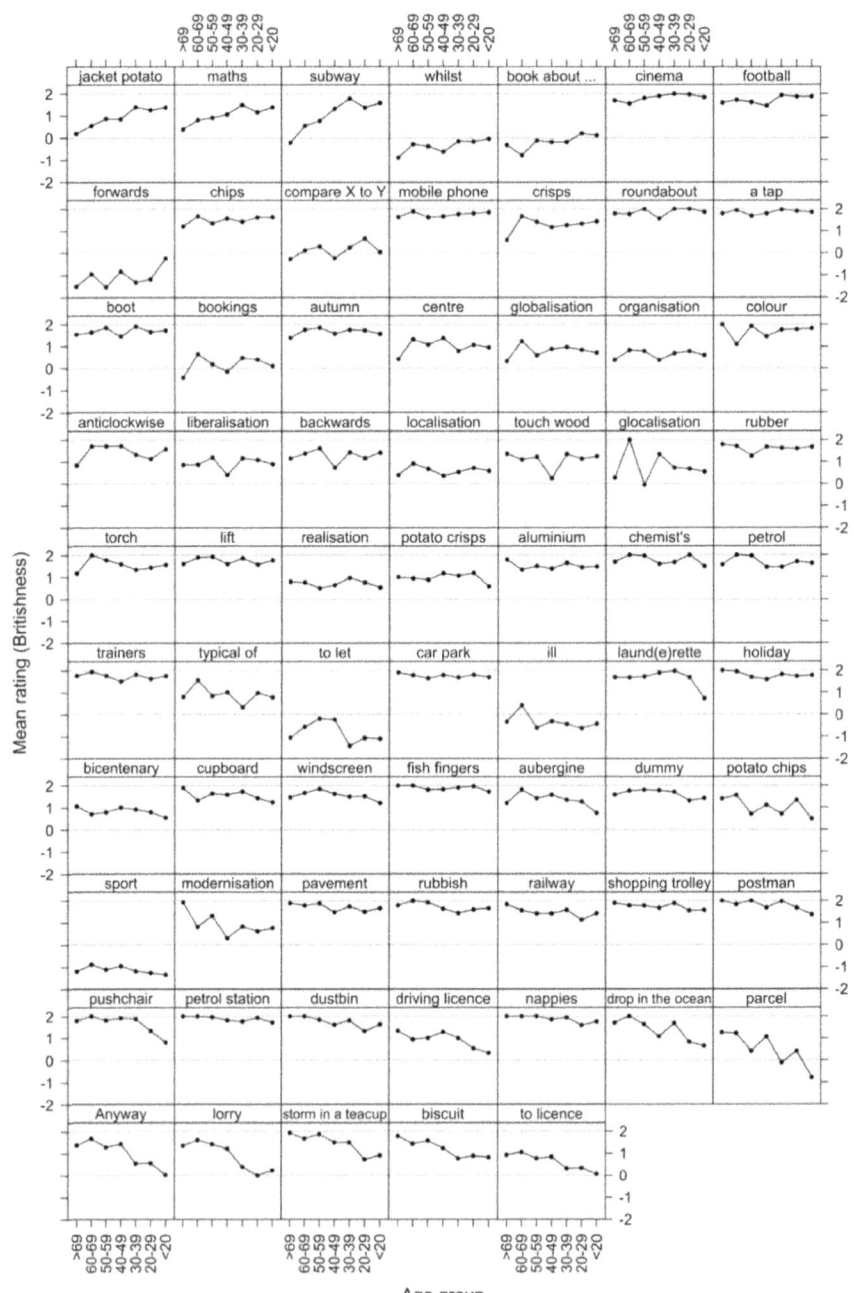

Age group

Notes

1   We dedicate this publication to Teresa Fanego, a linguist admirable for her ideas, perseverance, constructive communications, as well as the way in which she established and maintained academic networks and personal friendships. Teresa created an enduring link with the University of Bamberg through a project on variation, linguistic change and grammaticalization, which provided ample opportunities and invaluable support especially for junior researchers. This collaboration, formally as well as informally, became a constant source of inspiration that sparked reciprocal invitations and exchanges of ideas at all levels. We are grateful to two anonymous reviewers for their valuable comments. The usual disclaimers apply.

2   The most recent census data for the entire Gibraltarian population provide a value of *c.* 93 per cent English fluency based on self-reports (HM Government of Gibraltar 2012: xxxviii).

3   This contrasts strongly with figures for this item found in other L2 varieties like Maltese or Puerto Rican English, where English (or a combination of English and Maltese/Spanish) is submitted by only 5 per cent (Malta) and 13.5 per cent (Puerto Rico) of the raters. Note that, while not directly comparable, the findings of our questionnaire study are in line with Levey (2008: 59), but stand in stark contrast to Neidig (2008: 49–51), who claims that Spanish is the conversational language for two thirds of the Gibraltarian population and that near-exclusive use of Spanish characterizes parent-child interaction. However, even Neidig (2008: 55) acknowledges a growing influence of English in the latter domain (see also Weston 2012: 21).

4   For *parcel* vs. *package*, we considered as an alternative paraphrase 'something you send by *surface* mail' in order to avoid confusion with emails and computer programs. However, association tests with IT experts and students in 2008 and 2017 showed that both associate surface mail contexts for this test item rather than IT contexts. The longer paraphrase was therefore dismissed as minimal disambiguation gains were outweighed by extra efforts for explaining the term *surface mail* to older informants.

5   Of course, the expressions *binaries* and *British* vs. *American English usage* are simplifications which are used here for expository clarity. Some items have more than two alternatives, e.g., *dummy – pacifier – soother*, or *compare X with/to/and Y.* Similarly, we simplistically use *BrE* (or *AmE*, as the case may be) when we refer to more British (e.g., *backwards* vs. *backward*), exclusively (e.g., *-isation* spellings) or traditionally British terms (e.g., *lorry* vs. *truck*).

6   Alternative labels found in the literature are 'similarity matrix' or 'dissimilarity matrix'.

7   Thanks are due to Fabian Vetter for scripting. *MakeNex* is available upon request.

8   Originally, representations of this type were used in evolutionary biology and related areas to chart relationships between relevant categories, such as species or bacteria.

9   If the term were not laden with creolist associations, it would be tempting, in this investigation of lexical items, to speak of a 'lexifier' variety. See Krug, Schützler and Werner (2016: 45) for a similar interpretation based on a study of Maltese and Puerto Rican Englishes and their alignment with their BrE and AmE colonial 'parent' varieties. Note, however, that the alignment for those groupings is less close than the one observed between GibE and BrE here. We assume that this similarity is due to sociolinguistic factors applying to GibE, but also to language-external, historical factors (see further below and Weston 2011, 2015).

10 As we will see below, we are sometimes only dealing with alleged former norms. Often statistical preferences actually involve complex social patterns and sometimes they are even the inverse of what textbooks suggest.

11 The items *nappies, chips, backwards* and *bookings* receive only marginally higher ratings in GibE.

12 We plan to collect more British and American data, which in turn may lead to a reconsideration of individual items as well as to methodological adaptations.

13 The precise results of the linear regression model for male raters are INTERCEPT = .845 and AGE = .006 (p = .000); for female raters they are INTERCEPT = 1.055 and AGE = .003 (p = .019). That is, for example, a decrease of one year in the age of a male rater is expected to result in a rating that is lower by the value of .006.

14 For an alternative approach using Kendall's tau, see Hilpert and Gries (2009).

15 This does not mean that we take every rater's response at face value. In the case of our notorious UK-educated forty-nine-year-old lawyer with a PhD (see Section 4 for detailed discussion), whose parents were both teachers, for instance, we tend to believe that situational context impacts also on his usage of *while* vs. *whilst*, even though he reports to use only the latter. We do believe, however, that this rater indeed overwhelmingly uses traditionally BrE variants and that, over and above, our questionnaire results produce valuable data for charting variation and change, as the vast majority of raters do not report to use exclusively one variant in each case.

16 Apart from the items mentioned in this paragraph, only *forwards* and *whilst* show solidly negative ratings overall (see Figure 8.5). Both are special: the former has a nominal homograph *forward* used in sport(s); and *whilst* is a relatively formal variant that is probably less common than *while* in all present-day regional varieties.

References

Algeo, John (2006), *British or American English: A Handbook of Word and Grammar Patterns*, Cambridge: Cambridge University Press.

Braithwaite, David W. and Robert L. Goldstone (2013), 'Benefits of Graphical and Symbolic Representations for Learning and Transfer of Statistical Concepts', in Markus Knauff, Michael Pauen, Natalie Sebanz and Ipke Wachsmuth (eds), *Proceedings of the Thirty-Fifth Annual Conference of the Cognitive Science Society*, 1928–33, Berlin: Cognitive Science Society.

Central Intelligence Agency (2016), *The World Factbook*. Available online: https://www.cia.gov/library/publications/download/download–2016/index.html

Chambers, Jack K. (2009), *Sociolinguistic Theory: Linguistic Variation and its Social Significance*, Malden: Blackwell.

Dollinger, Stefan (2015), *The Written Questionnaire in Social Dialectology: History, Theory, Practice*, Amsterdam: Benjamins.

Fuchs, Robert and Ulrike Gut (2016), 'Register Variation in Intensifier Usage across Asian Englishes', in Heike Pichler (ed), *Discourse-pragmatic Variation and Change: Insights from English*, 185–210, Cambridge: Cambridge University Press.

Hilpert, Martin and Stefan Th. Gries (2009), 'Assessing Frequency Changes in Multistage Diachronic Corpora: Applications for Historical Corpus Linguistics and the Study of Language Acquisition', *Literary and Linguistic Computing*, 24 (4): 385–401.

HM Government of Gibraltar (2012), *Census of Gibraltar 2012*, Gibraltar: HM
  Government of Gibraltar. Available online: https://www.gibraltar.gov.gi/new/sites/
  default/files/HMGoG_Documents/Full%20Census%20Report%202012%20FINAL.pdf
Huson, Daniel H. and David Bryant (2006), 'Application of Phylogenetic Networks in
  Evolutionary Studies', *Molecular Biology and Evolution*, 23 (2): 254–67.
Kellermann, Anja (2001), *A New New English: Language, Politics, and Identity in Gibraltar*,
  Heidelberg: Books-On-Demand.
Kramer, Johannes (1998), *English and Spanish in Gibraltar*, Hamburg: Buske.
Krug, Manfred and Anna Rosen (2012), 'Standards of English in Malta and the Channel
  Islands', in Raymond Hickey (ed), *Standards of English: Codified Varieties around the
  World*, 117–38, Cambridge: Cambridge University Press.
Krug, Manfred, Ole Schützler and Valentin Werner (2016), 'Patterns of Linguistic
  Globalization: Integrating Typological Profiles and Questionnaire Data', in Olga
  Timofeeva, Anne-Christine Gardner, Alpo Honkapohja and Sarah Chevalier (eds), *New
  Approaches to English Linguistics: Building Bridges*, 35–66, Amsterdam: Benjamins.
Krug, Manfred and Katrin Sell (2013), 'Designing and Conducting Interviews and
  Questionnaires', in Manfred Krug and Julia Schlüter (eds), *Research Methods in
  Language Variation and Change*, 69–98, Cambridge: Cambridge University Press.
Krug, Manfred and Lukas Sönning (2017), 'Language Change in Maltese English: The
  Influence of Age and Parental Languages', in Patrizia Paggio and Albert Gatt (eds), *The
  Languages of Malta*, 247–70, Berlin: Language Science Press.
Labov, William (1990), 'The Intersection of Sex and Social Class in the Course of
  Linguistic Change', *Language Variation and Change*, 2: 205–54.
Levey, Stephen (2008), *Language Change and Variation in Gibraltar*, Amsterdam: Benjamins.
Levey, Stephen (2015), 'Gibraltar English', in Jeffrey P. Williams, Edgar W. Schneider, Peter
  Trudgill and Daniel Schreier (eds), *Further Studies in the Lesser-known Varieties of
  English*, 51–69, Cambridge: Cambridge University Press.
Loureiro-Porto, Lucía and Cristina Suárez-Gómez (2017), 'Language Contact in
  Gibraltar English: A Pilot Study with ICE-GBR', *Alicante Journal of English Studies*, 30:
  93–119.
McMahon, April and Warren Maguire (2013), 'Computing Linguistic Distances Between
  Varieties', in Manfred Krug and Julia Schlüter (eds), *Research Methods in Language
  Variation and Change*, 421–32, Cambridge: Cambridge University Press.
Neidig, Andrea (2008), *English und Spanisch im Kontakt: Das Yanito in Gibraltar*, Giessen:
  Herrmann.
Nevalainen, Terttu (1996), 'Gender Difference', in Terttu Nevalainen and Helena
  Raumolin-Brunberg (eds), *Sociolinguistics and Language History: Studies Based on the
  Corpus of Early English Correspondence*, 57–76, Amsterdam: Rodopi.
R Core Team (2016), *R: A Language and Environment for Statistical Computing*, Vienna:
  R Foundation for Statistical Computing. Available online: http://r-project.org
Raumolin-Brunberg, Helena and Arja Nurmi (1997), 'Dummies on the Move: Prop-ONE
  and Affirmative DO in the 17th Century', in Terttu Nevalainen and Leena Kahlas-
  Tarkka (eds), *To Explain the Present: Studies in the Changing English Language in
  Honour of Matti Rissanen*, 395–417, Helsinki: Société Néophilologique.
Ruette, Tom, Katharina Ehret and Benedikt Szmrecsanyi (2016), 'A Lectometric Analysis of
  Aggregated Lexical Variation in Written Standard English with Semantic Vector Space
  Models', *International Journal of Corpus Linguistics*, 21 (1): 48–79.
Schneider, Edgar W. (2007), *Postcolonial English: Varieties around the World*, Cambridge:
  Cambridge University Press.

Schützler, Ole (2015), 'Transforming Acoustic Vowel Data: A Comparison of Methods, Using Multidimensional Scaling', in Adrian Leemann, Marie-José Kolly, Stephan Schmid and Volker Dellwo (eds), *Trends in Phonetics & Phonology: Studies from German-speaking Europe*, 35–47, Bern: Peter Lang.

Suárez-Gómez, Cristina (2012), 'English in Contact with other European Languages (Italian, Spanish, Slavic)', in Alexander Bergs and Laurel J. Brinton (eds), *Historical Linguistics of English: An International Handbook, Vol. II*, 1738–53, Berlin: De Gruyter Mouton.

Szmrecsanyi, Benedikt (2011), 'Corpus-based Dialectometry: A Methodological Sketch', *Corpora*, 6 (1): 45–76.

Szmrecsanyi, Benedikt and Christoph Wolk (2011), 'Holistic Corpus-based Dialectology', *Brazilian Journal of Applied Linguistics*, 11 (2): 561–92.

Tagliamonte, Sali (2012), *Variationist Sociolinguistics: Change, Observation, Interpretation*, Malden: Blackwell.

Vessey, Iris (1991), 'Cognitive Fit: A Theory-based Analysis of the Graphs versus Tables Literature', *Decision Sciences*, 22 (2): 219–40.

Wainer, Howard (1992), 'Understanding Graphs and Tables', *Educational Researcher*, 21 (1): 14–23.

Wälchli, Bernhard and Benedikt Szmrecsanyi (2014), 'Introduction: The Text-Feature-Aggregation Pipeline in Variation Studies', in Benedikt Szmrecsanyi and Bernhard Wälchli (eds), *Aggregating Dialectology, Typology, and Register Analysis: Linguistic Variation in Text and Speech*, 1–25, Berlin: De Gruyter Mouton.

Werner, Valentin (2014), *The Present Perfect in World Englishes: Charting Unity and Diversity*, Bamberg: Bamberg University Press.

Werner, Valentin (2016), 'Overlap and Divergence – Aspects of the Present Perfect in World Englishes', in Elena Seoane and Cristina Suárez-Gómez (eds), *World Englishes: New Theoretical and Methodological Considerations*, 113–42, Amsterdam: Benjamins.

Weston, Daniel (2011), 'Gibraltar's Position in the Dynamic Model of Postcolonial English', *English World-Wide*, 32 (3): 338–67.

Weston, Daniel (2012), 'Code-switching Variation in Gibraltar', *International Journal of Bilingualism*, 17 (1): 3–22.

Weston, Daniel (2015), 'The Lesser of Two Evils: Atypical Trajectories in English Dialect Evolution', *Journal of Sociolinguistics*, 19 (5): 671–87.

Singular *they* in Asian Englishes:
A Case of Linguistic Democratization?[1]

Lucía Loureiro-Porto
University of the Balearic Islands

1. Introduction

Singular *they* is one of the linguistic devices used to refer to an antecedent whose sex is unknown or irrelevant, as in (1), in which the singular antecedent *a student* is referred to as *they* (their) in the immediate context:

(1)   But your sister said that that's not so common in Canada <,> for a student to travel a lot during *their* holiday. (ICE-HK:S1A-071)

Other linguistic devices used in the same context are generic *he*, as in (2), in which *the runner* is the antecedent of *him*, and the coordinate construction *he or she*, as in (3):

(2)   If we assume that the runner maintains a steady speed, the time intervals it takes *him* to cover these distances will also follow the same series and will converge to a finite limit. (ICE-IND:W2B-021)
(3)   Language is specific conferring and concise sentences which are clear at first glance If someone has to read a sentence twice then you've already lost *him or her* okay (ICE-SIN:S2A-036)

The focus of this chapter is singular *they*. Its use has been widely studied in British and American English (Bodine 1975; Green 1977; Gastil 1990; Meyers 1990; Zuber and Reed 1993; Balhorn 2004; 2009; Paterson 2011, 2014; Parini 2013, among others), and two main motivations have been proposed for its emergence and spread in the language. The origin of singular *they* can be traced back at least to Chaucer, who used it frequently with antecedents which are grammatically singular but notionally plural, such as the quantifier *every* (Balhorn 2004). This medieval use of singular *they* is, therefore, semantically justified, and has survived to the present day. However, the more recent spread of singular *they* can be attributed to social demands, namely a wish to make language more democratic by avoiding the use of generic *he* when the antecedent refers to a human being whose sex is unknown or not relevant (Leech et al. 2009: 263; Farrelly and Seoane 2012). Despite the fact that some prescriptive grammars have warned against it (see Curzan 2003: 76–9), singular *they* is nowadays generally acknowledged as an acceptable form in Standard English (e.g., Huddleston and Pullum et al. 2002: 494). Outer-circle varieties of English (Kachru 1985), though, remain unexplored in this respect. Hence, the current study examines this grammatical feature in three Asian Englishes, namely those spoken in Hong Kong (HK), India (IND) and Singapore (SIN).

The chapter is structured as follows. Section 2 reviews the history of singular *they* (2.1) and presents the two main social factors that have affected its frequency over time, namely prescriptivism and democratization (2.2). Section 3 provides some socio-linguistic background on the varieties spoken in the three Asian territories considered. After a brief discussion of language use in these ex-colonies in terms of Schneider's (2007) Dynamic Model (3.1), reference is made to the substrate languages that enter into contact with English and their pronominal paradigm (3.2). Methodological concerns are described in Section 4, and the results are presented in Section 5. Finally, Section 6 includes a discussion of the results and some conclusions.

2. Singular *they*: Diachronic and synchronic considerations

2.1. Origins of singular *they*

The exact moment in which singular *they* was first used in English is hotly debated in the literature. As Bodine (1975: 133) puts it, '[d]ozens of examples from several centuries of English literature are listed' in grammar books from the beginning of the twentieth century, quoted examples often being sentences by Walter Scott, Addison, Swift or Jane Austen (Leonard 1929: 225), in contexts such as (4) and (5), with two different kinds of antecedent:

(4) 'Every body was punctual, every body in *their* best looks: not a tear, and hardly a long face to be seen'. (Austen, *Emma*, 1815)

(5) 'Who is in love with her? Who makes you *their* confidant?' (Austen, *Emma*, 1815)

Nevertheless, these nineteenth-century examples are by no means the oldest. Balhorn (2004: 82) explores the *Oxford English Dictionary* (OED) and finds instances of this singular use over the past 400 years, and Sklar (1988: 420) claims that the use has been 'available to us for at least five hundred years'. Bodine (1975: 131) goes even further, arguing that 'English has *always* had other linguistic devices for referring to sex-indefinite referents, notably, the use of singular "they"' [my italics]. In an attempt to put a specific date on Bodine's claim of *always*, Curzan (2003: 70–1) explores epicene pronouns in the history of English and confirms that '[g]eneric *they* occurs as early as Old English in written texts', as seen in (6):

(6) Gif oxa ofhnite <u>wer (oððe) wif</u>, þæt *hie* dead sien, sie he mid stanum ofworpod
     (Alfred's *Introduction to Laws*, 32)
     'If an ox gores <u>a man or a woman</u>, so that *they* be dead, may he [the ox] be
     killed with stones' (from Curzan 2003: 70–1)

According to Curzan (2003: 71), *they* (*hie*) in (6) can be considered either plural or
singular, given the disjunctive coordinator *or* (*oððe*) in the antecedent:

> the pronoun *they* can also be used and interpreted as either plural (assuming a
> plural understanding of 'a man or a woman') or as singular and generic in this
> context (assuming the grammatical disjunction with "or" holds to require a singular
> generic pronoun). In fact, this kind of disjunctive construction seems particularly
> conducive to early uses of *they* to refer to a grammatically singular antecedent and
> it is the subject of discussion in nineteenth- and early twentieth-century grammars
> . . . In any case, *they* is being used in at least quasi-singular generic constructions in
> Old English, and the evidence becomes more prominent in Middle English.

The fact that Curzan herself considers Old English cases such as (6) instances of 'quasi-
singular generic constructions' has led authors such as Balhorn (2004) to argue that it
is difficult to find singular *they* before the fourteenth century. Thus, he explores two
Middle English texts, Chaucer's *Canterbury Tales* (written at the end of the fourteenth
century and copied at the beginning of the fifteenth century) and *Ancrene Wisse*
(thirteenth century). In the former he finds clear examples, such as (7):

(7) That <u>euery wight</u> hath deyntee to cheffare
     With *hem* and eek to sellen *hem* hir ware. (*Man of Law's Tale*, 139–40)
     'That everyone wanted to buy from them and also to sell them their
     merchandise'. (from Balhorn 2004: 93; Balhorn's translation)

According to Balhorn (2004), however, this is the only 'instance in the *Canterbury Tales*
where Chaucer has violated singular concord within the clausal domain of the
antecedent and where there are no particular pragmatic pressures that preclude the
singular' (Balhorn 2004: 93). In all other examples quoted in his article, singular *they*
may be motivated by pragmatic factors such as conjoined clauses, as in (8), in which
they cannot be devoid of plural meaning because of the following *iusten and daunce*
'jousted and dance':

(8) Made <u>euery wight</u> to been in swich plesaunce
     That al that Monday <u>iusten</u> *they* <u>and daunce</u> (*Knight's Tale*, 2486–7)
     'Made everyone so happy that they jousted and danced all that Monday'
     (from Balhorn 2004: 93; my translation)

Balhorn (2004) also considers *Ancrene Wisse*, an earlier Middle English text, in search
for cases of singular *they*. One of the singular qualities of this text is that in the
thirteenth century gender in English was still grammatical, and thus it is possible to

analyse cases of nouns whose grammatical gender does not correspond with the sex of the extra-linguistic referent, such as *þe deade, þe god* 'the dead, the good', which are grammatically masculine and refer to people of either sex. His findings in this respect are clear: 'there is no use of plural third-person pronouns with singular generic antecedents; instead, singular, grammatical concord is always maintained' (Balhorn 2004: 94–5). Nonetheless, *Ancrene Wisse* was written with a special focus on women (it is a guide for anchoresses), and the coordinate construction *he or she* is used to make clear references to women, as in (9):

> (9) weila he seiðwa is me þt *he oðer heo* habbeð swuch word icaht . . . þt is muchel
>   sorhe. for ifeole oðer þing *he oðer heo* is swiðe to herien (*Ancrene Wisse*, 47)
>   'Woe is to the one that *he or she* has caught such talk . . . that is a great sorrow,
>   for in many other ways *he or she* is greatly to be praised' (from Curzan 2003:
>   68; also quoted in Balhorn 2004: 96)

According to Balhorn (2004), the reason why singular *they* is not found in *Ancrene Wisse* while it is recorded in the *Canterbury Tales* must not be sought in social factors, but in strictly linguistic ones: while gender remains a grammatical issue, agreement between antecedents and pronouns is determined by grammatical gender, and explicit reference to both sexes is obtained through coordinating constructions (as in *Ancrene Wisse*). However, once gender is exclusively determined by the sex of the extra-linguistic referent, writers (and, supposedly, speakers) resort to available linguistic structures to establish agreement, as is the case in the *Canterbury Tales*, whose writer and copyist are very unlikely to have felt any kind of social pressure to use a specific epicene pronoun.

Thus, the first unquestionable instances of singular *they* are to be found in the late fourteenth century (Chaucer) and its use is justified exclusively in intra-linguistic terms. Nonetheless, its development has undergone the influence of two different social phenomena, namely linguistic prescriptivism and language democratization, as discussed in the following section.

2.2. Social factors affecting the use of singular *they*: Prescriptivism and democratization

Some aspects of grammar (and in particular, pronominal paradigms) are very sensitive to social factors such as changes in the hierarchical structure of society. This is the case, for example, with the second person pronoun in both English and in Russian. Before feudalism neither language had distinctive second person pronouns to mark superiority or non-intimacy, on the one hand, and inferiority or intimacy, on the other (Brown and Gilman 1960: 254–5; see also Bodine 1975: 141–2). However, in English the hierarchical structure of feudalism resulted in the introduction of *you* as a second person singular pronoun, used to address someone socially superior or non-intimate, when it had previously referred exclusively to plural referents (*thou* being the inferiority or intimacy counterpart). According to Bodine (1975: 142), '[t]hese analyses of change in second person pronoun usage rank among the most convincing demonstrations ever given of the social motivation of linguistic change'. Epicene pronouns are another example, and two social forces are usually identified in the evolution of singular *they*, namely the emergence of prescriptive grammar in the eighteenth century and second-wave feminism in the 1970s (Bodine 1975: 130; Paterson 2014: 76–112).

The publication of the first prescriptive grammars at the end of the eighteenth century constitutes an obstacle to the use of singular *they*, which until then had been both accepted and widespread (see Bodine 1975: 130; Madson and Hessling 1999: 571, among others). One of the earliest proscriptive first rules on the use of singular *they* can be found in Kirby (1746), who makes the following defence of the use of generic *he*: 'The masculine Person answers to the general Name, which comprehends both Male and Female; as *Any Person, who knows what he say*' (Kirby 1746: 117; quoted in Bodine 1975: 135). This eighteenth-century prescription continued to dominate English handbooks in the second half of the twentieth century. Bodine (1975: 139) looked at thirty-three high school grammars used in the US and found that twenty-eight of them advised against using singular *they*, prompting her to consider those authors 'the docile heirs to the androcentric tradition of the prescriptive grammarians'.

However, as usually happens with linguistic prescriptions, the avoidance of singular *they* did not extend to the oral language, and this epicene pronoun survived in British and American English, some grammarians even finding it 'not illogical', as noted by Paterson (2014: 86). In fact, singular *they* survived in non-written registers until second-wave feminism enhanced its use from the 1970s in an attempt to fight sexist language. The impact of this second social force is evident in different varieties of English. Regarding British English, for example, Quirk et al. accept some limited uses of singular *they* in their 1985 grammar (as do Biber et al. 1999: 316–17 and Huddleston and Pullum et al. 2002: 494), whereas they had 'questioned them in 1972' (Meyers 1993: 187, as quoted by Paterson 2014: 100). In American English, Sklar (1988) finds that the most recent handbooks she explores pay more attention to gender agreement and its social implications, while this was not the case earlier (Sklar 1988: 420). Australian English, another inner-circle variety of English, has also been explored in terms of the use of epicene pronouns. Pauwels (2001) found that in the 1990s radio stations reduced the use of generic *he* in accordance with non-sexist language reforms.

This kind of effect of changing social norms on language has been termed 'democratization', defined as 'the removal of inequalities and asymmetries in the discursive and linguistic rights, obligations and prestige of groups of people' (Fairclough 1992: 201), as 'a reflection, through language, of changing norms in cultural relations' (Leech et al. 2009: 259) and as the 'speakers' tendency to avoid unequal and face threatening modes of interaction' (Farrelly and Seoane 2012: 393). The feminist claim that singular *they* is the non-sexist option to refer to a generic antecedent (such as *person, anybody*, etc.) does indeed aim to remove inequalities (between males and females), to reflect through language a change in cultural relations (in that second-wave feminism fought against the invisibility of women in various respects) and to give speakers the option of avoiding an unequal mode of interaction (i.e. one in which females are subsumed by males). In fact, one of the clearest signs of the progressive democratization of the English language in the twentieth century has been the reduction of sexist linguistic features such as generic *he* and masculine professional terms (such as *fireman*, largely replaced by gender-neutral *firefighter*), as noted by Farrelly and Seoane (2012: 394).

So, singular *they* has been available as an epicene pronoun from the fourteenth century onwards, with speakers resorting to it once grammatical gender began to be replaced by natural gender. Its use was widespread, alongside generic *he* and coordinate constructions such as *he or she*, until eighteenth century grammarians advised against it, claiming that generic *he* should be considered the only valid epicene pronoun. Despite the proscription of singular *they*, it survived as an oral feature until the 1970s, when second-wave feminists revitalized its use as non-sexist linguistic practice. This has had an effect on different varieties of English, notably British, American and Australian Englishes, and as an example of language change it falls within the general process of democratization.

3. English in India, Hong Kong and Singapore: Development and language contact

This section describes the social and socio-linguistic background of the varieties of English analysed in this chapter, namely India, Hong Kong and Singapore, paying especial attention to their relation with their 'matrilect', or input variety, in this case British English (3.1), and to their substrate (3.2). Section 3.1 focuses on the different levels of evolution of the three Asian varieties regarding British English (according to Schneider's 2007 Dynamic Model), with the double aim of (i) describing the different developments of each variety (and their degree of dependence on or independence from the matrilect); and (ii) determining whether the potential 'democratic' uses of singular *they* are novel uses developed in these varieties or if they were inherited from the matrilect. Section 3.2, in turn, provides an overview of the different substrate languages with which English entered into contact in each of these regions and shows the possible third person singular pronouns in these varieties.

3.1. English in India, Hong Kong and Singapore: Development and current state

Schneider's (2007) Dynamic Model of Postcolonial Englishes places the different varieties of English spoken in ex-colonies around the globe into five evolutionary phases, these described in terms of socio-political background, identity constructions, socio-linguistic conditions and their linguistic effects. The five phases in Schneider's (2007) model are:

(1) Foundation: Native English-speaking settlers establish themselves in the new territory and use different regional varieties.
(2) Exonormative stabilization: English is stabilized in the territory according to British English rules, although the lexicon starts to incorporate localisms.
(3) Nativization: Mixed codes are commonly used and grammar sees the emergence of new word formation processes, varying prepositional usage, etc.

(4) Endonormative stabilization: After political independence, descendants of settlers consider themselves different from their country of origin and are aware of the new language variety they use; national dictionaries are published.

(5) Differentiation: New varieties emerge out of the newly standardized variety.

According to Schneider's (2007) model, the three Postcolonial Englishes studied in this chapter are presently at different developmental stages. HK is the least advanced variety, since it entered phase 3 in 1960 and exhibits no signs of phase 4 (2007: 135–9). IND, which entered phase 3 in 1905, still shows little evidence of entering phase 4 since an 'endonormative attitude as such is definitely gaining ground, but it is also far from being generally accepted' (Schneider 2007: 171).[2] Finally, SIN is considered to have been clearly in phase 4 since the 1970s (Schneider 2007: 160). Thus, SIN is the most advanced variety, followed by IND and, finally, by HK. Specific details of the socio-historical and socio-linguistic situation of these languages are given in what follows.

English officially arrived in India in 1600, when Queen Elizabeth I granted a very favourable charter for London-based merchants (Schneider 2007: 162). Hence it became a trade colony, one in which the variety of English that arrived during the first decades was spoken by 'mostly uneducated merchants, sailors, and soldiers' (Krishnaswamy and Burde 1998: 80). However, in the second half of the eighteenth century, the British interest in India moved from strictly economic matters to the political sphere, which turned the territory into an exploitation colony (Schneider 2007: 163). In the second half of the nineteenth century the teaching of English spread rapidly in large towns and cities (Mehrotra 1998: 3). Although English was typically considered the language of the upper classes, it was also required for communicative purposes by 'a wide range of middle-ranking functions (clerks, railway agents, military personnel, servants, etc.)' (Schneider 2007: 165). At the beginning of the twentieth century, English in India entered the nativization phase, and after independence (in 1947) it became a transitory official language, to be replaced by Hindi in 1965. However, this replacement never took place, and along with Hindi, English remained as an official language, coming to serve as an 'interethnic neutral link language' (Schneider 2007: 166–7). There are also some incipient symptoms of Indian English having entered phase 4. Thus, in a survey conducted by Kachru (1994) one quarter of respondents stated their preference for Indian English over the British model. However, the fact that three quarters still preferred British English and that this language still has a strong utilitarian purpose in India, functioning as 'an indicator of education and employability' (Collins 2013: 157), leads Schneider (2007: 173) to conclude that phase 4 is still far from our sight.

Hong Kong became a British colony much later than India, in 1841–1842, 'in the wake of the first Opium War' (Schneider 2007: 133), and English education arrived on the island soon after through missionaries (Bolton 2003: 192–4, 229–31). In 1898 Britain and China signed the Second Convention of Peking that guaranteed Hong Kong's colonial status for the next ninety-nine years. For the first seventy years of this period, education in English was restricted to a small, elitist section of the population, and, of course, education followed an exonormative approach (Schneider 2007: 135). The next phase, nativization, is considered to have started in the 1960s when Hong Kong began to become a 'wealthy, commercial and entrepreneurial powerhouse' (Bolton 2002: 33). Soon after, in 1970, negotiations between Britain and China regarding the handover of Hong Kong took place that had important socio-linguistic consequences, since a new middle class emerged, this involving the spread of education and the expansion of the role of English (Schneider 2007: 136), with the introduction of Anglo-Chinese secondary schools which fought back against the elitist character of English and led to 'mass bilingualism' (Bolton 2003: 84–7). Prescriptivism is evident in this last period of the twentieth century, which is a good indicator of Hong Kong entering phase 3, nativization, in that widespread complaints arose among academics in the 1970s regarding allegedly falling English standards (Bolton 2003: 108–11; see also Collins 2013: 157). The future of Hong Kong English is more difficult to predict than that of other Englishes, because Hong Kong did not gain independence, but rather was handed over to China. However, it exhibits enough features to indicate that it has clearly entered phase 3, nativization.

Singapore is a city-state island, with English arriving in 1819 when Thomas Stamford Raffles established a British trading post there. It became a British colony in 1867, and obtained its independence in 1963 (Deterding 2007: 2). Despite its relatively short history as a colony, Singapore is very advanced according to Schneider's (2007) Dynamic Model, since it entered phase 4 in the 1970s. The high speed in the development of this variety is rooted in its socio-historical context. Thus, at the beginning of the twentieth century many Chinese children began to attend English-medium schools, which is considered the likely origin of colloquial Singaporean English (or Singlish), as described by Gupta (1999: 1141–6; see also Schneider 2007: 154). During the Second World War, Singapore was occupied by the Japanese for three years (1942–1945), and by the time Britain assumed control, once more the population began to seek independence, which was obtained in 1965. The country was by now modernizing rapidly, to become a highly industrialized nation in which many ethnic groups coexist and in which 'Singaporean English has come to be the means of expression of this newly emerging Asian-cum-western culture' (Schneider 2007: 156). Singaporean English is considered very homogeneous (Ansaldo 2004), codification is in progress (Schneider 2007: 161), and there are also voices that anticipate phase 5, in that different ethnic varieties within Singaporean English can be identified. It is clear, then, that Singaporean English is the most advanced of the three varieties analysed in this chapter.

3.2. Language contact in India, Hong Kong and Singapore

Postcolonial Englishes are naturally contact varieties, since English was brought to different territories where other languages were the main vehicles of communication. These languages, which in contact linguistics are usually termed 'substratum' or 'substrate languages', are typologically very distant from English and also from one another. An outline of the substrates of the three Asian Englishes in relation to their typological family is shown in Table 9.1:

Table 9.1 Substrate languages in Asian Englishes (adapted from Lim and Gisborne 2009: 126)

Asian English	Austronesian Malay	Dravidian Tamil	Indo-Aryan Hindi	Sinitic		
				Cantonese	Hokkien	Mandarin
Hong Kong				✓		✓
India		✓	✓			
Singapore	✓	✓		✓	✓	✓

Table 9.2 Third person singular pronouns in Asian substrates

	Nominative	Oblique
Cantonese[3]	*kéuih (héuih)*	*kéuih (héuih)*
Hindi[4]	Proximal: *yəh*	Proximal: *is*
	Distal: *vəh*	Distal: *us*
Tamil[5]	Masculine: *avan*	Masculine: *avan*
	Feminine: *ava(ḷ)*	Feminine: *ava(ḷ)*
Mandarin[6]	*tā*	*tā*
Malay[7]	*dia / ia*	*dia / ia*
Hokkien[8]	*i*	*in*

An initial hypothesis in the analysis of singular *they* in these Asian Englishes is that the presence of singular *they* in each of them may be influenced by the existence or not of general third person singular pronouns in each of the substrates. Hence, Table 9.2 sets out the possible forms of each of these Asian languages which could enhance the use of singular *they*. A distinction is made between the nominative and the oblique forms, because, as can be seen, in some languages gender differences are shown in only one of the cases.

None of the substrates, with the exception of Tamil, has specific masculine and feminine third person singular pronouns. Therefore, it is possible to conclude that these languages do have a general way of referring to an epicene antecedent without compromising its gender and this may constitute a factor in favour of a higher frequency of singular *they*. The fact that Tamil, one of the main substrates of Indian English, does make a gender difference, could justify a lower frequency of epicene *they* in IND than in HK or SIN. Nevertheless, if any difference is found between HK and SIN, language contact cannot be considered a conditioning factor.

4. Methodology

This study follows a corpus-based methodology, because, although it has some drawbacks, as noted by Paterson (2014: 46–50), it is also the best way of conducting comparative studies among varieties for which similar corpora exist. In this respect, the study of World Englishes has the distinct advantage of being able to use the *International Corpus of English* (ICE), a project which aims to provide comparable representative corpora of varieties of English throughout the world (Greenbaum 1996; Nelson 2009). Each ICE corpus consists of one million words (60 per cent of spoken material, 40 per cent of written material) in twelve broad text-types, as shown in Table 9.3.

Therefore, ICE corpora provide many different contexts in which an epicene noun may be used and where speakers will have to choose an epicene pronoun from their grammatical inventory. Indeed, over 30,000 tokens were extracted from the three corpora scrutinized, namely ICE-IND (India), ICE-HK (Hong Kong) and ICE-SIN (Singapore), distributed per variety and morphological form, as shown in Table 9.4.

The large number of tokens in Table 9.4 was manually filtered by exploring the immediate context in search of a possible antecedent of the pronoun. On occasions, this very time-consuming task was not enough, and the context had to be enlarged to include up to several hundreds of previous words (especially, although not exclusively, in private dialogues), because the antecedent may be the topic of a conversation and is not repeated very often, or because the context may be misleading, as in (10):

Table 9.3 Text-types included in ICE corpora

SPOKEN	Dialogues	Private	S1A
		Public	S1B
	Monologues	Unscripted	S2A
		Scripted	S2B
WRITTEN	Non-printed	Student writing	W1A
		Letters	W1B
	Printed	Academic writing	W2A
		Popular writing	W2B
		Reportage	W2C
		Instructional writing	W2D
		Persuasive writing	W2E
		Creative writing	W2F

Table 9.4 Total number of forms scrutinized

	HK	IND	SIN
they	6,472	5,724	5,716
them	1,662	1,627	1,608
their	2,386	2,036	2,403
theirs	9	6	13
themselves	149	178	194
themself	3	1	0
theirselves	1	0	0
TOTAL	10,682	9,572	9,934

(10) We are arguing whether <u>Executive Councillors</u> of course as I said in the meeting last week I said there is a problem that has been built into the structure is that Executive Councillors are being appointed to the Legislative Council So they are in their own way Legco members as well and I find that very unfortunate I don't think that should be the case But anyway they are here and we cannot exclude them <?> So </?> <u>one member</u> suggested that okay *they* are also Legco members and these are Legco Committees (ICE-HK:S2A-033)

Thus, a cursory reading of the extract in (10) may lead to the wrong conclusion that the antecedent of *they* is *one member*. A more careful reading reveals, however, that the antecedent is in fact *Executive Councillors*, a plural noun phrase and, therefore, the example is not relevant for the present study.

Although the aim was to find singular antecedents, not all singular cases were included in the dataset. Hence countries, common collective nouns and companies were excluded because of their collective meaning.

In addition, the study of World Englishes requires extra caution, since many of these varieties have a variable nominal morphology that very often results in the absence of the plural suffix *-(e)s* in contexts in which it would feature in the Standard varieties (Mesthrie and Bhatt 2008: 52). On occasions, the context disambiguates the number of the antecedent, as in (11), where the determiner *those* signals a plural noun phrase:

(11) And common mistake made by <u>those average student</u> is *they* are careless *they* are little or no experience in application and applied type questions and *they* are poor in communication as well (ICE-HK:S1B-071)

However, there are cases in which the context does not offer much assistance. Those were included in the database as unclear examples. One of these is given in (12):

(12) The database engine will process the data uh directly with your hard disk make some uh transactions and then we 'll make the result back to the front-end tools and <u>user</u> can in this kind of format *they* can uh access the data in the remote site (ICE-HK:S2A-059)

In (12) the absence of the article preceding the noun *user* suggests that it is a plural noun without an inflectional marker, but since the use of the article in World Englishes also varies from Standard varieties, sequences such as (12) were included in the database as unclear examples of singular *they*. All in all, out of the 30,188 examples scrutinized (Table 9.4), only 321 were included in the database as cases of singular *they*, 284 were clear representatives of this use, and thirty-seven were unclear examples. All of these are discussed in the following section.

Table 9.5 Total number of valid examples of singular *they*

	HK	IND	SIN
Clear cases	117	75	92
Unclear cases	29	3	5
TOTAL	146	78	97

5. Results

The number of clear and unclear cases of singular *they* found in the corpora is shown in Table 9.5, which serves to indicate two facts. Firstly, unclear cases are much more common in HK than in IND or SIN. Secondly, HK features the highest number of cases of singular *they* and the difference is significant between HK and IND as well as between HK and SIN. The differences between IND and SIN, however, are not significant.[9]

The 321 examples of singular *they* represent 1.06 per cent of all tokens, a percentage considerably lower than that found in the first decade of the twenty-first century in press (3.06 per cent) and in prose (4.38 per cent) by Paterson (2014: 51). This difference may be due to diachronic reasons (Paterson's corpora and my own represent two different periods), a different kind of influence of politically correct language in the UK and in Asian ex-colonies, or the effect of the text-type (ICE corpora include many more text-types than press and general prose). This hypothesis is tested in Section 5.1.

5.1. Text-type distribution

Text-type has been found to be a determining factor in the use of singular *they* (Parini 2013; Paterson 2014). Figure 9.1 shows the normalized frequencies (per 100,000 words) of singular *they* according to the different text-types included in ICE (see Table 9.3), and it exhibits very interesting preliminary results. To begin with, singular *they* appears to be mainly an oral feature, not only because it has a higher frequency in spoken text-types, but also because its frequency decreases as spontaneity is reduced (notice the declining line in the histogram from S1A to S2B). Secondly, the written registers in which singular *they* features most often are student writing (W1A) and creative writing (W2F). While this high incidence in creative writing may be related to the fact that novels with a lot of dialogue will naturally tend to reflect oral language, the high frequency in student writing leads to another hypothesis: singular *they* might be so common in the latter text-type because students are (or tend to be) younger than other informants, and hence this could reflect a change in progress. This hypothesis is tested in Section 5.3 below, after discussing in Section 5.2 the role played by the type of antecedent.

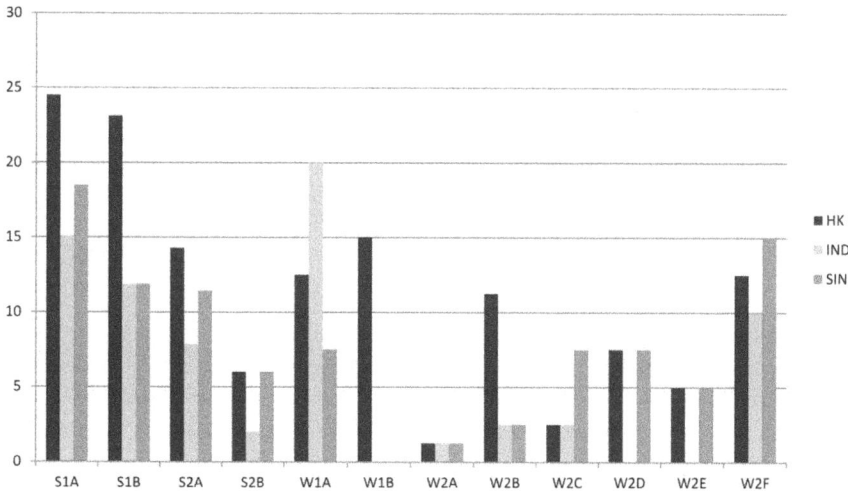

Figure 9.1 Normalized frequencies of singular *they* per text-type.

5.2. Type of antecedent

Singular *they* is co-indexed with a number of antecedent types, which Paterson (2014: 36–42) presents in a gradient from clear indefiniteness to increasingly syntactic definiteness. The four main types of antecedents are:

1. Indefinite pronouns: *everyone, someone*, etc.
    In this context, generic *he* is considered to add a masculine meaning to the antecedent (Balhorn 2004: 84; Paterson 2014: 37).

    (13) Now when <u>somebody</u><,> is treated in hospital *they* get rehabilitation there but *they* want *they* will have to go out of hospital (ICE-HK:S1B-025)

2. Noun phrase premodified by a quantifier: *any, some, every, no*.
    According to Paterson (2014: 39), singular *they* is also the epicene of choice in this context in British English:

    (14) If you go <u>any unknown <w> person</u>'s </w> house, no wonder *they* would ask <del> for </del> water for you. (ICE-IND:W1A-00)

3. Indefinite noun phrases: *a, an*.
    The use of other epicene pronouns (such as generic *he*), as in (15), is not so unexpected as in the previous types:

    (15) A: What do <u>a neurologist</u> does
         B: *they* treat non-surgical conditions of the nervous system (ICE-SIN:S1B-063)

4. Definite noun phrases: *the, this, that*.
    This is the most definite syntactic type, in which singular *they* serves three roles at the same time, according to Weidmann (1984: 68, quoted in Paterson 2014: 41), namely, 'it says nothing about the gender (or sex) of the referent,' it does not 'mark the referent for number' and 'it does not even specify whether a real referent exists'. See (16):

> (16) So if the students 're is uh quite bad they need to responsible for that that but but if <u>the teacher</u> is quite good uh *they* explain all the things in the book (ICE-HK:S1A-085)

The first two types of antecedent appear to justify the presence of singular *they* with specifically intra-linguistic reasons (namely a plural reading of the antecedent and the awkward collocation of generic *he*), while the exclusively singular reading of types 3 and 4 calls for social and pragmatic factors for the choice of singular *they*, such as a wish for a more democratic discourse or the avoidance of sexist forms. This division of the four types of antecedent into two large types justifies the representation of Figure 9.2 with lighter shades of grey (types 1 and 2) and darker shades of grey (types 3 and 4).

Figure 9.2 shows that not only does HK record more instances of singular *they* (as seen in Table 9.5), but its high frequency in this variety is also accompanied by over 60 per cent of occurrences with antecedents of types 3 and 4. The equivalent type of antecedents in IND represents some 25 per cent of all cases, and the proportion in SIN is 40 per cent. These differences in the collocation with specific types of antecedents can be interpreted as a symptom of a more advanced stage of democratization in HK than in IND and SIN.

This is reinforced by the text-type distribution of the definite and indefinite antecedents (which are better indicators of potential democratization) in the three varieties under analysis (Figure 9.3). Here HK again ranks higher than IND in all registers, and also higher than SIN in all text-types, with the exception of W2D (instructional writing) and W2E (persuasive writing).

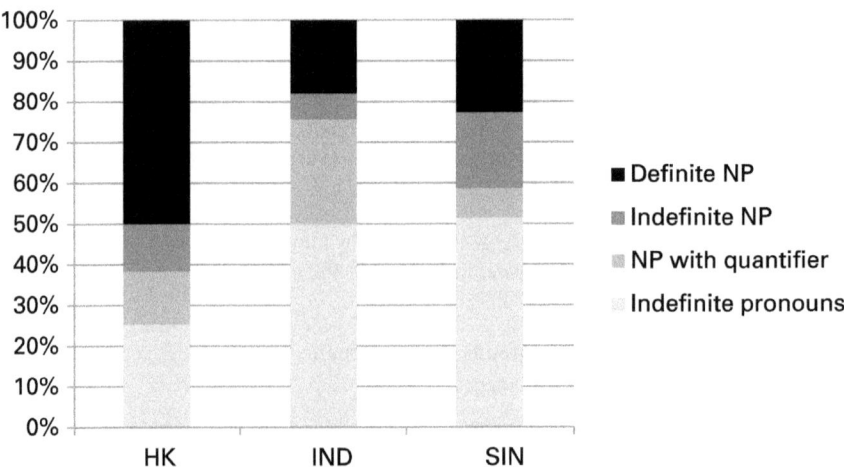

Figure 9.2 Types of antecedent found in the three varieties.

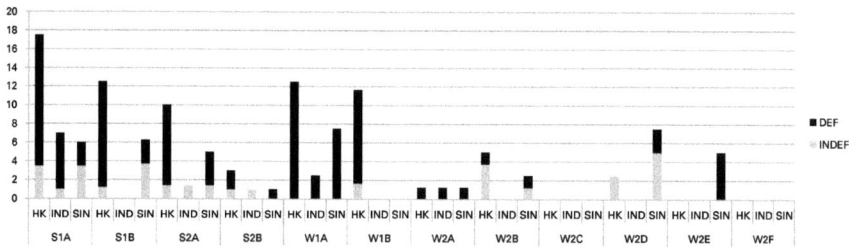

Figure 9.3 Definite and indefinite antecedents across text-types (normalized frequencies).

5.3. Age of the speakers

A useful advantage with ICE is that each corpus is accompanied by a metadata folder which includes extra-linguistic information about each text included in the corpus, such as the age and sex of the speakers. Unfortunately, this information is not available for ICE-SIN, so the results shown in sections 5.3 and 5.4 will be based solely on ICE-HK and ICE-IND. The interest of focusing on the age of the speakers relates to Labov's (1963) apparent time hypothesis, which establishes that a historical change can be studied using synchronic data from speakers of different ages, because the language of individuals tends to remain unchanged after a certain age. Since, as seen in 5.1, singular *they* features prominently in student writing in all three Asian varieties considered, it is hypothesized that this epicene pronoun will be more frequent in a couple of decades. Because age groups differ from one corpus to another (and there are inconsistencies within ICE-IND), I have merged both classifications so that their data can be compared, as shown in Table 9.6.

Table 9.6 Age groups in the corpora and classification proposed

HK classification	IND classification	Proposed classification
14–16		14–16
17–20	18–25	17–25
21–25		
26–30	26–33	26–35
31–35		
36–40	34–41	36–40
	35–41	
41–45	42–49	41–50
	45	
46–50	50	
51–55	52	51–59
	54	
56–60		
60 plus	60 plus	60 plus

In order to see which age group uses singular *they* most often, one cannot rely on raw numbers, because they may be biased by the differing presence of each age group in the corpus. Ideally, normalized frequencies per words uttered by each age group are needed, but since this information is not included in the ICE metadata, Figure 9.4 shows the percentage for each age group in terms of the number of speakers belonging to each of them, alongside the percentage of singular *they* uttered by each age group. In an ideal situation, if singular *they* were evenly distributed among the different age groups, the two columns of each variety would be identical, but they are not.

Figure 9.4 reveals that HK and IND speakers behave very differently. While the distribution of the proportion of speakers of a given age group and the frequency of singular *they* by age group is nearly the same in IND, in HK significant differences are found. Several age groups exhibit significantly higher frequencies of singular *they* than can be explained in terms of the number of informants in the corpus; these are group 17–25 (red bar), group 36–40 (green bar) and group 60 plus (brown bar). This makes it impossible to reach any conclusion from the apparent time hypothesis, since singular *they* exhibits higher frequencies with very young, young and older speakers.

Nevertheless, if we recall the findings in Section 5.2, we can make a distinction between cases of singular *they* with antecedents of types 1 and 2, and cases with antecedents of types 3 and 4 (where the influence of second-wave feminism, and, therefore, linguistic democratization, may be more visible). If we focus on the latter type, we obtain Figure 9.5, which shows that there is a sharp divide between HK 'younger' speakers (below 40) and 'older' speakers (above 41), in that the former exhibit a higher frequency of singular *they* with antecedents such as *the lecturer* or *a student* than expected from the number of speakers belonging to those groups. In IND, however, there are no significant differences, and the distribution of singular *they* with those kinds of antecedent corresponds roughly to the number of speakers of each age group.

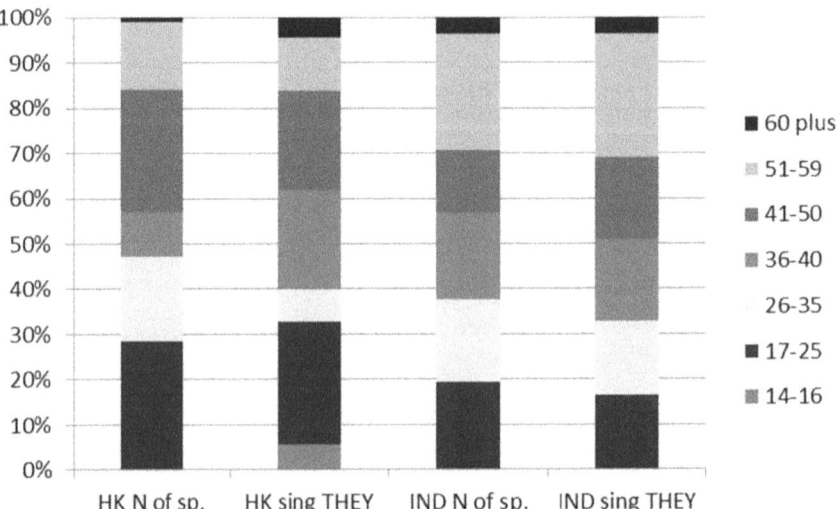

Figure 9.4 Correspondence between number of speakers and frequency of singular *they*.

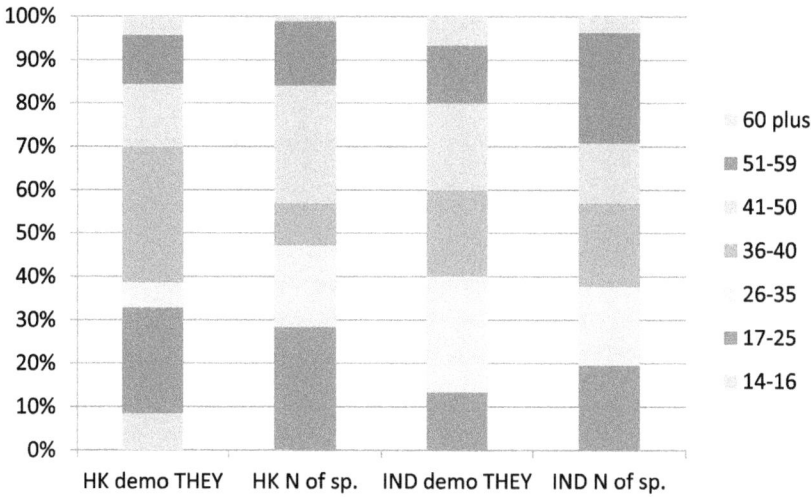

Figure 9.5 Correspondence between number of speakers and frequency of singular *they* with definite and indefinite NPs as antecedent.

5.4. Gender of the speakers

The last factor considered here to describe the situation of singular *they* in Asian Englishes is the sex of the speakers who use this epicene pronoun. According to the literature, women use gender-neutral pronouns more often than men (e.g., Laitinen 2007: 255), so this section considers the role played by gender (or sex) in the use of singular *they* in HK and IND, again because the metadata for ICE-SIN are not available.

Figure 9.6 illustrates the gender of the speakers who use singular *they* in HK and IND, and shows that women use this pronoun slightly more frequently than men in

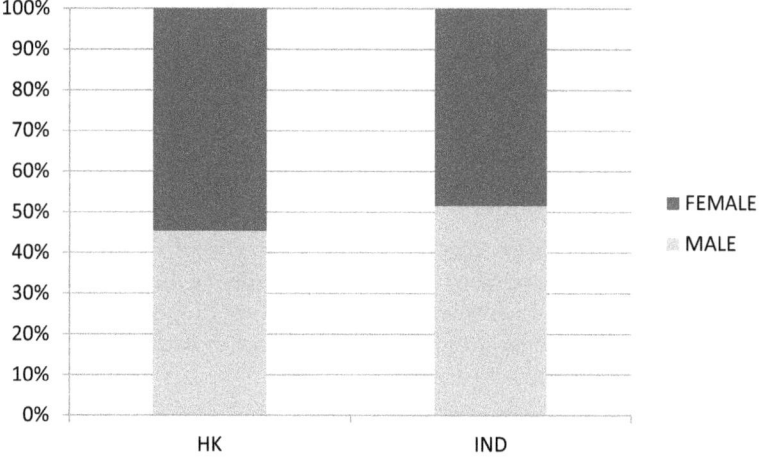

Figure 9.6 Gender distribution of singular *they* in HK and IND.

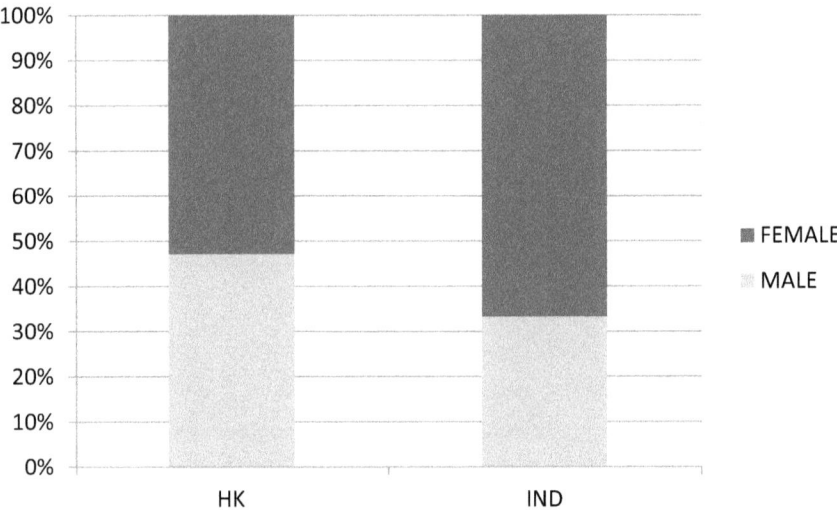

Figure 9.7 Gender distribution of singular *they* in HK and IND (only definite and indefinite NPs as antecedent).

HK, but not so in IND. However, the difference between both varieties is statistically non-significant.

We can proceed, as with the age of the speakers, to reduce the number of tokens to those which involve an antecedent represented by a definite or an indefinite noun phrase, because those contexts are expected to be more relevant for the identification of potential democratization of the language. In this way we obtain Figure 9.7, which shows a similar picture to that in Figure 9.6 for HK, but a considerably different one for IND; women in IND use singular *they* with a much higher frequency than men. If we consider that women are said to be the motors of language change (Labov 1990; Nevalainen 1996; among others), we could interpret this as a symptom of Indian women taking the lead in the rise of singular *they* as an epicene pronoun. Nevertheless, without further research this is a tentative suggestion rather than a firm conclusion.

6. Discussion and conclusions

This chapter has studied the frequency and use of singular *they* in three Asian Englishes as represented in the corresponding ICE corpora, considering the following variables: type of antecedent, text-type distribution, and age and sex of speakers. The data have been contrasted with those for British English from other sources whenever available. The main findings are summarized below:

- The frequency of singular *they* in the three Asian Englishes considered (data from the 1990s) is systematically lower than that shown in British English in the first decade of the twenty-first century.

- Among Asian Englishes, HK is the variety that ranks highest in the use of this epicene pronoun, while IND ranks lowest.
- Text-type distribution shows that singular *they* is much more common in oral registers and that its frequency decreases as the spontaneity of the speakers is reduced.
- The different sorts of antecedent analysed were divided into those which historically trigger singular *they* (indefinite pronouns and noun phrases with quantifiers), because they can have a plural interpretation, and those which are considered to be more susceptible to the application of democratizing changes (noun phrases with definite and indefinite articles). The fact that the latter type exhibits a much higher frequency in HK than in IND or SIN was interpreted as further evidence that the use of singular *they* is more extended in this Asian variety than in the other two.
- The apparent-time study conducted on HK and IND does not appear to suggest that singular *they* increased in frequency over recent decades, something which did happen in British English as a result of tendencies stemming from second-wave feminism.
- Analysis of the gender of the speakers reveals that there are no significant differences in HK, but that in IND women appear to be more willing to use singular *they* in cases considered more prone to be the result of democratization.

These findings suggest that HK is more 'advanced' in the use of singular *they* than IND and SIN. But can this be related to the alleged democratization of language? To begin with, we can exclude the influence of language contact, because, as shown in Section 2.1, differences between HK and SIN cannot be interpreted on the basis of the substratum. Secondly, it could be argued that it is no surprise that HK is closer to British English regarding the use of singular *they*, because it is less advanced according to Schneider's (2007) Dynamic Model (see Section 2.1 above). Yet this would ignore an important fact: the rise of singular *they* in the twentieth century is related to a social phenomenon that took place after HK entered phase 3, nativization, and therefore when it abandoned phase 2, exonormative stabilization. Thirdly, before we conclude that democratization is responsible to any extent for the use of singular *they* in Asian Englishes, we must at least explore other so-called democratic features. For the purposes of this chapter (and because of space constraints), we will only briefly comment on another grammatical feature which is considered to have undergone democratization, namely the use of modal *must* and the semi-modals *have to, need (to)* and *want to* (see, for example, Myhill 1995). Loureiro-Porto (2019) shows that the replacement of *must* with the semi-modals (and their corresponding grammaticalization) is more advanced in HK, followed by SIN and, at much greater distance, by IND. Therefore, the ranking of singular *they* would be HK > IND / SIN (because there are no significant differences between IND and SIN), while the ranking of the modals would be HK > SIN > IND. The only consistent result is that HK ranks higher in both 'democratic' features, but IND and SIN exhibit varying results for each of the variables. Having discarded factors such as language contact and the evolutionary phase, it seems plausible to conclude that democratization indeed seems to be more at work in HK than in IND and SIN (although the difference between IND and SIN is difficult to justify).[10] We must not forget, nevertheless, that democratization is directly linked to pragmatics and politeness, which has been found to exhibit different cultural interpretations in English-speaking communities (see Kachru 2017: 276–81, for example). Therefore, situations which are considered face threatening in western societies and which involve the use of sexist language may not be considered to have an undemocratic value in some Asian territories. In addition, the findings presented here are preliminary, and for a fuller description and analysis of singular *they*, a comparison must be made with the other main epicene pronoun, generic *he*, as well as with the coordinate construction *he or she*, both of which stand in clear competition with *they*. However, this must remain the subject of further research.

Notes

1   It was both a privilege and an honour to be 'raised' in Teresa's team. When she was my teacher, some 20 years ago, I admired her acute sense of rigour and her vast knowledge of language. However, it is through getting to know her as a colleague that I have been able to see her most extraordinary features: friendly leadership, vital enthusiasm, and extreme generosity. It is hard to imagine what my life (and the lives of many other scholars now spreading her approach to Linguistics throughout Spain and beyond) would be like without her inspiration. The dedication of an article to Teresa might be appropriate in the circumstances, yet it seems woefully insufficient as a means of conveying the enormous debt of gratitude that I, like many others, owe her.

    For financial support I am grateful to the European Regional Development Fund and the Spanish Ministry of Economy, Industry and Competitiveness (grant FFI2017-82162-P). Thanks are also due to two anonymous reviewers, whose comments have improved the original version of this manuscript to a large extent. Needless to say, errors or omissions that remain are my responsibility.

2   Against this, Mukherjee (2007: 182) claims that IND is 'endonormatively stabilized but showing some aspects of ongoing nativization', that is, it has entered phase 4, although it still exhibits features of phase 3.

3   Source: Yip and Matthews (2000: 17).

4   Source: Kachru (2006: 62–3).

5   Source: Schiffman (1999: 116, 118)

6   Source: Ross and Sheng Ma (2006: 24).

7   Source: Windstedt (1913: 107).

8   Source: Chappell (2019: 9, Table 7).

9   The Z-Score for the comparison between HK and IND is −5.6307. The *p*-value is 0, which means that the result is significant at $p < 0.05$. As for HK and SIN, Z-Score is −3.9873, *p*-value is 6E-05 (significant at $p < 0.05$). Finally, as for IND and SIN, Z-Score is 1.684, *p*-value is 0.09296 (*not* significant at $p < 0.05$).

10 An anonymous reviewer aptly notes that the phenomenon at work may be Americanization (see Leech et al. 2009: 252–9), rather than democratization. Though it may be difficult to disentangle both phenomena, because the 'democratic' uses of language seem to start in the US, for the sake of rigour I consider it safer to focus on democratization as the main factor behind these changes, without any reference to

whether such changes originated in America or not (the same could be applied to modal verbs, for example). A possible way to discern whether Americanization or democratization are behind these changes could require a clear list of markers which show the influence of American English on other varieties (e.g., quotative *be like*; Leech et al. 2009: 258) and democratic changes which do not originate in the US. That, however, falls out of the scope of this chapter and must be left for future research.

Corpora

ICE = *The International Corpus of English*. http://ice-corpora.net/ice.

References

Ansaldo, Umberto (2004), 'The Evolution of Singapore English. Finding the Matrix', in Lisa Lim (ed), *Singapore English. A Grammatical Description*, 127–49, Amsterdam: Benjamins.

Balhorn, Mark (2004), 'The Rise of Epicene *They*', *Journal of English Linguistics*, 32 (2): 79–104.

Balhorn, Mark (2009), 'The Epicene Pronoun in Contemporary Newspaper Prose', *American Speech*, 84 (4): 391–413.

Biber, Douglas, Stig Johansson, Geoffrey Leech, Susan Conrad and Edward Finegan (1999), *Longman Grammar of Spoken and Written English*, London: Longman.

Bodine, Ann (1975), 'Androcentrism in Prescriptive Grammar: Singular 'They', Sex-Indefinite 'He', and 'He or She'', *Language in Society*, 4: 129–46.

Bolton, Kingsley (2002), 'The Sociolinguistics of Hong Kong and the Space for Hong Kong English', in Kingsley Bolton (ed), *Hong Kong English: Autonomy and Creativity*, 29–55, Aberdeen: Hong Kong University Press.

Bolton, Kingsley (2003), *Chinese Englishes. A Sociolinguistic History*, Cambridge: Cambridge University Press.

Brown, Roger and Albert Gilman (1960), 'The Pronouns of Power and Solidarity', in Thomas A. Sebeok (ed), *Style in Language*, 253–76, Cambridge, MA: M.I.T. Press.

Chappell, Hilary (2019), 'A Sketch of Southern Min Grammar', in Alice Vittrant and Justin Watkins (eds), *The Mainland Southeast Asia Linguistic Area,* 176–233, Berlin: De Gruyter Mouton.

Collins, Peter (2013), 'Grammatical Colloquialism and the English Quasi-modals: A Comparative Study', in Juana I. Marín-Arrese, Marta Carretero, Jorge Arús Hita and Johan van der Auwera (eds), *English Modality. Core, Periphery and Evidentiality*, 155–69, Berlin and New York: De Gruyter Mouton.

Curzan, Anne (2003), *Gender Shifts in the History of English*, Cambridge: Cambridge University Press.

Deterding, David (2007), *Singapore English*, Edinburgh: Edinburgh University Press.

Fairclough, Norman (1992), *Discourse and Social Change*, Cambridge: Polity Press.

Farrelly, Michael and Elena Seoane (2012), 'Democratisation', in Terttu Nevalainen and Elizabeth C. Traugott (eds), *The Oxford Handbook of the History of English*, 392–401, Oxford: Oxford University Press.

Gastil, John (1990), 'Generic Pronouns and Sexist Language: The Oxymoronic Character of Masculine Generics', *Sex Roles*, 23 (11/12): 629–43.

Green, William H. (1977), 'Singular Pronouns and Sexual Politics', *College Composition and Communication*, 28 (2): 150–3.

Greenbaum, Sidney, ed. (1996), *Comparing English Worldwide: ICE*, Oxford: Clarendon Press.

Gupta, Anthea Fraser (1999), 'The Situation of English in Singapore', in Joseph A. Foley, Thiru Kandiah, Bao Zhiming, Anthea F. Gupta, Lubna Alsagoff, Ho Chee Lick, Lionel Wee, Ismail S. Talib and Wendy Bokhurst-Heng (eds), *English in New Cultural Contexts: Reflections from Singapore*, 106–26, Oxford and Singapore: Oxford University Press.

Huddleston, Rodney and Geoffrey K. Pullum et al. (2002), *The Cambridge Grammar of the English Language*, Cambridge: Cambridge University Press.

Kachru, Braj B. (1985), 'Standards, Codification and Sociolinguistic Realism: The English Language in the Outer Circle', in Randolph Quirk and Henry Widdowson (eds), *English in the World: Teaching and Learning the Language and Literatures*, 11–36, Cambridge: Cambridge University Press.

Kachru, Braj B. (1994), 'English in South Asia', in Robert Burchfield (ed), *The Cambridge History of the English Language. Vol. V. English in Britain and Overseas: Origins and Development*, 497–553, Cambridge: Cambridge University Press.

Kachru, Yamuna (2006), *Hindi*, Amsterdam: Benjamins.

Kachru, Yamuna (2017), 'World Englishes, Pragmatics, and Discourse', in Markku Filppula, Juhani Klemola and Devyani Sharma (eds), *The Oxford Handbook of World Englishes*, 272–90, Oxford: Oxford University Press.

Kirby, John (1746), *A New English Grammar*. Menston, England: Scolar Press Facsimile.

Krishnaswamy, N. and Archana S. Burde (1998), *The Politics of Indians' English. Linguistic Colonialism and the Expanding English Empire*, Delhi: Oxford University Press.

Labov, William (1963), 'The Social Motivation of a Sound Change', *Word*, 19: 273–309.

Labov, William (1990), 'The Intersection of Sex and Social Class in the Course of Linguistic Change', *Language Variation and Change*, 2: 205–54.

Laitinen, Mikko (2007), *Agreement Patterns in English: Diachronic Corpus Studies on Common-Number Pronouns*, Helsinki: Mémoires de la Société Néophilologique LXXI.

Leech, Geoffrey, Marianne Hundt, Christian Mair and Nicholas Smith (2009), *Change in Contemporary English: A Grammatical Study*, Cambridge: Cambridge University Press.

Leonard, Sterling Andrus (1929), *The Doctrine of Correctness in English Usage, 1700–1800*, Madison: University of Wisconsin Studies in Language and Literature.

Lim, Lisa and Nikolas Gisborne (2009), 'The Typologies of Asian Englishes. Setting the Agenda', *English World-Wide*, 30 (2): 123–32.

Loureiro-Porto, Lucía (2019), 'Grammaticalization of Semi-modals of Necessity in Asian Englishes', *English World-Wide*, 40 (2):115–42.

Madson, Laura and Robert M. Hessling (1999), 'Does Alternating between Masculine and Feminine Pronouns Eliminate Perceived Gender Bias in Text?', *Sex Roles*, 41 (7/8): 559–75.

Mehrotra, Raja Ram (1998), *Indian English. Texts and Interpretation*, Amsterdam: Benjamins.

Mesthrie, Rajend and Rakesh M. Bhatt (2008), *World Englishes. The Study of New Linguistic Varieties*, Cambridge: Cambridge University Press.

Meyers, Miriam W. (1990), 'Current Generic Pronoun Usage: An Empirical Study', *American Speech*, 65: 228–37.

Meyers, Miriam W. (1993), 'Forms of *They* with Singular Noun Phrase Antecedents: Evidence from Current Educated English Usage', *Word*, 44: 181–92.

Mukherjee, Joybrato (2007), 'Steady States in the Evolution of New Englishes: Present-Day Indian English as an Equilibrium', *Journal of English Linguistics*, 35 (2): 157–87.

Myhill, John (1995), 'Change and Continuity in the Functions of the American English Modals', *Linguistics*, 33: 157–211.

Nelson, Gerald (2009), 'World Englishes and Corpora Studies', in Braj B. Kachru, Yamuna Kachru and Cecil L. Nelson (eds), *The Handbook of World Englishes*, 733–50, Malden, MA: Blackwell.

Nevalainen, Terttu (1996), 'Gender Difference', in Terttu Nevalainen and Helena Raumolin-Brunberg (eds), *Sociolinguistics and Language History: Studies Based on the Corpus of Early English Correspondence*, 57–76, Amsterdam: Rodopi.

OED = *Oxford English Dictionary Online*. Available online: http://www.oed.com/.

Parini, Alejandro (2013), 'Epicene Pronominal Forms in Written English: Variation across Genres', *Documentos de Trabajo* (Universidad de Belgrano) 289. Available online: http://repositorio.ub.edu.ar:8080/xmlui/handle/123456789/2454 (accessed 15 September 2015).

Paterson, Laura Louise (2011), 'Epicene Pronouns in UK National Newspapers: A Diachronic Study', *ICAME Journal*, 35: 171–84.

Paterson, Laura Louise (2014), *British Pronoun Use, Prescription, and Processing. Linguistic and Social Influences Affecting 'They' and 'He'*, New York: Palgrave Macmillan.

Pauwels, Anne (2001), 'Non-sexist Language Reform and Generic Pronouns in Australian English', *English World-Wide*, 22 (1): 105–19.

Quirk, Randolph, Sidney Greenbaum, Geoffrey Leech and Jan Svartvik (1972), *A Grammar of Contemporary English*, London: Longman.

Quirk, Randolph, Sidney Greenbaum, Geoffrey Leech and Jan Svartvik (1985), *A Comprehensive Grammar of the English Language*, London: Longman.

Ross, Claudia and Jing-heng Sheng Ma (2006), *Modern Mandarin Chinese Grammar. A Practical Guide*, London: Routledge.

Schiffman, Harold F. (1999), *A Reference Grammar of Spoken Tamil*, Cambridge: Cambridge University Press.

Schneider, Edgar W. (2007), *Postcolonial English: Varieties around the World*, Cambridge: Cambridge University Press.

Sklar, Elizabeth S. (1988), 'The Tribunal of Use: Agreement in Indefinite Constructions', *College Composition and Communication*, 39 (4): 410–22.

Weidmann, Urs (1984), 'Anaphoric *They* for Singular Expressions', in Richard J. Watts and Urs Weidmann (eds), *Modes of Interpretation: Essays Presented to Ernst Leisi on the Occasion of his 65th Birthday*, 59–68, Tübingen: Narr.

Windstedt, Richard O. (1913), *Malay Grammar*, Oxford: Oxford University Press.

Yip, Virginia and Stephen Matthews (2000), *Basic Cantonese: A Grammar and Workbook*, London: Routledge.

Zuber, Shanon and Ann M. Reed (1993), 'The Politics of Grammar Handbooks: Generic 'He' and Singular 'They'', *College English*, 55: 515–30.

10

It is Important that Mandatives *(should) be studied* across Different World Englishes and from a Construction Grammar Perspective[1]

Marianne Hundt
University of Zurich

1. Introduction

In September 2017, the headline in a Reuters press release announced that *Saudi king decrees women be allowed to drive*. The ensuing discussion on Language Log was conducted under the topic of grammaticality in headlines, focusing mainly on the aspect of ellipsis and suggesting that a subordinating conjunction would improve grammaticality, as would an additional element in the verb phrase of the subordinate clause (such as a *to*-infinitival marker). Only later in the discussion did the possibility surface that the verb phrase might not actually be elliptical:

> And I completely missed the idea that this might be a 'mandative subjunctive'... In such cases, the verb is in the 'plain form', which for a passive would be simply 'be'. In my defense, the mandative subjunctive is kind of old-fashioned, not [to] say obsolete – and I don't think I've ever seen it with elided *that*. (Mark Liberman, *Language Log*, September 27, 2017; 'Headlinese grammaticality')

Interestingly, the first full sentence in the main text of the Reuters press release strongly suggests that the verb phrase in the headline was not meant to be elliptical. It uses a different verb in the main clause, supplies the subordinator *that* but – crucially – keeps the verb form used in the headline, i.e. the subjunctive:

(1) Saudi King Salman on Tuesday *ordered* that women *be allowed* to drive cars,
     (https://www.reuters.com/article/us-saudi-women-driving/saudi-king-
     decrees-women-be-allowed-to-drive-idUSKCN1C12SB)[2]

While the contributors to the Language Log entry discussed various non-finite alternatives to the original mandative subjunctive or suggested rephrasing the sentence with an active construction combining the modal *may* with *drive*, the modal passive alternative with *should* was not mentioned. This is surprising seeing that it provides a natural choice context here. In finite subordinate clauses following so-called mandative or suasive expressions like *important, decree* or *directive*, English speakers can use an unmarked form of the verb (as in (2) and (3)) or a periphrastic construction with a modal verb (typically *should*, as in (4)).

(2) Solomon was awed by Makada's beauty and *desired* that she *become* his queen and *bear* his child. (ICE-JAM:S2A-041)

(3) As a major *requirement* was that the corpus structure *be* user-definable, (ICE-GB:W1A-005)

(4) Now I had *directed* in fact that paragraph three *should read* at the fifth line (ICE-IRE:S2A-062)

Usage in this area of grammar has undergone change in English in the twentieth century, with English in America (AmE) being in the vanguard of change, British English (BrE) lagging significantly behind and other varieties typically lying somewhere in between the two epicentres, possibly as a result of influence from the 'matrilect' or historical ENL input variety (see Section 2 for details).[3]

Previous corpus-based research has looked into a number of variables, such as the lexical item triggering the subjunctive, register, the verb in the subordinate clause or negation. However, systematic investigation of the relative importance of these factors in predicting the choice between the subjunctive and the periphrastic construction with *should* is still lacking. This chapter adds evidence to a previous pilot study (Hundt 2018) from available components of the *International Corpus of English* (ICE) to address this gap in previous research. Additional material from the *Global-Web-based English* (GloWbE) corpus is used for a close-up on variation in South and South-East Asian varieties of English, with BrE and AmE as reference varieties.

Section 2 provides a brief overview of previous research. Background information on the data (corpora) and the methodology (particularly the definition of the variable, the predictor variables and data retrieval) is then given in Section 3. The results in Section 4, summarized in Section 5, show that the choice of a subjunctive strongly depends on the lexical trigger and the regional variety, with other factors being far less relevant. This calls for discussion within variationist construction grammar (Section 6). While construction grammar (CxG) is a framework that conceives of the syntax–lexis divide as a continuum and is thus ideally suited to model interaction of lexical meaning and constructional meaning, variation within constructions is an aspect that is relatively new to the framework. Moreover, previous research in variationist CxG has typically looked at word order variation rather than variation at the phrasal and morphological levels. The results on variation in mandative sentences can be used to expand CxG in this direction.

2. Previous research on mandative constructions: Variation and change in World Englishes

Variation in mandative constructions is something where regional differences were acknowledged early on (Quirk et al. 1972) and studied on the basis of the (American) Brown and (British) LOB corpora by Johansson and Norheim (1988), who confirmed the AmE preference for the subjunctive and the predominance of the periphrastic construction with *should* in BrE. Studies by Övergaard (1995) and Hundt (1998) provide evidence that synchronic regional variation is the result of relatively recent diachronic change, but while AmE sees a substantial increase in the use of the subjunctive early in the twentieth century, its spread in BrE can be observed only from the 1960s and at a slower rate. Waller (2017) replicates earlier research (albeit with a more rigorously defined variable) and extends it to the early twenty-first century, confirming the slower rate of change for BrE. In AmE, the relative proportion of the subjunctive variant against the periphrastic construction with *should* in mandatives was already approaching 80 per cent in the 1930s; in BrE it is still around 40 per cent at the end of the twentieth century and only at 56 per cent in the early years of the twenty-first century (Hundt and Gardner 2017; Waller 2017). Beyond the metropolitan varieties of AmE and BrE, research by Peters (1998) and Hundt (1998) shows that settler varieties in the southern hemisphere are between the two northern hemisphere varieties in this ongoing change, with Collins (2015) and Collins et al. (2014) providing long-term evidence for the change in Australian English (AusE). This drift towards a growing use of subjunctives world-wide is typically explained in terms of Americanization (see e.g., Övergaard 1995: 89; Mair 2006: 193), whereas Hundt (2018) argues that, with little evidence of speakers being aware that AmE is leading World Englishes (WEs) in the ongoing change towards greater use of mandative subjunctives, the change is unlikely to be due to conscious adoption of the subjunctive variant as an 'Americanism'.

Previous research has also looked at variation in mandative constructions in countries where English is an institutionalized second language, using two kinds of evidence: Brown-type corpora or components of ICE. Examples of the former are Sayder (1989) and Schneider (2000), who draw on evidence from the Kolhapur Corpus. They find that Indian English (IndE) resembles its matrilect in preferring periphrastic *should*-constructions over the subjunctive. In a similar vein, alignment with the matrilect has also been observed for Philippine English (PhilE) in studies based on Brown-type corpora of this variety (e.g., Schneider 2005, 2011; Collins et al. 2014). Peters (2009) uses ICE components for PhilE, IndE and Singapore English (SingE), comparing her findings for six lexical triggers with those from the corresponding British, Australian and New Zealand ICE components. Her study confirms matrilectal affinity for IndE and PhilE, but not for SingE. Similarly, Hundt (2018) is unable to substantiate lineage as a consistent explanation for variation once a larger range of institutionalized second-language varieties is taken into account. For IndE, Sedlatschek (2009: 281–9) uses data from the internet (Google searches and web archives of newspapers) for a small-scale study of four verbs (*demand*, *recommend*, *insist* and *suggest*), comparing usage patterns with those in BrE, AmE, SingE and South African

English. On his evidence, IndE is much more conservative than BrE in its rather restricted use of the subjunctive, and he observes 'a certain affinity among South and South East Asian Englishes meriting further investigation' (2009: 287). As the most likely reasons for the conservative nature of IndE in this area of grammar, he advances the bias towards the BrE variant in local textbooks, and usage guides warning against the use of the overly formal subjunctive (Sedlatschek 2009: 281–9). However, previous research on the subjunctive's stylistic connotations has cast some doubt on its formal connotations, as it is regularly attested in speech, including spontaneous conversations (see, e.g., Hoffmann 1997; Hundt 1998; Schneider 2005). As Peters (2009: 130) points out, evidence on the connection between stylistic connotations and regional variety is not conclusive. Crawford (2009) focuses on the relation between different triggers and trigger types and regional variation in his study of mandative subjunctives. He finds that regional differences are less marked for strong triggers (such as *ask, demand, require*), which are more likely overall to be used in mandatives, whereas weaker triggers (such as *advise* and *suggest*) show a more marked regional variation (Crawford 2009: 273). However, he only provides descriptive statistics in his study. It will be interesting to see whether trigger strength also plays an important role once a larger set of varieties are studied and how this relates to other factors.

Possible interaction of regional variation with other factors has generally been absent from previous research. Turner (1980: 276) suggests, for instance, that the verb *be* provides a stronghold for the subjunctive, but whether this holds across all regional varieties has not been investigated. *That*-omission has not been studied systematically across different WEs either, nor has it been correlated with other factors (such as register or regional variety). In this chapter, I expand on a pilot study (Hundt 2018) to investigate which factors predict the choice between the subjunctive and mandative *should* and how these predictors interact. In addition to regional variety, register and trigger, predictor variables that might play a role in the choice include the trigger type (verb, noun and adjective), the grammatical subject, the verb of the subordinate clause, negation and *that*-omission.

3. Data and methodology

3.1. Corpora

The data for this study come from several ICE corpora: five components sampled in countries where English is the first language of the majority of speakers (ENL varieties), four countries where it is an institutionalized second language (ESL) and one country where it is a regional standard variety that co-exists with an English-based creole in a diglossic situation and thus represents a second dialect (ESD). Table 10.1 gives an overview of the ten ICE components which provide the primary data for this study.

In order to be able to include the factor 'medium/register' in the analysis, only ICE components that provide a complete spoken and written sample (i.e. at approximately 600,000 and 400,000 words each per variety) were included. This means that only Canadian English (CanE) is represented as a North American variety. All ICE

Table 10.1 Overview of ICE corpora[4]

Country	ICE component	Variety type
Canada	ICE-CAN	ENL
Great Britain	ICE-GB	ENL
Ireland	ICE-IRE	ENL
New Zealand	ICE-NZ	ENL
Australia	ICE-AUS	ENL
Hong Kong	ICE-HK	ESL
India	ICE-IND	ESL
Philippines	ICE-PHIL	ESL
Singapore	ICE-SING	ESL
Jamaica	ICE-JAM	ESD

components used in this study belong to the first generation of ICE corpora, which were sampled in the early 1990s. For ESL varieties, there is a focus on Asian Englishes.[5]

Since individual ICE components run to only approximately one million words, the amount of evidence available for individual triggers varies greatly across varieties (see Section 4.1). As 'trigger' turned out to be a very important factor in the ICE material, supplementary data were collected from the GloWbE corpus for a follow-up study on the role that the trigger plays in the choice between a subjunctive and the periphrastic alternative in mandative constructions. The follow-up study is restricted to a subset of varieties used in the main study because the GloWbE corpus is not really comparable to the ICE corpora in terms of composition, size, date, etc. (see Davies and Fuchs 2015). More specific reasons relating to data retrieval (see Section 3.4) also necessitated limiting the follow-up study with respect to the number of WEs included. The focus is on the US and GB components as representatives of ENL varieties, and the same set of Asian Englishes as in the ICE-based part of the study.

3.2. Definition of the variable context

3.2.1. Subjunctives

Previous studies have taken slightly different approaches in their definitions of the variable in mandative constructions (see Hundt 2018). This provided one of the motivations for Waller (2017) to replicate earlier research into the Brown-family corpora, starting out with one of the clearest and most comprehensive discussions of the question of what to include as subjunctives. He distinguishes four identifying contexts for the subjunctive (2017: 83), which are given along with his labels and illustrated in examples (5)–(8):

- iNO-S: a third person singular noun phrase followed by an unmarked verb
  - (5) I think it's *important* that Cook *experience* winter in a Canadian context (ICE-CAN:W1B-012)

- iBE: unmarked use of *be*
  (6) It is also *essential* that those responsible for approving travel *be* given appropriate financial delegation. (ICE-AUS:W2D-003)
- iST: an unmarked verb following a past-tense trigger[6]
  (7) Men *desired* that these bourgeois women *drop* their current pursuit and resume their subservient role of yester-years. (ICE-CAN:W1A-006)
- iNEG: pre-verbal *not*-negation
  (8) Oh, but the crab catchers have suggested that you *not try* that method, have they? (ICE-JAM:W2F-006)

In the corpus data, identifying contexts also co-occur, as for instance in example (9), which combines a past-tense trigger (iST) with pre-verbal negation (iNEG) and the unmarked use of *be* (iBE):

> (9) he suggests opening up the least vulnerable part and *recommended* that all visitors *not be* concentrated on the same spot. (ICE-IRE:W1A-018)

One question is how nominal and adjectival triggers, which are not themselves marked for tense, should be treated. If the context in the main clause implies that the event took place in the past, a bare form is also considered to be unambiguously subjunctive after non-third person subjects. In other words, these cases are taken to be analogous to iST contexts (see example (10)).[7]

> (10) I have known Manuel for the last two months subsequent to his father's request that I *meet* with him to see if I could help orient him in his university studies. (ICE-CAN:W1B-022)

3.2.2. Should-*periphrasis*

While previous studies typically comment on their definition of the subjunctive in mandative constructions, the delimitation of modal variant is not always addressed. However, variationist studies require that the underlying variable be defined as a choice context, i.e. as true alternatives. This means that only those instances of periphrastic *should* in the subordinate clause can be included that would result in an unambiguous subjunctive if the modal were omitted. This is the case in example (11), which would be an instance of iST without the modal, but not in example (12), where the verb would be ambiguous between the subjunctive and the indicative if the modal were left out.

> (11) And in fact the Ghost of Singapore sold so well that my publisher *insisted* Ø I *should come* out with More Ghost of Singapore and this has been selling well too. (ICE-SING:S2A-029)
> (12) Well that's why I'm *suggesting* that may be in future we *should do* (ICE-HK:S1B-033)[8]

In addition to *should,* English occasionally uses periphrastic constructions with another modal in mandative constructions (see (13)–(17)), including some (i.e. *could, may, need* and *ought to*) that have very different semantics from the prototypical modal periphrasis in mandative constructions. Use of *could* instead of *should* in (13), for instance, stresses the possibility of the action rather than suggesting that the foodstuffs actually *be used* and is thus not really semantically equivalent with the subjunctive.

> (13) it was only after the blanket clearance given by the ... expert committee in 1981 *recommending* that all foodstuffs irradiated up to 10 kGy ... *could be used* without any further toxicological or nutritional testing, that food irradiation programmes really opened up the world over. (ICE-IND:W2B-035)
>
> (14) it may be advisable to return the Indian Post Office (Amendment) Bill of 1986 to both Houses of Parliament *requesting* that they *may reconsider* the Bill, especially clause 16". (ICE-IND:W2C-009)
>
> (15) I *urge* P that the State government *need to do* the same thing. (ICE-IND:S1B-054)
>
> (16) this threat *required* that these particular persons ... *ought to be interned* and held in camps for the duration of the war (ICE-CAN:S2B-026)
>
> (17) So I *urge* P members honourable members that we *must evolve* a viable national consensus for sound fiscal management of our economy. (ICE-IND:S1B-054)

Indicatives are an additional variant occasionally attested in mandative sentences, particularly in BrE. They were excluded from the model, as in most previous studies on the topic.[9]

3.2.3. False positives

The definition of the choice context requires that, once the data are retrieved from the corpus, false positives be excluded from the concordances. The following examples illustrate instances that, on closer inspection, do not satisfy the definitional criteria for a subjunctive or mandative *should* outlined above. The subordinate clause in example (18) has a second-person subject and a verb other than *be*; without a disambiguating past tense in the main clause, the verb *book* could therefore be indicative or subjunctive. Example (19) has a collective noun as the subject in the subordinate clause, and since collective nouns are ambiguous as regards number (there is variation between singular and plural concord), they were excluded from the data unless the context provided disambiguating clues (as in (20)).

> (18) Well I would advise you *book* your accommodation in advance (ICE-HK:S1A-002)
>
> (19) At any rate Mr Senate President I *move* that the Blue Ribbon <u>Committee</u> *open* investigations on this matter (ICE-PHI:S1B-056)
>
> (20) For Senator Button the focal point was the union's *demand* that the <u>Government</u> freeze <u>its</u> tariff reductions until unemployment is clearly declining (ICE-AUS:S2B-002)

As not all potential triggers invariably have mandative meaning (see examples (21)–(24)), any non-mandative instances retrieved with the triggers also need to be removed at the post-editing stage.

(21) I read my Lord in the circumstances the Petitioners have been *advised* [= 'informed'] that it *is* just an equitable[10] that the company be wound up (ICE-SING:S2A-067)

(22) Mr Calcutt had *advised* that the communication should not <u>have been hidden</u> (ICE-GB:W2C-001)

(23) They *propose* that contexts differ more from one another than do target lines presented alone, and it is <u>this fact</u>, and not the general structural properties of contexts, that underlies their effectiveness. (ICE-CAN:W2A-012)

(24) Also derived from demographic projections is the *suggestion* [= 'implication'] that health care costs will sky-rocket because resources are disproportionately expended for care of chronically ill elderly people (Schulz). (ICE-CAN:W2A-021)

The corpora yield additional false positives that are difficult to subsume under general headings. Some are typical of spontaneous spoken interaction. In (25), for instance, the speaker starts out with a subordinate clause introduced with *that* and then completes the move using an infinitive construction. A different kind of false positive is illustrated in (26), where the complement precedes the trigger and the following *that*-clause forms part of the construction *it is not until*. In other words, example (26) only superficially resembles the mandative construction.

(25) Mr Chairman Sir I beg to *move* that the sum to be allocated for head *to be* reduced by ten dollars in respect of code fifteen hundred of the main estimates (ICE-SING:S1B-053)

(26) It is not until one sits back and looks at <u>what he is</u> actually *proposing* [that you realize how barbaric it really is.] (ICE-CAN:W1A-012)

Finally, the study is limited to finite complement clauses following mandative triggers.[11] One way of avoiding the choice between the subjunctive and a modal is to use a non-finite complement (examples (27) and (28)), an option that is frequently employed.[12]

(27) They would insist on *ripping* this out and putting back the th the original box sash windows (ICE-GB:S1B-073)

(28) And we *propose to entrench* a continuing constitutional process for aboriginal matters (ICE-CAN:S2B-022)

The instance in (29) is interesting because the speaker sets out to use a finite *that*-clause after the trigger, introduces a long post-modifying relative clause after the subject of the subordinate clause, then repeats the trigger and switches to a non-finite construction:

(29) So we *advise that the ladies* who might have that kind of feeling with it the vomit they feel like they're nauseous and all of that *we advise them to take* it at night (ICE-JAM:S1A-054)

3.3. Data retrieval

Due to the complex interaction between the semantics of the trigger, tense in the matrix clause, number of the subject in the subordinate clause and negation, automatic retrieval of all mandative constructions from a corpus is not possible. Moreover, mandative subjunctives can also occasionally be used without overtly mandative triggers, as Övergaard (1995: 82) points out. The examples she gives all contain matrix nouns or verbs, though, and one could argue that they are coerced into a mandative construction (see Section 6 for details) and thus effectively function as mandative triggers.

Even though it is difficult to automatically retrieve all mandative subjunctives from a corpus, there are two previous studies which explore a bottom-up approach to deriving a set of possible triggers from a corpus. Hoffmann (1997) first retrieved instances of *be* in *that*-clauses. In order to balance precision and recall, he then used only the most frequently attested items from the list of 276 initially identified triggers to retrieve mandative constructions with verbs other than *be* (including instances where the subordinator was omitted).[13] Conceivably, Hoffmann's bottom-up approach might be refined by using a combination of clear-cut indicators (iNO-S, iBE, iNEG) to broaden the range of potential trigger expressions. However, the bottom-up approach to identifying trigger expressions typically also then has to use a subset of trigger expressions because extensive manual post-editing is necessary to single out true mandatives from false positives. Serpollet (2001) uses mandative *should* as her starting point for a bottom-up approach to retrieving trigger contexts from a corpus of BrE. However, such an approach assumes that the modal periphrastic variant is used after all triggers, an assumption that the corpus data in Section 4.1 show to be problematic.

All other previous empirical research on mandative constructions has relied on predefining a set of triggers. Table 10.2 compares the number and type of triggers used in studies on ENL varieties.

The figures in brackets for Crawford (2009) indicate the number of triggers that were actually attested with the subjunctive at least once in the corpora under investigation and subsequently formed the basis of the in-depth investigation. Interestingly, these correspond closely to the set of triggers on which Johansson and

Table 10.2 Overview of trigger expressions used in previous corpus-based research of mandative constructions[14]

	Verbs	Nouns	Adjectives
Johansson and Norheim (1988)	17	8	5
Algeo (1992)	25	29	18
Crawford (2009)	47 (16)	38 (11)	23 (6)

Norheim (1988) based their investigation of Brown and LOB. The triggers used for data retrieval in this study (cf. Table 10.3) are those that were shown in previous research to regularly trigger subjunctives. They largely overlap with those used in Johansson and Norheim (1988) and Crawford (2009). For the follow-up investigation on the role that the lexical trigger plays (Section 4.3), the dataset was limited to the items indicated in bold in Table 10.3. This further limitation is due to the relation of recall and precision: recall with the lexical retrieval approach is very high (100 per cent), whereas precision is low: out of the over 7,000 hits retrieved for forms of the verb *ask* in the ten ICE components, only thirty-seven are instances where either a subjunctive or a mandative *should* is used. As the aim was to retrieve ten variable contexts per trigger and variety, it was necessary to limit the set of trigger expressions to those where enough variable contexts could be retrieved in order to keep the amount of material to be post-edited within manageable bounds.

In his discussion of the Reuters example, Mark Liberman doubts that he has ever seen a mandative subjunctive in a subordinate clause lacking the conjunction *that*. Evidence that mandative *should* occurs without a subordinator can be seen in example (11) above and in examples (30)–(33) below. Corpus data thus show that, while instances of subjunctives without *that* might be rare, they are nevertheless a structural possibility.

(30) In these cases it recommended Ø smoking *should be* allowed. (ICE-NZ:W2C-007)
(31) You insisted Ø I *fill* your glass (ICE-AUS:S1A-033)
(32) He required Ø the singer *sing* in chord harsh and lyric note in contrast. (ICE-HK:W1A-015)
(33) Chinese language teachers *suggested* Ø they *be* sent to Beijing and Taiwan for visits and lecture programmes. (ICE-SING:W2C-004)

For the retrieval of mandative constructions this has the consequence that only the trigger can be used, as a combination of trigger and subordinator would fail to identify mandative clauses without subordinators and thus affect recall.

3.4. Coding for factors

Once false positives had been removed from the concordances, the remaining instances were coded with respect to the factors that might have an influence on the choice

Table 10.3 List of triggers used to retrieve mandative constructions from ICE and GloWbE (bold)

Verbs	advise, ask, beg, decree, **demand**, desire, dictate, **insist**, move, **order**, **propose**, **recommend**, **request**, require, stipulate, **suggest**, urge
Nouns	advice, demand, desire, motion, order, proposal, recommendation, request, requirement, stipulation, suggestion
Adjectives	anxious, essential, **imperative**, **important**

between the subjunctive and its modal periphrastic alternant: two external factors ('variety' and 'medium/register') and six contextual variables. The factor 'variety' has the levels for the different WEs (i.e. CanE, BrE, IrE, NZE, AusE, HKE, IndE, PhilE, SingE and JamE for the core study and, using the regional labels from GloWbE, US, GB, IN, PH, SG and HK for the follow-up study). The factor 'medium/register' made use of the four macro-text categories[15] applied in the sampling of the ICE corpora, i.e. spoken dialogue (S1), spoken monologue (S2), written unpublished (W1) and written published (W2). The six contextual variables were 'trigger' (with individual lexical items providing the level and morphologically related nouns and verbs treated as belonging to the same trigger), 'trigger type' (with the levels verb, noun and adjective), 'controlling subject' (making a binary distinction between third person singular and non-third person), the 'verb' in the subordinate clause (with the levels *be* vs. other), 'negation' (with the levels negative vs. affirmative) and 'subordination' (with the levels *that* vs. zero).

3.5. Modelling variable importance and factor interactions

The statistical analysis makes use of two different (but related) approaches to modelling complex variation (see e.g., Tagliamonte and Baayen 2012 or Bernaisch et al. 2014): a random forest analysis and a conditional inference tree (ctree) analysis. The first approach provides information on the overall importance of predictors and the second gives information on how these interact. Both can be calculated in R, using the party package for the forest and the party kit for the ctree (see Strobl, Hothorn and Zeileis 2009 and Hothorn, Hornik and Zeileis 2006, respectively).

The random forest analysis is a type of permutation testing that, instead of assuming a certain distribution in the data, builds the distribution by resampling the observed dataset. The advantage of the random forest analysis over traditional regression analysis (whether a generalized or a mixed model) is that it is able to cope even with highly correlated predictor variables and avoids overfitting (see e.g., Strobl, Malley and Tutz 2009). As Tagliamonte and Baayen (2012: 161) point out, a random forest analysis has the further advantage that it is particularly suited to datasets with relatively few observations but a large number of predictor variables, which is the case in much socio-linguistic research and in the present study (a total of only 519 choice contexts and a set of eight predictor variables). Finally, while empty cells or categorical responses for individual predictors pose problems for regression modelling (as is the case, for instance, with the triggers *ask*, *beg* and *necessary*), they do not pose a problem for random forests (see Tagliamonte and Baayen 2012: 161).

The random forest analysis models the overall importance of factors but does not provide any insight into how these factors might be interacting. In order to model interaction of factors, I fitted a conditional inference tree (ctree) to the data. The ctree approach makes use of recursive partitioning and predicts outcomes on binary splits of the data. These splits are made according to relatively homogeneous groupings of the data depending on the overall proportion of a particular dataset.

The random forest analysis requires setting two parameters: the number of predictor variables randomly selected at each split (mtry) and the number of trees to grow.

The recommendation for mtry (in classification modelling) is to set it to the square root of the predictor variables (rounded down, giving a setting of mtry=2). The recommendation for the number of trees to grow is that, with small datasets, even fifty trees might be sufficient but that increasing the number is advisable (Strobl, p.c.). To be on the safe side, I therefore set the parameter ntree to 500. For the ctree, it is useful to limit the depth of the tree (and thus limiting the number of splits) by specifying the values for "maxdepth" and "mincriterion" (see Hothorn et al. 2006).

4. Results

4.1. Summary statistics

The ten ICE corpora yield a total of 519 unambiguous choice contexts after the set of mandative triggers used for retrieval. The majority (69 per cent) of these are subjunctives. This section provides an overview of how the choice contexts are distributed according to the predictor variables. Table 10.4 shows that some regional varieties clearly prefer the subjunctive to mandative *should*: CanE, NZE and AusE are the ENL varieties where this is the case; PhilE, SingE and JamE are the non-ENL varieties that have the same preference. BrE is the only ENL variety that prefers the modal variant, as do the ESL varieties used in Hong Kong and India. IrE is the only variety without a clear preference for either option. The ICE data do not reveal a general trend for varieties to align with their matrilect or neighbouring variety. If that were the case, we should expect only PhilE and CanE to have a clear preference for the subjunctive.

The distribution across speech and writing (see Table 10.5) does not provide evidence of the subjunctive's preference for either medium. Surprisingly, the informal registers (spontaneous dialogues and unpublished written texts) yield slightly higher proportions of subjunctives than are found in monologues and published writing. This is a little counter-intuitive at first, as the subjunctive is typically associated with formal

Table 10.4 Summary of variants (*should*: subjunctive) in mandative constructions across varieties (raw frequencies) in ICE

	CanE	BrE	IrE	NZE	AusE	HKE	IndE	PhilE	SingE	JamE
should	7	**22**	26	18	6	**23**	**24**	13	13	11
Subjunctive	**46**	15	27	**52**	**52**	17	17	**52**	**34**	**44**

Table 10.5 Distribution of variants (*should*: subjunctive) across ICE registers (macro-categories)

	Dialogue	Monologue	Unpublished	Published
should	23 (22.1%)	56 (41.8%)	18 (23.4%)	66 (32.3%)
Subjunctive	81 (77.9%)	78 (58.2%)	59 (76.6%)	138 (67.7%)

Table 10.6 Distribution of subordination (zero vs. *that*) across varieties (numerical values/varieties = subjunctive)

	should	subjunctive	CanE	BrE	IrE	NZE	AusE	HKE	IndE	PhilE	SingE	JamE
that	152 (93.3%)	316 (88.8%)	50	36	53	56	44	35	39	57	44	54
zero	11 (6.7%)	40 (11.2%)	3	0	0	14	14	5	2	8	3	1

registers. When we consider the distribution of the subjunctive variants across the ICE macro-registers, however, the traditional association with formality is actually borne out: 38.8 per cent of subjunctives are from published texts, with 22.7 per cent, 21.9 per cent and 16.6 per cent coming from dialogues, monologues and unpublished writing, respectively.

That-deletion, a feature typically associated with informal use, is notably infrequent in mandative constructions (see Table 10.6): only 9.8 per cent of all mandative constructions lack overt subordination.

Table 10.6 further shows *that*-deletion to be more common in the two southern-hemisphere varieties than elsewhere. Individual examples from ICE-AUS and ICE-NZ indicate, however, that the feature is attested in both informal spoken ((34), (35)) and formal written ((36), (37)) contexts:

(34) he's aware of the problem and that's why he *ordered* Ø the studies *be* undertaken (ICE-AUS:S2B-010)

(35) the planning tribunal there is *recommending* Ø l and m mining *be* allowed to dredge a section of the river for gold (ICE-NZ:S2B-012)

(36) The impact on the inflow of funds to the party of legislation that *requires* Ø the identity of donors *be* revealed will be horrendous and it will be immediate. (ICE-AUS:W2C-004)

(37) the council's planning consultant *recommended* Ø the consent *exclude* general engineering fibre glassing spray painting and steam or sand blasting operations. (ICE-NZ:W2C-008)

Thus, in (34) and (35), the subjunctive co-occurs with features typical of colloquial speech, such as contractions and the progressive (where a written text, in this particular case, is more likely to have used a simple verb phrase). A typical feature of formal writing in (36) and (37) is the use of complex noun phrases such as *The impact on the inflow of funds to the party of legislation* and *general engineering fibre glassing spray painting and steam or sand blasting operations* (see e.g., Biber and Gray 2016), where speech prefers the use of clauses (e.g. *The impact that the inflow of funds has on the party of legislation*).

The summary statistics for the factor 'trigger' in Figure 10.1a combines the data for verbal and nominal triggers, on the assumption that it is the semantics of the trigger rather than the word class that is the relevant parameter.[16] Figure 10.1a reveals that some lexical triggers (e.g. *ask, demand, move, request, require*) clearly favour the subjunctive, whereas *advise* shows a preference for the *should*-variant. A third set of

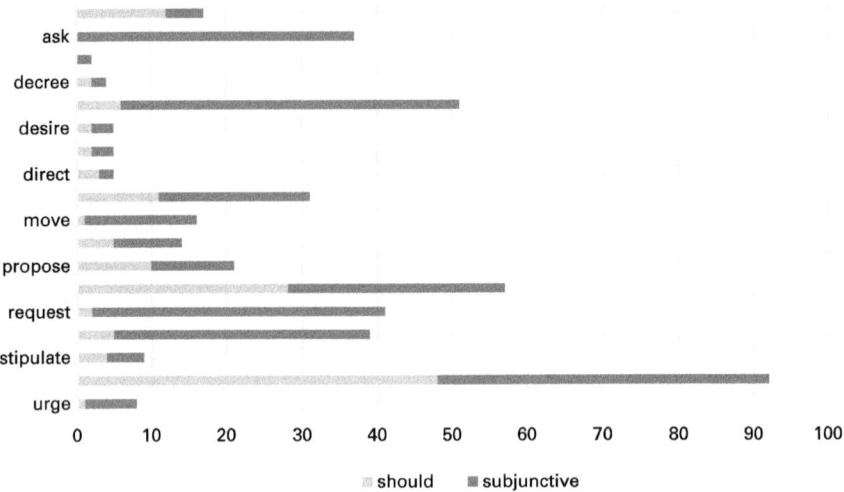

Figure 10.1a Distribution of choice contexts (raw frequencies) across verbal/nominal triggers in ICE.

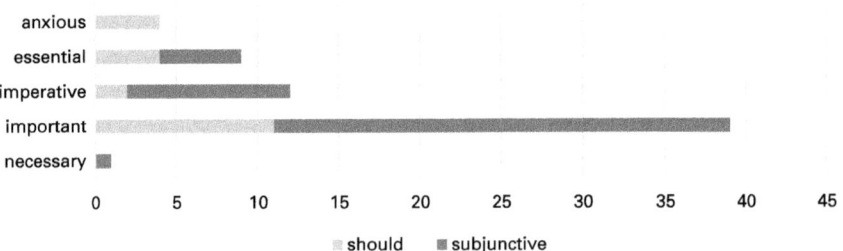

Figure 10.1b Distribution of choice contexts (raw frequencies) across adjectival triggers in ICE.

triggers (at least according to the rather limited ICE data) displays no clear preference for either variant (e.g. *propose, recommend, stipulate, suggest*).[17] Figure 10.1a also shows that two triggers (*ask* and *beg*) are attested with the subjunctive only.

The results for the adjectival triggers are a little more difficult to interpret, mostly because the overall raw frequencies of choice contexts are much lower (note the difference in scale between Figures 10.1a and 10.1b). That said, we can still observe that *imperative* and *important* are strong triggers for the subjunctive, whereas *essential* yields equal numbers of mandative *should* and subjunctives in the subordinate clause. Figure 10.1b further shows that *anxious* and *necessary* are only attested with *should* and the subjunctive, respectively.

It will be interesting to see how the factor 'trigger' interacts with other predictor variables, particularly regional variety (see sections 4.2 and 4.3).

Let us now turn to the role that the controlling subject in the subordinate clause may play (Table 10.7): it turns out that the subjunctive is, overall, more frequently used with third person singular subjects than with other subjects, which is not surprising given the fact that iNO-S is one of the identifying contexts. However, there is no substantial difference in the preference for the subjunctive over *should* when we compare the two kinds of subject: both third-person singular and other kinds of subject take subjunctives at a rate of around 70 per cent.

As pointed out in Section 2, Turner (1980: 276) suggests that the verb *be* provides a stronghold for the subjunctive. Again, this observation holds, in that *be* makes up a larger share of all subjunctives (at 241:115). However, when we compare the proportion of choice contexts across different types of verb, we see that *be* is not used proportionally more often as a subjunctive than other verbs (at ratios of 67.9 per cent to 70.1 per cent).

With respect to negation, finally, the ICE data reveal that the subjunctive strongly prefers affirmative contexts: only three (0.8 per cent) of the 356 subjunctives were negated (against 20 or 12.3 per cent of the 163 periphrastic *should*-variants). The three negated subjunctives are all from written texts (two unpublished, one published). A search for a noun followed by *not* and a bare verb ([nn*] not [vv0*]) in the *Corpus of Contemporary American English* (COCA) shows that, at least in AmE, iNEG is also attested in speech (see examples (38) and (39)).

(38) Well, if you had your *wish*, would it be that the president *not make* the first move here, give the Republicans a chance to do something first? (COCA, 2014, CBS, SPOK)

(39) So basically they're going to *ask* that the court *not allow* the election to be certified until those hand counts are completed. (COCA, 2000, CNN_SatMorn, SPOK)

Table 10.7 Distribution of choice contexts according to factor 'controlling subject' (ICE corpora)

	third person singular	other
should	109 (33%)	54 (28.4%)
Subjunctive	221 (67%)	136 (71.6%)

Table 10.8 Distribution of choice contexts (raw frequencies) across the factor 'verb' in ICE corpora

	be	other
should	114 (32.1%)	49 (29.9%)
Subjunctive	241 (67.9%)	115 (70.1%)

On the basis of the ICE data, we can still conclude that negated subjunctives are rarer than those found in subordinate clauses with *that*-omission (see Hundt 1998; Kjellmer 2009: 248).

4.2. Predicting the subjunctive

Figure 10.2 shows the results of the random forest analysis, which returns the 'trigger' as the overall most important predictor, with 'variety' coming a close second and 'subordination' and 'verb' below the level of significance.[18]

Testing for model accuracy with Somers2 Dxy returns a prediction accuracy of 0.755 and a C-index value of 0.877, which is above the level of 0.8 recommended e.g., in Tagliamonte and Baayen (2012: 156). In other words, the model already indicates a high level of fit. The best model fit (with a C-index of 0.889 and a prediction accuracy of 0.79) was obtained with only 'trigger', 'variety' and 'register' as predictor variables.

The result of the ctree analysis (with maxdepth=4, mincriterion=0.95) is given in Figure 10.3. The single tree selects 'variety', 'trigger', 'negation' and 'controlling subject' (but not 'register') as significant predictors, with 'trigger' chosen at the first split. Model accuracy of the single tree is somewhat lower at 0.784 than for the random forest and at a C-index of 0.711; the C-index is above the 0.5 random assignment level, but also somewhat below the 0.8 level recommended by Tagliamonte and Baayen (2012) for a good model fit. Removing predictor variables did not improve model fit, however. Notably, the model with only 'variety' and 'trigger' as predictors did not perform better, at 0.774 accuracy and a C-index of 0.694.

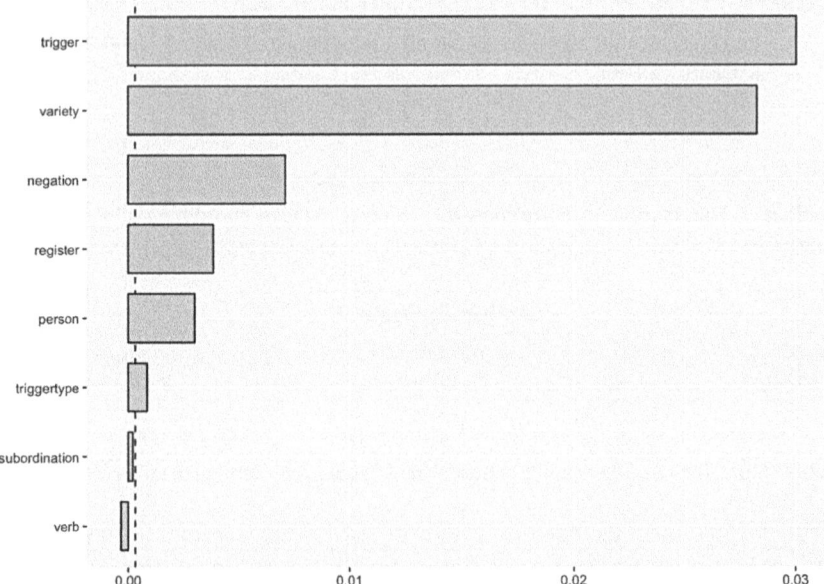

Figure 10.2 Overall variable importance (random forest analysis) for the mandative alternation in ICE.

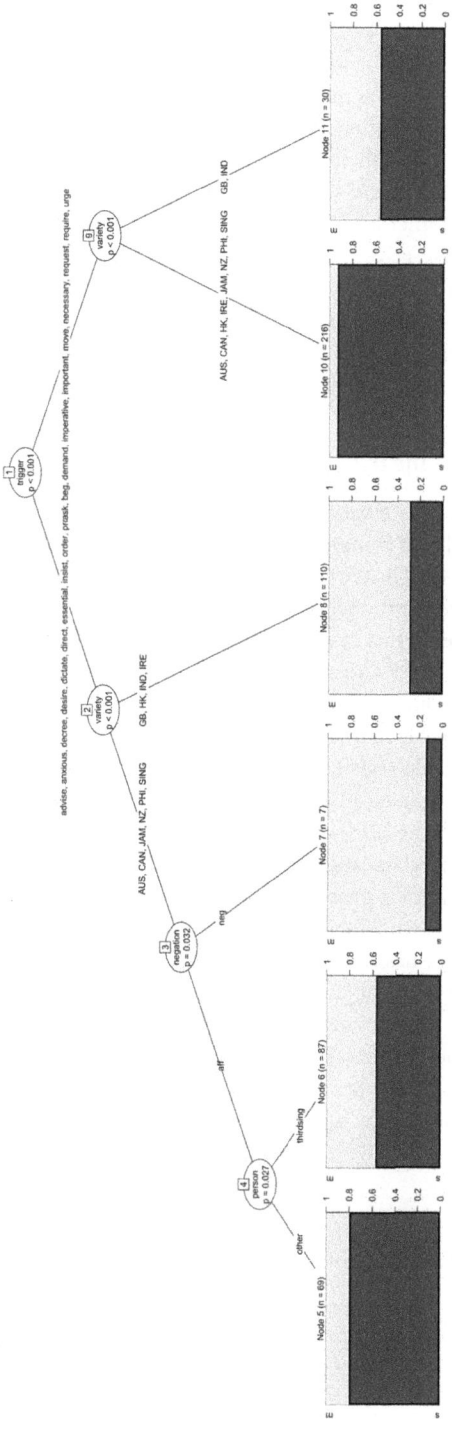

Figure 10.3 Plotting predictor interaction (ctree) in ICE (all predictor variables); s = subjunctive, m = *should*.

The single tree shows that a regional difference emerges for one set of mandative triggers (*advise, anxious, decree, desire, dictate, direct, essential, insist, order, propose, recommend, stipulate* and *suggest*) that groups BrE, HKE, IndE and IrE together as varieties preferring the modal over the subjunctive variant in these contexts (node 8). The remaining varieties show a preference for the subjunctive with these triggers (nodes 5 and 6), with the exception of negation (node 7), which acts as a strong predictor for the *should*-variant in these varieties (though the raw frequencies for this predictor are rather low). For the second set of triggers (*ask, beg, demand, imperative, important, move, necessary, request, require* and *urge*), the majority of varieties have an almost categorical preference for the subjunctive (node 10), and it is only the 'conservative' varieties BrE and IndE that regularly use mandative *should* in these contexts as well (node 11). The single tree does not substantiate Sedlatschek's (2009) hypothesis of a regional grammar in South and South East Asia.

4.3. Focus on the trigger as a factor

The ICE data have a very uneven distribution of triggers across varieties and overall numbers of choice context per trigger. In order to control for this, I collected a second dataset from the GloWbE corpus, taking care not to include material that was likely not to have been produced by local speakers/writers.[19] As pointed out in Section 3.3, data collection in this case was limited to nine triggers (*demand, insist, order, propose, recommend, request* and *suggest; imperative* and *important*), two ENL varieties (AmE and BrE) and four South Asian ESL varieties (IndE, PhilE, SingE and HKE). For this set I collected ten choice contexts per trigger and variety, i.e. a total of 540 observations. A predictor variable 'register' (general vs. blog) was not included as about 20 per cent of the material sampled in the 'general' category of the corpus also comes from blogs (Davies and Fuchs 2015: 4).

The summary statistics reveal a marked preference towards subjunctive use with this reduced set of triggers for AmE, PhilE and SingE, whereas BrE, IndE and HKE are more conservative (Table 10.9). The GloWbE data thus confirm general trends observed on the basis of the ICE data. The finding that the more conservative varieties, overall, also prefer subjunctives over mandative *should* is most likely due to the fact that GloWbE provides more recent data than ICE.

With respect to differences across triggers, the GloWbE data also confirm that *demand* and *request* are more likely to be followed by a subjunctive than weaker triggers like *propose* or *suggest* (see Figure 10.4).

Table 10.9 Distribution of choice contexts across varieties in the GloWbE dataset

	US	GB	IN	PH	SG	HK
should	15	38	40	18	15	39
Subjunctive	**75**	52	50	**72**	**75**	51

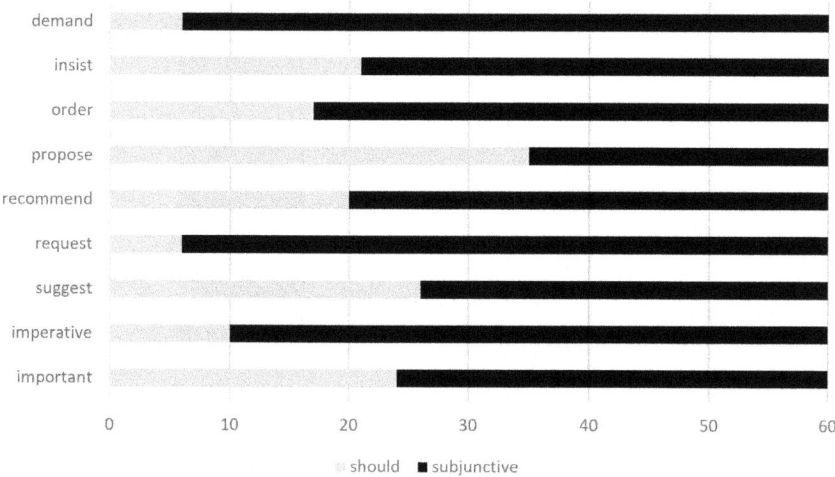

Figure 10.4 Distribution of choice contexts across triggers in the GloWbE dataset.

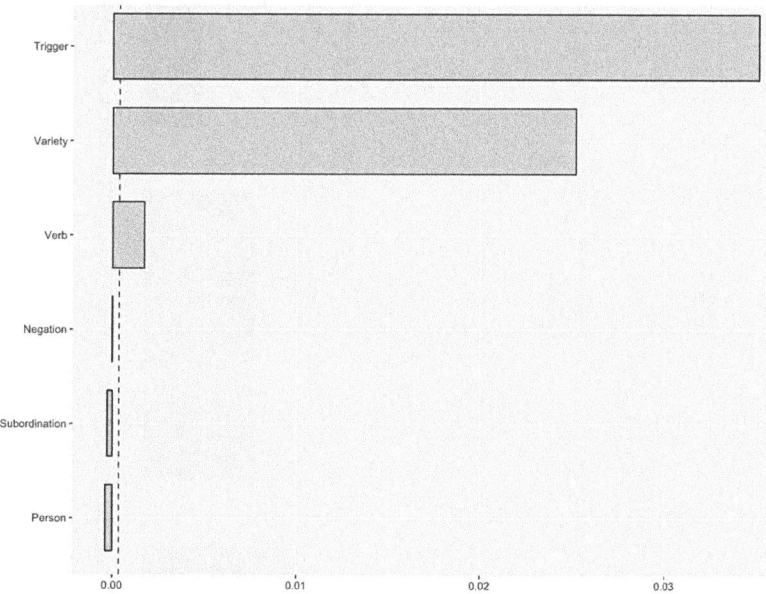

Figure 10.5 Variable importance (random forest analysis with mtry=2, ntree=500) for the mandative alternation in GloWbE.

The random forest analysis for the GloWbE data confirms that 'trigger' and 'variety' are much stronger predictors than any of the other variables (see Figure 10.5). The best model fit for the GloWbE data is achieved with 'variety', 'trigger' and 'verb' as predictors, at an accuracy level of 0.598 and a C-index of 0.799, i.e. just reaching the critical level recommended by Tagliamonte and Baayen (2012).

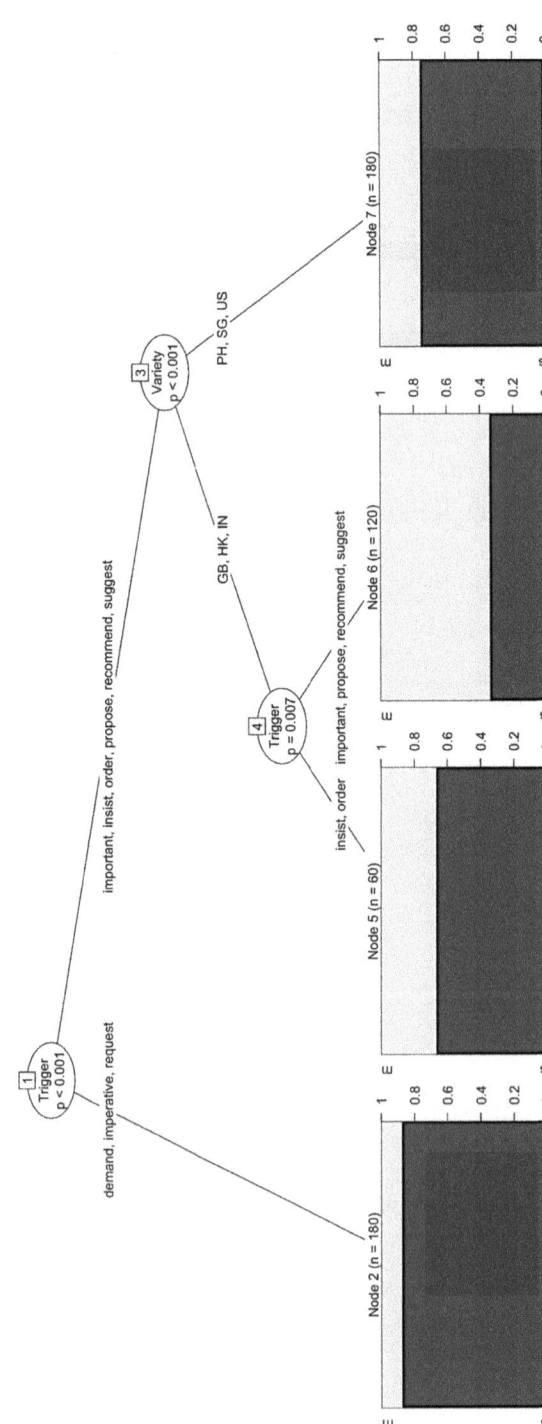

Figure 10.6 Plotting predictor interaction (ctree) for the mandative alternation in GloWbE; s = subjunctive, m = *should*.

The single tree (Figure 10.6) shows that the strong triggers (*demand, imperative* and *request*) do not interact with 'variety' as a predictor, i.e. there is no regional difference in the likelihood that a subjunctive will follow these triggers. For the remaining triggers, which also strongly prefer the subjunctive in AmE, PhilE and SingE (if at a somewhat lower level), we find that there is an additional split within the conservative Englishes, in that *insist* and *order* prefer subjunctives over the modal variant, whereas the weaker triggers (*important, propose, recommend* and *suggest*) predict the choice of the periphrastic construction with *should*. Interestingly, the factor 'verb' is not chosen as a predictor in the single tree (but this might be the case at a lower level if the depth of the tree were increased). Again, the single tree model performs slightly worse in the evaluation (with accuracy at 0.764 and a C-index of 0.684) than the random forest. All the same, it provides interesting information on how the two predictors 'trigger' and 'variety' interact in the GloWbE data.

5. Summary of the results

The present study of mandative constructions in WEs has shown that register and medium (i.e. speech vs. writing) do not play the role as predictors that might be expected, i.e. the subjunctive is not a feature typical of formal, written language, only. Contextual features (verb, controlling subject, *that*-omission, negation) also turn out to play a less important role than previous research suggested. The random forest analysis and the single tree reveal that the lexical trigger is the most significant predictor for the choice between a subjunctive verb or mandative *should* across all varieties of English. This finding emerged independently from both the ICE data and the follow-up study, in which the number of choice contexts per trigger had been controlled for. The data in the present study thus provide robust evidence that the strength of a trigger in predicting the subjunctive varies between strong (e.g., *demand, request, imperative, urge, move, ask*) and weak (e.g., *advise, anxious, desire, propose, important, suggest*), i.e. that triggers are biased towards a particular variant. The more recent GloWbE data suggest that with strong triggers, there might be no regional variation any more but that regional probabilistic grammars play out with weaker triggers. In other words, it is with these weaker triggers that we find interaction between lexical and regional variation. Finally, both the ICE and the GloWbE data do not provide evidence of a 'regional' grammar in the sense that Asian Englishes share an underlying probabilistic grammar. Instead, SingE turns out to be an innovative variety aligning with US and Canadian English, whereas IndE and HKE align with BrE in their bias towards the modal variant following weak triggers.

6. World Englishes and variationist construction grammar

The following discussion adopts the CxG definition of constructions as form–meaning pairings that can be found at different degrees of schematicity and that are attested with a sufficient degree of frequency (e.g., Goldberg 2006: 5). As CxG does not conceive of grammar as categorically separate from the lexicon, it is an approach that is inherently compatible with a view that allows for interaction at the lexis–grammar interface. The fact that the lexical trigger plays a key role in the choice between a subjunctive and *should* suggests that variation and change in this area of grammar can be fruitfully approached within the CxG framework.

Few studies so far explicitly aim to model variation in WEs within a CxG approach (see Ziegeler 2017: 715). Research by Ziegeler herself (e.g., Ziegeler 2010, 2015) focuses on constructional variation that can be attributed to language contact. However, she takes a qualitative approach rather than trying to integrate quantitative evidence with CxG modelling.[20] Moreover, Ziegeler looks at evidence from contact varieties of English to determine how this might be brought to bear on the theoretical notions (especially coercion) that are at the core of CxG, rather than using CxG to account for variation across contact varieties (see e.g., Ziegeler 2017: 715).

The discussion in this section takes the observed variation in standard varieties of WEs as its starting point and explores whether CxG provides a useful framework to account for the complex patterns of variation that emerge from corpus data. However, before we can model variation in mandative constructions within the CxG framework, we first need to look at how CxG conceives of variation.

If constructions are form–meaning pairings, variation in either form or meaning will, theoretically, result in a new or separate construction, i.e. alternations are not really possible (see e.g., Goldberg 2002). Studies that have looked at syntactic alternations within the CxG framework therefore argue for a level at which constructional variants or 'allostructions' are found (e.g. Cappelle 2006).[21] According to this view, constructions – typically at a higher level of abstraction, the 'constructeme' (Perek 2012: 629) – can be partially underspecified. So far, this concept has primarily been applied to link constructional variants that exhibit word-order variation, e.g. in the transitive verb-particle construction (Cappelle 2006) or the dative alternation (Perek 2012). According to Cappelle (2006: 18), variation between *pick up the book* and *pick the book up* can be captured in the representation proposed in Figure 10.7.

I propose that the same approach can be applied to morphological variants in a construction, in other words that the subjunctive and the periphrasis with *should* are allostructions of the mandative constructeme. The version given in Figure 10.8

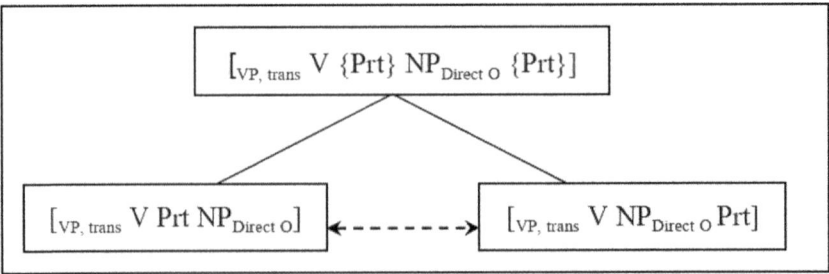

Figure 10.7 Example of constructeme–allostruction relation (Cappelle 2006: 18).

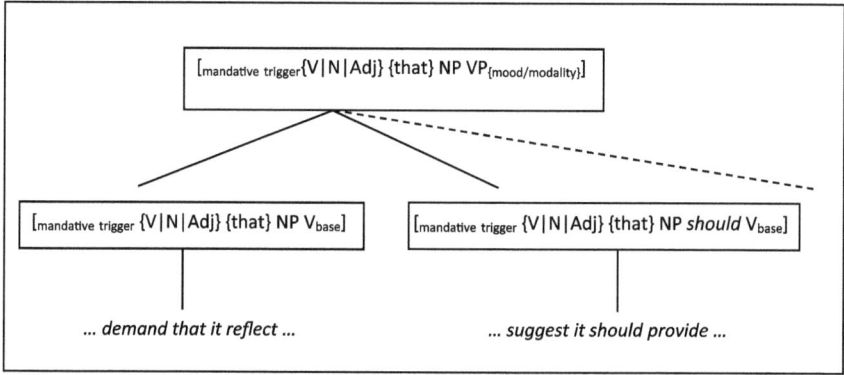

Figure 10.8 The (finite) mandative constructeme and its allostructions (schematic representation).

abstracts away from additional underspecification, i.e. the possibility that the verb phrase can be negated and that elements can occur between the subordinator and the subject of the subordinate clause, as well as the fact that the mandative construction itself is embedded in a matrix clause. Moreover, it is still underspecified at the allostructional level for the specific trigger expression, which is inserted into the construction at the level of the individual construct, i.e. the concrete realizations of the constructeme that are given at the bottom of the diagram. The two examples of mandative constructs illustrate how optional elements (such as the subordinating conjunction) can be realized (in the construct on the left) or not (in the construct on the right). The dashed line, finally, indicates that additional allostructions (e.g. with other modal verbs or the indicative) may also be included in the grammar (partly depending on the regional variety).

The quantitative approach taken in this study allows us to look at the relation between allostructions and the construct level in a more nuanced way, and to make the connection between constructional variation in the mandative constructeme and WEs: corpus data from ICE and GloWbE show that triggers are not neutral with respect to their preference for a particular allostruction of the mandative constructeme. Moreover, the trigger-specific bias was shown to interact with regional variety, particularly for triggers that are weak(er) predictors of the subjunctive, with all other predictors (register, negation) playing a less important role. In other words, while the underlying mandative constructeme is the same across WEs, the frequency patterns emerging from the corpus data reveal that there are region-specific effects at the allostructional level, with interaction effects playing out not only with the trigger but also between trigger, variety and negation. The ctrees in Figures 10.3 and 10.6 can thus be taken to complement the more abstract representation of the underlying schematic CxG grammar for individual varieties.

Notes

1   I am grateful to Nina Benisowitsch and Carlos Hartmann for help with the retrieval and initial post-editing, respectively, of data from the ICE components. Tim Waller and an anonymous reviewer provided valuable feedback on an earlier version.

2   Emphasis in the examples has been added throughout.

3   While the use of the subjunctive in the Reuters press release might be attributed to the company having been acquired by the Canadian media information company Thomson in 2008 (thus presumably coming under increased influence from American Englishes), Liberman's assessment of the construction's (near) obsolescence is a little surprising considering the linguist's American background.

4   Reliable, comparable word counts for ICE corpora are currently still a lacuna that will be addressed in the new online version to be made available at Zurich. For the present study, the variable is defined as a binary choice (see Section 3.2), which makes comparisons across corpora possible without normalization of raw frequencies.

5   There is only one complete first-generation African ICE corpus available. Since ICE-East Africa samples material from two countries (Kenya and Tanzania), which are not equally represented across the spoken and written registers, I decided not to include it in this study. For information on the divergent sampling for ICE East Africa, see https://www.tu-chemnitz.de/phil/english/sections/linguist/real/independent/ICE-EA/corpus.htm.

6   In one instance, the speaker self-corrected from a subjunctive to a past tense after a past-tense trigger. This instance was not included in my dataset.

7   Note that there were no occurrences in the ICE corpora of non-third person subjects with adjectives followed by a bare verb that would have needed a past-tense context to disambiguate them.

8   Note that spelling in all ICE examples is faithful to the version in the released corpus.

9   See Waller (2017: 88–9) for a critical discussion of this practice.

10 Note that the speaker repeats the phrase *just an equitable* (instead of *just and equitable*) several times in this recording. It can be considered an instance of coda-consonant cluster reduction (CCR), a feature commonly found in spoken SingE (Lim 2004: 33).

11 It is, in fact, a matter of dispute whether the mandative subjunctive is finite or not. For a comprehensive overview of the views on this matter, see Aarts (2012).

12 In ICE-CAN, for instance, the verb *propose* is followed by a finite *that*-clause twice, but there are five instances of non-finite complements following mandative *propose* (including example (28)). The question is how far one needs to cast the net in retrieving all possible alternatives to subjunctives and whether nominal complements as in the following would also have to be included (on the rationale that the sentence could be rephrased using a subjunctive): *I have proposed the use of a national referendum to ensure that we get the full participation and approval of Canadian people* (ICE-CAN, S2B-024) could be rendered as *I have proposed that we use a national referendum to ensure. . . .*

13 Kastronic and Poplack (2014) combine Hoffmann's approach with a set of predefined triggers. However, they do not provide a list of the 240 triggers they finally used. A footnote (2014: 77) suggests that the 240 items included 'triggers' such as *say, think* and *feel,* even though these were later excluded from the rate calculations because they were predominantly followed by an indicative. It is difficult to imagine contexts in which *say, think* and *feel* would have suasive meaning in the first place.

14 In the interest of comparability, the set of triggers used by Johansson and Norheim (1988) was used in diachronic studies of Brown-family corpora (i.e. Hundt 1998; Peters 1998; Hundt and Gardner 2017; Waller 2017).

15 For the micro-categories, see ICE (http://ice-corpora.net/ice).

16 Note, though, that Crawford (2009) found verbs, overall, to be stronger triggers for mandative sentences than nouns. I use the term 'strong trigger' below to mean 'showing a preference for the subjunctive'.

17 Raw frequencies for *beg, decree, desire, dictate* and *direct* are too low to warrant an interpretation here.

18 Note that the predictor 'controlling subject' (i.e. third-person singular vs. other persons) is given the shorthand label 'person' in Figure 10.2.

19 I generally excluded the websites of international companies and foreign embassies (e.g. the US embassy in Singapore, Hong Kong and the Philippines), as well as commercial websites that may simply be using the domain. On the basis of spot-checks, I also excluded expatriates' websites, such as http://marianne.hk/category/blog/ideas, written by a blogger living in Hong Kong and London who is originally from France but has a professional background that includes working in the US.

20 Exceptions are the case study on existential *ever*, which is based on survey data, and the case study on the past tense construction, where she uses internet blogs for a largely qualitative description of the range of verbs entering in the construction and a small set (a total of 129 verb phrases) for a preliminary evaluation of distributional frequency (Ziegeler 2015: Chapters 5 and 6, respectively). Recent studies that approach variation in WEs from a stochastic angle often do not explicitly make the connection with CxG, even though quite a few are amenable to it (e.g., Mukherjee and Gries 2009 and Röthlisberger et al. 2017).

21 Ziegeler (2015) adopts a complementary approach to modelling variation in language contact situations by introducing the concept of the 'merger construction' pairing a grammatical form with a meaning shared between a lexifier and the contact variety. This allows her to maintain construction integrity, albeit with different functions in the lexifier and the contact variety. In this way, merger constructions are a theoretical concept which allows to model variation across varieties in contact (in Ziegeler's case Standard and Colloquial Singaporean English) without having to postulate different constructions for each variety. Instead, constructions are shared in the contact situation, with extensions only affecting the distributional constraints on the form-meaning pairings. Her approach does not consider inter-dialect variation, however. The present study looks at both, inter- and intra-varietal variation, a context where the notion of 'allostructions' is more suitable.

Corpora

COCA = Davies, Mark (2008–), *The Corpus of Contemporary American English (COCA): 560 million words, 1990-present.* Available online: https://corpus.byu.edu/coca/.

ICE = *The International Corpus of English.* http://ice-corpora.net/ice.

GloWbE = Davies, Mark (2013), *Corpus of Global Web-Based English: 1.9 billion words from speakers in 20 countries (GloWbE).* Available online: https://corpus.byu.edu/glowbe/.

References

Aarts, Bas (2012), 'The Subjunctive Conundrum in English', *Folia Linguistica*, 46 (1): 1–20.

Algeo, John (1992), 'British and American Mandative Constructions', in Claudia Blank (ed), *Language and Civilization: A Concerted Profusion of Essays and Studies in Honour of Otto Hietsch, Vol. 2*, 599–617, Frankfurt: Peter Lang.

Bernaisch, Tobias, Stefan Th. Gries and Joybrato Mukherjee (2014), 'The Dative Alternation in South Asian English(es): Modelling Predictors and Predicting Prototypes', *English World-Wide*, 35 (1): 7–31.

Biber, Douglas and Bethany Gray (2016), *Grammatical Complexity in Academic English: Linguistic Change in Writing*, Cambridge: Cambridge University Press.

Cappelle, Bert (2006), 'Particle Placement and the Case for "Allostructions"', *Constructions*, Special Volume 1 (7).

Collins, Peter (2015), 'Diachronic Variation in the Grammar of Australian English: Corpus-based Explorations', in Peter Collins (ed), *Grammatical Change in English World-Wide*, 15–42, Amsterdam: Benjamins.

Collins, Peter, Ariane Macalinga Borlongan, Joo-Hyuk Lim and Xinyue Yao (2014), 'The Subjunctive Mood in Philippine English: A Diachronic Analysis', in Simone E. Pfenninger, Olga Timofeeva, Anne-Christine Gardner, Alpo Honkapohja, Marianne Hundt and Daniel Schreier (eds), *Contact, Variation, and Change in the History of English*, 259–80, Amsterdam: Benjamins.

Crawford, William J. (2009), 'The Mandative Subjunctive', in Günter Rohdenburg and Julia Schlüter (eds), *One Language, Two Grammars? Differences between British and American English*, 257–76. Cambridge: Cambridge University Press.

Davies, Mark and Robert Fuchs (2015), 'Expanding Horizons in the Study of World Englishes with the 1.9 Billion Word Global Web-based English Corpus (GloWbE)', *English World-Wide*, 36 (1): 1–28.

Goldberg, Adele E. (2002), 'Surface Generalizations: An Alternative to Alternations', *Cognitive Linguistics*, 13 (4): 327–56.

Goldberg, Adele E. (2006), *Constructions at Work: The Nature of Generalization in Language*, Oxford: Oxford University Press.

Hoffmann, Sebastian (1997), 'Mandative Sentences: A Study of Variation on the Basis of the British National Corpus', MA diss., Zurich.

Hothorn, Torsten, Kurt Hornik and Achim Zeileis (2006), 'Unbiased Recursive Partitioning: A Conditional Inference Framework', *Journal of Computational and Graphical Statistics*, 15 (3): 651–74.

Hundt, Marianne (1998), 'It is Important that this Study (*Should*) *Be* Based on the Analysis of Parallel Corpora: On the Use of the Mandative Subjunctive in Four Major Varieties of English', in Hans Lindquist, Staffan Klintborg, Magnus Levin and Maria Estling (eds), *The Major Varieties of English*, 159–75, Växjö: Växjö University.

Hundt, Marianne (2018), 'It is Time that this (*Should) Be Studied* across a Broader Range of Englishes: A Global Trip around Mandative Subjunctives', in Sandra C. Deshors (ed), *Modeling World Englishes: Assessing the Interplay of Emancipation and Globalization of ESL Varieties*, 217–44, Amsterdam: Benjamins.

Hundt, Marianne and Anne-Christine Gardner (2017), 'Corpus-based Approaches: Watching English Change', in Laurel Brinton (ed), *English Historical Linguistics: Approaches and Perspectives*, 96–130, Cambridge: Cambridge University Press.

Johansson, Stig and Else Helene Norheim (1988), 'The Subjunctive in British and American English', *ICAME Journal*, 12: 27–36.

Kastronic, Laura and Shana Poplack (2014), 'The (North) American English Mandative Subjunctive in the 21st Century: Revival or Remnant?', *University of Pennsylvania Working Papers in Linguistics*, 20 (2): 71–80.

Kjellmer, Göran (2009), 'The Revived Subjunctive', in Günter Rohdenburg and Julia Schlüter (eds), *One Language, Two Grammars? Differences between British and American English*, 246–56, Cambridge: Cambridge University Press.

Lim, Lisa (2004), 'Sounding Singaporean', in Lisa Lim (ed), *Singapore English. A Grammatical Description*, 19–56, Amsterdam: Benjamins.

Mair, Christian (2006), *Twentieth-century English: History, Variation and Standardization*, Cambridge: Cambridge University Press.

Mukherjee, Joybrato and Stefan Th. Gries (2009), 'Collostructional Nativisation in New Englishes: Verb-Construction Associations in the International Corpus of English', *English World-Wide*, 30 (1): 27–51.

Övergaard, Gerd (1995), *The Mandative Subjunctive in American and British English in the 20th Century*, Uppsala: Almqvist and Wiksell.

Perek, Florent (2012), 'Alternation-based Generalizations are Stored in the Mental Grammar: Evidence from a Sorting Task Experiment', *Cognitive Linguistics*, 23 (3): 601–35.

Peters, Pam (1998), 'The Survival of the Subjunctive: Evidence of its Use in Australia and Elsewhere', *English World-Wide*, 19 (1): 87–103.

Peters, Pam (2009), 'The Mandative Subjunctive in Spoken English', in Pam Peters, Peter Collins and Adam Smith (eds), *Comparative Studies in Australian and New Zealand English: Grammar and Beyond*, 125–37, Amsterdam: Benjamins.

Quirk, Randolph, Sidney Greenbaum, Geoffrey Leech and Jan Svartvik (1972), *A Grammar of Contemporary English*, London: Longman.

Röthlisberger, Melanie, Jason Grafmiller and Benedikt Szmrecsanyi (2017), 'Cognitive Indigenization Effects in the English Dative Alternation', *Cognitive Linguistics*, 28 (4): 673–710.

Sayder, Stefan (1989), 'The Subjunctive in Indian, British and American English: A Corpus-based Study', *Linguistische Arbeiten*, 69: 58–66.

Schneider, Edgar W. (2000), 'Corpus Linguistics in the Asian Context: Exemplary Analyses of the Kolhapur Corpus of Indian English', in Ma. Lourdes S. Bautista, Teodoro A. Llamzon and Bonifacio P. Sibayan (eds), *Parangalcang Brother Andrew: Festschrift for Andrew Gonzalez*, 115–37, Manila: Linguistic Society of the Philippines.

Schneider, Edgar W. (2005), 'The Subjunctive in Philippine English', in Danilo T. Dayag and J. Stephen Quakenbush (eds), *Linguistics and Language Education in the Philippines and Beyond: A Festschrift in Honor of Ma. Lourdes S. Bautista*, 27–40, Manila: Linguistic Society of the Philippines.

Schneider, Edgar W. (2011), 'The Subjunctive in Philippine English: An Updated Assessment', in Ma. Lourdes S. Bautista (ed), *Studies of Philippine English: Exploring the Philippine Component of the International Corpus of English*, 159–73, Mandaluyong City: Anvil Publishing.

Sedlatschek, Andreas (2009), *Contemporary Indian English: Variation and Change*, Amsterdam: Benjamins.

Serpollet, Noëlle (2001), 'The Mandative Subjunctive in British English Seems to Be Alive and Kicking . . . Is this Due to the Influence of American English?', in Paul Rayson, Andrew Wilson, Tony McEnery, Andrew Hardie and Shereen Khoja (eds), *Proceedings of the Corpus Linguistics 2001 Conference*, 531–42, Lancaster: University Centre for Computer Corpus Research on Language.

Strobl, Carolin, James Malley and Gerhard Tutz (2009), 'An Introduction to Recursive Partitioning: Rationale, Application and Characteristics of Classification and Regression Trees, Bagging and Random Forests', *Psychological Methods*, 14 (4): 323–48.

Strobl, Carolin, Torsten Hothorn and Achim Zeileis (2009), 'Party on! A New, Conditional Variable-importance Measure for Random Forests Available in the Party Package', *The R Journal*, 1 (2): 14–17.

Tagliamonte, Sali A. and R. Harald Baayen (2012), 'Models, Forests, and Trees of York English: *Was/Were* Variation as a Case Study for Statistical Practice', *Language Variation and Change*, 24 (2): 135–78.

Turner, John F. (1980), 'The Marked Subjunctive in Contemporary English', *Studia Neophilologica*, 52: 271–7.

Waller, Tim (2017), 'Studies of the Subjunctive in Present-Day English: A Critical Analysis of Recent Research, Leading to a New Diachronic Investigation of the Mandative Subjunctive', PhD diss., University College London.

Ziegeler, Debra (2010), 'Count-mass Coercion, and the Perspective of Time and Variation', *Constructions and Frames*, 2 (1): 33–73.

Ziegeler, Debra (2015), *Converging Grammars: Constructions in Singapore English*, Berlin: De Gruyter Mouton.

Ziegeler, Debra (2017), 'Are Constructions Dialect-Proof? The Challenge of English Variational Data for Construction Grammar Research', in Markku Filppula, Juhani Klemola and Devyani Sharma (eds), *The Oxford Handbook of World Englishes*, 715–34. Oxford: Oxford University Press.

11

The Stative Progressive in Singapore English: A Panchronic Perspective[1]

Debra Ziegeler and Christophe Lenoble
Sorbonne Nouvelle

1. Introduction

The presence of the progressive aspect in English has long endured a perennial quest for explanation. One of the reasons that this is so is because of the absence of a corresponding aspectual category in the modern languages which are amongst the closest neighbours of English, including German, Dutch, French and other Romance languages. As such, the category seems to emerge as having a specialized but redundant function capable of being grammaticalized using existing, non-progressive forms in other languages. But the real problems of the progressive in English, and those which are constantly under scrutiny in Anglicist research, time and again, are specifically related to two main areas: the diachronic development of the form and its synchronic dispersal in today's postcolonial heritage. In the present study, it is intended to provide an overview of these two main problems and to reveal something of the ways in which both the diachronic explanation and the synchronic situation across international dialects can be plausibly reconciled; in other words, to use the past to explain the present (a panchronic approach).

Alongside the emergence of the two central problems has been the emergence of new theoretical explanations for the presence of the progressive in today's English, and older works reflecting earlier philological traditions have, in many cases, yielded place to more contemporary, functionalist explanations of the history of the category, such as grammaticalization theory, and its underlying cognitive explanations of metaphor and metonymy (see, e.g., Bybee, Perkins and Pagliuca 1994). In the present study, such accounts are reconsidered, and it is questioned first why there should be a diachronic explanation in terms of grammaticalization theory, and second, how to explain the curious restrictions of today's progressive on the use of certain stative verbs and non-agentive, non-dynamic subjects using the evidence from diachronic patterns of development. Given the conviction in many accounts of a grammaticalization account, it may also be questioned why grammmaticalization is necessary as an explanation when the lexical sources of the progressive are not even apparent in the earliest appearance of the construction in Old English. What is more, the synchronic dispersal of the progressive in international dialects of English today appears not to be constrained by any lexical retention, and freely uses the progressive with stative and dynamic verbs alike. This usage is not illogical and should be explained within the framework of a cross-linguistic overview.

The present study takes such factors into consideration, looking first at the current state-of-the-art on the historical development and then at the arguments surrounding the use of the progressive in the 'new' dialects of English, such as Singapore English and Indian English. An earlier study, Ziegeler (2017), in which the extended use of the progressive in these dialects was associated with a replication of historical pathways, is reviewed in the light of new research on the process of reanalysis. The data from Singapore English and Indian English will be reviewed with respect to the types of semantic environments associated with one of the most frequent verbs appearing in the progressive, *have*. Amongst other things, it was observed in Ziegeler (2017) that *be + having* may occur frequently due to the bias of a particular semantic context in which it is used, that of adversity. If such contexts are in the majority, then the use of the progressive in such situations may require a specific interpretation. The present study will examine such contexts using a corpus in order to determine if there is a numerical preference for *be + having* to occur in adversative contexts and whether or not this may be said to be affecting the overall usage patterns of the stative progressive in international or 'new' dialects of English.[2] What is uncertain, then, is whether (i) the stative uses seen in present-day international dialects can be attributed to a replication of earlier uses in Old English and Middle English, (ii) whether they are indicative of faster grammaticalization towards temporary states or (iii) if there is otherwise a particular semantic field relevant to such uses in today's international dialects which is creating the illusion of a greater usage of stative progressives generally.

The chapter consists of the following sections: Section 2 reviews historical accounts previously discussed in Ziegeler (1999, 2006) of the early development of the progressive. Section 3 focuses on the current arguments on the role of the substrate vs. other explanations for the occurrence of the progressive with stative verbs in international dialects of English. Section 4 presents previous data from Ziegeler (2017), obtained from corpus sources showing the use of the *be + having* progressive in Singapore and Indian English. In Section 5 the studies in Ziegeler (2017) are taken further to quantify the use of progressive *have* specifically in adversative contexts. In Section 6, the question is raised whether the frequent use of the progressive with statives in Singapore English may be due only to its frequency with a restricted lexical pool of statives or whether, on the other hand, the stative progressive in international Englishes may be illustrative of a universal stage of the development of imperfectives which reflects a broader aspectual range dating back to Old English times.

2. The historical situation

Arguments over the diachronic development of the English progressive in late twentieth-century studies were generally divided into two camps: those who believed that the progressive began to emerge in Middle English, through the gerund construction, and those who believed that its origins could be established much earlier in Old English. The former hypothesis, which has been labelled the 'Locative Source' hypothesis in Ziegeler (1999, 2006) has been taken up by proponents of a grammaticalization account, e.g., Heine (1994), Bybee, Perkins and Pagliuca (1994) and later in studies such as Bertinetto (2000; cited in Killie 2014). The grammaticalization account rests on the presupposition that the pathway of the progressive follows universal patterns realized in other languages. This is also alluded to in Comrie (1976), amongst others, referring to the Celtic substrate construction which was similar to the gerund construction believed to be the source of the progressive. While there is often a valid argument for the comparative approach which underlies such research, it should not, on the other hand, be considered that grammatical constructions across languages must always be submitted to a universal explanation. The idiosyncrasies of their individual histories may be equally significant in determining the routes of change that take place at later stages.

The Locative Source hypothesis relied on a schema source to explain grammaticalization, known as the Location Schema (Heine 1994): X is at [on, in] Y, where Y represented a place or location. This was interpreted in Bybee, Perkins and Pagliuca (1994: 137) roughly as '[a]n agent is located spatially in the midst of an activity at reference time', in which they suggested that to be located spatially in an activity is to be located temporally in it (using a Space-to-Time metaphor). However, it may be questioned how a referent can become an agent if only located somewhere: agentivity involves a dynamic infusion of energy, and this is not understood in the interpretation, particularly in thirteenth-century examples such as (1):

(1) that contre is in quakynge (*The Romance of Sir Beues of Hamtoun*, MS. M, 1.2647)
     'that country is quaking'

Example (1) is no more dynamic than *That country is in South America*. In addition, the examples usually associated with such hypotheses, involving gerund forms preceded by a preposition, were not common in Old English and Early Middle English, according to Denison (1993), who also notes the absence of direct objects with such types, as well as the absence of co-occurrence with verbs prefixed by telic prefixes, such as *a–*, *be–*, *for–*, *ge–*, *ofer–*, *of–*, *on–* and *to–*, and such prefixes would have been associated with more dynamic actions and events. It is well-known that a grammaticalization path is usually initiated in sources having an increased frequency of use (Bybee 2011). The verbal noun or gerund was derived from a verb with a suffix such as *–ing/–yng/–ynge*, with *–ing* and *–ung* suffixes being found in Old English, according to Núñez-Pertejo (2004). Núñez-Pertejo (2004) maintains, at the same time (citing Brussendorf 1930: 243), that the prepositional form with the gerund complement was virtually unknown before 1300, around about the time that the Old English periphrasis, *be + V–ende*, started to disappear. Another reason for dismissing such an account is that agentivity typically involves transitivity, and the number of transitive cases relative to intransitive at the time were very few: according to Visser (1973; cited in Ziegeler 1999), only five examples out of sixty-seven were not intransitive.

Accounts which have traced the progressive back to Old English include: Nickel (1966), Scheffer (1975), Mitchell (1976; 1985), Nehls (1988), Traugott (1992), Denison (1993) and Warner (1993). Others include Núñez-Pertejo (2004) and, more recently, Kranich (2013), Killie (2014) and Petré (2015), Kranich (2013) suggesting that the locative source construction type (as in (1)) was not functionally equivalent to the progressive at the time. Some accounts allow for a different explanation for the process by which the construction developed – rather than grammaticalization, it may have been a case of reanalysis that determined the ultimate direction that the progressive was to take. Studies such as Kranich (2013), Killie (2014) and Petré (2015) suggest a secondary grammaticalization, Kranich proposing the original primary grammaticalization to have begun long ago, prior to Old English times, since it is not possible to trace the origins of the progressive to a true lexical source using available resources.[3] However, if so, the path of development must have taken place at a relatively slow pace, compared with other aspectual classes in English.

Amongst the accounts that refer to reanalysis as being instrumental in the early stages of the progressive in Old English, there have been many which have described the Old English form as a type of imperfective aspect (e.g., Traugott 1992; Núñez-Pertejo 2004). Their rendering of an early imperfective aspect is quite plausible given its observed associations in Old English mainly with intransitive verbs expressing an inherent lexical semantics of duration: Traugott notes that verbs such as *wunian* 'dwell' and *libban* 'live', *faran* 'go', *cweþan* 'speak', *feohtan* 'fight' and *growan* 'grow' were frequently found in the *be + V-ende* form.[4] The definition of imperfective adopted in the present study subsumes both Comrie's (1976) and Bybee, Perkins and Pagliuca's (1994) definitions of a situation viewed from within which focuses on the internal structure of the situation rather than on its bounded limits and includes sub-categories such as habitual and continuous aspect, as well as progressive. What is often overlooked is that many such examples may be translated in Present-Day English (PDE) without the use of a progressive, for example:

(2) a. & hie þa ymb þa gatu *feohtende wæron* oþþæt hie þær inne fulgon, (HC, *Two of the Saxon Chronicles Parallel*, O2)
'And they went on fighting around the gates until they forced their way in',

   b. & þy ilcan geare ferde to Rome mid micelre weorþnesse, & þær *was xii monaþ wuniende*, (HC, *Two of the Saxon Chronicles Parallel*, O2)
'And the same year he proceeded to Rome in great state, and remained there twelve months',

In both (2a) and (2b), the translations are by Garmonsway (1967), but while in (2a) the periphrasis is translated using the *go*-progressive in PDE, in (2b) it is translated using the simple past form of the verb. (2a) could well have been translated using the simple past form also, and not lose any of the original meaning ('and they fought around the gates until they forced their way in'). The same apparently redundant use of the ancestor to the progressive is found in another text:

(3) & þær ealle neaht *wæs restende*: & þa on morne gehælde witte aras & ut eode. (HC, *Bede's Ecclesiastical History*, O2)
'and he rested there all night; and then in the morning he arose in his sound senses and went out'.

The 'redundancy' of the form is an illusion created by the fact that the lexical meaning of the verbs with which it co-occurs is already durative, and so expresses precisely the aspectual meaning that is also conveyed by the periphrasis itself. That such redundancy is possible is due to the initial attraction between lexical and grammatical aspects sharing semantic harmony in the early stages of grammaticalization. According to Bybee (1985: 13–16), the harmony is governed by a principle of relevance, by which a grammatical category may be packaged together with a lexical item if the semantics are mutually relevant.

The presence of aspectual harmony in the use of the progressive is also seen in Old English examples expressing habitual, or characterizing uses (cited in Ziegeler 1999, 2006):

(4) Sume *syndan creopende* on eorðan mid eallum lichoman, swa swa wurmas doð. Sume gað on twam fotum, sum on feower fotum, sume fleoð mid fyðerum. (Bybee, Perkins and Pagliuca 1994: 135, from *Ælfric's Lives*, I, II. 52–55)
     'Some creep on the earth with their whole body, as worms do. Some go on two feet, some on four feet, some fly with wings'

Such uses were also found in Middle English, with reference to timeless geographical facts:

(5) the flode *is* Into the grete See *rennende* (Mustanoja 1960: 595, from John Gower's *Confessio Amantis*)
     'the river runs into the great sea'

In today's English, again, the use of the progressive would be unacceptable in such contexts; however, the reason may be not because of its incompatibility with such lexical verbs, but related more to its obviously redundant, functional compatibility with verbs expressing duration, whether permanent or temporary. Thus, the present-day use of the progressive is somewhat more restrictive than in earlier times, when any type of duration, permanent or temporary, could attract the use of the progressive marker.

Some of the earliest research, as mentioned above, attributed the origins of the progressive aspect in today's English to the periphrastic be + V–*ende* construction in Old English, with a continuity involving an amalgamation with the then-existing gerund or verbal noun. Much of the history of the gerund is comprehensively described in Fanego (2004) and need not be reviewed again, but the be + V–*ende* construction appears to have had a variety of possible sources: Nickel (1966) discusses three apart from the gerund source: (i) be + predicative adjective, as in *hie wæron blissiende* 'they were happy', occurring alongside *hie wæron bliþe*, with roughly the same meaning and resulting in the reinterpretation of the adjectival predicate as a verbal predicate; (ii) appositive participles: *þa he on temple wæs lærende his discipulas* 'when he was in the temple teaching his disciples', in which the word order resulted in the be verb falling alongside the be + V–*ende* form; and (iii) the agentive predicate nominal, which bore a curious similarity to the participle form, with the exception that the case suffixes for an agent noun needed to be plural (*–ende* rather than just *–end*) to correspond exactly with the participle form. However, the fact that a phonological merger between the Old English participle form and the gerund might have taken place is almost indisputable, given not only the formal similarities (*-ende/-en/-in/-ing*) but also the semantic or functional similarities between the two forms, the disappearance of the *be + V-ende* form taking place almost simultaneously with the emergence of the gerund complement, as noted above (Núñez-Pertejo 2004).

The possibility of an agent noun source for the periphrasis at the time is well supported by the parameters of semantic continuity, discussed in Ziegeler (1999, 2006). Exactly when this form was reanalysed is less certain, but if, as Kranich (2013) observes, the Old English periphrasis was already functioning to express durative aspectual meanings, then the reanalysis from an agent noun (also supported by Núñez-Pertejo 2004) must have taken place prior to Old English, and the agent nominals found in Old English may be indicative of a period of overlap, in which one form could have expressed both functions. This reanalysis is discussed in Ziegeler (1999, 2006) as attributable to a shift along the noun-to-verb continuum of Haspelmath (1994), in which a nominal form may gradually acquire verbal features through the intermediate stages of adjectives and participles. The question is how this change might have taken place.

The following is a summary of the hypothesis detailed in Ziegeler (1999, 2006). Certain forms in Old English were ambiguous between categories and could readily be interpreted as either agent nouns or adjectives:

(6) hwæt oððe hu mycel ælc mann hæfde þe *landsittende wæs* innan Englalande. On lande. (HC, *Two of the Saxon Chronicles Parallel*, O4) 'and what or how much each man who was a landowner/was land-owning here in England had in land'

The shift from agent noun to durative aspectual functions is not too difficult to reconstruct, if it is considered, as Vendler (1967) had done, that agent nouns encode dispositions, occupations, habits and abilities, all states. According to Vendler, there are two types of agent nouns, one referring to specific states, which refer to smokers, painters and dog-catchers, none of whom need to be performing the activity at the moment of speaking to be still called painters, dog-catchers, etc. The activity is habitual and takes place at specific points in time. The other refers to generic states, states of rulers, servants and educators, whose activities of ruling, serving and educating are less easily defined in terms of specific time points; i.e., they are enduring across time. It was the category of generic agent nouns which appeared to have given rise to a reanalysis into a durative imperfective participle in Old English, since a durative state, of land-owning for example, entails temporary duration over speaker time, as seen in the following stages (Ziegeler 1999):

(7) a. Nominal: He is [land-owning] (*land-owning* is a generic agent noun = 'land-owner').
b. Adjective: He is [land-owning] (*land-owning* is a denominal generic adjective = 'he land-owning/is a land-owning one').

therefore,

c.   Participle: He [is land-owning] now (*land-owning* is a participle expressing an
     on-going situation extending over speaker reference time).

Quirk and Wrenn (1994: 113) list a large number of agent nouns belonging to the
group of generic types, according to Vendler's (1967) classifications; for example:
eardiend 'dweller', *hælend* 'saviour', *healdend* 'chief', *nergend* 'saviour', *rædend* 'ruler',
scyppend 'creator', *wrecend* 'avenger', *agend* 'owner', *buend* 'dweller', *hæbbend* 'owner',
folc-, foldagend 'ruler of people, of land' and *woruldbuend* 'world-dweller'. It was clear
that the periphrasis was already functioning as a copula and participle construction by
Old English times; the main difference between the Old English usage and that of
today's English is the use with habituals and permanent states (and even iteratives,
according to Killie (2014), though she emphasizes that they were notably infrequent).
The once broader range of aspectual uses, though much debated, appears to reflect a
function of general imperfectivity, which has since gradually narrowed over more than
a thousand years to express more restricted imperfective functions in the present-day
progressive. This is the position taken in Ziegeler (2006).

The gradual shift in categorial distinction from noun to verb (also discussed in
Ziegeler 1999, 2006) is highlighted in the fact that the more agentive lexical aspectual
types, Accomplishments and Achievements, did not begin to become frequent in
combination with the progressive until after 1600 (Ziegeler 1999, 2006), and these are
the lexical aspectual types believed to be less imperfective in their inherent semantics.
The question is whether we can associate such shifts with grammaticalization; in the
present study, the possibility of a gradual reanalysis is also considered. Gradualness in
reanalysis has been observed in previous studies (see e.g., Fanego 2004; De Smet 2012),
and is not unlikely in the case of the progressive, as it diffused through a range of
classes of lexical aspect, first co-occurring mainly with Activities or States (see below)
and later extending its range of uses to Accomplishments and Achievements. The
hypothesis of secondary grammaticalization proposed by Kranich (2013) is not
inconsistent with the present perspective apart from her interpretation of the fact that
stative progressives are slowly making their way back into the paradigm. Kranich cites
Quirk et al. (1985: 202) as discriminating between acceptable statives and unacceptable
statives, on the basis of whether or not they involve the speaker's judgement on a
situation:

(8)   a.   Ellen is being nosey.
      b.   *Ellen is being brunette.

Apart from 'special' interpretations in which temporary hair colouring may be used,
(8b), asterisked by Kranich (2013: 9), is unacceptable: the distinction now seems to
depend on whether the states express opinions or facts. The present-day extension,
creeping as it is through a range of stative situations of limited duration in standard
varieties of English, is only a recent phenomenon (dated only to the eighteenth century,
according to Kranich 2013: 23), and is estimated by Kranich and others to reflect a later
stage of grammaticalization, in which the present-day stative contexts are temporally
limited. According to Bybee, Perkins and Pagliuca (1994), amongst others, the

progressive may grammaticalize on to become a general imperfective marker, thus broadening the narrower or more restricted range of functions it once commanded. However, the temporal delimitations of today's stative verbs call to question this possibility, according to Kranich (2013: 23).

A shift along the noun-to-verb continuum would not preclude such a development, and the proposal of a continuum development allows quite feasibly for a reversal of direction, unlike a grammaticalization path, which is obligatorily unidirectional. If the progressive were grammaticalizing on to include other types of imperfectives, the grammaticalization path would appear to be bi-directional. The return to stative uses, albeit only those expressing subjective opinions of the speaker, is curiously reminiscent of the earlier stages we encountered in Old and Middle English, in which statives occurred quite happily with the progressive, e.g., in Middle English (Mustanoja 1960: 595, as cited in Ziegeler 1999: 79):

(9) we holden on the Crysten feyth and *are bylevyng* in Jhesu Cryste (Caxton, *Blanchardyn and Eglantine*)
'we hold onto the Christian faith and *believe* in Jesus Christ'

(10) They sayd thre men ansuerd them with grete fere that the paleyce and the ysle *was belongynge* unto the Kynge of Fryse. (Caxton, *Blanchardyn and Eglantine*)
'They said three men answered them with great fear (saying that) the palace and the isle *belonged* to the King of Frisia'.

A stative predicate is less agentive than a non-stative predicate, hence less verbal in nature, and may reflect the first steps back towards the time-stable, nominal end of the continuum once more. This is also apparent in the fact that the progressive can now occur in some habitual situations, observed as contingent uses by Comrie (1976), and reminiscent again of the range of uses found in Old and Middle English. What is also interesting in today's English is the presence of statives in international contact dialects. The following section reviews some of the earlier discussion on the international spread of the stative progressive, in the light of the diachronic evidence above.

3. The use of stative progressives in international dialects: An overview

The over-extension of the progressive to stative verbs in international Englishes has been long observed in the literature, and it continues to be used in a wide range of varieties. From as early as Platt, Weber and Ho (1984: 73), it was seen in Singapore English in examples such as (11a), and was also found in Indian English, Papua New Guinean English, and East and West African English. Although acknowledging the presence of substrate influence to a certain extent, the universality of the feature led Platt, Weber and Ho (1984) to hypothesize the cause of its ubiquity in the effects of postcolonial 'over-teaching' or analogy with what are commonly used expressions of stative progressives in standard varieties such as (11b) or (11c):

(11) a. I am having a cold.
    b. She's having a good time.
    c. I'm having a meal.

More recently, there has been a return to substrate language diagnostics, as shown in accounts such as Sharma (2009). Other more recent surveys find it an almost insurmountable problem to determine why certain uses of the stative progressive are acceptable in established varieties of English and yet others in the new, international Englishes are not (Siemund 2013: 148). Siemund's (2013: 148) proposal of a continuum of uses seems to be an appropriate means of describing the representation of stative uses across the varieties.

Van Rooy (2014) focuses on three varieties of English in particular: Indian English, Kenyan English and Black South African English. He shows that the use of the *be* + *–ing* form with state verbs 'conveys a sense of extended duration' (2014: 157) which is far less frequent in British English. He also makes it clear that stative progressives are on-going and that on-going states stand in sharp contrast to temporary states, which are prototypical for Inner Circle varieties (using Kachru's 1985 classifications of international dialects). In addition, his study reveals that the concept of extended duration fits both state verbs and dynamic verbs so that all types of lexical verbs can be affected by it, even though Achievements are rarely used in the progressive (Van Rooy 2014: 165) and even though language register is often a determining factor. For example, it is in Black South African spoken English that stative progressives are used the most, as seen in Van Rooy's data, which brings to light the fact that they are even three times as frequent as Accomplishment progressives in this diatect (2014: 165).

The use of the progressive with state verbs is therefore not the only criterion which sets apart the two main circles in Kachru's (1985) classification. The search for 'angloversals' (Mair 2003: 84, discussed in Ziegeler 2017: 319) in the domain of progressivity has to be extended to a whole series of uses, as Sharma (2009) shows. Sharma specifically focuses on Indian English and Singapore English. According to her study, two other avenues of research are worth exploring, that is, the omission of the auxiliary *be* of the progressive, particularly in the past (Sharma 2009: 178), and the use of the progressive to express perfective aspect, as in (13) below, in cases in which there is no backgrounding context. Sharma (2009: 180–1) gives the following examples from Indian English:

(12) My son [is] driving his own car. [*be* omission in variation]
(13) I was moving to Miami in 1998.

It should be noted that (13) is grammatical in standard English provided it has a backgrounding effect such as:

(14) I was moving to Miami in 1998 when I met the woman who was to become my wife.

Yet, the perfective meaning intended in (13) would require the simple past in standard English:

(15) I moved to Miami in 1998.

Just like Van Rooy (2014), Sharma (2009) studies the extension of the progressive to stative verbs and to habituals which are not delimited by such temporal adverbials such as *these days*, *always*, etc., adverbs which usually accompany such uses in standard varieties. Sharma (2009: 180) gives the following example:

(16) a. *I'm eating meat.
     b. I'm eating meat these days.

(16a) is non-delimited, while in (16b) the progressive is acceptable because of the delimited adverbial *these days*. Other Indian English examples from Sharma (2009: 181) include (17), where habituality in the present is more standardly expressed by the simple present *I call*, and (18), in which the progressive is used instead of the bare infinitive *know*.

(17) Every week I'm calling [my parents].
(18) Japanese patients . . . would not be knowing English at all.

Thus, Sharma (2009) shows that in Indian English, as well as in Singapore English, the use of the progressive is less constrained and is highly dependent on the substrate language of the variety at stake, that is, Hindi and Mandarin respectively (although her 2009 study provides no examples of the corresponding substrate language constructions). However, she also considers that similarities between varieties may be only superficial and that differences can be highlighted if the data are more closely examined. Her approach is intended to analyse the interaction between the substrate and what she labels the superstrate (Sharma 2009: 190), the so-called standard English variety that Weinreich (1953) had termed the 'source-language' or 'lexifier'. Sharma then establishes that the search for universal phenomena in variation – which is equally dear to generativists – can be successful if and only if all possibility of transfer from the substrate to the new variety has been ruled out in the first place (Sharma 2009: 171).

The extension of the progressive to uses that are different from those to be found in standard English is connected to an even wider range of phenomena according to Paulasto (2014: 248), who adds the narrative function and the perfective function to those previously mentioned. Paulasto's analyses (2014) are grounded on a comparative study of three different varieties: Welsh English, Indian English and spoken, rural English English, with standard British English as a control. The narrative function has a foregrounding effect in narration, which builds up suspense and signals greater involvement on the part of the narrator (Mesthrie 2013: 242), quoted by Paulasto (2014: 248). This is a feature of South African Indian English, according to Mesthrie (2013). As for the perfective function, according to Paulasto (2014: 248), referring here to Sharma (2009) and to Hundt and Vogel (2011: 158–9), it consists in replacing the simple present, the simple preterite or the present perfect by the progressive form. Paulasto (2014: 258) gives the following example from rural English that she collected in the Survey of English Dialects Spoken Corpus, in which the progressive past is used instead of the simple past, with an achievement verb, which is telic, dynamic but non-durative:

(19) Coming down there one night, one ... middle of the night, we ... one more go at rabbits. I was hurting my back. Down in the road. # In the mud and water.

This example shows that variation in the English progressive actually extends to the vernacular varieties of British English as well. Paulasto uses such examples to point out that the angloversal approach needs to be underpinned by a study of regional linguistic ecologies (Paulasto 2014: 157), as the extension of the progressive reveals structural, functional and lexical properties which differ according to the variety under scrutiny, and thus current research should not be confined to just the environment of stative verbs alone.

The phenomenon of the co-occurrence of the progressive aspect with stative verbs, then, can either be considered as a universal feature of international Englishes or related to contact features in particular substratum languages, and shows that there are other interesting features associated with the progressive in regional varieties of English besides the extension to stative verbs. Variation in the use of the progressive in Singapore English is mainly concerned with the extension of stative progressives to cases where the speaker expresses his or her objective opinion, which is deemed to be unacceptable in PDE by Quirk et al. (1985). Indeed, the latter regard subjectivity as the only semantic feature making stative progressives grammatical.

However, even these cannot serve as reasonable distinguishing criteria for the use or non-use of progressive *have*, since in examples like *I'm having a meal/shower* the speaker's opinion is of little relevance and a fact is still being expressed. It seems it is more specifically the criterion of temporary duration which is governing the present-day restrictions on the use of the progressive and the capacity of the subject to enter into or move out of a particular situation, dynamic or stative (Ziegeler 1999: 65). However, (11a) is still dubious because of the sense of agentivity it carries, which is in conflict with the undesirable state of having a cold, an adversative context. It must therefore be considered at this stage whether there is an additional semantic factor governing the use of the progressive in such examples, which were amongst the most frequently appearing examples in previous research.

4. Previous research on stative progressives in Singapore English

Sharma (2009) observed only two non-standard uses of the progressive with stative verbs in her study of the entire ICE-Singapore corpus, and Bao (2005) attested that the stative progressive was not found at all in the ICE-Singapore corpus. In his (2015) study, Bao explains that the imperfective aspect in Singapore English is little different from the (standard) English use of progressives, apart from the occasional absence of the copula verb. Comparing Singapore English with Mandarin Chinese, he finds parallels in the use of the *zai-* imperfective in Chinese, which co-occurs with dynamic verbs, but the *zhe-* imperfective is not transferred in any way into Singapore English, and its use occasionally with stative verbs does not parallel that of Singapore English stative progressives. For example, *zhe-* can be suffixed to stative verbs to express an on-going state, but these are unlike the transitory conditions described in English stative progressives:

> (20) a. He is being naughty again. (Bao 2015: 96, citing Quirk and Greenbaum 1973: 21)
>
>   b. Nahaizi pi-zhe   ne.
>   that   child naughty-ASP PRT
>   'That child is naughty'.

Note that the English gloss in (20b) does not have a progressive form, even though it contains an imperfective aspect marker (ASP) accompanied by a reinforcing particle (PRT). For this reason, it is agreed with Bao (2015) that there are no substrate reasons for the emergence of stative progressives in Singapore English. On the other hand, there are many studies (e.g., Sharma and Deo 2010; Van Rooy 2014; Van Rooy and Piotrowska 2015) which do find functional parallels in substrate languages. Their pervasiveness in various international dialects seems to suggest that the patterns of imperfective aspect exhibited across the many completely unrelated substrate languages are reflected in the international dialects with which they are in contact and that the extended progressive is a universal feature of the majority of international, outer-circle varieties. This leads to the argument, in that case, that L1 varieties of English currently have an extremely specialized use of the imperfective relative to a more universal, typological situation, in which imperfective marking reflects more the 'continuous' aspectual level of Comrie's (1976: 25) hierarchy (or perhaps the even higher level of a general imperfective). Hence the universality of the stative progressive across the international dialects is related to the more generalized imperfective categories found in languages other than English. The continuous aspect, according to Bybee, Perkins and Pagliuca (1994: 139) would encompass both stative and non-stative progressives, though they found no language in their data with such a feature. However, it could also be argued that, diachronically, earlier stages of English, as shown in examples such as (9)–(10), once had a continuous imperfective, which has narrowed its functional range to a non-stative progressive over time. As such, there are only a limited number of functional directions into which the progressive can now be extended, and the possibility that in international dialects these are influenced by substrate functions or are simply following a universal trajectory of all imperfectives to include a broader imperfective function is a matter for more intensive research. A continuum-like development would not rule out the latter possibility.

The present study was considered to provide a necessary continuation of Ziegeler (2017), in which a survey of the use of the progressive with verbs of state in Singapore English, Indian English and East African English was undertaken and in which some examples were found. The survey used the Singapore, Indian and East African components of the International Corpus of English, as well as the Flowerpod Corpus, a personal corpus of over 700,000 words compiled at the National University of Singapore using internet blog-spot data from Singapore postings.[5] The original survey used a wide range of lexical participles: *having, containing, believing, belonging, remaining, owning, smelling, hearing* and *seeing,* but for most of these lexical items, only one or two tokens of each were found, the highest degree of lexical variation being attested in the East Africa component of ICE, which recorded at least one token each of *remaining, smelling, hearing* and *seeing,* with the last item yielding six tokens. The Flowerpod Corpus also contained one token of *owning,* and the ICE India two tokens of *remaining.* This left the largest number to come from having forty-two tokens in the Flowerpod Corpus, which is compared in Table 11.1 with the frequency of the same verb in the three ICE corpora.

The data do not reflect a particularly frequent use of stative progressives, vis-à-vis the use of progressives generally, with the exception of Indian English which revealed as many as 40.5 per cent of *have*-progressives. It is likely that substrate influences have affected the increased usage in Indian English, though they do not explain the reason for the presence of stative progressives in Singapore English, as the Indian population makes up only around 6 per cent of the ethnic composition of Singapore.[6] It is clear, though, that *have* supplies the most frequent usage of stative progressives across all the dialects. The higher frequency of *have* in the progressive was possibly attributable to its generally higher frequency as a light verb, though it must be noted that its use in cases such as *having problems* or *having trouble,* in which it is found in standard use everywhere, was not included, as were those in which it expressed the duration of sustained state, as in *JL is having 20% off now* (from the Flowerpod Corpus, referring to the holding of a sale by a local department store in Singapore). However, the 'standard' uses of *have* in the progressive are worth considering, since the over-extensions could be considered to be analogized on these to some extent in the international dialects of English. Although there was no control corpus used in the previous study, since the particular use of the stative progressive under investigation in the 'new' international dialects is not expected to be found in the more established varieties, three examples were found in the ICE-Great Britain describing physical conditions of suffering or adversity that could be typical of uses on which the over-extension to examples such as (11a) above could be analogized. These are given as (21)–(23) below:

Table 11.1 Tokens of extended stative progressive *have* across four international dialectal corpora as illustrated in Ziegeler (2017: 328), showing frequency as a percentage of the total number of *having* forms overall

	Flowerpod	ICE-SG	ICE-India	ICE-E.Africa
Extended *have*-progressives	42/232=18.1%	12/76=15.7%	62/153=40.5%	66/216=30.5%

(21) So that's not the problem,
　　　Are you still *having* the tremor? (ICE-GB:S1A-051)
(22) Is she still *having* hallucinations? (ICE-GB:S1A-080)
(23) Now I saw you was it a year ago when you were *having* back pain?
　　　(ICE-GB:S1A-089)

It may well be questioned why such uses can be readily expressed using the progressive aspect in most standard varieties of English, and yet examples like (11a) are considered to reflect regional variation. All such uses refer to health conditions of an adversative nature. In the previous study, it was found that in a restricted portion of the Flowerpod Corpus, the Health Thread, a total of 11.4 per cent of the uses of *have* were in the progressive vs. 88.6 per cent of non-progressive uses of the same verb, to express possession of a physical condition. This is not a very high proportion; however, we also see that it is frequent with expressions such as *having problems/trouble/difficulty*, and thus could be more related to adversity of a general nature than to merely adversative health conditions.

Verbs of possession have often been associated with adversative uses in previous accounts. In Ziegeler (2004: 181), it was noted that the Old English uses of the ancestor of *have* had the polysemous meanings 'hold', 'get', 'keep' and 'take' when co-occurring with a human agent. It was also shown in that study that the causative meanings in causative *have*-constructions started to weaken during Early Modern English and that it was often the case that a subject was no longer causative but merely the passive recipient of an act which he or she did not instigate:

(24) Another had one of his hands burnt. (OED, 1719 Defoe. *Robinson Crusoe* II, x)

In such cases the subject of *have* is considered to represent a similar sentence role to those of the progressive examples in (21)–(23) above; thus, it would not be surprising to see such a function extended to other uses of *have* in international dialects such as Singapore English. What is questionable, though, is whether this function is the main reason for the frequent use of *have* in the progressive in Singapore English. In Section 5, we investigate the Flowerpod Corpus again in order to determine if the adversative function of the *have*-progressive can also be found in other sections of the corpus that were not covered in the Health Thread subsection of the corpus.

5. *Have*-progressives in the Flowerpod Corpus

Although, as noted in Ziegeler (2017), the largest proportion of stative progressives was observed to have come from the use of the verb *have* in the progressive, it was not possible to measure this proportion against all other possible stative progressives in the same corpora, as this would require a survey of much greater scope. The restriction to just three verb types (*be having*, *be containing* and *be belonging*) was based on the comparison observed between their appearances in the international dialects and the diachronic appearance of the same verbs, also in the progressive in Middle English, in previous historical texts, as seen in Ziegeler (2017). We note that *have* was the only verb with data worth recording in the previous survey for Singapore English, with 18.1 per cent of uses in the Flowerpod Corpus occurring in the progressive, and 15.7 per cent in the ICE-Singapore corpus (out of a total of all forms of *having* found in the corpora, including gerunds and non-finite forms). This is why it was felt necessary to investigate whether the semantic tendency of adversity associated with (21)–(23) was influencing the lexical bias for *have* in the extracted tokens from the Flowerpod data. The Flowerpod Corpus was therefore investigated once more with the objective of teasing out those instances which were particularly illustrative of an adversative use of the progressive *have*, as discussed above. Unlike in the previous study, the data were sorted according to whether or not the *have*-progressive could be considered as in common standard usage (e.g., in *having problems*, *having fun*, etc.), and these data were included in the total count in Table 11.2 under standard progressive *have*; those not considered compatible with standard usage were categorized as Singlish examples. The criteria for distinguishing adversative uses from non-adversative uses were based on whether the role of the subject could be described as a passive experiencer/possessor of an unfortunate event or state rather than an agent, as is illustrated below in the difference between the use of the *have* progressive in (26) vs. that in (33a). Thus, the attributing of misfortune to the subject referent could not be readily explained as adversative if the subject was the causer of the event described in the predicate.

Note that both the extended uses and the non-extended uses of progressive *have* appear in the corpus, and that we are not comparing two different dialects but illustrating the range of variation possible in one dialect, in which both standard and non-standard usage appear together. This entails, therefore, that the extended usage of the *have*-progressive is not categorical, but in a state of variation alongside the non-extended use, and the comparisons between the adversative and non-adversative uses of the *have*-progressive illustrate that there is a higher probability for extended uses to express adversity than non-adversity (69.04: 30.95). The extended adversative use, in the present account, is thus hypothesized to be an over-generalization of the non-extended adversative uses, already found in other dialects of English besides Singapore English. The results in Table 11.2 are further illustrated in Figure 11.1 below.

Table 11.2 Frequency of the total use of *have* in the progressive in the Flowerpod Corpus of Singapore English, and differentiated for adversative contexts, comparing frequency of extended uses (Singlish) with non-extended, standard usage of the *have*-progressive[7]

	extended (Singlish) progressive *have*	non-extended(standard) progressive *have*	Totals
	42	67	109
adversatives	29/42=69.04%	24/67=35.82%	53/109=48.62%
non-adversatives	13/42=30.95%	43/67=64.17%	56/109=51.37%

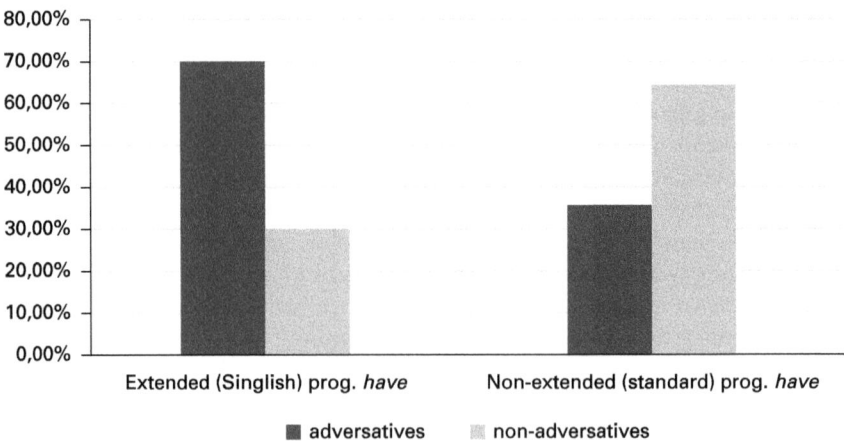

Figure 11.1 Comparisons between extended (Singlish) *have*-progressives and non-extended (standard) *have*-progressives in the Flowerpod Corpus, showing stronger tendencies for extended uses to appear in adversative contexts than in non-adversative contexts.

Examples of adversative uses in Singlish included (25) to (27):

(25) Posted by: Mermaid Oct 18 2005, 09:46 AM
I think it comes in many forms. I had a mild one few months ago. I cant sleep, keep thinking my problems, cant eat and easily *having headache*.

(26) Posted by: Kacey Nov 6 2005, 08:29 PM
If u r having pimples on ur face, then u can consider using acne med powder since it has anti inflammatory effect and wun worsen ur pimples.

(27) Posted by: Earl Feb 8 2008, 03:39 AM
She somewhat has to do so these days as the mom has very little income and *her father is having another woman out of the house* and contributes very little to the household expenditure

Adversative uses which could be found (standardly) in other varieties included (28) to (30):

(28) Posted by: HOPES Nov 10 2005, 04:01 PM
Me too ... *i m having a serious problem now*

(29) Posted by: summer33 Nov 3 2007, 12:13 PM
Besides all those problems I've stated, *I'm also having a relationship problem*[8]

(30) Posted by: kiddyu15 Mar 10 2008, 09:27 AM
In my current company (which is a pretty big one), the pple [people] in my dept do not lunch together ... They go for lunch separately [sic] ... And *I've been having lunch alone* or trying to find my frens

Non-adversative, Singlish uses are illustrated in (31):

(31) Posted by: wklee Apr 12 2008, 10:31 PM
i feel that *too many people are still having the old thinking* that Uni grads must be well paid JUST BECAUSE THEY STUDY FOR A FEW MORE YEARS AND GOT A DEGREE

Finally, (32) illustrates non-adversative uses that could be found in other varieties:

(32) Posted by: AnG3L Aug 20 2006, 04:58 PM
My fren happens to have a 3rd eye. Went clubbing with her last week. Initially *we were having fun* ... but after awhile she starts to get really quiet and keep wanting to leave.

6. Discussion

From the data above, it is clear that there is a strong lexical tendency for the use of the stative progressive with *have*, and moreover, that the majority of Singlish uses of the progressive *have* come mainly from adversative meanings. In at least four examples it is quite difficult to decide whether a use was specific to Singlish or not. Borderline cases included examples such as those in (33), which might be heard in standard varieties, though preference would probably be given to an alternative expression such as *I'm on holiday*; however, these discrepancies have not affected the tendencies shown in the Singlish data.

(33) a. Posted by: miSS pOOh Sep 3 2006, 09:56 PM
Hi, may i noe if there is any part time job now? *i'm now having my holiday.*
b. Posted by: babyhugss Sep 9 2007, 05:00 PM
PING, i'm 17 this year only. *And currently having my school holidays* till next year. I want to find a part time job in a hotel.

The data also included examples in which the *be-* auxiliary was absent and understood from the context; it did not include tokens of *keep* + progressive, and gerund and non-finite forms were also eliminated completely. It is shown in the frequency table above (11.2) that 35.82 per cent of the uses of adversative *have* in the progressive in the Flowerpod Corpus were found in standard contexts such as *having problems*, etc., but that the Singlish data might have over-extended the functions of adversity and misfortune, these contexts being represented by 69.04 per cent of such uses, leaving only 30.95 per cent of Singlish non-adversative uses for the *have*-progressive (χ^2=11.41, p<.001). The high frequency of use of the progressive of *have* in adversative contexts overall (48.62 per cent) makes it unsurprising that such a function could be over-extended in Singlish.

As discussed above, the range of meanings for the verb *have* may vary from those meaning 'hold', 'get', 'keep' and 'take', according to the context. Many of these meanings appear in standard uses, as in (34a), in which a meaning of 'holding' (an event) is intended. Others included the Singlish, non-adversative meanings of acquisition in which standard usage would probably employ a verb meaning 'get', as in (34b):

(34) a. Posted by TheoDR 27-01-2008 02:58 PM

Forgot to add, *Nikko is having a clearance sale* for a limited range of minichamps and autoart 1/18th scale models for $65.

b. Posted by: smurfect Jun 2 2008, 04:24 PM

gals r jealous creatures n they tend 2 hate *the gal who is pretty n having all the bees* (guys) *swarmed ard* [around] *them.*

The progressive use of *have* in Singapore English seems to exhibit an entire range of functions in this respect, including causativity (in (34a)), possession and adversity, with an exaggerated usage of the latter function. There could be more than one reason for this extension. The observation of such examples in standard usage might have provided the basis for the analogical extension by speakers of Singlish to any kind of ailment or adversity, as seen in the data above. If that is the case, a further question needs to be asked, and that is why some instances are tolerated in standard usage (e.g., (28)) and others are less likely to be (e.g., (25)). This definitely remains a question for future research to explore. The possibility of substrate influence is ruled out, only because of the obvious universality of the stative progressive, found across all the 'new' dialects of English, as noted above. So, if there is a tendency for *have*-progressives to occur when they express adversity, it may be linked to the meanings of temporality or contingency associated with its present-day meaning. It would be natural, thus, to want to use a grammatical expression linked with temporal meanings of short-term duration, in order to 'lighten up' the sense of misfortune conveyed in the message. The element of positive evaluation in many linguistic expressions has been discussed under Boucher and Osgood's (1969) 'Pollyanna Hypothesis', by which speakers, when given the choice, often tend to select positively-evaluated words or expressions over negatively-evaluated ones (the operation of an E+ factor, also discussed in Ziegeler 2016). It is quite possible that this factor may be motivating, to a certain extent, the progressive use of adversative *have* in Singlish. However, it does not explain the occurrence of non-adversative uses, which, though apparently fewer in the Flowerpod Corpus, are still there. In the first instance, it is recalled that an internet blog site is likely to attract all manner of personal accounts of affliction, misfortune and ailments of various kinds (one of the Health Thread sections was entirely devoted to the topic of 'constipation'). The mere nature of the subject matter discussed by the anonymous bloggers could well have influenced a tendency for the expression of adversity in whatever grammatical form, and a further count of the non-progressive uses of *have* which express adversity certainly reveals that the expression of adversity is not restricted to progressive forms. For example, for the non-progressive form *have* alone, there were 167 tokens of adversative uses in the Flowerpod Corpus, a number which far exceeds the fifty-three tokens of adversative *be + having* for the same corpus, and this does not count the other forms possible, such as *has* (twenty-five tokens) or *had* (eighty-four tokens). The difference thus indicates that it is not obligatory to use a progressive form of the verb *have* to express adversative states or conditions, although at the same time, when a progressive form of the verb *have* is used, it is shown (in the data in Table 11.2) to be more than 200 per cent more likely to express an adversative state than anything else. The alternation between the progressive and the non-progressive is seen in examples such as (26) above and (35):

(35) Posted by: HashBrown Jul 7 2006, 12:08 PM
Funny, I always eat veg, drink loads of water ... *And my face now have some pimples* ... last time only a little or dun have.[9]

The contingency function of the progressive for *have* is clearly visible in some examples, in which the same speaker may use either the progressive or the non-progressive form:

(36) Posted by: starssy_stella Dec 22 2006, 02:14 PM
I too *had* depression when something big happened to me this yr ... I took 3mths to walk out of it
Now *is my brother having depression*, he had anxiety disorder ... My mum had no choice but to bring him to see psychatrist

In (36) the speaker uses the simple form of the verb, *had*, to indicate that the state had passed. It could be argued that the choice made of *have* in (35) indicates that there has been a change of state, particularly as the adverb *now* has been used inchoatively here, but on the other hand, the progressive is used with the adverb *now* in (36): *now is my brother having depression*, and the use of the progressive suggests that the state is on-going. Thus, there may be aspectual reasons for the avoidance of the progressive, but it is not clear that they may apply in every case.

Nevertheless, another question which arises is how to explain the occurrence of the numerous other stative lexical verbs which appear in the progressive in other international dialects, which may have nothing to do with the notion of expressing adversity at all. Some examples from Ziegeler (2017) include the following:

(37) a. Therefore in Tanzania we have two document documents. The Our constitution [sic.] is *containing* that is in the act two documents the nineteen seventy-seven and the nineteen sixty- six act of union. (Conversation T, ICE – East Africa corpus)
b. And the key the key of that basati is given to one of the persons who is not *belonging* to that sect uhm I mean Jain. (ICE-IND:S1A-063)
(38) For example okay we have done our MA and all that ... suppose we do get married with someone who is not *having* any education. (ICE-IND:S1A-024)

The verb in (38), although it may be adversative in the context, expresses primarily an abstract state of (non)-possession. Thus, the many other uses of the stative progressive in international dialects of English, that are not centred around the use of adversative *have* and use other stative verbs instead, require alternative explanations.

The remainder of the uses of the stative progressive in other dialects had been attributed to a different reason in the earlier study: the possibility of historical replication across time. Replication in grammaticalization has been discussed at length in Heine and Kuteva (2003, 2005) and in the majority of the cases they discussed, it was replication of a substrate path of grammaticalization (in the model language) that was being reproduced, often stage-by-stage, in the language of contact (the replica language). In their 2003 seminal article on the subject, they discuss contact-induced grammaticalization as a strategy for transferring some grammatical concept from the model language (M) to the replica language (R) (2003: 533). This strategy involves the following stages:

(39) Contact-induced grammaticalization:
  a. Speakers of language R notice that in language M there is a grammatical category Mx.
  b. They develop an equivalent category Rx, using material available in their own language (R).
  c. To this end, they draw on universal strategies of grammaticalization, using construction Ry in order to develop Rx.
  d. They grammaticalize construction Ry to Rx.

One example they provide (citing Corne 1995: 125–8) is that of the Melanesian French-based creole, Tayo, which has a system for marking dual pronouns that does not exist in metropolitan French, but does exist in the substrate model languages, Drubéa and Cèmuhî. The speakers of Tayo recruited the French numeral form *deux* (Ry) and grammaticalized it to the Tayo dual suffix, -*de*. The result was that the Tayo form had the grammar of the substrate or model languages and the lexicon of French, e.g., *nu-de* 'we two' – Rx – (French *nous deux*); *u-de* 'you two' (French *vous deux*). This process draws on a universal strategy of grammaticalization and creates a category that does not exist in the lexifier language.

In another process described by Heine and Kuteva (2003, 2005), replica grammaticalization, it is not just a grammatical concept that is transferred from the M-language to the R-language, but an entire grammaticalization process. It is shown in the following stages (Heine and Kuteva 2003: 539):

(40) Replica grammaticalization
  a. Speakers of language R notice that in language M there is a grammatical category Mx.
  b. They develop an equivalent category Rx, using material available in their own language (R).
  c. To this end, they replicate a grammaticalization process they assume to have taken place in language M, using an analogical formula of the kind [My> Mx] = [Ry > Rx].
  d. They grammaticalize category Ry to Rx.

The difference between the two processes is essentially in the fact that in the latter case, replica grammaticalization, the two contributing languages actually share the same lexical source concept, which means that the grammaticalization stages it will go through are expected to be the same in both the substrate and the replica language. In Irish English, for example, the model process in the substrate Irish language, the Location Schema (My), is grammaticalized into a perfect aspect marker [Mx]. In Irish English in the late seventeenth century, the same process was replicated (Ry > Rx). The fact that no other language in the world is known to have undergone a similar process indicates that it is not a universal strategy, but a replication of the entire process of grammaticalization in the model language. The following examples are given by Heine and Kuteva (2003: 540):

(41) a. Irish (Harris 1991: 205)

Tá	sí	tréis	an	bád	a dhíol
be: NON-PAST	she	after	the	boat	selling

'She has just sold the boat'
   b. Irish English (Harris 1991: 205)
      She's after selling the boat
      'She has just sold the boat'

As further evidence for the stage-by-stage replication of substrate grammaticalization patterns, they propose the appearance of an intermediate stage between (41a) and (41b), in which there is a noun phrase complement: *He's after the flu* ('he's just had the flu'). The presence of a noun phrase is a likely antecedent stage before a verbal complement starts to appear, and so justifies the gradual nature of the grammaticalization path in contact.

In the model proposed in Ziegeler (2014, 2017), it is the lexifier language rather than the substrate language in a situation of contact which is acting as the model language – i.e. the path of grammaticalization of a functional morpheme follows the same route as in the language from which it derived the lexical form in the first place. In the example from Irish above, the category Rx is developed on the basis of lexical similarity between the substrate model language, Irish, and the selected item from the lexifier, *be after V-ing*. But the construction does not exist in standard English, so in other words, it is like a calque which has undergone a grammaticalization path modelled on the substrate grammaticalization path. But what happens to grammaticalizing items which do not appear to be modelled on any substrate patterns of development? In the replica grammaticalization model shown in (40) above, the grammaticalizing item follows the same pathway as the lexical source concept in the substrate language. It would not be surprising, then, to find that in cases where there is no substrate model of grammaticalization involved, the pathway of replica grammaticalization in items directly inherited from the lexifier language must surely model, on a certain scale, the same stages of development as in the lexifier itself. It was this proposal that was used to explain, in Ziegeler (2014, 2017), the extended frequency of the modal *will* in habitual contexts in Singlish, as well as the use of the numeral *one* to express specific indefinite reference and the present case, which is the use of stative verbs in the progressive.

If we return to the Old and Middle English examples discussed above, we see that it was common to find stative verbs used in the progressive at the time (examples (9) and

(10) above). Visser (1973: 2011) provides another example of a stative verb in the progressive, dated *c*. 1475, using *have*:

> (42) He cosyn vnto the hy king of fraunce, By the which branche honour *is hauing*.
> (The Romans of Partenay, 6266)
> 'He, being cousin to the noble king of France, by which connection he has honour'.

Although these examples do not come from Old English, they are reflective of the range of uses at earlier times in the history of the progressive when the construction was used more as a general imperfective. Rather than representing new linguistic environments for the progressive, the situation of the international (new) dialects of English may be one of replication, and replication in grammaticalization will mean that certain forms which do not replicate patterns of usage in the substrate model languages will be found replicating, on a schematic level, the diachronic developmental patterns of their lexifiers. A lexical source, then, will forge the same pathway of grammaticalization universally, no matter where it is used.[10]

It may be questioned, though, how the progressive in English can be described as a consequence of grammaticalization when there is no obvious lexical source concept or schema from which it appears to have evolved. We are reminded of Kranich's (2013) observations that it might well have been grammaticalized as a durative aspect marker long before Old English, and of Núñez-Pertejo's (2004) hypothesis that the Old English participle was related to an adjectival form in existence at the time. The pathway of development proposed in Ziegeler (1999) of a reanalysis along a noun-to-verb continuum is sustainable alongside these hypotheses, since the path from noun to adjective to participle and then to verb involves a necessarily weaker sense of agentivity to be associated with the form in its early stages. Thus, it is more likely that a stative progressive will reflect diachronically earlier periods of its history, as a stative verb is lexically imperfective, and thus is harmonious with the function of expressing grammatical imperfectivity at its early stages.[11] This is why, in the early stages of its development in a new language situation, as is seen in the development of English varieties internationally, a broader range of uses may be found than in the older varieties of English, in which the functional range has narrowed over time. The pathway of development may be a secondary grammaticalization (broadening of functions), as Kranich (2013) suggests, and one that involves an extended reanalysis. However, such a diagnosis does not account so well for the regression to a broader, imperfective stage that was more typical of its uses in Old and Middle English. It seems that the jury is still out on such possibilities. For this reason, it must also be recalled, as noted in Fanego (2004), that not only grammaticalization but also reanalysis may occur gradually and over an extended period of time, and the English progressive is clearly illustrative of such processes.

It was hypothesized, then, as in Ziegeler (2017), that the universal use of the progressive with stative verbs in international Englishes still remains a problem for diachrony to sort out and that if there is any replication at all, it will be of the early developmental stages of the form in the history of the language. These stages may not be exactly parallel in both diachrony and synchrony, but there is sufficient evidence to suggest that the broader range of uses in international Englishes is at least reminiscent of such early stages. The replication seen in Ziegeler (2017) involving grammaticalization pathways could well apply to a continuum situation as well, and international dialects of English may be seen to replicate reanalysis in the same way as other diachronic processes are replicated.

However, as far as Singapore English is concerned, the frequency of the progressive with *have* is certainly higher than with other lexical types, as shown in the Flowerpod data, and this was thought to be due to the increased use of adversative contexts, analogized to similar uses found in L1 varieties of English, as the data above demonstrate. But given that other varieties of English show the same over-generalization of uses with a wider lexical range, it is possible that the analogical model of adversative progressive *have* interacts with the replication model for other cases of extended progressives. The explanations for the extended uses of the progressives may therefore be considered to be due to multiple factors, according to the findings of the present study:

(i)   A particular lexical context of high frequency, based on a similar context in standard usage (adversity).
(ii) The role of replication of universal, diachronic stages of development in a new dialect situation.
(iii) The role of aspectual broadening and narrowing as a universal, typological feature of imperfectives generally.

The last possibility, (iii), could require verification from other languages where the same narrow range of English imperfective functions is currently found. It should be remembered that PDE is unusual in having such a restricted functional range for imperfective uses, and as such, any form of extension to other imperfective sub-categories found either in contact or in earlier diachronic periods would not be an unexpected development.

7. Conclusions

A lot of stones remain unturned for future research – amongst them, questions may be asked such as the nature of the replication processes in international dialects of English – whether recapitulation of diachronic processes in new language varieties is restricted to grammaticalization alone, and if not, how other processes are motivated (e.g., reanalysis). A lexical item may be propelled on the same trajectory towards a grammaticalized item merely because that is its destiny, whatever the situation in which it is found, and that may explain its retreat to historically earlier stages of development in the creation of international dialects of English. However, it is questionable that the English progressive has been grammaticalized, given the absence of evidence of a lexical source and the fact that constraints on stative verbs cannot be attributed to lexical persistence. It is possible to conjecture, instead, that the process of diachronic reanalysis alone may also invite replication in new language varieties, in the same way as grammaticalization has been replicated. But a great deal more detail of the theoretical underpinnings of such a hypothesis would be needed before such a conjecture could be explored. The present study only serves to eliminate one possible factor that may have resulted in the bias of the data in a previous study, the bias towards the use of *have* in the progressive in international dialects, and it has only proven that in Singapore English, at least, there may be an interaction with a certain semantic domain, that of adversity, which may be interfering with the generalization of the replication hypothesis. Thus, it is necessary to reconsider the case for universal explanations in the light of each individual dialect. It is further shown that it is essential in corpus studies of this kind to be able to separate the biases of corpus subject matter from the frequency data which are created by such biases. It remains then for more studies to investigate the factor of semantic domains in other dialects of English in order to determine if the same hypothesis can be applied elsewhere.

Notes

1   This article is offered as a tribute to the significant contribution made by Teresa Fanego to the promotion of English linguistics research and to her role in the creation of a thriving and successful, international research community in Spain.

   We are grateful to the efforts of two anonymous referees who have significantly contributed to the refinement of the ideas presented in this chapter. We also wish to thank the audience at the workshop 'Morphosyntactic variation in World Englishes: Apparent time and diachronic studies', convened by Cristina Suárez-Gómez, Lucía Loureiro-Porto and Robert Fuchs, at the 7th Biennial Conference on the Linguistics of Contemporary English, University of Vigo, 28–30 September 2017, where the paper was first presented.

2   The term 'international dialects/Englishes' will be used throughout to refer to indigenized, L2 varieties of English, sometimes referred to as 'new' Englishes (e.g., Platt, Weber and Ho 1984). The term 'Singlish' will be used to distinguish language examples reflective of the non-standard, contact sub-variety of Singapore English from those of Standard (Singapore) English. It is not considered to be used pejoratively, and holds a covert prestige in Singapore today.

3   Primary and secondary grammaticalization are defined in Brinton and Traugott (2005: 78, citing Givón 1991 and Traugott 2002), primary grammaticalization transforming a lexical item into a grammatical one and secondary grammaticalization defined as the change from a grammatical status to a more grammatical status.

4   *Be + V–ende* will be used as a cover term for the many forms of the periphrasis which represented the original imperfective form in Old English. The two auxiliaries concerned were *beon* and *wesan* and the progressive suffix was represented in a number of variants, of which *-ende* was only one.

5   Acknowledgements are owing to the National University of Singapore Staff Research Support Scheme, 2008, and to Amelyn Thompson for her assistance in compiling the corpus. Some of the forum sites used are no longer available for public searching. The ICE-corpora used included only sections S1a-001 to S1b-020 in the Singapore component and the India component, since they were felt to be the most colloquial

spoken usage of the dialects in the entire corpora. The East African corpus of ICE is structured slightly differently and therefore was not restricted in the same way.

6 According to Bao (2015), only 7 per cent of the population of Indians brought Hindi, Bengali or Punjabi with them in the colonization of Singapore. These were the substrate languages considered by Sharma (2009) to have influenced the use of the stative progressive in Indian English. Bao (2015) considers the influence of Indian languages on Singapore English to be negligible, in any case.

7 The reliability of the data is unquestionable, as $\chi^2=11.41$ (p<.001), as pointed out by an anonymous referee.

8 Similar examples to (28) and (29) appear in the British National Corpus (accessed online 16/10/2017). They include *having problems* (114 hits), *having a problem* (16 hits), *having difficulty* (125 hits), *having difficulties* (23 hits), *having trouble* (156 hits), *having second thoughts* (29 hits) and *having doubts* (12 hits). Non-adversative examples include *having fun* (131 hits), *having a good time* (97 hits) and *having success* (1 hit). The clear difference in frequency between *having problems* (plural) and *having a problem* (singular) in the BNC is interesting and shows a preference for either a recurrent or a habitual time frame (see also (21)–(23) in the expansion of the progressive in adversative contexts). However, the singular object may also be found, as is seen in the frequency of non-adversative *having a good time*.

9 *Last time* in Singlish means 'before' and does not necessarily refer to a particular time point in the past. *Dun* means 'don't' or 'doesn't'.

10 It must be noted that the parallels viewed in this way are often superficial and that the absence of diachronic data from Singapore English rules out any prospect of observing the replication described, stage by stage. The replication merely states that diachronic recapitulation is possible because Singapore English is a 'new' language variety and that therefore, for grammaticizable notions, the same pathways of development may be forged anew whenever a particular lexical source is pressed into service. It is not, on the other hand, viewed as 'retentionism' (see, e.g., Pietsch 2009), where the grammaticalization stage reached by the lexifier at the time of contact is preserved and fossilized in the new variety relative to developments proceeding elsewhere the language is spoken.

11 The association between stative verbs and lexical imperfectivity is made in Langacker (2002: 86–7).

Corpora

BYU-BNC = Davies, Mark (2004–) *BYU-BNC*. (Based on the *British National Corpus* from Oxford University Press). Available online: https://corpus.byu.edu/bnc/.

HC = *The Helsinki Corpus of English Texts* (1991), Department of Modern Languages, University of Helsinki. Compiled by Matti Rissanen (Project leader), Merja Kytö (Project secretary); Leena Kahlas-Tarkka, Matti Kilpiö (Old English); Saara Nevanlinna, Irma Taavitsainen (Middle English); Terttu Nevalainen, Helena Raumolin-Brunberg (Early Modern English).

ICE = *The International Corpus of English*. http://ice-corpora.net/ice.

The Flowerpod Corpus. (Not available online).

References

Bao, Zhiming (2005), 'The Aspectual System of Singapore English and the Systemic Substratist Explanation', *Journal of Linguistics*, 41: 237–67.

Bao, Zhiming (2015), *The Making of Vernacular Singapore English: System, Transfer and Filter*, Cambridge: Cambridge University Press.

Bertinetto, Pier Marco (2000), 'The Progressive in Romance, as Compared with English', in Östen Dahl (ed), *Tense and Aspect in the Languages of Europe*, 559–604, Berlin: De Gruyter Mouton.

Boucher, Jerry and Charles E. Osgood (1969), 'The Pollyanna Hypothesis'. *Journal of Verbal Learning and Verbal Behavior*, 8 (1): 1–8.

Brinton, Laurel J. and Elizabeth C. Traugott (2005), *Lexicalization and Language Change*, Cambridge: Cambridge University Press.

Bybee, Joan (1985), *Morphology. A Study of the Relation between Meaning and Form*, Amsterdam: Benjamins.

Bybee, Joan (2011), 'Usage-based Theory and Grammaticalization', in Heiko Narrog and Bernd Heine (eds), *The Oxford Handbook of Grammaticalization*, 69–78, Oxford: Oxford University Press.

Bybee, Joan, Revere D. Perkins and William Pagliuca (1994), *The Evolution of Grammar: Tense, Aspect and Modality in the Languages of the World*, Chicago: University of Chicago Press.

Comrie, Bernard (1976), *Aspect*, Cambridge: Cambridge University Press.

Corne, Chris (1995), 'A Contact-induced and Vernacularized Language: How Melanesian is Tayo?', in Philip Baker (ed), *From Contact to Creole and Beyond*, 121–48, London: University of Westminster Press.

De Smet, Hendrik (2012), 'The Course of Actualization', *Language*, 88 (3): 601–33.

Denison, David (1993), *English Historical Syntax: Verbal Constructions*, London: Longman.

Fanego, Teresa (2004), 'On Reanalysis and Actualization in Syntactic Change. The Rise and Development of English Verbal Gerunds', *Diachronica*, 21: 5–55.

Garmonsway, George Norman (ed) (1967), *The Anglo-Saxon Chronicle*, London: Dent.

Givón, Talmy (1991), 'The Evolution of Dependent Clause Morphosyntax in Biblical Hebrew', in Elizabeth C. Traugott and Bernd Heine (eds), *Approaches to Grammaticalization, Vol. II*, 257–310, Amsterdam: Benjamins.

Harris, John (1991), 'Conservatism versus Substratal Transfer in Irish English', in Peter Trudgill and Jack K. Chambers (eds), *Dialects of English: Studies in Grammatical Variation*, 191–212, New York: Longman.

Haspelmath, Martin (1994), 'Passive Participles across Languages', in Barbara Fox and Paul J. Hopper (eds), *Voice. Form and Function*, 151–77, Amsterdam: Benjamins.

Heine, Bernd (1994), 'Grammaticalization as an Explanatory Parameter', in William Pagliuca (ed), *Perspectives on Grammaticalization*, 255–87, Amsterdam: Benjamins.

Heine, Bernd and Tania Kuteva (2003), 'On Contact-induced Grammaticalization', *Studies in Language*, 27: 529–72.

Heine, Bernd and Tania Kuteva (2005), *Language Contact and Grammatical Change*, Cambridge: Cambridge University Press.

Hundt, Marianne and Katrin Vogel (2011), 'Overuse of the Progressive in ESL and Learner Englishes – Fact or Fiction?', in Joybrato Mukherjee and Marianne Hundt (eds), *Exploring Second-Language Varieties of English and Learner Englishes: Bridging a Paradigm Gap*, 145–65, Amsterdam: Benjamins.

Kachru, Braj B. (1985), 'Standards, Codification and Sociolinguistic Realism: The English Language in the Outer Circle', in Randolph Quirk and H.G. Widdowson (eds), *English in the World: Teaching and Learning the Language and Literatures*, 15–39, Cambridge: Cambridge University Press.

Killie, Kristin (2014), 'The Development of the English *be* + *V–ende/V–ing* Periphrasis: From Emphatic to Progressive Marker', *English Language and Linguistics*, 18 (3): 361–86.

Kranich, Svenja (2013), 'Functional Layering and the English Progressive', *Linguistics*, 51: 1–32.

Langacker, Ronald W. (2002), *Concept, Image and Symbol*, Berlin: De Gruyter Mouton.

Mair, Christian (2003), 'Kreolismen und verbales Identitätsmanagement im geschriebenen jamaikanischen English', in Elisabeth Vogel, Antonia Napp and Wolfram Lutterer (eds), *Zwischen Ausgrenzung und Hybridisierung*, 79–96, Würzburg: Ergon.

Mesthrie, Rajend (2013), 'Transfer and Contact in Migrant and Multiethnic Communities: The Conversational Historical *be* + *–ing* Present in South African Indian English', in Daniel Schreier and Marianne Hundt (eds), *English as a Contact Language*, 242–57, Cambridge: Cambridge University Press.

Mitchell, Bruce (1976), 'Some Problems Involving Old English Periphrases with *Beon/Wesan* and the Present Participle', *Neuphilologische Mitteilungen*, 77: 478–91.

Mitchell, Bruce (1985), *An Old English Syntax*, Oxford: Clarendon.

Mustanoja, Tauno F. (1960), *A Middle English Syntax*, Helsinki: Société Néophilologique.

Nehls, Dietrich (1988), 'On the Development of the Grammatical Category of Aspect in English', in Josef Klegraf and Dietrich Nehls (eds), *Essays on the English Language and Applied Linguistics on the Occasion of Gerhard Nickel's 60th Birthday*, 173–98, Heidelberg: Julius Groos.

Nickel, Gerhard (1966), *Die Expanded Form in Altenglischen. Vorkommen, Funktion und Herkunft den Umschreibung 'Beon/Wesan + Partizip Präsens'*, Neumünster: Wachholtz.

Núñez-Pertejo, Paloma (2004), *The Progressive in the History of English*, Munich: Lincom Europa.

OED = *Oxford English Dictionary Online*. Available online: http://www.oed.com/.

Paulasto, Heli (2014), 'Extended Uses of the Progressive Form in L1 and L2 Englishes', *English World-Wide*, 35 (3): 247–76.

Petré, Peter (2015), 'Grammaticalization by Changing Co-text Frequencies, or Why [BE Ving] Became the "Progressive"', *English Language and Linguistics*, 20: 31–54.

Pietsch, Lucas (2009), 'Hiberno-English Medial-Object Perfects Reconsidered: A Case of Contact-induced Grammaticalisation', *Studies in Language*, 33: 528–68.

Platt, John T., Heidi Weber and Mian Lian Ho (1984), *The New Englishes*, London: Routledge.

Quirk, Randolph and Sidney Greenbaum (1973), *A University Grammar of English*, London: Longman.

Quirk, Randolph, Sidney Greenbaum, Geoffrey Leech and Jan Svartvik (1985), *A Comprehensive Grammar of the English Language*, London: Longman.

Quirk, Randolph and C. L. Wrenn (1994), *An Old English Grammar. With a Supplemental Bibliography by Susan E. Deskis*, DeKalb: Northern Illinois University Press.

Scheffer, Johannes (1975), *The Progressive in English*, Amsterdam: North Holland.

Sharma, Devyani (2009), 'Typological Diversity in New Englishes', *English World-Wide*, 30: 170–95.

Sharma, Devyani and Ashwini Deo (2010), 'A New Methodology for the Study of Aspect in Contact: Past and Progressive in Indian English', in James Anthony Walker (ed), *Aspect in Grammatical Variation*, 111–30, Amsterdam: Benjamins.

Siemund, Peter (2013), *Varieties of English. A Typological Approach*, Cambridge: Cambridge University Press.

Traugott, Elizabeth C. (1992), 'Syntax', in Richard Hogg (ed), *The Cambridge History of the English Language, Vol. 1: The Beginnings to 1066*, 168–289, Cambridge: Cambridge University Press.

Traugott, Elizabeth C. (2002), 'From Etymology to Historical Pragmatics', in Donka Minkova and Robert Stockwell (eds), *Studies in the History of the English Language: A Millennial Perspective*, 19–49, Berlin and New York: De Gruyter Mouton.

Van Rooy, Bertus (2014), 'Progressive Aspect and Stative Verbs in Outer Circle Varieties', *World Englishes*, 33 (2): 157–72.

Van Rooy, Bertus and Caroline Piotrowska (2015), 'The Development of an Extended Time Period Meaning of the Progressive in Black South African English', in Peter Collins (ed), *Grammatical Change in English World-Wide*, 465–83, Amsterdam: Benjamins.

Vendler, Zeno (1967), *Linguistics in Philosophy*, Ithaca: Cornell University Press.

Visser, F. Th. (1973), *An Historical Syntax of the English Language. Part 3, ii: Syntactical Units with Two and More Verbs*, Leiden: Brill.

Warner, Anthony R. (1993), *English Auxiliaries. Structure and History*, Cambridge: Cambridge University Press.

Weinreich, Uriel (1953), *Languages in Contact*, The Hague: Mouton.

Ziegeler, Debra P. (1999), 'Agentivity and the History of the English Progressive', *Transactions of the Philological Society*, 97 (1): 53–101.

Ziegeler, Debra P. (2004), 'Grammaticalisation through Constructions: The Story of Causative *have* in English', *Annual Review of Cognitive Linguistics*, 2: 159–95.

Ziegeler, Debra (2006), *Interfaces with English Aspect. Diachronic and Empirical Studies*, Amsterdam: Benjamins.

Ziegeler, Debra (2014), 'Replica Grammaticalisation as Recapitulation. The other Side of Contact', *Diachronica*, 31 (1): 106–41.

Ziegeler, Debra (2016), 'Intersubjectivity and the Diachronic Development of Counterfactual *almost*', *Journal of Historical Pragmatics*, 17 (1): 1–25.

Ziegeler, Debra (2017), 'Historical Replication in Contact Grammaticalisation', in Daniel Van Olmen, Hubert Cuyckens and Lobke Ghesquiere (eds), *Aspects of Grammaticalization: (Inter)subjectification, Analogy and Unidirectionality*, 311–52, Berlin: De Gruyter Mouton.

Index

Ingram Content Group UK Ltd.
Milton Keynes UK
UKHW051457150623
423417UK00015B/164